INDO-TIBETAN BUDDHISM

INDO-TIBETAN BUDDHISM

Indian Buddhists and Their Tibetan Successors

David Snellgrove

VOLUME ONE

Shambhala
Boston
1987

SHAMBHALA PUBLICATIONS, INC.
314 DARTMOUTH STREET
BOSTON, MASSACHUSETTS 02116

9 8 7 6 5 4 3 2 1
FIRST EDITION
Printed in the United States of America
Distributed in the United States by Random House
and in Canada by Random House of Canada Ltd.

Library of Congress Cataloging in Publication Data
Snellgrove, David L.
Indo-Tibetan Buddhism.
Bibliography: p.
Includes index.
1. Buddhism—China—Tibet—History.
2. Buddhism—History. I. Title.
BQ7576.S64 1987 294.3′09515 85-2453
ISBN 0-87773-311-2 (v. 1)
ISBN 0-87773-379-1 (v.2)

Cover art: Padmasambhava with Mahāsiddhas.
Tibetan thangka, collection of Samuel Bercholz.

CONTENTS

ABBREVIATIONS

AF	Asiatische Forschungen (publication series on the history, culture, and languages of the peoples of East and Central Asia, issued by the Seminar für Sprach- und Kulturwissenschaft Zentralasiens, University of Bonn)
AOH	Acta Orientalia, Hungarian Academy of Sciences
ASP	*Aṣṭasāhasrikā Prajñāpāramitā*
BEFEO	Bulletin de l'École française d'Extrême Orient
Blue Annals	See Roerich in Bibliography
BSOAS	Bulletin of the School of Oriental and African Studies, London
CAJ	Central Asiatic Journal, The Hague and Wiesbaden
DTH	*Documents de Touen-houang relatifs à l'histoire du Tibet*, see Bacot, J. in the Bibliography
EFEO	École française d'Extrême Orient
GOS	Gaekwad's Oriental Series, Baroda, India
GST	*Guhyasamāja Tantra*
HJAS	Harvard Journal of Asiatic Studies
HT	*Hevajra Tantra*
IHQ	Indian Historical Quarterly, Calcutta
JA	Journal Asiatique, Paris
JAOS	Journal of the American Oriental Society, Baltimore
JASB	Journal of Proceedings of the Asiatic Society of Bengal
JRAS	Journal of the Royal Asiatic Society, London
MCB	Mélanges Chinois et Bouddhiques, Brussels
MK	*Mañjuśrīmūlakalpa*, ed. Gaṇapati Śāstri
MMK	*Mūlamadhyamakakārikā*, see Prasannapadā in Skr/Tib Bibl
MVP	*Mahāvyutpatti*, ed. A. Sakaki, Kyoto, 1916 and 1925, together with Tibetan index by K. Nishio, Kyoto, 1936
OUP	Oxford University Press
PTS	Pāli Text Society, London
RAS	Royal Asiatic Society, London
SBB	Sacred Books of the Buddhists, PTS, London
SBE	Sacred Books of the East, PTS, London and Max Müller, Oxford
SDPS	*Sarvadurgatipariśodhana Tantra*
Skr/Tib Bibl	Sanskrit/Tibetan and Pāli Bibliography
STTS	*Sarvatathāgatatattvasaṃgraha* ("Symposium of Truth" = STTS)
TT	*Tibetan Tripitika*, Tokyo-Kyoto, 1958
ZAS	Zentral Asiatische Studien, Wiesbaden
ZDMG	Zeitschrift der deutschen Morgenländischen Gesellschaft, Berlin

LIST OF PLATES

(Between pages 528 and 617)

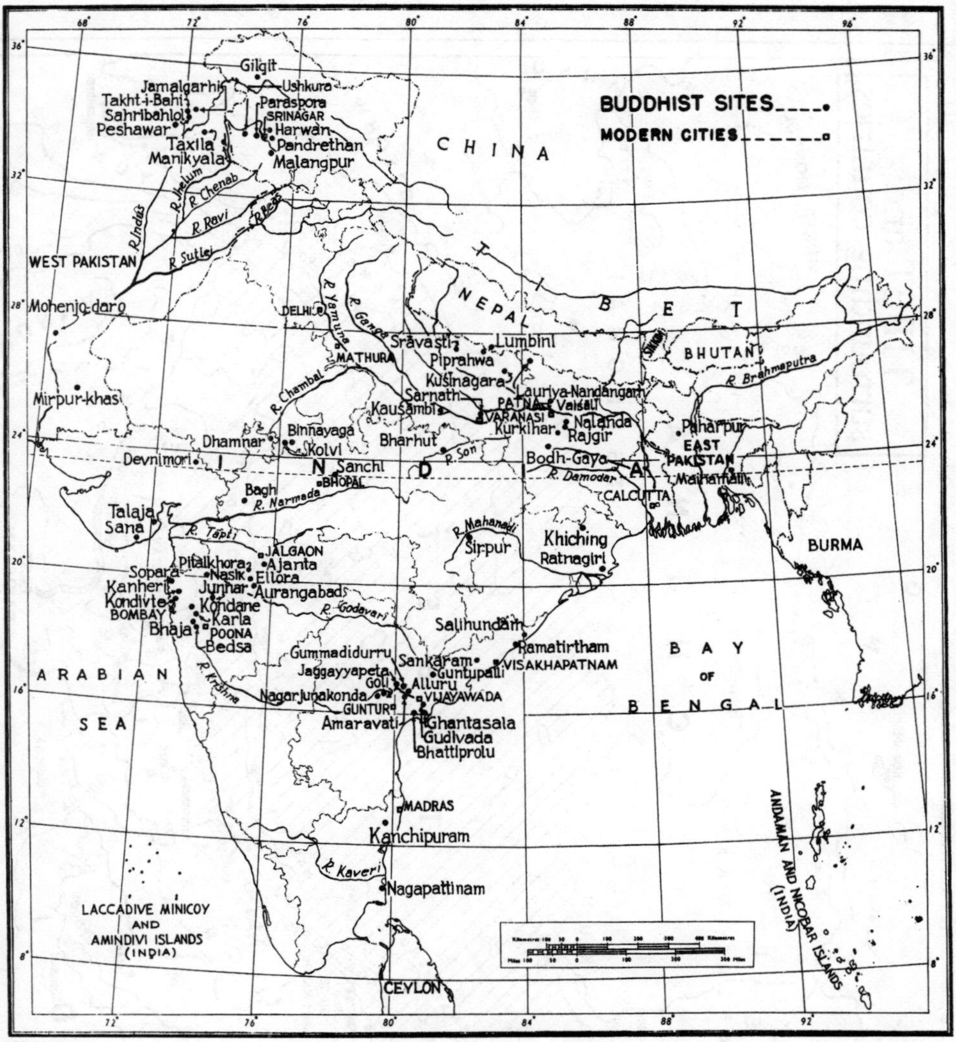

BUDDHIST SITES......•
MODERN CITIES------□

Gilgit
Jamalgarhi Ushkura
Takht-i-Bahi Paraspora
Sahribahlol SRINAGAR
Peshawar Harwan
Taxila Pandrethan
Manikyala Malangpur

CHINA

WEST PAKISTAN

Mohenjo-daro

R. Indus
R. Jhelum
R. Chenab
R. Ravi
R. Beas
R. Sutlej

Mirpur-khas

Devnimori

TIBET

NEPAL

DELHI
R. Yamuna
R. Ganges
MATHURA
Śrāvastī Lumbini
Piprahwa
Kuśinagara Lauriya-Nandangarh
Kauśāmbi Sarnath PATNA Vaiśālī
VARANASI
Bhitargaon Kurkihar Nalanda
Dhamnar Skolvi Bharhut R. Son Bodh-Gaya Rajgir
Sanchi R. Damodar
BHOPAL
Bagh
R. Narmada
R. Chambal

BHUTAN
R. Brahmaputra

Paharpur
EAST PAKISTAN
Mainamati
CALCUTTA

Talaja
Sana
R. Tapti

Sopara
Kanheri Pitalkhora JALGAON
Kondivte Nasik Ajanta
BOMBAY Junhar Ellora
Bhaja Kondane Aurangabad
POONA Karla
Bedsa

R. Godavari

Khiching
Sirpur Ratnagiri
R. Mahanadi

BURMA

ARABIAN

SEA

R. Krishna

Salihundam

Gummadidurru Sankaram Ramatirtham
Jaggayyapeta Guntupalli VISAKHAPATNAM
Goli
Nagarjunakonda Alluru
GUNTUR VIJAYAWADA
Amaravati Ghantasala
Gudivada
Bhattiprolu

BAY
OF
BENGAL

ANDAMAN AND NICOBAR ISLANDS
(INDIA)

MADRAS

Kanchipuram

R. Kaveri

Nagapattinam

LACCADIVE MINICOY
AND
AMINDIVI ISLANDS
(INDIA)

CEYLON

© 1967 by Government of India, courtesy of Debala Mitra.

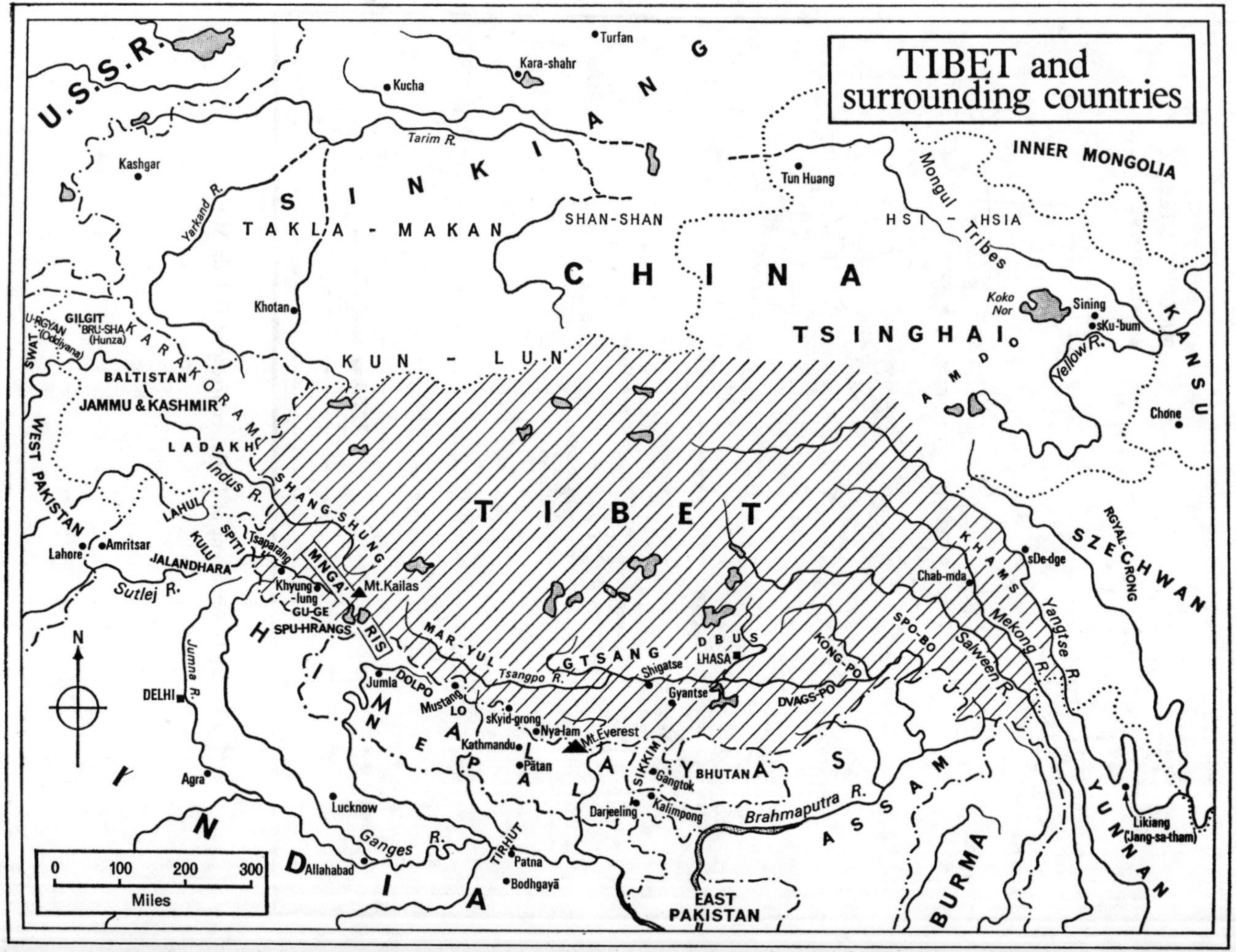
TIBET and surrounding countries
U.S.S.R.
SINKIANG
TAKLA-MAKAN
CHINA
TSINGHAI
INNER MONGOLIA
KANSU
TIBET
KUN-LUN
KARAKORAM
HIMALAYA
NEPAL
BHUTAN
SIKKIM
ASSAM
BURMA
YUNNAN
SZECHWAN
INDIA
WEST PAKISTAN
EAST PAKISTAN
Turfan
Kara-shahr
Kucha
Kashgar
Tarim R.
Yarkand R.
Khotan
SHAN-SHAN
Tun Huang
Mongul Tribes
HSI-HSIA
Koko Nor
Sining
sKu-'bum
Yellow R.
Chone
AMDO
GILGIT
'BRU-SHA (Hunza)
U-RGYAN (Oddiyana)
SWAT
BALTISTAN
JAMMU & KASHMIR
LADAKH
Indus R.
SHANG-SHUNG
LAHUL
SPITI
KULU
JALANDHARA
Lahore
Amritsar
Sutlej R.
Tsaparang
MNGA'-RIS
Mt. Kailas
Khyung-lung
GU-GE
SPU-HRANGS
MAR-YUL
Jumla
DOLPO
Mustang
LO
sKyid-grong
Nya-lam
Mt. Everest
Kathmandu
Pātan
Tsangpo R.
GTSANG
Shigatse
Gyantse
DBUS
LHASA
KONG-PO
DVAGS-PO
SPO-BO
Chab-mda
KHAMS
sDe-dge
RGYAL-RONG
Salween R.
Mekong R.
Yangtse R.
Likiang (Jang-sa-tham)
Gangtok
Kalimpong
Darjeeling
Brahmaputra R.
DELHI
Jumna R.
Agra
Lucknow
Ganges R.
Allahabad
TIRHUT
Patna
Bodhgayā
N
0 100 200 300
Miles

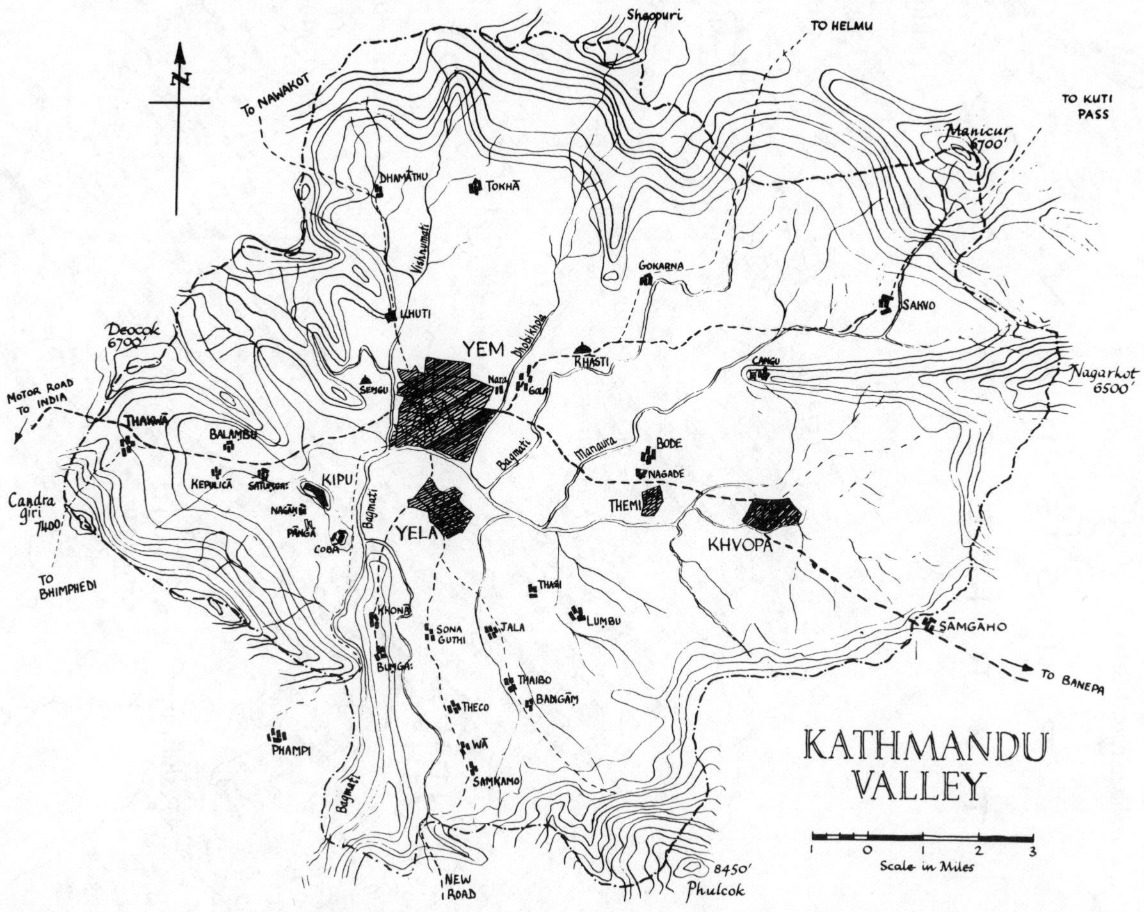
KATHMANDU VALLEY
Scale in Miles
1 0 1 2 3
N
Shaopuri
TO HELMU
TO KUTI PASS
Manicur 6700'
Nagarkot 6500'
TO BANEPA
TO NAWAKOT
Deocok 6700'
MOTOR ROAD TO INDIA
Candra giri 7400'
TO BHIMPHEDI
8450' Phulcok
NEW ROAD
YEM
YELA
KHVOPA
KIPU
THEMI
DHAMATHU
TOKHA
LHUTI
GOKARNA
SAKVO
CANGU
KHASTI
BODE
NAGADE
SEMGU
THAKWA
BALAMBU
KEPULICA
NAGAM
PANGA
COBA
KHONA
BUNGA:
SONA GUTHI
JALA
THASI
LUMBU
THAIBO
BADIGAM
THECO
WA
SAMKAMO
PHAMPI
SAMGAHO
Vishnumati
Dhobikhola
Bagmati
Manaura
Nara
Gola

CENTRAL ASIA

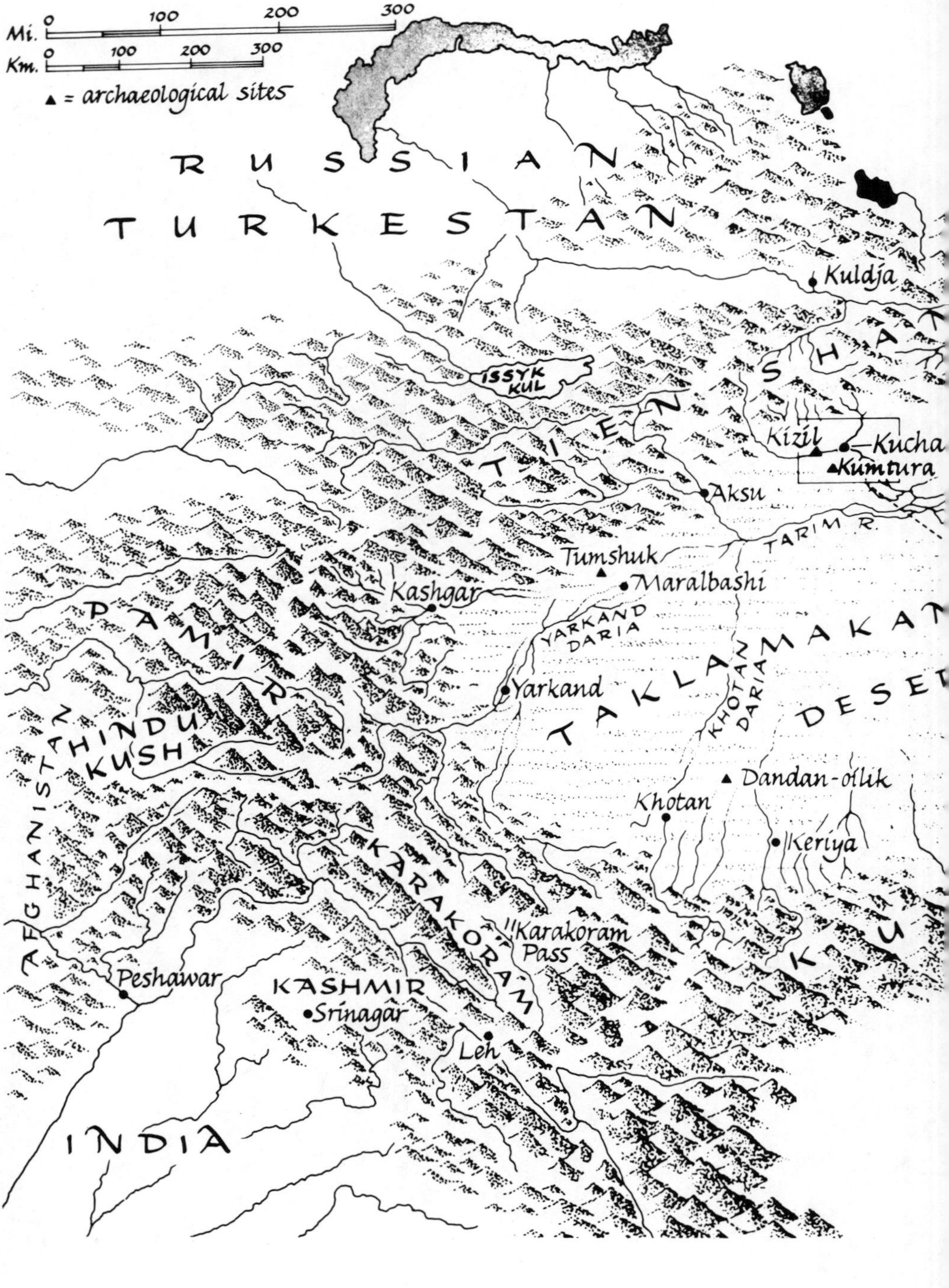

Mi. 0 100 200 300
Km. 0 100 200 300
▲ = archaeological sites
RUSSIAN TURKESTAN
Kuldja
ISSYK KUL
TIEN SHA
Kizil
Kucha
Kumtura
Aksu
TARIM R.
Tumshuk
Maralbashi
Kashgar
YARKAND DARIA
PAMIR
Yarkand
TAKLAMAKAN DESE
KHOTAN DARIA
HINDU KUSH
AFGHANISTAN
Dandan-oilik
Khotan
Keriya
KARAKORAM
Karakoram Pass
KU
Peshawar
KASHMIR
Srinagar
Leh
INDIA

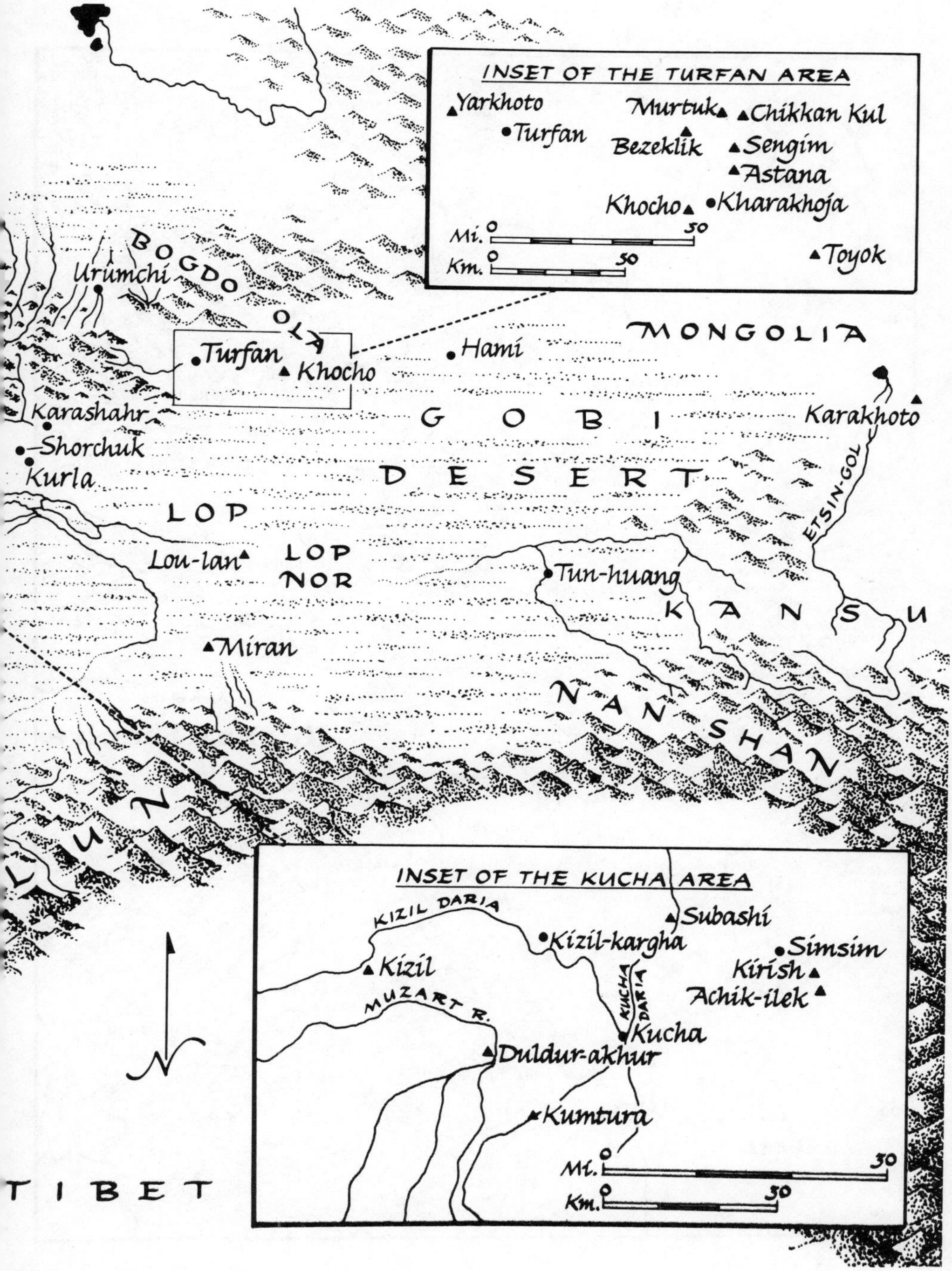
INSET OF THE TURFAN AREA
Yarkhoto
Turfan
Murtuk
Chikkan Kul
Bezeklik
Sengim
Astana
Khocho
Kharakhoja
Toyok
Mi. 0 50
Km. 0 50
BOGDO OLA
Urumchi
Turfan
Khocho
Hami
MONGOLIA
GOBI
DESERT
Karakhoto
ETSIN-GOL
Karashahr
Shorchuk
Kurla
LOP
Lou-lan
LOP NOR
Tun-huang
KANSU
Miran
NAN SHAN
KUN LUN
INSET OF THE KUCHA AREA
KIZIL DARIA
Subashi
Kizil-kargha
Simsim
Kizil
Kirish
Achik-ilek
MUZART R.
KUCHA DARIA
Kucha
Duldur-akhur
Kumtura
Mi. 0 30
Km. 0 30
N
TIBET

ARAL
SEA

KHWAREZM

Jaxartes R.

LAKE BALKASH

45

40

Oxus R.

Bukhara •

SOGDIANA
• Samarkand

FERGHANA

Tien Shan Range

• Kucha

LAKE ISSIK-KUL

• Marw

KHORASAN

• Kash

Balkh • • Termez

• Kunduz

Pamir Mts.

• Kashgar

TARIM BASIN

40

35

BACTRIA

Paropamisadae Mts.

Surkh Kotal

Hindu Kush Mts.

Herat •

Bamiyan • • Begram (Kapisa)

Kabul •

Jelalabad •

• Yarkand

Kun Lun Range

• Khotan

• Niya

35

SEISTAN

ARACHOSIA

Swat R.

Peshawar • • Taxila

KASHMIR

• Srinagar

30

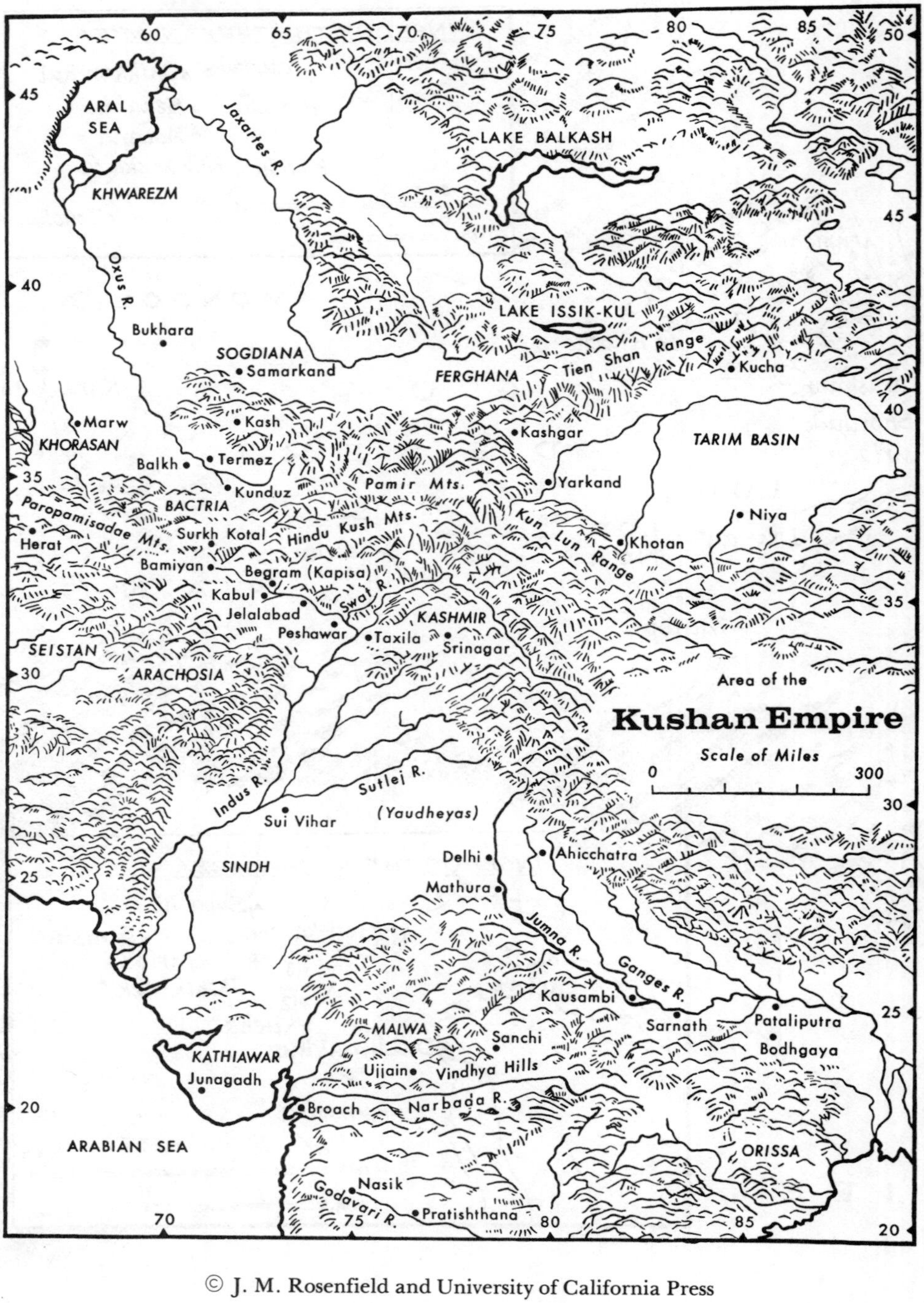

Area of the

Kushan Empire

Scale of Miles

0   300

Indus R.

Sutlej R.

• Sui Vihar

(Yaudheyas)

SINDH

Delhi •

Mathura •

Ahicchatra •

30

25

Jumna R.

Ganges R.

Kausambi •

Sarnath •

• Pataliputra

• Bodhgaya

25

KATHIAWAR

Junagadh •

MALWA

Ujjain •

Sanchi •

Vindhya Hills

• Broach Narbada R.

ORISSA

20

ARABIAN SEA

Nasik •

Godavari R. • Pratishthana

20

© J. M. Rosenfield and University of California Press

PREFACE

Since 1959 when the fourteenth Dalai Lama followed by some one hundred thousand of his subjects began his life of exile in India, there has been a great upsurge of interest in Tibetan culture generally and especially in Tibetan religion. Meanwhile Tibetan culture and religion in Tibet itself have been ruthlessly subverted by the new Communist régime, and although recently the Chinese authorities have been expressing regrets for the damage that has been done, it has already been done on so vast a scale, that such regrets come far too late. Writing earlier (1957) about the importance of the Himalayan regions for an understanding of Tibetan Buddhism, I observed that "these regions which once saw the passage of Buddhism to Tibet, have now become dependent on Tibet for the very life of their religion. The source in India has long been dead, and only the Tibetans possess the living traditions which can enliven the ancient places." Now over the last twenty years the Tibetan exiles have not only been enlivening the ancient places by means of new communities that they have established there, but they have also founded monasteries in many new areas as well as reprinting vast quantities of the literature that has been accumulating in Tibet over the last ten centuries and more. Much was brought out by the exiles themselves and much more has come to light in Himalayan lands that were subject to Tibetan cultural and religious influences in the past, but which, not being part of political Tibet, have not fallen under Chinese control. Such lands include Bhutan, much of northern Nepal, Ladakh and Zangskar, Spiti and Lahul. Moreover, the accessibility of so many Tibetan lamas and monks has led to an enthusiastic interest in Tibetan religion on the part of many young Western "truth-seekers," some of whom have become dedicated translators with facilities available to them that were unthought of thirty years ago. Such is this present-day enthusiasm for Tibetan religion, that it is easily forgotten that Tibetan Buddhism is not only of Indian origin, but has perpetuated forms of Indian Buddhism long since lost in the land where Buddhism originated. The works of many great European scholars of the past who have done so much to prepare present-day understandings are now scarcely read by a new generation and the essentially Indian nature of Tibetan Buddhism is often forgotten altogether, even though all great Tibetan lama-scholars have never ceased to draw their inspirations and their teachings from Indian sources, albeit for a long time now available to them in Tibetan translation. We now have the extraordinary situation that just as Buddhism finally disappeared from India largely as a result of foreign conquest, so Buddhism, which survived in Tibet as a remarkable Indian inheritance, has now suddenly disappeared from Tibet once again as a result of foreign conquest. Thus it seems to me suitable to attempt a general survey in historical perspective of that great religious inheritance, built up in the land of its origin during a period of some seventeen hundred years, which having been earlier transferred more or less complete to Tibet, has now been restored to India in a sadly fragmented form.

As work proceeds with a self-imposed task of such wide scope, one becomes increasingly aware of one's own limitations in some of its parts and the need for further personal investigation of original sources where one's competence is adequate for dealing with them. Delay and a sense of frustration are caused when one finds that one is dealing with textual problems that are of interest in some cases to fewer qualified scholars than one can count on one's fingers. In other cases so much reading of obscure early texts is required before one can express a reasonably acceptable general account of the kind that is suitable for a book of this nature, that one almost takes fright at the prospect before one. The various parts of this book are affected in different ways by these considerations. For the first chapter on Buddhist origins in India there is already a very large amount of published work available, mainly in English, but also in French and German. This subject is thus comparatively easily treated, and one's main task in this case is to correct the liberal-minded rationalizing approach, from which the retelling of Śākyamuni's life may suffer distortion. For later developments in India some material is available in European translations and textual editions, whether Sanskrit or Tibetan. I have drawn largely on these, but always retranslating the sources used, to maintain a consistent vocabulary. Tantric Buddhism has never yet been dealt with adequately within the whole context of Indian Buddhism, since books on this subject tend to treat Buddhist developments after the eighth century as a period of decline and corruption, which is not worth the time spent on it. This was the very period during which Buddhism was transferred in its almost total availability from India to Tibet, and the absence of any readable account of these times results in an apparent cultural gap between the two traditions, which it is the main purpose of this book to bridge. Thus the chapter on tantras is the longest in the book. Very little of this material has been translated into English or any other European language. I have used this wherever it was available and have otherwise drawn on untranslated Sanskrit editions of various works, always checking them against Tibetan translations and also upon other Tibetan translations, available in the Tibetan canon, but of which the Sanskrit original is unknown. Here the material available still in unedited Sanskrit manuscripts and in ever larger quantities in the Tibetan Canon as well as in noncanonical Tibetan collections, is so vast, that a reasonable limit has to be set to one's work, if a book of this kind is ever to be finished. It will be a long time before a more comprehensive account can be given, whatever the limitations of the present one. Competence in both Sanskrit and Tibetan as well as familiarity with the philosophical concepts and strange patterns of thought are required, and in Britain there is now only one young scholar who continues this work. Including others in Europe and the U.S.A. we might reach the number of ten, but unhappily no university seems to encourage these particular studies at the present time. Considerable work is done in Japan on Buddhist studies generally, including much work in Sanskrit and Tibetan, but this is done usually through the medium of Japanese, thus adding enormously to the linguistic burden of any Western scholar who wishes to make use of their publications.

The chapter on Buddhist communities in India and beyond has been included partly to restore the balance in the impressions given concerning Indian Buddhism, following upon the long chapter on tantras, and partly to prepare the way for the final chapter on the conversion of Tibet. Tibet was converted to Buddhism as much from the Central Asian and Chinese side as from the Indian, although Indian Buddhism later predominated almost totally. Apart from one or two brilliant and scholarly studies, referred to in the notes, on some aspects of these developments, no general survey has been attempted before as part of a history of Buddhism. Here fortunately a knowledge of Tibetan will take one a fair way in dealing with available source materials. Much relevant material from Chinese sources is available in French and English translations, while Professor Emmerick of Hamburg has been helpful in the matter of Khotanese literature. I have also drawn on the published results of the labours of earlier European archaeologists, and I should mention the time spent with Mr. Kenneth Eastman in going carefully through a new five-volume Japanese publication of illustrations of the wall paintings of the Tun-huang Caves, so as to gain an impression of the range of iconography in Chinese Central Asia during the period leading up to the conversion of Tibet and continuing beyond it, when the Tibetans in their turn added their literary and cultural achievements to the history of Central Asian Buddhism. Hsüan-tsang's account of his travels across Central Asia and throughout the Indian subcontinent during the first half of the seventh century provide a constantly recurring theme throughout this chapter and I thank Dr. Katherine Whitaker for checking the Chinese text with me, wherever an extract from an English or French translation has been used.

The conversion of Tibet to Buddhism was a long process, just as was the conversion of Europe to Christianity, a task which was never really completed in either case. I have dealt with the early period of the seventh to the tenth century in some detail, because here again no coherent account using the available source materials is generally available. Much information is, however, available in the form of articles in learned journals, to which an interested reader would not find easy access. Moreover, in order to tell their full story they need to be brought together against a general historical background. With this chapter Dr. Hugh Richardson has been of great help and encouragement to me in the interest which he has taken in checking my translations of early Tibetan manuscript material and in drawing my attention to related references. Also Mr. Kenneth Eastman of Berkeley, California, who is one of the rarest of young scholars able to use Japanese publications in his work on Tibetan Buddhism, and who is now working on early Tibetan Buddhist works of the eighth to tenth centuries, surviving as rediscovered manuscripts in the Tun-huang collection, has done much to keep me on a steady course in my brief treatment of this material. Here again there is a desperate need for interested support for these studies, if any further progress is to be made. This rare material is divided between London and Paris; work certainly proceeds in Paris, while in Britain there is now no one in any of our universities who makes use of our collection.[1] The later period of the conversion of Tibet from the eleventh century onward is well dealt with in Tibetan religious histories, and the most useful of them all for this period, namely *The Blue Annals* of a famous Tibetan scholar and translator, gZhon-nu-dpal (1392-1481), is happily available in an English translation. This later period leads straight through to what becomes in effect a history of Tibetan Buddhism, which would be quite beyond the scope of the present book and would require a second volume. Also, owing to an extraordinary increase in interest in Tibetan religion and culture, following upon the exodus of some one hundred thousand Tibetans from their country when it was finally taken over by the Chinese Communist government in 1959, the amount of Tibetan source material now available for writing a history of Tibetan religion is already overwhelming. There is only one scholar in the whole world who has been taking stock of the greater part of this material, as it has gradually appeared in print in India, and that is Mr. E. Gene Smith, Field Director of the Library of Congress Office in New Delhi, who happens also from personal interest to be a highly qualified Tibetan scholar. His breadth of knowledge is displayed in several introductory essays to some of these Tibetan publications, and one only hopes that one day he will produce a general survey of all that has appeared. There are now Tibetan religious centres scattered over Western Europe and the United States, and some of these have encouraged the production of useful surveys and selected translations of Tibetan texts. This work proceeds mainly outside university life, and one might mention an unusual exception in this regard, namely Jeffrey Hopkins of the University of Virginia, who does much to further the cause of the dGe-lugs-pa (Yellow Hat) Order and so has the special blessing of no less a person than the Dalai Lama himself. Western scholars generally find the works of the earlier Tibetan religious orders more interesting because of their more eclectic approach and their freer manners of religious life. Several useful publications have come forth from Boulder, Colorado, where this book is also being published, and one can scarcely omit all reference to this remarkable center of Tibetan studies. Trungpa Rinpoche, now the head of an extensive religious network covering much of the U.S.A., seems to have inspired Mr. Samuel Bercholz to devote his publishing interests mainly to books on Buddhism, and his company now has a high

[1] This is hardly a criticism of those who occupy university posts, when for Tibetan they are reduced to one in the whole of the British Isles, and when Buddhist studies are usually taught by those who have no knowledge of any oriental language. There are probably some four or five exceptions.

degree of competence in this rather specialized field. Publishers now usually want diacritical marks and difficult foreign spellings reduced to a minimum, unless they are going to be helped on the way with quite a substantial financial subvention, and in the course of my now quite long publishing life, no publisher has ever asked me before to restore Sanskrit names and titles, where I thought it more prudent to use English equivalents. Thus my thanks are more than due to Mr. Larry Mermelstein of this friendly publishing company for the considerable amount of work that he has done on the whole typescript before publication, checking and rechecking with detailed care and uncomplainingly inserting into my text the many changes that we have agreed upon. Incidentally he has also introduced American spellings throughout, thus undoing some of the work that my sister, Una Snellgrove, had done by looking for spelling and typing errors through the whole text.

I can hardly allow to appear in print a book of this kind, which represents an overall survey of all the work done throughout my university career, without some words of appreciation for the School of Oriental and African Studies in London, which has largely sponsored my activities for over thirty years. Without the use of its magnificent library and related facilities, the writing of this book would have been a far more tedious task. Also I want to thank those other institutions that have come to our assistance with grants for research work and travel over the last decade. The British Academy has come to our help in this way on several occasions, and recently the Leverhulme Trust has saved us—at a time that has been financially very difficult for our particular studies—from losing the momentum of personal initiative, which alone keeps our work in a thriving condition when direct government support is reduced to a bare minimum in subjects such as ours. Finally I must again thank the British Academy for their generous help toward the cost of publication of this book by Serindia Publications in the United Kingdom.

In the preface to *A Cultural History of Tibet* by Hugh Richardson and myself (first published in 1968 in London and reprinted in Boulder, Colorado, in 1980) we referred to our founding of a modest Institute of Tibetan Studies in Tring (England). Owing to changed circumstances since its foundation eighteen years ago it was decided in the course of 1983 to reconstitute this charge of ours as an Institute of Buddhist Studies, while inviting Dr. Tadeusz Skorupski to assume the responsibility of directing activities. What the future will bring we have yet to see, but in the meantime I hope that this book, the first to be published in the name of the newly constituted Institute, will not only supply a need wherever there is interest in the great variety of teachings and practices which may be called Buddhist, but also that it will draw attention to the vast amount of scholarly labor by others, which alone makes the writing of a general survey of Indo-Tibetan Buddhism a feasible task for its author.

David L. Snellgrove
Torre Pellice (Italy)
14 January 1985

NOTE ON TRANSCRIPTION

Sanskrit and Pāli are given in the normally accepted Anglo-American transcription. The letters most likely to be mispronounced by the uninitiated are:

c which represents a soft unvoiced *j* sound, as in Vairójana (correctly spelt *Vairocana*); by contrast *ch* represents fully aspirated Anglo-American *ch*.

th which represents an aspirated *t-h*, as in English "goatherd" and in the term *tathāgata*, pronounced tatágata, breathing heavily on the second *t*.

Tibetan terms are spelt according to the system shown in my *Buddhist Himālaya*, pp. 299-300, where some simplified rules of pronunciation are also given. It is regrettable that such spellings appear formidable to anyone unfamiliar with the Tibetan language, but there is no satisfactory solution to this problem. Artificial spellings which are intended to provide easier means toward the actual present-day pronunciation of such names (e.g., writing Thri-de-song-tsen instead of the correct spelling *Khri-lde-srong-brtsan*) assist the uninitiated reader very little, while tending to bewilder anyone familiar with Tibetan. It is exactly as if one were to spell the English word "knight" as "nait" for the benefit of readers who do not know how to pronounce English. In any case, the reader must then become familiar with the rules applying to such phonetic spellings. I have however occasionally added in brackets such spellings, and even used them in the text, where the same name occurs frequently, e.g., *bKa'-brgyud-pa* (Ka-gyü-pa) and *bKa'-gdams-pa* (Ka-dam-pa). The rules for such phonetic spellings are given in my *Himalayan Pilgrimage*, pp. 275-9.

It may also be noted that while my system of reproducing correct Tibetan spellings corresponds almost entirely with that now generally in use by British and American scholars, it differs in several respects from the systems still used by French, German, and Italian scholars. To avoid further confusion I have normally transposed their transliterations into the Anglo-American system when I have occasion to quote their works, to preserve consistency. The Anglo-American system is often referred to as the Wylie system, as it was set out by Turrell Wylie, "A Standard System of Tibetan Transcription," HJAS, 1959, pp. 261-7. He reproduced my own system of a few years earlier, with the one important difference in the use of capital letters, used by him for the first letter of a name even when this is a silent prefix, instead of for the radical letter under which words are always listed in Tibetan dictionaries. Thus whereas I write *bSam-yas*, pronounced Sam-yä and correctly listed under S, he writes *Bsam-yas*. Such differences may seem petty to the uninitiated, but, especially in a book of the present size, one has to choose one system and attempt to be consistent.

I
ORIGINS IN INDIA

1. THE REDISCOVERY OF INDIAN BUDDHISM

Anyone who writes nowadays about the history of Buddhism takes for granted its promulgation by Śākyamuni Buddha in the central Ganges Valley as the starting point of this religion, and it is all too easily forgotten that this great event which probably occurred about 500 B.C. was scarcely known of in the western scholarly world until the early nineteenth century and that it was only since then that several decades of laborious research, mainly in Sanskrit, Pāli and Tibetan Buddhist literature supported by extraordinary archeological discoveries all over the Indian subcontinent, have given substance to that belated discovery. The problem of establishing the origins of this great pan-Asian religion was by no means as easy as it may now appear to us in retrospect. Christian missionaries had encountered Buddhist monks at the Mongol court of Kublai Khan and his successors in the thirteenth and fourteenth centuries, but the origins and nature of Buddhist religion remained totally obscure. Three centuries later when the first Christian missionaries reached Tsaparang, capital of the old kingdom of Gu-ge in western Tibet, in 1624, their interpretations of the religious life that they saw there remained just as naïve. Knowing no Tibetan, they suspected that they were perhaps confronted by some strange debased form of Christianity, for might not the image of Tārā (the Saviouress) be a weird form of the "Mother of God," or the set of three images of Tsong-kha-pa and his two chief disciples be some outlandish representation of the Trinity? From the sixteenth century onward there appear many descriptions of local religious beliefs, mainly the work of missionaries, who, following in the wake of European adventurers, established themselves, often precariously enough, in India and Ceylon, in Burma, Thailand, China and Japan, but operating only by hearsay and without any precise knowledge of the relevant literary sources, they found no obvious connection between the Buddhism of China and that of Ceylon.[1] As for India, the "holy land" where Buddhism had indeed originated, all local memory of it had been lost long since its final eclipse in northern India in the thirteenth century. Some ancient Buddhist sites were certainly known locally, but were quite wrongly interpreted by popular tradition. Thus the now famous Buddhist

[1] The best account of these early gropings after the truth will be found in Henri de Lubac, *La Rencontre du Bouddhisme et de l'Occident*, p. 51 ff.

caves at Nāsik (about one hundred miles northeast of Bombay) were associated with the Pāndava brothers of the Indian epic, the Mahābhārata, and the magnificent Buddhist cave-temple at Karlā (easily reached nowadays from Lanavla half way between Bombay and Poona) was accepted as a Shaivite shrine, in that the rock-hewn stūpa in the apse was assumed to be a huge Śiva *lingam*. Many other now well-known ancient Buddhist sites, such as Sāñcī and Ajantā, were totally lost in the jungle and were discovered often accidentally by British officers in the course of the nineteenth century.

As early as 1784 due to the enthusiasm of Sir William Jones, a judge of the Supreme Court in Calcutta, an institution known as the Asiatic Society was founded for the purpose of investigating "the history and antiquities, arts, sciences and literature of Asia," but it was a long time before sufficient pressure could be brought upon the British administration in India to give support to such operations. However, as soon as responsibility for government passed from the old East India Company to the British Crown (1858) it was decided to establish an archaeological department with Sir Alexander Cunningham as the first Archaeological Surveyor of India (1862).[2] A few years earlier a French Sinologist, Stanislas Julien, had completed the translation of the travels of the now famous Chinese scholar-pilgrim Hsüan-tsang, whose personal record of all the many Buddhist sites that he visited in the seventh century throughout Central Asia and northern India at a time when they were mainly flourishing, remains the best description to this day. There could have been no better guide to the archaeological treasures of a past Buddhist age than this work, and amongst his many other activities Cunningham set himself the task of identifying as many as possible of these ancient sites on the ground. Government support of archaeological work remained unhappily rather hesitant, and it was not until the first years of the twentieth century under the viceroyalty of Lord Curzon that adequate funds were at last made available for the repair and preservation of the many Buddhist sites all over India, which the present-day visitor can reach with comparative ease. Despite other pressing demands on its resources, the Government of India since the year of independence (1947) has maintained the work of the Archaeological Survey, which is concerned not only with Buddhist monuments (of special interest to us in this book), but also Hindu, Muslim as well as many significant prehistoric finds.

Meanwhile the scholarly investigation of textual source material was gaining momentum, and at long last this newly discovered literature combined with archaeological investigation began to reveal the long forgotten history of the Buddhist religion on Indian soil covering some seventeen hundred years from approximately 500 B.C. to 1,200 A.D. Three names stand out significantly during the pioneering work of the first half of the nineteenth century. Firstly perhaps one should think of Brian Hodgson, who lived in Kathmandu over a period of some twenty-three years from 1820 onward, first as an assistant at the British

[2] For "The Story of Indian Archaeology" one may refer to the chapter by N. P. Chakravarti in *Archaeology in India*, an Indian Government publication, Calcutta, 1950.

Residency and later as accredited British Resident.[3] Whereas Buddhism had largely disappeared in northern India from the thirteenth century onward, it has survived in the Nepal Valley until the present day. Moreover, from the seventh century onward the Nepal Valley served as a halfway house for the transmission of Buddhism from India to Tibet and thus considerable accumulations of Buddhist Sanskrit manuscripts are to be found there. The oldest of these are palm-leaf manuscripts from India dating back to the period of the Pāla dynasty (eighth to twelfth century) of Bengal, whose monarchs were generally staunch supporters of Buddhism during the very centuries that Sanskrit Buddhist literature was passing into Nepal for its eventual translation into Tibetan. Since Buddhist traditions have survived in Nepal up to the present time the latest manuscripts are copies of the nineteenth and twentieth centuries. However, apart from the inevitable textual errors attributable to so many generations of copyists, these later works have quite as much significance for the lost history of Buddhism in India as do the earlier ones. It was Brian Hodgson who first discovered for the outside world this enormous accumulation of Indian and Nepalese Buddhist materials, and having obtained as many hundreds of such works as he could, he distributed them between Calcutta, London, Oxford and Paris. Little account was taken of them except in Paris, where Eugène Burnouf had become the incumbent of a Chair in Sanskrit at the Collège de France. His eventual publication in 1844 of his *Introduction à l'histoire du Bouddhisme indien* opened the whole field of study with which this present book is mainly concerned. He also produced the first translation of any known Mahāyāna sūtra, namely the *Lotus of the True Law*, to which several references will be made below. Mainly a collector of widely ranging interests, Hodgson produced merely a number of articles on the subject of Buddhism as revealed by his Nepalese sources, and although he refers to it as Nepalese or even Tibetan Buddhism, its true Indian origin is in no doubt. His perspicacity was truly amazing and much of what he wrote remains fully valid in terms of the considerable amount of later scholarly work to which his discoveries gave birth. It may be noted that this work on Sanskrit Buddhist materials was initiated at a time when the Theravādin traditions of the Pāli Canon of Ceylon were still practically unknown.

The third outstanding name during the first half of the nineteenth century is that of Csoma de Kőrös, a Hungarian who set out on an adventurous journey overland eastwards in search of the origins of his own Hungarian race and ended up from 1823 onward leading an ascetic life in the Indian Tibetan-speaking borderland of Zangskar, making an inventory of the contents of the Tibetan Buddhist Canon, as well as compiling a grammar and a dictionary of Tibetan. Csoma's work showed conclusively that the Tibetan canonical works were almost entirely translations from Buddhist Sanskrit, and thus another large chapter was opened in the history of Buddhism in India. Csoma may fairly be regarded as the founder of Tibetan studies in the outside world, but in fact this honor should

[3] For his life story see the Introduction by Philip Denwood to Brian H. Hodgson, *Essays on the Languages, Literature and Religion of Nepal and Tibet*.

rightly have gone to the Jesuit missionary scholar Ippolito Desideri who lived in Lhasa from 1716 to 1721. He was the first foreign scholar to master the Tibetan language, both in its colloquial and its literary form, and as well as celebrating Mass and disputing on friendly terms with learned Tibetan monks, he acquired an amazing knowledge not only of Tibetan religion but also of Tibetan life and customs. He knew well the Indian origins of Tibetan Buddhism, but owing to the lack of interest of his superiors, none of his work was published until the beginning of the twentieth century, and thus what he himself knew, remained unknown to the outside world until a century later, when Csoma de Kőrös made his appearance.

In the second half of the nineteenth century serious studies on the Pāli literature of Ceylon were undertaken, leading to the founding of the Pāli Text Society by T. W. Rhys Davids in 1881, thanks to whom the whole of the Theravādin Canon has gradually been made available in Western-style editions, much of it also translated into English. This has been a stupendous work of three generations of Pāli scholars, of whom the last staunch English representative, Miss I. B. Horner, died only recently. Already in 1879 the great orientalist Max Müller founded his impressive series of translations under the general title of *Sacred Books of the East*, in retrospect a vast work that extends right up to present times, when the many reprints are taken into account. It is interesting to note that interpretations of Buddhism in the English language have been mainly based on Theravādin (Pāli) sources, presumably as a result of the spectacular productions of the Pāli Text Society. Interest in Indian Buddhism, especially of the Mahāyāna and Vajrayāna periods, has been mainly a European preserve with most of the scholarly works on the subject appearing in French. One thinks at once of Sylvain Lévi, Louis de la Vallée Poussin and Paul Demiéville, of Jean Filliozat, Alfred Foucher and Jean Przluski, of Étienne Lamotte, Constantin Régamey and André Bareau, whose works will receive special mention in the footnotes throughout this book. Without doubt the one great scholar in Indo-Tibetan Buddhism is my old revered professor Giuseppe Tucci, whose expeditions in western and central Tibet during the 1930s and 1940s brought to light hitherto unknown treasures of Tibetan religion, history and art. His literary works range from editions of Sanskrit, Tibetan and Chinese texts to impressive works on all aspects of Indo-Tibetan civilization. Amongst Indian scholars one thinks of Rājendra Mitra (1822-91) from the last century, and from this present one Benoytosh Bhattacharyya who has made easily available a useful number of Buddhist tantric works, or Shashi Bhusan Dasgupta, who has ranged more widely over similar religious materials, or again Nalinaksha Dutt, who has worked particularly on the relationship of the Mahāyāna to the earlier Buddhist period. Without the work of these and of many other scholars, whose names appear in the bibliography, it would have been an even more exacting task to attempt this general survey of Indian Buddhism. Special attention must also be made of Edward Conze, who devoted so many years of his life to translating large quantities of the "Perfection of Wisdom" literature, which provides the philosophical basis for the whole Mahāyāna period both in India and in Tibet.

Especially relevant to any study of Indo-Tibetan Buddhism are the remarkable discoveries of earlier Buddhist civilizations brought to light mainly by the labors of British, French and German expeditions at the beginning of the present century. Thus not only has the significance of Khotan and other city-states on the ancient Silk Road linking India as well as western Asia with China become known, but also much of the pre-Buddhist history of Tibet itself, previously unknown to the Tibetans themselves, has been revealed through remarkable discoveries of remains of Tibetan manuscripts throughout the area going back to the time when Tibet was a major power in Central Asia (seventh to ninth centuries). Here Sir Harold Bailey, the guide and teacher of my Cambridge years, has achieved renown not only for his vast linguistic scholarship but especially for the painstaking work that he has done over many years specifically on Khotanese materials. Those to whom we are primarily indebted for their work on the earliest known Tibetan literary remains (and this includes the early stone inscriptions in Tibet itself) are Jacques Bacot, Paul Pelliot, F. W. Thomas and Hugh Richardson, who was the last British representative in Tibet, remaining there until 1949. Much of this early Tibetan material is influenced by Buddhism simply because the development of local scripts seems to have occurred simultaneously with the more general introduction of Buddhist culture into Tibet as well as into Central Asia. Although we shall be concerned primarily with Buddhism in India and its eventual transfer to Tibet, one must remember that Indian civilization, whether in its Hindu or Buddhist form, was at the same time penetrating the whole of Southeast Asia, not to mention the Far East whither it was transmitted mainly across Central Asia. The great Indian gods, Viṣṇu and Śiva, had their followers in some countries of Southeast Asia, but it was the person of Śākyamuni Buddha whose teachings have had by far the most extensive influence throughout all Asian lands. It is interesting to note that the eclipse of Buddhism in India coincided more or less with the gradual weakening of its hold on the rest of Asia, so that nowadays it survives only in Ceylon, Burma, Thailand and Cambodia in a form deriving from one of the early Buddhist schools (the Theravādins) and in Himalayan regions and in Japan in its Mahāyāna form. Thanks to the many Tibetan exiles now settled there, it is even now reestablishing itself in the land of its origin.

2. ŚĀKYAMUNI: BUDDHA OF THE PRESENT WORLD-AGE

The group of followers who gathered around their teacher and leader, referred to as Gautama by others, but revered by them as "Lord" (*Bhagavan*), represented one of many such ascetic groups who appeared on the Indian scene round about 500 B.C. The accounts of their wanderings and of their Lord's teachings, as committed to writing very much later, represent probably the earliest Indian historical material of a literary kind, and thus they provide their own historical and geographical context. It is difficult to test their authenticity, except perhaps by bringing them into archaeological relationship with certain sacred places, which were known to be famous in subsequent centuries.

No attempt at a coherent "biography" of Gautama, the Sage of the Śākya Clan (*Śākyamuni*) was made until some five centuries after his decease. The much earlier canonical writings, most of which would seem to have been accumulated within the rather vague period of one to two centuries after his decease, relate incidentally certain essential stories about him, especially his miraculous birth in the Lumbini Garden near Kapilavastu, the chief town of the Śākyas, his realization of Enlightenment (*bodhi*) under the famous tree of enlightenment at Bodhgayā (in modern Bihar), his preaching of the First Sermon in the Deer Park just outside Vārānasi, and the Great Decease (*parinirvāṇa*) at Kāsia (close to the northwestern boundary of Bihar, see pls. 1 and 2). The circumstances that led up to these four main events were also described in some detail, but there was never any consecutive account of events between the preaching of the First Sermon and the Final Decease, a period of forty-five years, if this last tradition is accepted. At the same time the canonical texts contained numerous stories of teachings given, of hospitality received, of visits made to persons of note and so on, and it was by arranging such as these in some coherent, but by no means necessarily correct historical order, that a form of overall biographical account was eventually produced. It may be important to note that the earliest attempts at a form of "biography" were as much concerned with Śākyamuni's previous lives, which no modern scholar and few "modern" Buddhists would regard as in any way historical.[4]

It is possible to draw interesting analogies between the "life" of Jesus Christ as presented in the Four Gospels and the life of Śākyamuni Buddha, as presented in this later Buddhist tradition. In both cases certain essential events received at an early stage a more or less fixed traditional form, in the one case the events of the miraculous birth, the baptism scene and the temptation in the wilderness, then the crucifixion and resurrection narratives, while in the other case we have the four main events of miraculous birth, the renunciation of a worldly life and the scene of the enlightenment, followed by the first sermon and with a very long gap indeed finally the events leading up to the Great Decease. Apart from these main events, nothing else was recorded in a consecutive historical manner, and in order to produce a coherent story, later Buddhist writers, in an analogous way to the authors of the Four Gospels, drew upon the large available stock of isolated stories, which were associated with collections of sayings and teachings, arranging them in the order which suited their overall purpose.

Yet a further important analogy can be drawn, for in neither case was the

[4] Two such early productions that have survived in Sanskrit are the *Lalitavistara* ("Extended Version of his Display") and the *Mahàvastu* ("The Great Matter"). The first coherent "lives" in any truly biographical sense are the *Buddhacarita* ("Acts of the Buddha"), one composed by *Saṅgharakṣa* and another one, better known, by Aśvaghoṣa. See the Bibliography.

overall purpose the producing of an historically acceptable biography. Just as the main interest in the Gospels is their christological trend, so the overall purpose in producing a "life" of Śākyamuni was doctrinal and buddhalogical. In both cases mythological concepts precede and condition the form that the story shall take. The Gospel story is told as it is, because those who told it already conceived of this Jesus in terms of the concepts of "suffering servant," "son of man" and "son of God." Similarly the story of Śākyamuni's life is cast in the form of the ideal last life of a "would-be Buddha" (Bodhisattva) who after an innumerable succession of previous lives eventually achieves his goal. It is for this reason that the earliest formulations of a consecutive kind are concerned as much, if not more, with tales of previous lives, leading up to the final great event of the Enlightenment under the famous tree at Bodhgayā. Thus the final story assumes certain fundamental doctrinal concepts, which are expressed mythologically, and apart from these the story itself has no particular significance. It is the story of a wealthy young man, a prince of the Śākya Clan, who tires of the meaningless luxury of the royal court, and abandoning secretly at night his wife and young son, goes to seek out a religious teacher, who can restore his peace of mind, disturbed as it is by thoughts of disease, old age and death, the inevitable afflictions of all living creatures. He finds teachers, but surpasses them in wisdom, proclaims himself enlightened and gathers followers, who become under his direction a recognized order of mendicant ascetics. He directs his monks for a period of forty-five years, during which time a considerable amount of teaching is given, which being first preserved orally, becomes the basis for the later scriptures, comprising monastic rules, doctrinal utterances and philosophical disquisition. Except for his remarkable success as a religious teacher, there is nothing extraordinary or personally biographical about such a story.[5] The same theme reoccurs in Indian religious literature, and indeed the story was regarded, once it was formulated, as representing the set course that any Buddha should follow in his last life in this world. It was defined as the Twelve Acts of a Buddha, listed thus:

1. The Bodhisattva resides in the Joyful (*Tuṣita*) Heaven.
2. He decides to descend into the world to save it from false teachings.
3. He enters the womb of Queen Mahāmāyā, chief wife of King Śuddhodana of the Śākya Clan, while she dreams that a white elephant is descending within her.
4. He is born from his mother's side while she supports herself against a tree in the Lumbini Gardens outside Kapilavastu. As soon as he is born, he takes seven firm steps to the north, and surveying the four directions, he proclaims: "I am the chief in the world. I am the best in the world. I am

[5] Exactly the same story but with a variant setting is told of one of Śākyamuni's own disciples, namely Yasa. The son of a wealthy gildmaster in Vārānasi, he wakes up one night with feelings of disgust for the life of licentious luxury that surrounds him. He escapes from the house and the city gates open miraculously for him. However, instead of having to search for a religious teacher, he goes straight to Śākyamuni who is teaching in the Deer Park. For the whole story in its various early versions, see André Bareau, *Recherches* I, pp. 199 ff.

the first in the world. This is my last birth. There is now no existence again."

5. His prowess in arts and sports leading to his marriage.
6. His life in the palace and the resulting sense of revulsion.
7. He flees from the palace with the help of his groom Chandaka and his horse Kantaka and practices meditation under two different teachers.
8. He practises severe asceticism, but finally accepts food from the village-girl Sujātā.
9. He goes to the Tree of Enlightenment and taking his seat beneath it, engages upon his successful battle with the forces of the Evil One (Māra).
10. He wins through to Supreme Enlightenment.
11. He preaches, or to use the technical term, "turns the wheel" of the doctrine.
12. He passes into total nirvāṇa.

Apart from the contents of item 11, which was ever more extended in teaching scope in order to accommodate the later developments of the doctrine, all the rest is composed of traditional materials going back to the earliest known phase of Buddhism, including the extraordinary claim to preeminence in item 4. Thus it is important to emphasize that the idea of an agnostic teacher of ethics of entirely human proportions who was later divinized by the enthusiasm of his followers, remains a liberal nineteenth-century European creation, corresponding to the similar efforts that were made to find a purely human ethical teacher behind the Jesus Christ of the Gospel accounts. In both cases the "mythological" interests are primary, and since they dictate, as it were spontaneously, the form in which the story is told, not only does the story become trite when deprived by critical scholarship of its religious significance, but also a gap begins to yawn between the "founder" himself and his believing followers. According to the traditional accounts only superhuman intervention can explain the extraordinary early success of the teaching, and of this liberal-minded scholarship will know nothing. Thus, the subsequent development of the religion has to be explained away as mainly the work of overcredulous followers, who choose to conceive of their teacher within the categories of preconceived concepts. To what extent such a thesis is theoretically possible is really beside the main point. For the main point is the fact that there is nothing substantial in the earliest traditional accounts to support any such thesis. The notion of "the Buddha," as though there were only one, just as there is traditionally only one Christ, is entirely a modern nineteenth-century Western idea. Whether the previous Buddhas who are named in the early scriptures can be shown to be historical or not, is once again beside the point, since the followers of Śākyamuni Buddha throughout the whole history of Buddhism in Asia have never doubted that he was one of many. He was certainly regarded as the most recent and in this sense the most important during the early Buddhist phase, subsequently referred to as the Hīnayāna by those who had faith in later dispensations, but it was never forgotten that he was one in a series. The concept of the world as part of a beginningless series of time-cycles was fundamental to Buddhism, and thus it was taken for granted that there were other Buddhas in other world-ages. Fundamental too is the concept of continual rebirth, which Desideri found so "pestiferous,"[6] and thus it was assumed that any living being who achieved final enlightenment and proclaimed himself as "Buddha," must have progressed through a very long series of previous lives. Since the earliest form of Buddhism that we know of makes these basic assumptions, it is a not unreasonable assumption that they were already taken for granted by Śākyamuni Buddha himself. Thus his views on the problems of life can hardly coincide with those ascribed to him by certain nineteenth- and twentieth-century interpreters. Nor can they possibly coincide, except for a bare statement of ethical principles, with those of Jesus Christ as portrayed in the Gospels. Thus while one can draw interesting analogies between the ways in which their very different life stories were conditioned by the cosmological, mythological and religious ideas, which they apparently and quite understandably accepted as the basis for their teachings, these very ideas that were fundamental to the subsequent development of their very different religions, being totally diverse, limit considerably the scope for doctrinal similarity.

However, one further analogy relating to what was already said earlier may be mentioned, as it is particularly relevant to any study made of the life of Śākyamuni. It was observed that the accounts of certain events in his life, in so far as they may be treated as historical, represent some of the earliest known Indian "history," and since there are no other literary sources against which to check them, they provide their own historical context. There are, however, two other contexts, geographical and archaeological, by which they can be judged, and in these respects they survive very well the tests that can be applied. Thus, all the place-names associated with the main events of his life and his various journeyings are to be found within the limits of the middle Ganges Valley, corresponding more or less to modern Bihar. Much later "apocryphal" traditions envisage him traveling as far as Sri Lanka in the South and even to the city of Khotan in Central Asia, but no such extravagances occur in the early materials.[7] Thus, the geographical extent of his activities would seem to be historically certain. More than this, several of the actual sites associated with some of the main events in his life were certainly well known as major places of pilgrimage before the third century B.C., when they were visited by the great Emperor Aśoka who had inscriptions made in stone to mark the occasions. Thus, in the tenth year of his reign (259-8 B.C.) he visited the Tree of Enlightenment at Bodhgayā,

[6] For his account of "the abominable belief in metempsychosis" see *An Account of Tibet, the travels of Ippolito Desideri S.J.*, p. 226 ff.; but for his overall more balanced view of Tibetan religion, see p. 300: "although I believe the articles of Faith to be absolutely wrong and pestiferous, yet the rules and directions imposed on the will are not alien to the principles of sound reason; they seem to me worthy of admiration as they not only prescribe hatred of vice, inculcate battling against passions, but, what is more remarkable, lead man towards sublime and heroic perfection."

[7] Similarly, the place-names associated with the life of Jesus Christ as given in the New Testament limit convincingly the range of his personal activity. The apocryphal stories, however, bring him into personal contact with Tiberius in Rome and with King Abgarus of Edessa. See e.g., M. R. James, *The Apocryphal New Testament*, p.158 and pp. 476-7.

and in the twenty-first year he visited Śākyamuni's birthplace in the Lumbini Gardens.[8]

Eight such great places of pilgrimage remained famous so long as Buddhism endured in northern India, that is, up to about 1200 A.D., and meticulous descriptions of the sites have been preserved thanks to the travelogues of certain Chinese pilgrim-scholars, especially Hsüan-tsang, who made a tour of Buddhist India toward the middle of the seventh century A.D. Finally, a Tibetan monk-pilgrim, Chos-rje-dpal, the translator from Chag, visited Bodhgayā, the most important of the holy places, in the early thirteenth century, when it was already practically abandoned following upon the latest Moslem incursions. As already noted above, four main sites, Lumbini, Bodhgayā, Sārnāth (the Deer Park near Vārānasi) and Kāsia, represented the places of Śākyamuni's birth, enlightenment, first preaching and final decease. Four secondary sites represented the places where certain miracles were believed to have occurred, namely Śrāvasti, where Śākyamuni had defeated six heretical teachers by means of an extraordinary magical display, Rājagṛha, where he had quelled the wild elephant set upon him by his jealous cousin Devadatta, Vaiśāli, where a monkey had offered him a dish of honey, and Sāṅkāśya, where he descended by a heavenly flight of steps from the Heaven of the Thirty-Three Gods after delivering a sermon to his mother, who having died only seven days after his birth, had been happily reborn there. All these eight places were graced with stūpas (memorial mounds), temples and monastic enclaves in the past, but with the disappearance of Buddhism from India, they soon sank into neglect and ruin. In the nineteenth century the Archaeological Department of the Government of India began to take an interest in these as well as other ancient Indian sites, some of which have been so well reconstituted that pilgrims from countries beyond India have begun to come again. Bodhgayā, the place of the Enlightenment and thus the center of the Buddhist world, has been most successfully restored. Already in the thirteenth to fourteenth centuries the Burmese were responsible for substantial repairs, and yet again toward the end of the nineteenth century. This led to the active interest of the Archaeological Survey, which restored some of the ancient railings, a large number of small votary stūpas, several images and even the Diamond Seat (*vajrāsana*) itself. This is a sandstone slab, placed once more beneath the pipul tree, which one may not unreasonably suppose to be the lineal descendant of the original Tree of Enlightenment, under which Śākyamuni sat twenty-five hundred years ago. In recent years several religious communities, mainly Tibetan monks who have been exiles from their own country for the last twenty years and more, have built new monasteries, and thus it has become once more a major center for enthusiastic followers of Buddhist teachings. Sārnāth has also benefited from the attentions of the Archaeological Survey of India and

[8] See Romila Thapar, *Aśoka and the Decline of the Mauryas*, pp. 37-8 and 49-50. For the actual inscriptions one may turn to A. Sen, *Aśoka's Edicts*, pp. 84 and 122. One may also note that one of Aśoka's other inscriptions (see Sen, pp. 124-5) confirms the existence of the cult of previous Buddhas, since we are informed that he enlarged the already existing stūpa of the Buddha Kanakamuni, next but one before Śākyamuni.

more recently from the presence of Tibetan exile communities. Lumbini, the birthplace, and Kāsia, the site of the Great Decease, have also become once more favourite places of pilgrimage. The four other secondary places of pilgrimage in the past have not been neglected by the Archaeological Survey, but they do not appear to stir the imagination of modern Buddhists in any way comparable to the four major sites, for which the historical justifications are so much stronger. It is indeed significant that the main events of Śākyamuni's life story, which is so permeated with mythological concepts, should be so firmly anchored to these particular places, which thus bestow upon it a sense of reality, combining satisfactorily history and mythology. One may note too that one of the best accounts of the life of Śākyamuni produced during this century is that of the famous French archaeologist, Alfred Foucher, who tells the story in direct relationship with the ancient set of places of pilgrimage.[9] He also enunciates the interesting theory that many of the legends that found their way into the early traditional cycles of tales may have derived from the actual storytelling of the ciceroni who showed pilgrims so many centuries ago around the sacred places. It should be emphasized that since we are primarily concerned with the development of Buddhism in India and beyond prior to its promulgation in Tibet, nothing is achieved by reducing Śākyamuni's proportions to those that suit modern rationalizing views. The problem of the origins of Buddhist faith and religious practice would merely be transposed to a later period, which on firm evidence has to be pre-Aśokan, and in effect nothing whatsoever would be achieved. Crucial to the development of Buddhism from its earliest known beginnings is what Śākyamuni's followers believed him to be and what they believed him to have taught, and not the speculations of those, who seem determined to separate him from the whole cultural and religious background in which he most certainly lived and taught. Thus our familiarity with the main places of pilgrimage, which were closely associated with him before Aśoka's time, help to keep us on a far surer historical basis, relating cosmological, mythological and religious concepts with the period to which they properly belong, and thus not attributing to the central figure social and political ideas which would have been totally foreign to him.[10]

3. THE CONCEPTS OF *SAṂSĀRA* AND *NIRVĀṆA*

a. *The Nature of Śākyamuni's Enlightenment*

Taking the four major places of pilgrimage as points of reference, we can now make a survey of fundamental Buddhist beliefs, which have remained practically unchanged during the spread of this great religion throughout Asia. Some of these beliefs have been developed in various ways, sometimes quite

9 See A. Foucher, *La vie du Bouddha d'après les textes et les monuments de l'Inde.*

10 Two examples may be given of books which attempt to over-humanize Śākyamuni but with such different intentions that they may be said to confute one another. These are Mrs. Rhys Davids, *Sakya or Buddhist Origins*, and Trevor Ling, *The Buddha*.

logically, sometimes rather curiously. Also new beliefs have been added from the enormous store of Indian religious experience. However, despite such developments and changes, which we shall describe in due course, certain basic beliefs have remained. They may be listed thus:

Relative to the birth of Śākyamuni at Lumbini, we may note that:

(i) A Buddha is not a unique being and his birth at a suitable time and place is in a certain sense predestined.

(ii) The final life during which he realizes Supreme Enlightenment is the result of heroic striving throughout a long series of previous lives. As such a heroic striver he is known as a Bodhisattva ("Enlightenment-Being") and this quality of heroic concern for all living beings is not necessarily lost when he realizes the state of nirvāṇa in this life. The early believers were aware of the possibility of achieving enlightenment for oneself alone, and a "Buddha" of such a kind was referred to as a Pratyekabuddha ("Lone Buddha").

Relative to his realization of Supreme Enlightenment at Bodhgayā, we may note:

(iii) Enlightenment was won by his own efforts understood as conditioned by his heroic strivings in previous lives and by his acts in this his last life. These inevitably include the progress made under two teachers, Ālāra Kālāma and Uddaka Rāmaputta, as well as the subsequent practice of the severest austerities, although he is represented as turning deliberately away from them before entering upon the final stages of trance.

(iv) Enlightenment is characterized by a threefold knowledge: knowledge of his own previous births, knowledge of the births and deaths of all living beings, and knowledge of his release from the whole process. The process of birth and death and rebirth continuing endlessly, unless stopped in the way which Śākyamuni now knew he had stopped it, is described as a twelvefold causal nexus, which he runs backward and forward in his thoughts.

Since this threefold knowledge, in terms of which a Buddha's Enlightenment is described, is the very basis on which the whole superstructure of Buddhist developments through the centuries has been raised, it certainly requires more detailed elucidation. Moreover it was the acquisition of this knowledge that won for Śākyamuni preeminence over gods and men. It was this that earned him the title of "Lord" (*Bhagavan*) and the faith and devotion of his followers. This certainty of knowledge is said to have so transformed his physical appearance, bestowing upon it such radiance and majesty that the five fellow-seekers after truth, who had turned away from him when he abandoned the practice of extreme austerity, now suddenly found his presence irresistible, and accepting his claims without question, became his first group of disciples. It is made abundantly clear from the early canonical accounts that Śākyamuni was believed, and believed himself to have solved, the mystery of human existence, and indeed of all forms of phenomenal existence. What he saw with his divine eye was the interminable meaningless succession of life and death in all its various forms and he knew that he was now released from the whole wretched process. His earlier experience, when still surrounded by the luxuries of his father's court, was that kind of aversion to the meaninglessness of such human pleasures when seen within the context of the inevitable process of old age and death, which afflicts all living beings. This experience lies at the root of much religious effort, not only among the followers of Śākyamuni. The worthlessness of riches, indeed the spiritual dangers of riches were certainly preached by Jesus Christ, and some of his followers also throughout the centuries have drawn the full logical implications of such teachings, abandoning the world as resolutely as did the early Buddhist monks. It may be tempting to make comparisons between one such as Saint Benedict, who drew up his Rule according to a kind of "middle way" avoiding self-indulgence on the one side and excessive asceticism on the other. But here we anticipate our story, for what we are concerned with now is the fundamental mystical experience, which is the raison d'être of all later Buddhist developments. The difference between Śākyamuni's earlier feeling of revulsion for the world, which is by no means an uncommon human experience, and the certainty of knowledge that he had now acquired is as fundamental as the difference between sorrow and joy, between darkness and light. Thus, writers who treat Buddhism as a religion of pessimism are seeing only one half of the picture. The earliest form in which Buddhist philosophy came to be expressed (we go into more detail below) is a form of dualism familiar to the early Christian Fathers, and resolutely attacked by them as the Gnostic heresy. Thus, with their fundamental view of existence, Buddhism and Christianity never join company, whatever similarities may be noted in forms of religious practice. At the moment of the Enlightenment Śākyamuni was aware of two planes of existence, absolutely distinct the one from the other. There was the continual circling of phenomenal existence, known as saṃsāra (continual revolving) and as something quite other the state of nirvāṇa (the extinction of the continual process), which despite the negative terminology refers to that state of serenity that is the essential attribute of a Buddha. Some Western critics of Buddhism fail to take seriously enough the positive qualities of the state of a Buddha, which are listed in much detail in the earliest known texts. Moreover, there is a tendency to compare the aversion to the world with that form of pessimism that can lead a human being to the destruction of his own life. Such pessimism is quite unknown in Buddhism and in any case the taking of one's own life could only lead to rebirth in a more wretched condition than one suffers at present, for it must never be forgotten that the doctrine, or rather the dogma, of inevitable rebirth (transmigration) is fundamental to Buddhism in all its forms. There is certainly an early tradition of an arhat (literally meaning "worthy" but used as a title of Śākyamuni's early disciples who won through to nirvāṇa) disappearing in an act of self-conflagration, but this was no act of despair, but a sign that once all that bound the personality to the world had been dispersed, continuing existence in it could be pointless. Only a Buddha remains by a deliberate act of will in order to lead other living beings along the path of deliverance.

The twelvefold causal nexus (*pratītyasamutpāda*) announced at the time of Enlightenment as the formal expression of a Buddha's intuitive insight into the whole process of saṃsāra is by its very nature a kind of dogmatic statement, which requires no proof for believers. Thus it is a form of revelation, and efforts by Buddhist commentators as well as non-Buddhist scholars to discover a logical relationship between the various terms of the nexus are probably misdirected. The list is best understood just as it is presented, namely as a spontaneous searching back into the origins of death and rebirth, and apart from the stimulation of desire which maintains the process and the transitory existence of the mental and physical components of which a personality is formed, no origin exists except for the absence of knowledge (*avidyā*), which is precisely the negation of the threefold knowledge achieved at the moment of Enlightenment. Such knowledge and such ignorance have a kind of absolute existence in early Buddhist philosophy, just like the pairs of light and darkness, sorrow and bliss. As they are the primary data of experience, they simply relate to one another as opposites and no further explanation is necessary. Śākyamuni instructed his monks on occasions concerning the nature of nirvāṇa and the closest one comes to logical deduction is the famous saying:

> There is, monks, an unborn, an unbecome, an unmade, an uncompounded; if, monks, there were not this unborn, unbecome, unmade, uncompounded, there would not here be an escape from the born, the become, the made, the compounded. But because there is an unborn, an unbecome, an unmade, an uncompounded, therefore there is an escape from the born, the become, the made, the compounded.[11]

Here it is assumed that the phenomenal world (as born, become, made and compounded) is an object of personal experience, and it is from this sense of objectivity, experienced as fundamentally tragic, that release is sought. Śākyamuni's analysis of the whole process of becoming as expressed in the twelvefold causal nexus has been used throughout the history of Buddhism as a means of evoking aversion to the world and turning the thought toward those aspirations that lead to release. The term saṃsāra (continual revolving) suggests at once the idea of a wheel, and thus it is as the "wheel of existence" (*bhavacakra*) that the whole phenomenal process has been envisaged. This wheel-like design, clasped by Māra, the Evil One, is regularly portrayed in the porch of every Tibetan Buddhist temple (see *Pl. 3*) and the survival of a similar painting in Cave XVII at Ajantā suggests that such a practice was well established in Indian Buddhist monasteries.

The wheel is divided into six segments, representing six possible spheres of rebirth: the realm of the gods, that of the titans or nongods, the human world,

[11] From the *Udāna* (*Khuddaka-nikāya*). For the whole context see E. J. Thomas, *Early Buddhist Scriptures*, pp. 109-111.

the animal world, the world of tormented spirits and the realm of the hells. Such component parts clearly derive from the general world view of the early Buddhist centuries, of which it is a considerable simplification arranged as a symbolic design.[12] At the center of the wheel are depicted a cock, a snake and a pig, representing passion, wrath and delusion, the three fundamental evils that result in the continual process of rebirths in the various realms. The realm of the gods comes as a reward for virtuous acts, but these alone are not sufficient to secure one release, and when one's store of merit is exhausted, one falls on rebirth into a lower realm. The realm of the titans is associated with quarrelsomeness and jealousy, while the world of men offers the only real hope for salvation, depending upon one's condition of birth in it.[13] Rebirth in the animal world results from stupidity, amongst tormented spirits from avarice, and in the various hells from anger and cruelty.

The twelve interrelated causes, which represent, as it were, the mechanism of this wheel of existence, together with their symbolic representation, are:

1. ignorance (*avidyā*)	a blind old woman
2. elemental impulses (*saṃskāra*)	pots being made by a potter
3. consciousness (*vijñāna*)	a monkey plucking fruit
4. personality (*nāmarūpa*)	a boat on the journey
5. the six sense-organs (*ṣaḍāyatana*)	a house with many windows
6. contact (*sparśa*)	the act of kissing
7. feeling (*vedanā*)	a man with an arrow in his eye
8. desire (*tṛṣṇā*)	a drinking scene
9. appropriation (*upadāna*)	plucking fruit from a tree
10. the process of becoming (*bhava*)	a pregnant woman
11. birth (*jāti*)	a birth scene
12. old age and death (*jarāmaraṇam*)	a corpse being carried to its place of disposal

The interpretation of the relationship between the various terms is assisted by the little symbolic illustrations, as listed above, which are set around the rim of the wheel. Logical interpretation may appear to be difficult because of the way in which the relationship fluctuates between the general and the particular or between rather more philosophical concepts than psychological ones. Interpreted however as a process of actual experience as one reflects upon the inevitably unhappy lot of all living beings as they passs form the prenatal state into life and thence on to decay and death, where they fall once more into the prenatal state of ignorance leading again to unhappy rebirth, interpreted thus, no great difficulty need be found.[14] The list is presented as a statement of

[12] For a succinct description of the Buddhist cosmological system, see H. Kern, *Manual of Indian Buddhism*, pp. 57-60.

[13] All such conditions were later carefully listed. See my *Four Lamas of Dolpo*, vol. I, pp. 18-19.

[14] A sympathetic and quite helpful discussion of the whole matter is found in Waddell, *Lamaism*, pp. 105-122, if only one tempers his emphasis on "the inveterate pessimism of Buddha's ethics" by reminding oneself that this is but one side of the coin.

Śākyamuni's vision of the continual cycle of rebirths, couched in terms that soon acquired, if indeed they did not already possess them, quite precise meanings. Since it is fundamental to an understanding of the Buddhist world view, it certainly merits serious treatment.

Ignorance refers in this context to the absence of the saving knowledge of the Buddhist doctrine, which alone can bring the endless cycle to a stop. It is the fumbling ignorance typical of the intermediate state between death and rebirth, known in later Tibetan tradition as the Bardo. Indeed efforts were made by later spiritual guides to lead the befuddled departed from such a state of ignorance to at least some glimmerings of recognition.[15] The elemental impulses (*saṃskāra*) or perhaps more literally "coefficients," are conceived of as the basic factors, external as well as internal to the living being, which make possible the appearance of his existence. Thus, without the external "visible" factors, his sense of sight would be inoperative. We shall meet this term again, used in a more restricted sense, in the set of five aggregrates (*skandha*) of which a living being (*sattva*) is composed. Here it is used in a wider sense to include all factors, physical and mental, which operate under the controlling influence of "consciousness" (*vijñāna*), the next on the list. The result is the apparent "personality," literally "name and form." Such a complete "personality" by means of the six sense organs (eye, nose, ear, tongue, body, mind) makes "contact" with their respective spheres of activity, thus producing "feeling," which results in "desire." Desire leads to grasping or the "act of appropriation," which is the root cause of the whole "process of becoming," involving "old age and death." Interpreted in this straightforward way, items 2 to 9 may appear to refer to any apparent individual living being, while items 10 to 12 and relinking to item 1 refer to the concomitant general nature of existence. However, from a Buddhist point of view there is nothing essentially illogical about this, since the individual living being is already a false conception enmeshed in the general process of becoming.

Illogicality, if any, exists at another more fundamental level, and this prevents any clear definition of the "living being" (*sattva*), who becomes manifest in the "series" (*santāna*) of rebirths. On the one hand Śākyamuni is represented as viewing the process of existence as a continuing flux in which there is no abiding entity, and yet on the other hand he taught quite clearly the doctrine of *karma*, namely the inevitable effect of one's actions in this and especially in succeeding lives. Moral responsibility for one's actions is a cardinal Buddhist teaching and it is driven home in a wealth of "rebirth stories," which relate the person of one birth with the person of the next. This doctrine is clearly stated in an incontrovertible way:

> Beings, student, have their own karma, they are heirs of karma, their origin is karma, they have karma as their kinsman, as their resource. Karma distributes beings, that is, according to lowness and greatness.

[15] For further details see the section V.2.c.

Asked for a fuller explanation, Śākyamuni continues:

> There is the case of the person, a woman or a man, who takes life, cruel with blood-stained hands, given to striking and killing, and without mercy to living things. When that karma is worked out and completed, with the dissolution of the body after death, he is reborn in a state of misery, in an unhappy destiny, in a state of punishment, or in hell; or if he is not thus reborn, but attains the state of man, wherever he is reborn he is short-lived . . .
> There is the case of a person, a woman or a man, who has put aside and refrains from taking life, who has laid aside the use of a stick or a knife and dwells modest, full of kindliness, and compassionate for the welfare of all living beings. When that karma is worked out and completed, with the dissolution of the body after death, he is reborn in a state of happiness or the world of heaven, or if he is not reborn in heaven but attains the state of man, wherever he is reborn he is long lived.[16]

It is precisely a vision of this whole process on a cosmic scale which is vouchsafed to Śākyamuni at the moment of his enlightenment. Having recalled as the first aspect of his special knowledge all his own previous existences reaching back endlessly through many cycles of the dissolution of the universe, he is able to recall the related fates of all other living beings.

> With divine, purified, superhuman vision I saw beings passing away and being reborn, low and high, of good and bad colour, in happy or miserable existences according to their karma. Those beings who lead evil lives in deed, word or thought, who speak evil of the noble ones, of false views, who acquire karma through their false views, at the dissolution of the body after death are reborn in a state of misery and suffering in hell. But those beings who lead good lives in deed, word and thought, who speak no evil of the noble ones etc. etc. are reborn in a happy state in the world of heaven . . . This was the second knowledge that I gained in the second watch of the night.[17]

The third knowledge, namely Śākyamuni's realization of his release from the whole process, is associated with the destruction of the three so-called pollutions (*āsrava*) of sensual desire, of desire for existence and of ignorance.

> There arose in me emancipated the knowledge of my emancipation. I realized that destroyed is rebirth, the religious life has been led, done is what was to be done, there is nought (for me) beyond this world. This was the third knowledge that I gained in the last watch of the night. Ignorance was dispelled, knowledge arose. Darkness was dispelled, light arose. So it is with him who abides vigilant, strenuous and resolute.

It is scarcely just to label such an expressed realization of "truth" as pessimistic except from the viewpoint of a hedonistic man who regards all higher religious striving, whether Christian or Buddhist, as a total waste of human effort.

[16] See E. J. Thomas, *Early Buddhist Scriptures*, pp. 127 ff. (= *Majjhima-Nikāya* III, 202).

[17] See E. J. Thomas, *Life of Buddha*, pp. 67-8; also André Bareau, *Recherches* I, pp. 75-91.

Although one may question the foundations of Śākyamuni's apparent belief in the interminable nature of the cycles of rebirth and of the strict karmic connection within the various series of the rebirth process, the vanity of all human striving in the affairs of this world has been taught by many other religious teachers, and if one allows for the often considerable differences in the cosmological and philosophical background to their experiences, the positive, indeed optimistic, answer given is that one should direct one's striving toward those things, however differently conceived, that are beyond this world. Nor can this involve neglect of concern for other living beings who find themselves in the same world. Even the monk who abandons the world at Śākyamuni's behest is dependent upon an accumulation of previous beneficial actions in this and in previous lives for reaching the time and place, where such an act of abandonment becomes the next inevitable step. The emphasis on high standards of morality was fundamental to Buddhism from its origins, but here again Śākyamuni has not been the only great religious teacher who sees the limitations of the practice of good actions for their own sake.

Also associated with the gaining of Enlightenment is the contest with the Evil One, Māra, signifying both Death and Desire, in that Desire holds one prisoner in the endless round of death and rebirth. The description of this contest underwent very colorful development, and the scene as depicted in later Buddhist art and the pose of Śākyamuni, seated crosslegged, and touching the earth with the tips of the fingers of his right hand in order to summon the earth-goddess as witness against the assertions of Māra, became in due course the primary symbolic representation of the Enlightenment scene. In the earlier period the Tree of Enlightenment itself was considered an adequate symbol. However, E. J. Thomas has drawn attention to a text in the Pāli canon referring to the Māra incident, and thus it is clearly part of an early tradition. Thus, Māra approaches Śākyamuni, when he is exerting himself in meditation, and says:

> Lean art thou and ill-favoured, near to thee is death, Death hath a thousand parts, only one part of thee is life. Live, good sir; life is better. Living thou shalt do good works. If thou livest the religious life, if thou sacrificest the fire-sacrifice, much good is stored up. What hast thou to do with striving?
>
> Śākyamuni replies: Friend of the slothful, evil one, for thine own sake hast thou come hither. No need for even the least work of merit is found in me. Them that have need of merits let Māra deign to address. Faith is found in me and heroism and wisdom. Why doest thou ask about life from me, who am thus intent.[18]

Māra thus appears as a subtle tempter urging conventional "good works" as more profitable than the rigors of the ascetic life, and his full role is represented by the illustrations of the "Wheel of Existence," mentioned just above, which he is regularly shown as holding in his grasp. He is of the very essence of saṃsāra, as typified by the three evils of ignorance, desire and anger, and he stands opposite

[18] For this extract and its wider content see E. J. Thomas, *Life of Buddha*, pp. 72 ff. An admirable study of Māra's significance is provided by T. O. Ling, *Buddhism and the Mythology of Evil.*

Śākyamuni, whose title of "Victor of Māra" signifies his victory over the whole phenomenal world by the achieving of nirvāṇa (*Pls. 4a, 5b*). One may note that as the dichotomy of saṃsāra and nirvāṇa disappears in the Mahāyāna teachings of "relativity" and "universal sameness", so the significance of Māra as the chief embodiment of evil tends to lose its doctrinal usefulness. His significance is in fact greatly weakened by his subdivision into four Māras, and in Tibetan Buddhism he becomes little more than one of many malignant demons (*mDud*). However, he continues to survive in his earlier robust form as holder of the "Wheel of Existence," which decorates the porch of every Tibetan temple.

b. *The Doctrine of "Nonself" and the* Dharma-*Theory*

Continuing our survey of fundamental Buddhist beliefs with the four major places of pilgrimage as points of reference, we now come to the preaching of the First Sermon in the Deer Park near Vārānasi, in respect of which we may note:

(v) The basic teachings as given to the five first converts consist of the assertion that the Buddha recommends a middle way, avoiding laxity on the one hand and excessive hardship on the other, combined with certain stereotyped sets of teachings known as the Four Noble Truths and the Eightfold Path.[19]

The four may be simply listed as (1) the existence of misery as defining the normal conditions of saṃsāra, (2) the cause of misery which is desire as further elaborated in the twelvefold causal nexus, (3) the end of misery, which is the uprooting of this desire, and (4) the way of uprooting misery as represented by the Eightfold Path. This Path consists of right views, right intention, right speech, right action, right livelihood, right effort, right mindfulness, right concentration.

(vi) Śākyamuni is said to have then immediately taught the five monks concerning the nature of the apparent personality in terms of "nonself."[20]

This basic teaching may be seen as the foundation of "right views," the first member of the Eightfold Path, on which the success of the religious practice depends. It thus forms the basis, as a kind of dogmatic assertion, on which the whole later edifice of Buddhist philosophical investigation has been raised. Now the "personality" of living beings (human beings come first to mind) is analyzed as fivefold, consisting of body (*rūpa*), feelings (*vedanā*), perceptions (*saṃjñā*), impulses (*saṃskāra*) and consciousness (*vijñāna*). These are the Five Aggregates (*skandha*) of personality, and they play an important part in Buddhist physio-pyschological theory right through all Buddhist developments into the Vajrayāna (tantric) phase where they become crucial to the elaboration of the maṇḍala. In giving the five first converts this primary lesson in "right views" Śākyamuni declares that none of the five aggregates may be identified as the Self (*ātman*),

[19] See E. J. Thomas, *Life*, pp. 87-9 and André Bareau, *Recherches* I, pp. 172-82.

[20] See André Bareau, *Recherches* I, pp. 192-8.

and we touch immediately upon the fundamental Buddhist teaching of "non-self" (*anātman*), which differentiated it from the very start from the more orthodox forms of Hindu teaching.

The term Hindu is an exceedingly general one embracing all aspects of Indian culture prior to the Moslem invasions, which resulted in the disappearance of organized Buddhism from the land of its origin and gradually resulted in the more restricted use of the term Hinduism as referring to Brahmanical religion distinct from other religious developments which have remained active in India.[21] However, it is important to emphasize the earlier connotation of the term, observing that Buddhism developed throughout the whole of its history on Indian soil (approximately the fifth century B.C. to the twelfth century A.D.) within a more general Hindu context. Once this is realized, both Buddhist origins as well as the whole later complicated development of the doctrine become much more comprehensible. Buddhist thinkers were often provoked into opposition to the teachings of other schools and precisely for this reason it is within the context of the teachings of other schools that Buddhist teachings must be understood. The "nonself" doctrine, also interpreted as the doctrine of "no soul", has been understood all too often in terms of neo-Platonic or Christian medieval philosophy, and while this may well be one legitimate kind of comparison, it should not be taken as the only one or even as the main one.

In an interesting study published more than thirty years ago[22] Herbert Guenther draws attention to the various meanings of *ātman* in Śākyamuni's time and in the following centuries. None of these need come as a surprise to anyone who is familiar with forms of local religious beliefs which have not been superseded by the special teachings of some "higher religion." In Europe in earlier times, as much as in Asia, Africa and the Americas, people have believed in all kinds of "souls" in trees, in stones, in animals as well as in various parts of the body. While some of the Upaniṣads were already teaching a doctrine of a superior form of "soul" (*ātman*), which should realize its ultimate potential in unity with a kind of "universal soul" (*brahman*), such ideas were scarcely current amongst the wandering ascetics who formed the first groups of Śākyamuni's disciples. Although the "great god Brahmā" is mocked in early Buddhist texts for imagining falsely that he is eternal, I believe I am correct in saying that no such early text has yet been found where the term *brahman* is used in the

[21] One might draw interesting analogies between Hinduism before the Moslem conquest and Jewish religion before the destruction of the Jewish state in A.D. 70. Whereas before this time Jewish religion included a variety of groups and sects, some of whom, such as those of Qumran, cut themselves off entirely from the temple cult of Jerusalem, thus exhibiting a kind of religious freedom which only became insufferable when the whole Jewish way of life was under threat, so Hinduism began to manifest itself in similarly harsher forms, when all its most sacred traditions were liable to be overthrown by Moslem rulers and when such formal direction of Hindu life as was still possible became the responsibility of leading Brahmins instead of the far more liberal-minded Hindu rulers who had previously stood at the head of Hindu society. Just as Christianity had its origins in this freer form of Jewish religion, so Buddhism had not only its origins but also underwent all its later Indian developments within the context of a freer form of Hinduism.

[22] *Das Seelenproblem im älteren Buddhismus.*

sense of a tranquil absolute in which the individual *ātman* is absorbed. It is thus likely that the early Buddhists were understanding the term *ātman* in an equally popular sense and scarcely in the sense which we have learned to associate with it from reading modern works about the higher forms of Hindu teachings. Śākyamuni's sermon to the five first converts is quite suggestive in this respect:

> The Body, monks, is not the *ātman*. If the Body, monks, were the *ātman*, this body would not be subject to sickness, and it would be possible in the case of the body to say: 'Let my body be thus! Let my body be thus!'[23]

The same argument is used of the other four aggregates, Feelings, Perceptions, Impulses and Consciousness. Similarly elsewhere he teaches:

> The eye, O monks, is not the *ātman*. That which is not the *ātman* is not mine; that belongs not to me; what I am not, that is not my *ātman*. Thus should one who possesses right knowledge, regard his own being. The nose, O monks, is not the *ātman*, etc.

The same argument continues for the ear, the tongue, the body and the mind.[24] In many such teachings the meaning of *ātman* comes close to "life force" (*jīva*), which is yet another of the contemporary terms for "soul" rigorously rejected by Śākyamuni's followers.

Quotations such as those just cited have been used in an effort to prove that Śākyamuni did not himself deny a higher principle in man and that the Buddhist doctrine of "no self" as developed in the early canonical scriptures is the creation of scholastic minded followers who could not understand the subtleties of his teaching.[25] But for this the texts are being pressed too hard. Before commenting further, we may allow ourselves one more quotation, which has been often cited, where Śākyamuni is asked directly whether the *ātman* exists or not.

> Then the wandering monk Vacchagotta came to where the Blessed One was staying, and when he had come, he greeted the Blessed One. After exchanging friendly words of greeting, he sat down by his side. Seated thus at his side, the wandering monk Vacchagotta asked the Blessed One:
>
> "How is it, noble Gotama, is there an *ātman*?"
>
> When he spoke thus, the Blessed One remained silent.
>
> "How is it, noble Gotama, is there then no *ātman*?"
>
> Again the Blessed One remained silent, so the wandering monk Vacchagotta rose from his seat and went away.
>
> Not long after he had gone away the worthy Ānanda asked the Blessed One: "How come's it, Lord, that the Blessed One failed to reply to the question asked by the wandering monk Vacchagotta?"
>
> "If I had replied to him, Ānanda, when he asked the question: 'Is there an *ātman*?' by saying that there is, then I would have been supporting the teachings of those ascetics and brahmans, who speak of permanence. If I had

[23] See E. J. Thomas, *Life of Buddha*, pp. 88-9 and compare Guenther, *op. cit.*, p. 20.

[24] Guenther, *op. cit.*, pp. 50-51 (*Saṃyutta-Nikāya* IV.2); see also E. J. Thomas, *Early Buddhist Scriptures*, pp. 192-9.

[25] For example see C. A. F. Rhys Davids, *Sakya or Buddhist Origins*, pp. 195ff.

replied to him, when he asked the question: 'Is there no *ātman*?' by saying that there is not, that would have been supporting the teachings of those ascetics and brahmans, who speak of annihilation. If I had replied to him, when he asked the question: 'Is there an *ātman*?' by saying that there is, would that have served the purpose of awakening in him the realization that all the elements (*dharmas*) are non-self?"

"It would not, Lord."

"If I, Ānanda, had replied to him, when he asked: 'Is there no *ātman*?' by saying that there is not, that would have resulted in his falling from one delusion into a still greater one: 'Alas, the *ātman* that I once had, that is no more.' "[26]

There is nothing agnostic about this argument, which is perhaps best understood by considering the third possibility given, namely if an *ātman* is asserted, this is liable to be understood as somehow existing in or adhering to the elements (*dharmas*), a view, which Śākyamuni was at pains to refute, when he said that the Body and the other four aggregates, the eye and the other five organs of sense were not the *ātman*.

The whole of saṃsāra is conceived as fluctuating conglomerations of "elements" known as *dharmas*, which manifest themselves momentarily something like the dots of which the images on a television screen are composed.[27] The dots are conceived of as "impulses" (*saṃskāra*) and the resulting image is impermanent and so "self-less" (*anātman*). The five aggregates (*skandha*) of which the transient personality is composed, are either themselves elements, as in the case of "consciousness," or conglomerations of elements, as in the case of "body." Body, for example, consists of earth (= hair, flesh, nails, teeth, bones, etc., in fact whatever is hard), water (gall, pus, blood, sweat, etc., whatever is fluid), fire ("that by which a man heats himself, consumes himself, worries himself and digests his food") and wind ("in the stomach, in the lower body, that which passes through the limbs and that which is breathed in and out")' Moreover the "body," referring to form of any kind, possesses sense-data, visual, auditory, olfactory, flavorous and tactile, all of which are conceived of as "elements." A silent bell will comprise visual and tactile elements. If it is struck the action causes auditory-type elements to become manifest, and the bell then appears to be heard as well as to be touched and to be seen. Accordingly an eye possesses visual-sense elements and an ear auditory-sense elements necessary for the apparent seeing and hearing of the bell. Thus bodily form can comprise a

26 *Saṃyutta-Nikāya* IV.400ff. Compare Guenther, *op. cit.*, pp. 25-6.

27 It is very difficult to find a suitable translation for the term *dharma*, but some attempt is necessary in order to assist readers who are unfamiliar with it. Its interpretation as something like "firm reality" will cover both its chief Buddhist meanings of Sacred Law or Religion as well as that of "existential element." These last are the "ultimate realities" of all existence. Kenneth K. Inada in his work on *Nāgārjuna* protests against the translation "elements of existence" because of its association with the earlier Western materialistic conceptions of the ultimate elements of existence (pp. 7-9). Thus he prefers a translation "factors of experience." However, since the rather more recent progress in physics has dispersed these materialistic conceptions, I retain the translation "elements." Perhaps "manifesting elements" might be more precise, but it is too cumbersome.

total of four gross elements, earth, water, fire and air, and ten subtle elements, five sense-elements and five sensation-elements, which create the relationship between subject and object.

Mental elements are far more numerous and are listed in more or less arbitrary groups. The principle followed suggests that whatever quality can be named, may be accepted as an "element." There are ten general elements, headed by feeling and perception (two of the five aggregates) and continuing with will, sensation, understanding, memory, etc. There are ten good elements, belief, courage, attentiveness, etc., six obscuring elements, ignorance, carelessness, indolence, etc., ten vicious elements, anger, hypocrisy, deceit, etc., and so on. No difference is suggested between what we would call physical and mental elements. If a name can be given, the name suggests a *thing*, and it is of such *things* or "realities" (*dharmas*) that the whole of phenomenal existence is momentarily composed in a continuous succession of moments.

c. *The Relativity of Philosophical Explanations*

Neither Śākyamuni nor even his followers invented such a system purely out of ideas of their own. They were accepting the philosophical conceptions of their times, when everything was conceived of materialistically. Indeed variant forms of such materialistic pluralism are found not only in other Indian schools but also in the pre-Socratic philosophy of Greece. No suggestion of influence either way need be implied, for we are simply concerned with the same kind of early efforts to explain phenomenal existence, whether in India or in Greece. The early Buddhists certainly strove to be carefully analytical in their philosophical reasoning, but while saṃsāra (phenomenal existence) could be analysed within the terms of current ways of thought, nirvāṇa as it was experienced could not be, as it came about precisely when the whole analyzable saṃsāra was brought to a stop. Thus at best it could be conceived philosophically as a blank like space or as the nonmanifestion of something that was previously manifest (e.g., a light which is extinguished). Since nirvāṇa is known as a state of which nothing can be predicated, nothing is gained by attempting a definition. It was known by experience to be attainable and that in itself is all that matters. Some early Buddhist schools listed nirvāṇa, space and "nonmanifestation" as elements (*dharmas*) for the only reason that they were thus nameable, but they were defined as "unconditioned" (*asaṃskṛta*) as opposed to all the conditioned (*saṃskṛta*) elements of which the saṃsāra was fleetingly composed. These two terms, the conditioned and the unconditioned, were often used later as synonyms for saṃsāra and nirvāṇa.

Any religion that posits a kind of "supernatural" state as distinct from the "natural" phenomenal state confronts philosophical problems at one point or another when its exponents attempt to establish a possible relationship between the two. The early Buddhists avoided certain problems by admitting no analytical relationship between saṃsāra and nirvāṇa. Any conception of a "self" or a "person" existing as a permanent or even as a quasipermanent element would have introduced a contradiction into their whole elaborate scheme of conditioned and nonconditioned elements.[28] However, the contradiction, or at least an apparent contradiction, is thereby removed to the level of practicalities and of general religious belief. Expressed rather more dramatically, the apparent contradiction exists between Śākyamuni's revelation at the time of the Enlightenment and the Doctrine as formulated in consequence of his first preaching. According to his revelation:

1. Phenomenal existence (saṃsāra) is a continual process of birth, death and rebirth. Whatever joys there may be in life are inevitably transitory. Suffering predominates even here, and it certainly predominates overall as a result of the continuing circle of sickness, old age and death.
2. A human being can escape from this wretched process by following the path that Śākyamuni has shown. Salvation of this kind may require several or even many rebirths but throughout, the person is responsible for his own destiny and real progress can thus be made from one life to the next.
3. Unhappily most human beings as well as all other living things remain in ignorance of the true state of affairs, and at the time of his enlightenment Śākyamuni could see them passing from one life to another in the wretched round of existences.
4. Śākyamuni also had a vision of his own previous lives going back into a limitless past. Throughout his own series of lives just as throughout the series of lives of others, he was aware of a personal connection between one life and the next. In his teachings Śākyamuni often refers to the previous lives of his interlocutors, connecting them with events in their present lives. Moreover the early Buddhist scriptures contain whole collections of linked stories, illustrating the principles on which the process of rebirth can be seen to operate. Western scholars and some modern Buddhists tend to dismiss these stories as mere legends. Even though they are legends, they cannot be so lightly dismissed, since they are employed in all seriousness to illustrate certain fundamental teachings which relate essentially to Śākyamuni's enlightenment.

According to the Doctrine formulated as a result of his preaching:

1. Phenomenal existence is a continual process of birth, death and rebirth, quite as wretched in its effects as he proclaimed it to be.
2. Phenomenal existence is analyzed as a fluctuating totality of transient elements (*dharmas*). These elements are the only "realities" in this transient world, and persons and things apparently complete in themselves (a favorite example is a cart) are nothing more than temporary conglomerations of certain basic elements. There is thus no "being" (*sattva*), "self" (*ātman*), "life-force" (*jīva*) or "person" (*pudgala*) who can provide a link from one life to the next.

[28] One Buddhist school known as the Vātsīputrīyas did indeed posit a person (*pudgala*) as neither eternal, nor noneternal, as neither identical with the five aggregates of personality, nor different from them, but such an idea was easily shown to be nonsensical by their opponents and thus the *pudgala* remained a sectarian notion. For references see Nalinaksha Dutt, *Buddhist Sects in India*, pp. 197-222.

3. The effective link is provided by *karma* (action) understood as the sum total of a person's actions, good or bad, in his present and all preceding lives of the series. The effects of such *karma* result in separate series of lives, which give the false impression of a person actually being reborn from one life to another. It is interesting to note therefore that the word for series (Sanskrit *santāna*; Tibetan *rgyud-pa*) comes to have the actual meaning of "transmigrating soul" or something very similar. There is no other strictly orthodox term available.
4. Since a human being inherits *karma* and is thus endowed as a result of his *karma* with moral responsibility, he can change the direction that his "life-series" would otherwise have taken if only he will act in a suitable manner. Here external influences can be all important, such as preeminently being born in a place and at a time that a Buddha is preaching his doctrine, but even this happy circumstance is the result of previously accumulated *karma*.

Christian thinkers have wrestled with the problem of God's foreknowledge of events inevitably suggesting a doctrine of predestination as against the apparent factor of human free will. Buddhist thinkers on the other hand seem to accept placidly the anomaly of *karma* as an all-controlling force and the everyday experience of a man's seeming ability to make a free decision to do right or wrong. Moral responsibility is thus accepted as one of the given data of experience, as represented by such "elements" in the human being's transient make-up as belief, courage and attentiveness. It may safely be assumed that no greater proportion of practicing Buddhists than of practicing Christians have concerned themselves with abstruse doctrinal problems, and that is why those that write about Buddhism as though it were nothing more than a severely rational system of doctrine and practice can be very misleading, if their views are taken as anything more than a particularized interpretation. The rationalizers were always in a minority in previous centuries, and it is only in this modern rationalizing age in which we now find ourselves that their arguments have been given a significance that they did not previously have in earlier times when the rationalizers themselves were usually men of religion. Such considerations have considerable bearing upon the devotional aspects of the Buddhist religion, which surely had their beginnings during Śākyamuni's lifetime, when he was already honored by his followers with the titles of *Bodhisattva* and *Buddha*.

The elaborated theory of *dharmas* as impersonal fluctuating elements, although representing the earliest known Buddhist philosophical system, is nonethelesss a later compilation, and its attribution to Śākyamuni himself remained a matter of dispute among the early schools. From the start there was not only a majority of Buddhists unconcerned with abstruse analytical notions, but also a vocal minority who refused to accept such doctrinal formulation as "canonical." The earliest collections of the Buddhist scriptures consisted of books on monastic order (*Vinaya*), although these contained much else besides in illustration of how the various rules came to be formulated, and books containing anecdotes and teachings of Śākyamuni and of his disciples and followers. These last, known as *Sūtras* or "Threads (of Discourse)," contained much doctrinal matter of a spontaneous kind. Gradually a third collection was compiled, known as *Abhidharma* ("Further Dharma"), in which attempts were made to codify the doctrine in a more scholastic form. This last collection was rejected by some groups as noncanonical. Thus in the earliest times it must have caused considerable controversy, although it was not until three or four centuries later that other collections of texts began to make their appearance, claiming to be the "Buddha Word" and deliberately refuting the whole theory of "real *dharmas*" with all its pluralist and materialist implications. This new literature, known as the "Perfection of Wisdom" (*Prajñāpāramitā*) provided the doctrinal basis for the great religious movement which was self-named the "Great Way" (*Mahāyāna*) as opposed to the "Inferior Way" (*Hīnayāna*), which its followers now claimed to surpass.

Although many of the aspects of the Mahāyāna will be covered in the next chapter, we cannot delay reference to it now, since most of its roots must be held to lie in the earlier period that we are now considering. Hīnayāna and Mahāyāna are all too often described as though they were two quite distinct forms of Buddhism, and this separate treatment has been assisted by the accidental survival due entirely to historical circumstances of one Hīnayāna school, namely that of the Theravādins, in Sri Lanka and other countries of Southeast Asia. However, there were many other early Buddhist sects, traditionally numbering eighteen, and some of these were responsible for the gradual transition of their Master's teachings from the early stage, where they were directed primarily to a group of personal followers, to the latter stage when they were reinterpreted and made available to a very much larger number of adherents of very different cultural backgrounds in lands where the first few groups of disciples had never traveled. Such an expansion of any religious teaching that is on its way to becoming a world religion is inevitable, for if the expansion and consequent development of the original doctrine had not taken place, it would simply have run its own course on its own limited territory and probably have been heard of no more. Those who have the fairest claims to represent a form of the original teachings are usually those who for accidental reasons have been cut off from the main historical streams of the religion in question.[29] Their claims may be on many scores genuine, but they have lost much by clinging to them.

Probably the most poignant description of the differences between Hīnayāna and Mahāyāna is that given by the great Russian scholar Th. Stcherbatsky and it deserves to be quoted at this point, despite its calculated exaggeration, as presenting a problem that requires solution.

[29] So far as the history of Christian developments is concerned, this might be said to apply to those early groups of Christian adherents of exclusively Jewish background who surviving the fall of Jerusalem in A.D. 70 continued to remain cut off from the "Great Church" of the Mediterranean world. The Theravādins of Sri Lanka were cut off in a similar way from later Buddhist developments on the Indian mainland, but they enjoyed a far more glorious future thanks to their contacts with other Southeast Asian countries, notably Burma, where Buddhist influences continued to be very strong.

> It has never been realized what a radical revolution has transformed the Buddhist church when the new spirit, which however for a long time was lurking in it, arrived at full eclosion in the first centuries A.D. When we see an atheistic, soul-denying philosophic teaching of a path to personal Final Deliverance consisting in an absolute extinction of life, and a simple worship of the memory of its human founder, when we see it superseded by a magnificent High Church with a Supreme God, surrounded by a numerous pantheon, and a host of Saints, a religion highly devotional, highly ceremonial and clerical, with an ideal of Universal Salvation of all living creatures, a Salvation not in annihilation, but in eternal life, we are fully justified in maintaining that the history of religions has scarcely witnessed such a break between new and old within the pale of what nevertheless continued to claim common descent from the same religious founder.[30]

It is noteworthy that this Russian scholar's invaluable books on Buddhism are concerned almost exclusively with philosophical disquisition and that he was writing this particular book as a vigorous rebuttal of the arguments published by that great French scholar, Louis de la Vallée Poussin, in his book entitled *Nirvāṇa*, where far greater consideration is given to those aspects of early Buddhism which are not strictly doctrinal. It may be observed that exclusively doctrinal considerations become all the more misleading when they are interpreted in Western terms. Thus while such terms as "atheistic" and "soul-denying" may be in some respects applicable to certain early Buddhist teachings, they are totally misleading when applied to early Buddhist beliefs as a whole. We have noted above how Śākyamuni himself was careful not to deny or assert the existence of a "soul" (*ātman*), and he can scarcely be called atheistic in any way comprehensible to a Westerner, when he seemingly claimed to be, and was certainly acclaimed by his early followers as, the superior of gods and men.

Not only was the central doctrine of rebirth together with that of personal moral responsibility for one's acts clearly stated, but a belief in personal survival throughout one's future rebirths was also firmly inculcated. The whole course of a Bodhisattva (would-be Buddha) leading through many lives up to the final life where buddhahood is achieved, assumed just such a form of personal continuity, and this was precisely the course that Śākyamuni had run, and which others could and would run after him. Scholastic teachings of real but ever vanishing elements, which are supposed to explain the whole cosmological process, leave untouched the central religious convictions, and it was inevitable that such philosophical views should be challenged as untenable. This was done by turning against them one of their central arguments, namely their contention that if the whole being or the person is not real, then the elements of which it is composed

[30] *The Conception of Buddhist Nirvāṇa*, p. 36. The exaggerated distinctions that he draws between Hīnayāna and Mahāyāna may have some substance if one contrasts the modern practice of Buddhism in Sri Lanka and its practice in Tibetan communities today (those now in exile, let it be understood). For my own total rejection of any idea of such a dichotomy existing even in seventh century India, Central Asia or even during the early period of Tibet's conversion to Buddhism, see below section IV.1.a. Such differences are unthinkable in the "first centuries A.D.," whatever the strange word "eclosion" may mean.

must be real. The answer to this is simply why? If the *ātman* has no self-existent nature, then why should the *dharmas* (elements) possess one? They are even more transitory and unreal in their manifestation. Śākyamuni had rejected all questions concerning the eternity or noneternity of the universe, of the existence or nonexistence after death of one who has achieved nirvāṇa, as meaningless. If indeed he had taught the nonexistence of a self, how could he have clung to belief in the existence of real elemental particles? Such a belief was held in particular by the adherents of the sect known as the Sarvāstivādins and its was presumably in reaction against so extreme a view that the reality of the elemental particles (*dharmas*) came to be so fervently denied. Such a denial inevitably came after such an affirmation, but those who denied the validity of these materialist principles could claim with good reason that they were in effect reverting to a fairer expression of Śākyamuni's teachings. The way to rectify such wrong views was to produce suitable teachings and promulgate them as the word of the Buddha just as their opponents had done earlier on. Thus, later in time as it certainly is, the Perfection of Wisdom literature can make as good a claim as the Abhidharma texts to represent genuine Buddhist teachings. The phenomenal world had been described from the earliest period as misery (*duḥkha*), as transient (*anitya*) and as "self-less" (*anātman*). Another term came into use, namely "void" (*śūnya*). Applied by the Sarvāstivādins to entities, which were diagnosed as "empty" conglomerations of real elemental particles, this term came to be used by their opponents to describe the particles themselves. Thus was developed the use of the all-important word *śūnyatā* ("voidness"), which was said to characterize everything that could be named whether relating to saṃsāra or to nirvāṇa. Here we touch on developments which must be considered in the next chapter, but it is important to remember that such later developments have direct references to beliefs held in the earlier period. There is no clear break between the two.

The later descriptions of Śākyamuni's first preaching, as preserved for us in Tibetan histories of Indian Buddhism, which can only draw on Indian traditions, many of them lost, tell how Śākyamuni turned the "Wheel of the Doctrine" three times. First he taught according to the terminology that was suitable for the early disciples as represented by his five first converts. Next he taught the doctrine of universal "voidness" as represented by the Perfection of Wisdom literature and finally he taught the doctrine concerning Pure Consciousness, which was a combination of the previous two. More will be told of these doctrines later on, but it is important to realize that while the main tenets of his religion have remained unchanged over the centuries, there has been a considerable shift in their philosophical exposition.[31]

[31] This last must be regarded as normal and healthy in the case of any great religion. Christianity likewise would be in a sorry pass if it continued to express itself solely in the cosmological and philosophical theories of the first three centuries, or even if it were bound to the doctrines of medieval philosophers.

4. THE PREEMINENCE OF BUDDHAHOOD

a. *Śākyamuni as Buddha and Man*

Turning now to the last of the four major events of Śākyamuni's life, namely his passing into final nirvāṇa at Kuśinagra (identified with the present-day village of Kāsia thirty-five miles due east of Gorakhpur), we may note that

(vii) The tomblike mounds (*stūpa*) erected over his remains became the primary symbol of his passage into a supramundane state, thus coming to be accepted as the supreme symbol of otherworldly aspiration.

(viii) Śākyamuni himself, as Bodhisattva and Perfected Buddha, was the inspiration for the formulation of Buddhist doctrines concerning the nature of a Buddha. Complex buddhalogical theories were developed and these gradually assumed generally accepted formulation over the next seven centuries.

According to undisputed early Buddhist tradition Śākyamuni's physical remains, having been cremated, were divided between ten townships, who each built a stūpa over their share. There were said to be eight shares of the actual relics, but the brahman who shared them out claimed for his village of Droṇa the vessel which had contained them, and a brahman boy who had assisted at the ceremony claimed the burning ashes for his village of Pippalāyana. It is altogether a rather curious story and perhaps results from a firm tradition that prior to the Emperor Aśoka's interest in Buddhism in the third century B.C. there had been originally just ten stūpas reputed to contain the relics of Śākyamuni himself.[32] There were, however, probably many more in existence by that time, containing the relics of some of the leaders of the community who succeeded him. It is certain that from the time of Aśoka onward, such stūpas were being built all over the Indian subcontinent, wherever the doctrine spread and established itself. The relics in their casket seem to have been placed not under the commemorative mound but in a square shrine on the summit, which was in turn surmounted by an umbrella fashioned out of wood in order to emphasize the august nature of the relics. The mound itself was surrounded by a wooden palisade with entrances to the four directions in order to mark the separation of the sacred and the profane. Stonework modelled upon the earlier work in wood survives at several sites from the second century B.C. onward. Famous examples of such early stoneworked stūpas are found at Sāñcī (near Bhopal in Madhya-pradesh), one of the best preserved Buddhist sites in India thanks to the reconstruction carried out by the Archaeological Survey (*Pls. 2, 5, 6*); the remains of the famous stūpa of Bhārhut (near the small town of Satna nearly 100 miles SW of Allahabad) were taken in the old British days to the Indian Museum in Calcutta, which now contains a remarkable collection of Buddhist sculptures representing the changes that took place during the seventeen hundred years

[32] A number of useful bibliographical references to the events will be found in a short article of mine, "Śākyamuni's Final Nirvāṇa," *Bulletin of the School of Oriental & African Studies*, vol. XXXVI (1973), pp. 399-411.

and more that Buddhism continued to thrive on Indian soil. The stone railings, replacing the earlier wooden palisade, and especially the ornate stone gateways are of primary importance for the history of early buddhalogical concepts, for their sculptures fix with a certainty which no early texts can do, subject as these are to a continual process of reformulation, the beliefs which were already held concerning the nature of a Buddha by the second century B.C. Two features of these early stone carvings are especially significant: firstly Śākyamuni himself is never represented in human form and secondly the inset scenes, when not concerned with the great events of his last life, are largely concerned with illustrating the more famous of his previous lives. Where Śākyamuni would be expected to appear either as Bodhisattva or Buddha there is simply a blank. Thus the scene illustrating his winning of enlightenment shows an empty throne with the Tree of Enlightenment behind it and that illustrating the preaching of the first sermon shows an empty throne with a Wheel of the Doctrine. These two symbols, the tree and the wheel, as well as carvings of the stūpa itself, come to represent a Buddha according to his main activities, winning enlightenment, preaching and passing into nirvāṇa. Thus not only Śākyamuni, but also previous Buddhas, making up a set of seven in these early times, are represented by a row of seven trees or a row of seven stūpas. Other beings, whether men or local gods and goddesses (*yakṣa* and *yakṣinī*), whether the gods of Brahma's heaven or denizens of the animal world, all these are shown in realistic detail, but a Buddha cannot be shown because he consists of pure invisible *dharmas* and even when operating in the present world he transcends it in his true being. The preoccupation with stories of his earlier lives can clearly be related to the form which the earliest "biographies" received, as referred to above. Thus the earliest archaeological remains seem to support the early texts in bearing witness to a mythological rather than a historical interest in Śākyamuni's activities.

Many modern accounts of Buddhist developments (of which the quotation above is an extreme example) give the impression that in the early Buddhist period, often referred to inadequately as "Theravādin Buddhism," Śākyamuni was regarded as a mere man, while in the later period known as the Mahāyāna, he became divinized as the focal point of an ever more elaborate cult. Such a suggestion falsifies the true state of affairs not only by its gross oversimplification (the Theravādins were certainly an important early sect, but only one of many), but also in that it interprets Buddhist beliefs in terms of a largely Christian conception of God and Man as distinct spheres of being. There can never be any question in a real sense of "deifying" Śākyamuni. According to the earliest attested beliefs he was already superior to all gods, including the great god Brahmā, the first and highest being to reappear in every succeeding world age, in that he had already attained the summit of existence. The least that can be claimed of a Buddha may be quoted from a passage which occurs several times in the Theravādin canon, thus:

> The Lord is an Arhat, Perfectly Enlightened, perfect in his knowledge and his doings, the Blessed One, supreme knower of the universe, a competent

charioteer who controls men, a teacher of gods and men, Buddha, the Lord. He knows this universe with its gods, with Brahmā, with Māra, the world with its ascetics and brahmans, with its men and its gods, and realizing it [for what it is], he declares it to others.

It is difficult to understand how, having quoted such a passage as this, an eminent scholar can comment that "a description like this does not suggest that Buddha was originally more than a man, a mortal," and that thereby "the Hīnayānists do not attribute any transcendental or theistic element" to him.[33] Surely it is clear that as a man Śākyamuni was mortal, but that he was also more than man, for he was a Buddha, who transcends the whole universe. As noted already, the reference to theistic elements is irrelevant and obscures the real significance of a Buddha.

It would be an easy matter to accumulate extracts from the Theravādin canon, of which in any case so much is available in English translation already, which assert without any reasonable doubt the supramundane nature of Śākyamuni. It is equally easy to find passages where he appears as a mere mortal, and perhaps one of the most touching of these relates to his last journey on the way to Kuśinagara. At a place called Pāvā he and his followers accept a meal in the house of a smith, practically an outcaste in Hindu society then as now. He alone partakes of a certain dish and afterwards he is ill. "He bore with fortitude the pain, the sharp pain even unto death." However, they continue on their way until "the Blessed One went aside from the path to the foot of a certain tree; and when he had come there he addressed the venerable Ānanda and said: 'Fold the robe, I pray you Ānanda, and spread it out for me. I am weary, Ānanda, and must rest awhile'."[34] Extracted from its context no passage suggests more forcibly the fragile humanity of Śākyamuni. But when writing about Buddhism, we have no mandate to extract such texts and draw conclusions from them, based on the mere assumption that the more human the representation, the earlier the text must be. All one can fairly do is to accept the whole tradition as presented in any particular sect of Buddhism at its face value, and when this is done the humanity of Śākyamuni is clearly subsumed within his supramundane nature.

Apart from the titles of Lord (*Bhagavan*) and Blessed One (*Sugata*) and Conqueror (*Jina*) there is one title that he is represented, maybe quite historically, as using when speaking of himself. This is the title *Tathāgata*, which

[33] See Nalinaksha Dutt, *Aspects of Mahāyāna Buddhism and its Relationship to Hīnayāna*, pp. 97-9. Despite my strictures at this point, this book represents a most useful study of the development of Buddhist doctrines, and there will be occasion to refer to it below. His translation of the passage under discussion here tends to weaken its force. In this respect one may refer helpfully to T. O. Ling, *op. cit.*, pp. 96-7. Nalinaksha Dutt repeats the whole passage unchanged in the revised edition of his work entitled *Mahāyāna Buddhism*, pp. 142-3.

[34] For the story as recounted in the Pāli canon, see T. W. Rhys Davids, *Buddhist Suttas*, pp. 70-73. It also occurs in the same form in the Sanskrit version of the Mūla-Sarvāstivādins, as also reproduced in the Tibtan canon. See Ernst Waldschmidt, *Das Mahāparinirvāṇasūtra*, pp. 252ff. It is not impossible that even this story, which appears to be so realistically historical, may be a later rationalization of a mythological concept concerning a Buddha's special food. See A. Bareau, "La transformation miraculeuse de la nourriture" and also his *Recherches* II, vol. 1, pp. 27-81.

cannot be translated satisfactorily into any European language unless we translate literally as did the Tibetans (*Thus-Gone*) or the Chinese (*Thus-Come*). The Sanskrit could mean either of these two translations (as indeed the Tibetan might also), implying either the meaning of "Predestined" or more likely "The One who has won through" to Perfect Enlightenment.[35] This title becomes in any case a mere synonym for Buddha and so it comes to be applied to any other Buddha, wherever he may appear. Thus it is regularly used of the set of Five Cosmic Buddhas (*pañca-tathāgata*) to whom we shall refer in scetion III.11 and who can in no way be treated as human beings.

Tradition has always insisted that Śākyamuni's birth was immaculate in a physical sense. Thus he was born not from the womb of his mother but from her right side. Later tradition went even further, envisaging him as enshrined in a precious casket while inside her body. There is no specific doctrine of a "virgin birth," but this is implied when his mother dreams that he enters her body from the heavens in the guise of a white elephant. His claim to preeminence in the world, made as soon as he is born, seems to belong to the earliest known tradition. He was certainly believed to have from birth the marks of a "great man" (*mahāpuruṣa*), thirty-two major ones and eighty minor ones. These too came to be a cliché as a description of any Buddha, whether human or celestial, for all are described as "possessed of the marks of perfection." Some of the more significant of these marks influenced the representation of a Buddha in stone, when such images began to be produced. One may note especially the long ear lobes and the "wisdom bump" (*uṣṇīṣa*).[36] The nonrepresentation of Śākyamuni during the first three to four centuries, when mythological concepts concerning him seem to have predominated, is most significant for the high regard in which he was held as pertaining to a supramundane state. Gods and men might be represented sculpturally, but not a Buddha. In this respect it is interesting to note that the creation of the first Buddha images corresponds more or less in time with the production of the first biographies which attempt to be consistently historical. Yet both these developments belong to the period when the Perfection of Wisdom texts, those basic works of the Mahāyāna, were also becoming known, On no reckoning can one convincingly treat Hīnayāna and Mahāyāna as two distinct phases. They may be regarded, however, as two fluctuating tendencies, usually mingling together, and only kept strictly apart in certain philosophical texts.

Despite the considerable differences between Buddhist and Christian cosmological assumptions, certain interesting analogies can be usefully drawn between the ways in which buddhalogical and christological doctrines generally

[35] Searching for a passable English translation I have thought of "Prize-Winner" despite the rather more concrete implication. The "Predestined One" as used e.g. by Alfred Foucher (as "le Prédestiné") in his life of the Buddha, sounds well, but it is doubtful if this represents the original meaning. Such an interpretation might appeal to those who look for Buddhist and Christian parallels, for it would then correspond very closely to the term *ho erchomenos* (the one who is to come) as used in Luke VIII.20. It is, however, noteworthy that Jesus is represented in the Gospels as referring to himself as "Son of Man," yet another rather mysterious mythological title.

[36] One may refer to my observation in *The Image of the Buddha*, pp. 48-54 *passim* and 75-6.

developed and in particular in one basic common feature. Orthodox Christianity over the centuries has insisted that Jesus Christ was both Man and God, and thus texts that clearly assert his manhood, of which there are many in the New Testament, are not allowed to contradict the equally clear teaching in other passages of his divinity. A similar situation must be allowed to exist in the early Buddhist scriptures, not to mention the later ones. No Buddhist in any period doubts that Buddhas appear in the world as men and that Śākyamuni was thus far a man and so mortal.[37] But it cannot fairly be shown that he was ever regarded by his followers as a mere man, that is to say no more than a man. The whole Buddhist doctrine would disintegrate into the moralizing and philosophizing of a handful of intellectuals, just as Christianity, once Jesus Christ is reduced to a mere human teacher, becomes a rather unusual assortment of ethical teachings often of quite impractical implications. Thus to the same extent that Jesus Christ can be regarded as both Man and God on the basis of the writings of the New Testament, so Śākyamuni can be regarded, indeed must be regarded if the success of the Buddha is to be explained at all, as both Man and Buddha. Furthermore just as many of Christ's contemporaries and indeed some of his actual followers never gave credit to ideas of his divinity, so many of Śākyamuni's contemporaries, especially his adversaries, continued to see him as no more than a mortal man, as well as mistaken in his teachings. There is, however, no indication that any of his followers regarded him as anything less than a Buddha together with all the attributes associated with this title. Within such a context as this one may note the absurdity of applying to him such epithets as "atheistic" or even "agnostic." On the contrary his followers believed him to be omniscient, far from agnostic. Also to refer to his teachings as "pessimistic" is no true judgement of his teachings, but rather an indication that the person who uses this term concerning him sees nothing but phenomenal existence and the extinction of phenomenal existence in the sense that death may be said to extinguish it. If he envisages nirvāṇa as a goal to be striven for, to be earned, he would realize that optimistic might be a more appropriate description of a Buddha's striving towards enlightenment. But all such value-judgements become irrelevant when one writes of Buddhism in the terms in which it presents itself, not attempting to force it into alien thought-forms. On the other hand, analogies can be helpful, and it will become clear in the next chapter how Buddhist doctrines were developed and formulated over a long period of several centuries in much the same way that Christian doctrine was gradually established.[38]

37 In this respect one may note that Śākyamuni claims to be able to continue living for a whole world age and thus his death at the age of eighty is voluntary. One may certainly argue that such teaching must be a later development, but it is firmly stated in the Pāli canon of the Theravādins (*Mahāparinibbāna-sutta)*, III.43-55. See also André Bareau, *Recherches* II, vol. 1, pp. 151-6.

38 Such analogies do not diminish at all the essential differences between these two great religions. Analogies are not to be understood as similarities. One might justly claim that they are never in conflict for the reason that they never really come into contact, except in the human world, which for both religions represents a transient state, which must eventually be transcended. The goal of enlightenment might conceivably be equated with the mystical union with the Godhead as described

Just as the much later Christian formulations could be shown to be foreshadowed or even envisaged in the earlier beliefs, which were subsequently judged orthodox, so likewise the followers of the Mahāyāna can without difficulty be shown as consistent in their formulations with views that were known to be held in the earlier period. Again, just as the subtle distinctions made by the supporters of opposing schools of thought were often quite irrelevant to the faith and practice of the majority of Christian believers, so the arguments between the various Buddhist schools deal mainly with abstruse points of doctrine, which would seem to leave the central beliefs untouched. A major group that split off perhaps some hundred years after Śākyamuni's decease, known as the Mahāsāṃghikas (members of the Great Assembly) as opposed to Sthaviravādins (Pāli: Theravādins, members of the Group of Elders), is usually credited by Western scholars with inventing the idea of "a transcendent Buddha, a supernatural being who has nothing in common with the world and whose terrestrial life is a mere fiction." However, as can be easily verified, the Theravādins themselves preserve many early canonical scriptures in Pāli where the transcendent nature of a perfected Buddha, referring specifically to Śākyamuni, is clearly asserted. It would seem that none of the early schools known to us denied such an assumption, although their more scholarly members were certainly preoccupied with the nature of Śākyamuni's physical form here in this world. However, this could never be a dispute between some followers who believed that he had really lived as man and those who believed that his life on earth was mere appearance. To present the dispute in such a way is to transfer to the case of Śākyamuni the arguments of orthodox Christian believers in the real human nature of Jesus Christ as against those who held views, usually defined as "docetic," which taught that his suffering and dying were not those of a real human being but just semblance.[39]

Such a comparison between the two religions is not doctrinally possible, for the fundamental reason that there can be no real "person" at all according to Buddhist theory, whether of Śākyamuni or of any other living being. As has been noted above, all such apparent entities are dissolved into elemental particles (*dharmas*) and thus the argument about the nature of Śākyamuni's physical presence in this world is bound up with the theory of the nature, either real or unreal, of the *dharmas*. Some thinkers, such as the Sarvāstivādins, held that all

in the writings of certain Christian contemplatives, but such an equation does violence to the teachings of both religions in different ways. Perhaps the Christian doctrine of the absolute distinction between created and uncreated being causes the main difficulty in this respect.

[39] Compare Étienne Lamotte, *Histoire du Bouddhisme Indien*, pp. 713-4: "les Mahāsāṃghikas ont inventé un Buddha transcendant, être surnaturel n'ayant plus rien de commun avec le monde et dont la vie terrestre n'est que fiction." However, the following section (up to p. 759) provides a most useful discussion of the development of the "Buddha legend."

For a detailed discussion of Mahāsāṃghika views on the nature of a Buddha see N. Dutt, *Buddhist Sects in India*, pp. 75-105. Here again it is significant that Dutt begins this chapter by quoting a Theravādin text as leading in the same "transcendental" direction: "I am the Lord of All, the Omniscient. I am untainted by all *dharmas*. I am the Worthy One in the world, the Teacher Supreme. I alone am the Perfect Buddha, tranquil in the state of nirvāṇa" (*Ariyapariyesanā-sutta* from the *Majjhima Nikāya*).

dharmas, the conditioned (saṃsāra) as well as the unconditioned (nirvāṇa), were essentially real. For them a Buddha logically consisted of real *dharmas*, albeit only purified ones. Other beings, no more or less real as apparent conglomerations of *dharmas*, consisted of combinations of pure and impure *dharmas*. However, some thinkers were already contesting the "reality" of *dharmas* that at best only manifested themselves momentarily, and those belonging to the sect known as Lokottaravādins (followers of the Supramundane) urged the essential unreality of conditioned *dharmas* and treated the unconditioned ones (which means nirvāṇa) as real. Thus the *dharmas* composing Śākyamuni's physical body would be regarded as unreal like those composing all other apparent combinations of *dharmas* in the phenomenal world. There could never be a question of Śākyamuni's appearance in this world being regarded as unreal while those of all his contemporaries were regarded as real, and this is precisely what the use of the term "docetic" implies according to Christian usage.[40] This provides one more example of the inadvisability of applying Western terminology uncircumspectly to any exegesis of Buddhism.

b. *The Cult of Relics*

The Buddhist cult of human relics, which cuts it off so markedly from more orthodox forms of Hindu religion, certainly suggests that the body of a Buddha, or at least the cremated remains, were regarded as real enough for practical purposes as well as exceedingly valuable. It is related that the other seven contenders for a share of Śākyamuni's relics were prepared to fight the Mallas of Kuśinagara for their part of the sacred spoils, if these townsfolk near whose town he has happened to expire were not willing to share them. In an interesting article[41] Jean Przyluski refers to the account of the sharing of the bodily relics of Śākyamuni's favorite disciple Ānanda. According to the Vinaya of the Mūla-Sarvāstivādins, when he was about to enter nirvāṇa, Ānanda reflected:

> If I enter into nirvāṇa here, King Ajātaśatru (of Magadha) will quarrel for a long time with the town of Vaiśāli. He will certainly not share my relics with them. But if I enter nirvāṇa in the town of Vaiśāli, King Ajātaśatru will in that case not get a share. Thus I must obtain nirvāṇa in the middle of the Ganges."
>
> By means of his miraculous powers Ānanda created an island in the middle of the river, where he entered nirvāṇa. Having thus expired on neutral territory the two contestants each received a share of his relics.

Such relics must have been in considerable demand in order to "activate" the numerous stūpas which from the third century B.C. onward were being built all over India. Some of them have even survived to our times. Thus the great stūpa of Sāñcī (mentioned above) was found to contain a casket holding the relics of Śāriputra and Maudgalyāyana, two of the most famous of Śākyamuni's

40 See e.g. Aloys Grillmeier, *Christ in Christian Tradition*, pp. 93-4 and 115ff., also concerning Clement of Alexandria and his curious suggestions, pp. 161-3.

41 "Le partage des reliques du Buddha," *Mélanges chinois et bouddhiques* 4 (1936), pp. 341-67. For the supposed actual citing of this story see below pp. 311-12.

disciples.[42] From the time that Sāñcī was being restored in the last century the casket with its relics was kept in the British Museum. In 1956 on the occasion of the great Buddhist festival in India, celebrating twenty-five hundred years of Buddhist expansion, these relics were solemnly returned and reenshrined at Sāñcī. Also, in 1898 an ancient mound at Piprāwā (some fourteen miles SE of the Lumbini site) was excavated and found still to contain relics in a casket inscribed with an Aśoka-style inscription translatable as: "This deposit of relics of the blessed Buddha of the Śākyas is of Sukiti and his brothers with their sisters, their sons and their wives."[43] Uncertain as the meaning may be, there was certainly at this place a deposit of relics going back at least to the third century B.C., which the founders of the stūpa presumably believed to be those of Śākyamuni himself. We are not concerned with the problem of to what extent such relics may have been genuine or whether the oft repeated story is true of how the Emperor Aśoka had the earlier stūpas opened so that the relics could be shared out in the innumerable stūpas that he himself is said to have founded. That such stories were current is more than evidence enough, especially when combined with that of archaeological finds, to suggest that relics were needed at a very early period to "activate," as it were, any newly erected stūpa. This practice has continued to this present day, for at least in Tibetan-speaking regions stūpas (Tibetan *mChod-rten*, pronounced chöten) are activated with religious texts, representing the Buddha Word. Often however they contain the relics of deceased lamas, thus continuing a tradition going back to the earliest times.

The cult of relics, as evinced in so remarkably similar a manner in Buddhism and Christianity, represents a kind of spontaneous devotion to the holy person deceased and in both religions miraculous powers are attributed to them. It may seem strange that the cult was so widespread in early Buddhism, for not only would human remains be regarded as impure in themselves in contemporary Hindu society, but also in accordance with philosophical notions of the *dharma* theory, they are simply composed of elemental particles, which are supposedly essentially impure. We surely have here a particularly cogent example of the irrelevance of such scholastic disquisition where the actual practice of Buddhist religion was concerned. A Buddha is of supramundane dimensions, and once he has left this world, the most fitting representation of his presence is this hemispherical mound, for others conceived of as a tomb, but in his case the symbol of the ineffable state, transcending life and death, into which he has withdrawn.

A corresponding theory was developed of two kinds of Buddha-manifestation, known as "Bodies" (*kāya*), where this term is used in a restricted buddhalogical sense rather as the term "Person" is used in a special sense for the Christian Trinity. A later development resulted in a trinity of "Buddha-Bodies," but in the earlier phase of the Doctrine only two were formulated, those of the "Body of Appearance" (*rūpa-kāya*) and the "Body of the *Dharma*" (*dharma-kāya*), where

[42] See Debala Mitra, *Buddhist Monuments*, pp. 97-8.

[43] See E. J. Thomas, *Life of Buddha*, pp. 160-163 and L. de la Vallée Poussin, *L'Inde aux temps des Mauryas*, pp. 144-5. Especially D. Mitra, *op. cit.* pp. 79-82.

dharma refers not to transient elemental particles, whether considered real or unreal, but to the absolute Buddha nature, which is the *alpha* and the *omega*, the source and the goal, of the whole sacred Law (*Dharma*) as taught by Śākyamuni. The stūpa is conceived of as the symbol of this absolute Buddha-nature (*dharma-kāya*), activated, as it were, by the sacred relics of Śākyamuni's "Body of Appearance" (*rūpa-kāya*). Thus a "real presence" is suggested in a sacramental sense with the result that stūpas were worshipped with offerings of flowers and garlands, of lamps and of incense. One may refer to this, if one will, as a Mahāyāna tendency in pre-Mahāyāna Buddhism, but this is merely a circuitous way of admitting that there is no early phase of Buddhism known when there was no cult of a Buddha as a supramundane being.

It is interesting to note that it is precisely the followers of the Mahāyāna, if only perhaps the more thoughtful ones, who realize the essential "emptiness" of the whole cult of relics. In an early Mahāyāna sūtra Śākyamuni says:[44]

> The Buddha-sphere is inconceivable.
> The Buddhas are incomparable.
> All Buddhas are always at peace.
> All Buddhas emerge in perfection.
> All Buddhas are alike in hue.
> Such is the *Dharma*-nature of Buddhas.
> The Lord is no created being.
> The Prize-Winner is never born.
>
> He reveals his "Body of Appearance,"
> A body as hard as adamant.
> The relics of this Great Sage
> Cannot be assessed even to the size of a sesame seed.
>
> If such a Body has neither bones nor blood
> How can relics be found?
> But in order to benefit living beings
> He leaves relics as a mere device.
>
> The *Dharma*-body of a Perfect Buddha
> Is the *Dharma*-Sphere of the Prize-Winning Buddhas.
> As one in the act of teaching the Dharma,
> Even such is the Body of the Lord.

Reading this one should bear in mind that those who promulgated such teachings insisted that all appearances in the phenomenal world, all living beings as much as a Buddha, were mere appearance since the elements of which they are here said to be composed were "void" (*śūnya*) of essential content. Relics are therefore left as a device or "method" (*upāya*) of instilling faith so that men shall hold to the religious life and eventually find a way out of the maze of false views in which they would otherwise be lost. The essential need for committed religious practice is certainly not denied, but is identified as "relative truth," as it

44 Extracted from the *Suvarṇaprabhāsottama-sūtra*, vol. I, Tibetan Texts, edited by Johannes Nobel, pp. 16-17.

is relative to the state in which the world appears to be.

No traditional Buddhist of any School appears to have discounted the importance of relics, and the doubt suggested concerning them in the Perfection of Wisdom literature is by no means special to them, for it applies to all material things and intellectual concepts. Relics may even be regarded as the most prized things after the Perfection of Wisdom itself. Thus the Lord asks Indra, Chief of the Gods:

> "If on the one hand, someone were to present you with this world filled to the top with relics of the Buddha and if on the other hand you were presented with a copy of the Perfection of Wisdom, which of the two would you take?"
>
> Indra replies: "The Perfection of Wisdom, and why? It is not, O Lord, that I lack in respect for these relics of the Buddha, and it is not that I am unwilling to honour, revere and worship them. But I am fully aware, O Lord, that the relics of the Buddha have come forth from the Perfection of Wisdom and that therefore they are honoured, revered and worshipped. I am aware that they are saturated with the Perfection of Wisdom, and therefore they become an object of worship."[45]

Wisdom (*prajñā*) comes to play a very important part in buddhalogical concepts. In the earlier teachings it is linked with morality (*śīla*) and mental concentration (*samādhi*) as representing a threefold formulation of well-ordered religious life. Wisdom, however, is both the beginning and end, for without "right views" to start with, efforts in morality and mental concentration will be wasted. But wisdom is also the result of religious practice in that it culminates in the threefold knowledge of a Buddha. From a philosophical viewpoint the *dharma* theory was wisdom according to those who accepted it as representing "right views" and as an accurate analysis of a Buddha's insight into saṃsāra. But for those who rejected the materialistic realism of the *dharma* theory, regarding all concepts as "void" (*śūnya*), wisdom, named now the Perfection of Wisdom,[46] signified the ultimate state where all apparent contradictions are resolved in the state of buddhahood. As a Sanskrit term "Perfection of Wisdom" (*Prajñā-pāramitā*) is feminine and thus its identification as the "Mother of all Buddhas" will logically follow. However, here we anticipate doctrinal developments which will come within the purview of the following chapter.

[45] Extracted from Edward Conze, *The Large Sūtra on Perfect Wisdom*, chapter 31 (p. 249). More or less the same wording is found in the earliest of the "Perfection of Wisdom" Sūtras, that in 8,000 verses, which may be generally dated in its origins to the second or first century B.C. See Edward Conze, *Aṣṭasāhasrikā Prajñāpāramitā*, p. 35. A rather different version of the same teaching, which may or may not be even earlier, occurs in the verse-form version of the same "Perfection of Wisdom." For this see Edward Conze, *The Accumulation of Precious Qualities*, published in Indo-Iranian Studies, Part I, pp. 162-278.

[46] It is of interest to note that when the Tibetans translated the Sanskrit term *pāramitā*, meaning supremity or perfection, they understood it as a derivative of *param ita*, meaning "gone beyond" and therefore they invented the technical term *pha-rol-tu phyin-pa*, which is a literal translation.

5. THE BUDDHIST COMMUNITY

From early times a Buddhist convert signified his adherence to the religion by the threefold refuge-taking formula: "I take refuge in the Buddha. I take refuge in the Dharma. I take refuge in the Community." Of the nature of the Buddha and the Dharma some account has been given, and we must now consider the Community. The same problem of historical origins arises, as in the case of the other two, because the community appears in Aśoka's time (third century B.C.) already with its main features fixed. There is in existence a well-established order of monks, living in settled communities, bound by a recognized code of rules, known in Sanskrit as the *prātimokṣa*, which is the essential text for monastic discipline in the Vinaya, the first part of the three-part Buddhist canon.[47] By this time too the Community had begun to split into different sects, partly as a result of internal disputes concerning precisely which teachings were strictly canonical, but also as a result of the vast distances that now separated the various communities. By the end of Aśoka's reign such communities were established in Gandhāra in the far northwest of the Indian subcontinent (representing in modern times Pakistan and eastern Afghanistan), in Sri Lanka in the far south, and over large parts of the rest of India, where the comparative peace of the later years of Aśoka's rule had opened routes of trade and the whole country to greater prosperity. The Buddhist communities were usually established near enough to towns to ensure lay interest and support, but not so close that distraction to the religious life might result. It is significant that merchants proved the most generous benefactors whose support could be generally relied upon. Kings and local rulers could outdo them in their benefactions, if they chose to support the Buddhist order, and it is in fact the support of certain great monarchs, of whom Aśoka was the first, that enabled Buddhism to become first a great pan-Indian religion and later the greatest pan-Asian one.

The *Prātimokṣa*, which consists of a list of approximately two hundred and fifty rules, arranged in groups, according to the severity of the punishment which their breach entails, survives as part of the Vinaya of several different Buddhist sects, and thus it clearly goes back to that very early period when Buddhism had not yet spread beyond the region of the central Ganges, where Śākyamuni had lived and taught.[48] Since he is said fairly reliably to have watched over his growing community for the space of forty-five years, it is scarcely conceivable that he himself did not draw up the first list of rules, probably compiled gradually as occasion demanded. The list is headed by the four major sins which demand expulsion from the order, namely unnatural

[47] *Prātimokṣa* is a later Sanskritization of the early term which occurs in Pāli as *pātimokkha*, interpreted as "that which should be made binding" (Rhys Davids and Stede, *Pāli-English Dictionary*, p. 450). Understanding the prefix *prāti-* in a different sense, the Tibetan translation of the term comes to mean "individual release" (*so-sor thar-pa*).

[48] The early Vinaya collections that are known are: the Theravādin (in Pāli), the Mūla-Sarvāstivādin (in Sanskrit and Tibetan), the Sarvāstivādin, Dharmaguptaka, Mahāsāṃghika, Mahiśāsaka (in Chinese translation).

sexual intercourse, theft, murder and a false claim to miraculous powers. Sins demanding temporary suspension from the order include sexual intercourse with a woman, self-abuse, acting as intermediary in the sexual relations of others, building a shelter for oneself without having it formally approved, building a monastic compound without having the site formally approved, accusing another falsely of wrong conduct, causing dissension, causing local scandal, contradicting harshly a just rebuke. Lesser sins, such for example as asking a nun who is not related to wash or iron one's robe, or begging for a new robe from unrelated layfolk, except when this is justified (as when one's robe is lost or destroyed), result in the forfeiture of the article concerned. Another set of lesser sins, such as trivial lying or slandering or gossip, preaching to a woman in more than five or six words when no other witness is present, using an article that belongs to the community without replacing it afterwards, etc., all these require expiation. All these and the many other minor rules which make up a total of two hundred and twenty-seven in the Theravādin collection and two hundred and fifty-eight in that of the Mūla-Sarvāstivādins, were clearly drawn up over quite a number of years, but there need be no reason to doubt that the original core, although no longer ascertainable, goes back to Śākyamuni himself.[49] These rules were recited monthly in the different communities, and the presumed adherence to them constituted formal adherence to the community of monks. This is still so today when the Theravādin collection is recited by religious communities in Sri Lanka, while the Mūla-Sarvāstivādin collection is even now recited in present-day Tibetan monasteries. Despite the later tantric developments, there still remain close historical connections between early Buddhism and certain aspects of Tibetan Buddhism today. To these attention will be drawn in due course.

It is from the general situation of the various Buddhist communities in Aśoka's time that one has to try and trace back to the still earlier period, simply interpreting the accounts as given in a reasonable manner. It would appear that the first communities were indeed established in the time of Śākyamuni himself. There is no good reason to doubt the tradition that King Bimbisāra of Magadha was well disposed to the new order and that he himself donated one of his parks (the Veluvana) to Śākyamuni. Another park, also on the outskirts of the royal city of Rājagṛha, known as the Udambarikārā, was made available to wandering ascetics generally. Other parks, famous in early times as donations to Śākyamuni himself, were the Jīvikārāma, also near Rājagṛha and given by the physician Jīvaka, the Jetavana near Śrāvasti, given by the rich merchant Anāthapindaka,

[49] Sukumar Dutt in his excellent book *Buddhist Monks and the Monasteries of India* draws attention (pp. 66-7) to an earlier use of the term *pātimokkha*, which has survived in the *Mahāpādana Suttanta* (*Digha Nikāya*), 3.28, where it is attributed to the previous Buddha Vipaśyin. It probably belongs to the general religious lore of wandering ascetics, including the first Buddhists, but it can scarcely deprive Śākyamuni of the honor of being the first formulator of detailed rules for the conduct of his monks (viz. the *prātimokṣa* somewhat as it is now known), as Sukumar Dutt would seem to suggest.

and the Ambapālivana near Vaiśāli, given by the courtesan Ambapali.[50] Śākyamuni's followers were but one of several groups of mendicant ascetics, some of whom can have been little better than wandering vagabonds of the kind that one still meets in India today, while others were organized under a recognized teacher in much the same way as were "the sons of the Śākya." The only other such community to have survived to this day is represented by the Jains, whose traditions go back to the Teacher Vardhamāna, known by his followers as the "Conqueror" (*Jina*, whence the term *jaina* is derived) and as "Hero" (*mahāvira)*. Both titles were applied to Śākyamuni by his particular followers, and the two movements had much in common, including the same cosmological and philosophical ideas, belief in the process of rebirth and in a succession of world-teachers, as well as the cult of stūpas. To an outsider, and such in a real sense were most benefactors, whether local rulers, wealthy merchants or ordinary householders, there might very well appear to be little difference in the actual beliefs of the various wandering teachers, but what would presumably be noted would be the standards of behaviour of their followers.[51] Here one gains the impression that not only were Śākyamuni's followers well ordered and controlled, but also they had an air of social respectability, which other groups seemed to lack. Not only did Śākyamuni himself come from an aristocratic family, but so too did many of his early followers according to canonical accounts, and even if such stories are suspected of being legendary, they nonetheless indicate the manner in which the new movement presented itself to others. Moreover in his first sermon Śākyamuni is said to have taught that his doctrine was a "middle way," avoiding excessive laxity on the one hand and excessive hardship on the other.[52] The comparatively easy life of the Buddhist monk made him a butt for the followers of other sects, but it probably contributed largely to the success of the doctrine in a worldly sense. It seems to have succeeded in preserving a fair balance between genuine religious practice and lay respectability, thus attracting to its ranks men of good family and talent as well as of religious aspiration. The establishing of a new order that was destined to succeed in such a way certainly requires a wise and tactful founder, and it is precisely in this respect that one might draw a limited comparison between Śākyamuni and St. Benedict, for just as St. Benedict fixed a Rule for his monks, so too must surely have Śākyamuni.

[50] The term *ārāma* (Tibetan *kun-dga'-ra-ba*) as e.g., in *Jīvaka-ārāma*, means a pleasure park, and because of the use to which such places were sometimes put, it came to have the meaning of "monastic compound." For more on the subject, see Sukumar Dutt, op. cit., pp. 58-65.

[51] Concerning other seemingly well-constituted groups, who were opponents of Śkyamuni, one may refer to A. L. Basham, *History and Doctrine of the Ājīvakas.*

[52] It should be observed that there was always a tendency in Buddhism (just as in early Christianity) to a highly strict ascetic way of life. Indeed arguments concerning the extent to which this was necessary produced one of the causes of splits in the order thus resulting in different sects. There is reference to a rule involving dressing only in rags, living only in the open air, sleeping in a sitting posture, etc. See e.g., T. W. Rhys Davids, *The Questions of King Milinda*, Part II, p. 268. See also the interesting article by J. Przyluski, "Vêtements de religieux et vêtements de rois," *Journal Asiatique*, vol. XIII, pp. 365ff. However, it seems scarcely likely that Śākyamuni himself urged such practices upon his followers.

It was the practice of wandering ascetics to stay put in one place during the monsoon period (mid-June to mid-September) when travel was unusually difficult, and thus the first settlements were needed only during the resulting three-month period. At some stage these settlements came to be used for extended periods and thus regular monastic communities came into being. How soon this occurred it is impossible to know, but it is not at all unlikely that the process had already begun during Śākyamuni's lifetime. It is certain that by Aśoka's time many such communities were well established, that they were soon being rendered permanent by the constructions of buildings in brick and stone, and that organized Buddhism had already assumed those outward forms of the religious life that have persisted right through to the twentieth century. In India building continued on many of these ancient sites so long as Buddhism survived in the land of its origin, and in recent years much archaeological work has been done on the ruins, often only foundations of buildings, thus providing reliable material substantiation of the very early traditional accounts of such foundations and of the later descriptions of visiting pilgrim-scholars. Fortunately however some early communities constructed their monasteries by cutting them out of solid rock.. This was only possible where the type of rock-formation permitted the elaborate hollowing-out of temples and cave-dwellings, notably in the present-day state of Maharashtra. Three such sites, at Bhaja, Bedsa, and Karla, in close proximity to one another, are to be found about half way between Bombay and Poona (*Pls. 7, 8*). Another important site of Kanheri is about twenty miles north of Bombay. Rather further afield are Nāsik and especially Ajantā and Ellora, which nowadays figure on all tourist programmes. These cave-monasteries, like those elsewhere consisting of free-standing buildings, underwent long periods of development, at least from the second century B.C. until the eighth century A.D., changing their styles and their iconography in an exactly similar way. Thus the early rock-cut temples have no Buddha image and the central object of worship is the domed stūpa, cut out of the solid rock just as the rest of the building has been. The Karla pillars have a kind of pot-base and are surmounted by elaborate capitals in the form of elephants with noble couples on them and horses with their riders. Horses and riders are a favorite motif and the massive pillars at the entrance to the Bedsa caves are likewise adorned. Worthy of note too are the deep-cut bas-reliefs that cover the walls on either side of one of the Bhaja cave-cells. The sun-god in his chariot appears on the left and Indra as the god of war riding his elephant on the right. The early carvings are largely decorative, as are many of the subsidiary carvings at the ancient site of Sāñcī, already mentioned above. We shall deal in the next chapter with the later iconographical developments, and all we need emphasize here is that just as Buddhism emerges into history with the ideal of a supramundane Buddha and with a Doctrine which teaches of saṃsāra and nirvāṇa associated with a complicated theory of fluctuating "real elements," so it also emerges with a fully constituted monastic order, already split into various sects, but all clearly following the same pattern of religious life, a pattern that has remained unchanged in essentials to this day.[53] Early Buddhist belief in a plurality of Buddhas who appear in succeeding world-ages makes it impossible to conceive of Śākyamuni in any traditional religious sense as the founder of his religion in the way in which Jesus Christ is certainly the founder of Christianity and Mohammed of Islam, but he may certainly be regarded as the founder of an order of monks and later of nuns, and on the future wellbeing of his monks all the subsequent success of his religion has depended.

Nāgārjuna (see pp. 81 ff.)
"Salutation to Nāgārjuna, proclaimed as the second wondrous teacher of the doctrine of the incomparable Śākya-Lion,
For he transmits reliable and profound interpretations."

[53] For typical plans of early Buddhist temples and monasteries one may conveniently refer to Debala Mitra, *Buddhist Monuments*, pp. 21-56.

II

LATER DEVELOPMENTS IN INDIA

1. BUDDHISM BECOMES A PAN-ASIAN RELIGION

During the first five hundred years, that is to say up to approximately the beginning of the Christian era, Buddhism spread over the whole of the Indian subcontinent. Well within the next one thousand years it established itself as the main religion throughout Asia. From the first century A.D. onward it spread across Central Asia to China, moving on to Korea and Japan in the fourth century. Perhaps as early as the fourth century it became established in Nepal,[1] and in the seventh century the long work of the conversion of Tibet was begun. All this work of conversion was a slow process, as vast areas were being covered over long and difficult trade routes and through different countries where a great variety of different languages were spoken. Thus an enormous amount of translation work was involved over these centuries.

From the third century A.D. onward Buddhism, together with Hinduism, found its way across the Indian ocean to all the countries of Southeast Asia as represented nowadays by Burma, Thailand, Laos, Cambodia, Vietnam and Indonesia. By marked contrast with the conversions that followed long land routes, there was far less need for translation work. Thus, just as Buddhism had been preached in Sri Lanka in the Indian dialect (Pāli) in which the scriptures were being recited (and eventually written down) so now the main medium for instruction remained the Indian language then in use, by this time mainly Sanskrit.

The one country, later to become Buddhist, that was not penetrated during these thousand years is Mongolia, where not until the thirteenth century did the Tibetans begin this new work of conversion. It may be of interest to note that this last work of foreign conversion coincided closely in time with the destruction of Buddhism in India itself, and although the ancient links with the center of their faith were never entirely forgotten, the various Buddhist or now partly Buddhist countries of Asia tended to develop their own particular traditions in an ever more exclusive manner. However, up to this time and in so far as it was humanly

[1] Modern works on the history of Buddhism often state that Śākyamuni was born in Nepal and this rather anachronistic assertion may cause a misunderstanding. Lumbini, his birthplace, has since the mid-nineteenth century, thanks to a British donation, fallen a few miles inside the frontier of Nepal with India. However, modern Nepal is a creation of the Gorkha Rājas, dating back only to the end of the eignteenth century. See below, Section IV.3.a.

possible most of the countries of Asia, where Buddhism was now an established religion, maintained some kind of contact whether through individual monk-pilgrims or state-sponsored missions with the ancient places of pilgrimage in the central Ganges valley, as well as with the many other sites, especially in Gandhāra, which had since become important in Buddhist tradition. Up to the end of the seventh century intrepid Chinese scholar-pilgrims visited the "Holy Land" at various times. From the tenth century until the thirteenth century the Tibetans were maintaining the closest possible scholarly contacts in India. The great Indian scholar Dīpaṅkaraśrījñāna, nicknamed Atiśa, who came to Tibet in 1042 after studying and teaching at the great Indian monasteries of Vikramaśīla, Bodhgayā and Odantapuri, had also studied earlier under a certain Dharmakīrti of Suvarṇadvīpa (= Sumatra), thus suggesting far-flung relationships across the Buddhist lands of Asia. The Tibetan monk-pilgrim Chos-rje-dpal, who visited Bodhgayā in the thirteenth century not long before its final abandonment, met with a strong community of monks from Sri Lanka who were still there, and up to the end of the same century repairs were being carried out on the main temple at the instigation of the king of Burma. Such interesting information tends to be scanty as no one in any one country has had an interest in producing any general account, but judging by the suggestive material already available as well as by the vast numbers of pilgrims from all over Asia who have been returning to the ancient Indian Buddhist sites since they were reconstituted in the late nineteenth century, there must have been very many more visitors in those earlier centuries of whom nothing is recorded. Throughout these centuries too, a truly vast amount of translating was done mainly from Sanskrit into Chinese from the second century onward and from Sanskrit into Tibetan from the seventh century onward. Much of our knowledge of the later Indian Buddhism as described in this chapter is in fact derived from Tibetan materials originating from lost Indian sources.

While we shall be concerned in this chapter with the later Buddhist developments in India itself, one should bear in mind that they continued to provide the materials for the progress of the religion in all the other countries of Asia so long as contact could fruitfully be maintained. Just as there can be no "original Buddhism" promulgated once and for all in the land of its origin, as some sectarians have tried to insist, so there has not been one form of Buddhism transported to any other country at any one particular time. Attempts were made at various times to resolve doctrinal differences, and there are traditional accounts of various "councils" that were held in order to establish a recognized orthodoxy.[2] The first is supposed to have been held at Rājagṛha immediately after Śākyamuni's decease, the second at Vaiśāli perhaps some hundred years later, and a third one at Pātaliputra under Aśoka (according to Theravādin

[2] For a succinct account of these councils one may turn to H. Kern, *Manual of Indian Buddhism*, pp. 101-112 and 121-2. Although this was written more than eighty years ago, there is little or nothing to add to Kern's conclusions. For a far more recent account where up-to-date references are given, see E. Lamotte, *Histoire du Bouddhisme indien*,, pp. 136ff and pp. 296ff., noting that his history does not reach to Kushāna times.

accounts) or at Jālandara in Kashmir under Kaniṣka (according to Sarvāstivādin accounts). Just as Aśoka must have played an effective part in the propagation of Buddhism throughout the Indian subcontinent, so Kaniṣka of the Kushāna Dynasty, reigning in Gandhāra in the second century A.D., played at least indirectly as effective part in the further spread of Buddhism from northwest India through Central Asia and beyond. However, both the Theravādin account of a general council held under the auspices of Aśoka in the third century B.C. and the Sarvāstivādin accounts of the much later council under Kaniṣka remain equally tendentious. In this respect it may be interesting to quote the very open view of the first great Tibetan historian, namely Bu-ston (1290-1364), who representing the Indian Buddhist tradition as current in Kashmir, knows nothing of any third council at Pātaliputra.

> The Mūla-Sarvāstivādins say that up to the time of the Second Council there was only one school, viz., the Mūla-Sarvāstivādin. Thereafter, owing to the fact that the Scriptures were recited in different dialects, there arose the seventeen other sects, which do not represent the Buddha's teaching. . . . .
>
> We refute this statement of the Sarvāstivādins thus: The texts of the other seventeen sects are the Buddha-Word. They are to be found in the Vinaya since they teach moral discipline. They are contained in the Sūtras in that these teach mental discipline. Also they are not in conflict with the true essence of the Doctrine, since they accord with the teaching concerning nirvāṇa and contain the treatises relating to Wisdom.[3]

According to Bu-ston there was a general recitation of scriptures at the Third Council (meaning the one held under Kaniṣka in Kashmir) and it was settled that all the texts acknowledged by all the eighteen sects represented the Buddha-Word. While such a happy conclusion to the gathering may seem to be historically unlikely, the fact that Bu-ston thus records it indicates the wide catholicity of the later converts to Buddhism. On one of his edicts Aśoka had announced: "Whatever has been spoken by the Lord Buddha, all is well spoken."[4] By the time of Kaniṣka some three centuries later there was an even greater accumulation of scriptures claimed as Buddha-Word by those who subscribed to them, and the openness shown, as described by Bu-ston, was the only reasonable approach to the religion on the part of those who came from outside India. Thus the sects as they had developed in India and as they continued to develop over the remaining centuries so long as the religion flourished there, remained peculiar to India.[5]

[3] For the whole context of this extract see Bu-ston, *History of Buddhism*, translation by E. Obermiller, vol. II, pp. 97-8.

[4] See A. Sen, *Aśoka's Edicts*, p. 134.

[5] The best available accounts of these sects are: André Bareau, *Les sectes bouddhiques du petit véhicule*; N. Dutt, *Buddhist Sects in India*.

2. THE BUDDHA IMAGE

a. *The Earliest Representations in Human Form*

The Emperor Kaniṣka of the Kushāna Dynasty, famous in local tradition as a great supporter of Buddhism, ruled over an empire that stretched from what is now eastern Afghanistan, across Pakistan and including the upper Ganges Valley with the important city of Mathurā (thirty-five miles NW of modern Agra). The far northwest has always been the main approach route toward India and thus its population has been continually absorbing fresh waves of non-Indian stock. Interesting arrivals in the late fourth century B.C. were the Greeks (or Macedonians) led there by Alexander the Great. During the reign of Aśoka when India became for a short while as great an empire as in the very much later Moghul days, the Greek-speaking rulers of the far northwest had been forced to withdraw west of the Hindu Kush into what is now western Afghanistan. Here was the ancient kingdom of Bactria, Greek in culture and language at least so far as the ruling classes were concerned. On the breakup of Aśoka's empire, which soon followed his death, these Greeks again advanced, taking over the land of Gandhāra (modern eastern Afghanistan and Pakistan). However, they were soon overrun by a barbarian people from the north known as the Scythians, who in turn found themselves in constant warfare with the Parthians to their west. Finally, around about the beginning of the Christian era all these various peoples, the earlier inhabitants (whom one may describe as generally "Indian" in so far as they had been included earlier in Aśoka's empire), the Greeks, Scythians and Parthians, succumbed before the advance of yet another barbarian race, known by the Chinese as the Yüeh-chih (they had already caused trouble on China's western borders) and by the Indians as the Tushkaras. These people rapidly established a large empire that included an extraordinary variety of religions—Zoroastrian, Greek, Buddhist, Jain and Hindu, and became in the process highly civilized themselves, practicing and encouraging the various cultures with which they found themselves surrounded. The greatest of their kings was Kaniṣka I, who probably ruled in the first half of the second century A.D., and it is quite possible that he himself showed a predilection for Buddhism, as Buddhist tradition so firmly asserts.

It is certain that Buddhism achieved considerable success in Gandhāra and throughout the outlying regions of the Kushāna domains, especially across the Pamirs to the east, where it was gradually propagated in the series of city-states that linked West Asia with China the whole length of the ancient "Silk Route" to China (see section IV.2.a). Westward, it pressed into Persian territory, however with rather less success, as here it was confronted with the well-established and often state-protected Zoroastrian religion. Owing to Persian military advances during the third century A.D. under its new Sassanid dynasty, the Kushānas lost their hold north of the Hindu Kush and thus their empire was restricted to Gandhāra itself with twin capitals, Kapiśa and Taxila, on the two sides of the Khyber Pass, the mountain gateway that nowadays connects Afghanistan with

Pakistan.[6] However, toward the end of the fifth century a fresh wave of barbarian people, the Ephthalite Huns, overran the whole area and from this onslaught Buddhism never fully recovered. Then from the early eighth century Moslem pressures made themselves felt ever more strongly and throughout the far northwest of the Indian subcontinent Buddhism and Hinduism rapidly disappeared. Only in the fastnesses of Kashmir did they hold their own until the mid-fourteenth century. Vast quantities of archaeological remains, ruined stūpas, the foundations of monasteries and broken Buddha-images, continue to bear witness to the earlier extraordinary success of Śākyamuni's teachings. However, before Buddhism disappeared from Gandhāra, some of its special features were absorbed into the mainstream of later Buddhist developments in the central Ganges Valley and throughout the rest of India, and although it may not always be easy to isolate these features altogether, their effects can be quite clearly noted.

It was noted in the previous chapter that early interest in Śākyamuni's person was largely mythological. Thus, he was envisaged as the latest Buddha of a whole series, while his own final life in this world had been conditioned by a whole succession of previous lives, during which he gradually progressed toward buddhahood. The earliest attempts at his biography, therefore, showed more interest in his supposed previous lives, leading up to the high points of his enlightenment at Bodhgayā and his first preaching at Sarnāth. No apparent interest was shown in producing a biography in the modern sense of the word. This attitude is confirmed by the archaeological remains. Śākyamuni is represented by symbols and the stone carvings illustrate mainly mythological concepts and legendary scenes from previous lives. Thus it may not be without significance that the first biographies of Śākyamuni, telling his story from the events leading up to his birth right through to the final nirvāṇa, were written in Gandhāra presumably for a more realistically minded people who wanted to know more about Śākyamuni as a person. This more realistic interest also becomes manifest in the sudden appearance of Buddha-images showing Śākyamuni for the first time in human form. This event took place in northwest India during the Kushāna period, and it is very likely that the initial inspiration came from converts to Buddhism whose cultural background was Hellenistic. While stating this, one has to bear in mind the strange fact that two very different kinds of Buddha-image seem to have been produced at more or less the same time (*Pls. 9, 10*). One kind is undoubtedly Hellenistic in origin, for Śākyamuni appears as Apollo in Buddhist guise, clad in a Roman toga. Images of this kind were produced in vast numbers, of which so many have been discovered since the last century. The other kind is thoroughly Indian in style, for the sculptors have taken as their model, not Apollo, but earlier images of the local divinities known as *yakṣa*. Understandably, images of this kind were produced at Mathurā in the

[6] For our present purposes the most relevant study of the Kushāna Empire is that of J. M. Rosenfield, *The Dynastic Arts of the Kushans*, to which further reference will be made in Chapter IV.

extreme southern limits of the Kushāna empire where Hellenistic influence was at its weakest. Few of such images are known, but famous as Mathurā certainly was for its creations, the output was inevitably far less than throughout the rest of the Kushāna empire where the Hellenistic-style Buddha certainly prevailed. Archaeologists, both Indian and European, have disputed for many decades concerning which of these two kinds of Buddha-image, the Gandhāran Buddha or the Mathurā Buddha, came first. If the original inspiration of creating an image of a Buddha in human form was non-Indian, as would seem to be almost certain, then the Hellenistic Buddha must surely come first.[7] Its creation, however, inspired other craftsmen of Indian background to produce at once a Buddha-image in the style in which they were accustomed to carve. This is surely the most likely solution of the problem. In any case the fact remains undisputed that it was in northwest India at the time of Kushāna rule that the first Buddha-iamges in human form were produced.[8] It is also evident that their creation relates to no doctrinal position of any particular school. It is quite incidental that the beginnings of the Mahāyāna have been attributed by most Western scholars to more or less the same period.

Quite apart from the human representation of Śākyamuni there are other clear proofs that the earlier mythological interest in the person of a Buddha was now being replaced by a realistic interest in his more recent life-story on earth. In the Gandhāra sculptures scenes from his historical biography are appreciably more common than scenes from the previous legendary lives. These include many scenes associated with his birth, with his youthful prowess and marriage, with his abandonment of life in the palace, his flight and his religious practice,

[7] More on this interesting subject together with useful references will be found in *The Image of Buddha*, pp. 59ff. I may perhaps quote once more the few lines from A. Foucher, *L'art gréco-bouddhique du Gandhāra*, vol. 2, p. 283, which I quoted previously:

> Is it not as though the Hellenizing master-craftsman, whose skilful chisel-cuts produced this Buddha image from a block of blue schist, had left his own thoughts imprinted on the stone? Standing before his finished work, we think we understand how he conceived it and why he executed it in such a way. For one matter had he not something of us in him, with the result that it is easier for us to read his thoughts? For another matter, do we not know in advance what those who ordered the images would have suggested to him? When they encountered the figure of the Buddha, he was not just fading in the mists of the past; he was rather beginning to lose his clear outlines in the clouds of incense that everywhere arose towards his divine nature now being realized. So after all, what one needed to represent was someone like a young prince, a descendant of the solar dynasty and more glorious than the day, who in former times, filled with loathing for the world and compassion for living creatures, had assumed the garb of a monk and had become by the power of his intellect a kind of saviour god. . . .
>
> Apollo, Saviour God, God of mysteries so learned,
> God of life and God of all salutary plants,
> Divine Conqueror of Python, God triumphant and youthful . . .
>
> Remembering these fine ancient verses of André Chénier (*Bucoliques*, VI), no one would be surprised that our artist should have thought at once of using as his model in such circumstances the most intellectual of his own youthful Olympian gods.

[8] The latest addition to the long continuing argument over the place of origin (Mathurā or Gandhāra) of the Buddha-image is a compelling article by J. E. van Lohuizen-de Leeuw, "New Evidence with Regard to the Origin of the Buddha Image," in *South Asian Archaeology 1979, Papers from the fifth conference of the association of South Asian archaeologists in Western Europe*, Berlin, 1981, pp. 377-400. This article supports the priority of the Mathurā type of image.

the onslaught of Māra, his enlightenment and first preaching, his many miracles and conversion-scenes leading up to his final decease and the distribution of relics (*Pls. 4b, 13a & b*). Scenes like these clearly predominate, although a few still hark back to his previous lives. Of the latter the most popular is perhaps that of the future Śākyamuni, then the Brahman youth named Mègha (or Sumegha), making a vow before the previous Buddha Dīpaṅkara that eventually he will himself become a Buddha. This previous Buddha Dīpaṅkara (literally "Light-Maker") is not one of the earlier set of six previous Buddhas, but appears in later extended sets. His name suggests a connection with a possible Gandhāran origin in that light is a very primary attribute of the divine nature in Persian religion [9] (*Pls. 11, 15*). Also very popular in Gandhāra, in so far as one may judge by archaeological remains, is the future Buddha Maitreya (*Pl. 12*), who while not unknown in the earlier canonical tradition,[10] embarks now upon his glorious future as prophesied by Śākyamuni. These three Buddhas, Dīpaṅkara, Śākyamuni, Maitreya, later become a stylized set representing the so-called "Buddhas of the Three Times," past, present and future. Maitreya is logically Buddha in a future sense, and apart from this particular context, he is normally represented as a Bodhisattva, and it is as such that he appears in many Gandhāran images.

The full development of the classical Buddha image was achieved during the period of the third great empire to be established in the Indian subcontinent, namely that of the Guptas who reigned from the fourth to the seventh centuries in an earlier period from Aśoka's old capital of Pātaliputra (Patna) and in the later period from Kānyakubja (modern Kanauj) in the upper Ganges valley. The two periods are separated by the devastating invasions of the Ephthalite Huns, referred to above, and although the two Gupta dynasties seem to be scarcely related, it is sufficient for our purposes to treat as one this new empire which embraced the whole Ganges valley and most of Central India. It was during these centuries that Buddhism attained a kind of maturity on Indian soil, India becoming the "holy land" for foreign pilgrims and traveling scholars from all the other Asian countries, listed at the beginning of this chapter, where the Buddhist religion had by now spread. The various traditions associated with this "classical" period, namely the established use of Sanskrit for a great scholarly literature, the founding of monasteries as centers of learning and religious practice, the embellishment of stūpas and temples, the fixing of the canons of Buddhist art, all these traditions continued to develop and flourish from the eighth century on, especially in eastern India, Kashmir and Nepal, where they existed side by side with the tantric developments which we shall be considering in the next chapter.

We tend to associate with the Mahāyāna a plurality of Buddha-forms with the

[9] This connection is emphasized by the flames that are shown emerging from some Buddha images. See e.g., *The Image of Buddha*, pp. 186-7. For those who read Italian an article on "Notes on the iconography of some luminous manifestations of Buddhas" by Maurizio Taddei is available in *Gururāhamañjarikā: Studi in onore di Giuseppe Tucci*, 2, pp. 435-49.

[10] E.g. in the *Dīgha Nikāya*, III.76.

suggestion that Śākyamuni has already lost his central position as the one and only Buddha of our present world-age. However, neither the literature, as represented by the great Mahāyāna sūtras, nor the iconography, as represented by the images retrieved from ruined sites all over India, bear this out. We are also fortunate in having a detailed description of religious practices in Indian monasteries provided by one of the Chinese pilgrim-scholars who came to India at the end of the seventh century.[11] Such a description confutes altogether the views that tend to be promulgated nowadays of "early Buddhism" and the Mahāyāna as two irreconcilable factions. Such views may be derived from the considerable differences that separate now the Theravādin Buddhism of Sri Lanka from the Buddhism of Tibet, but here the gulf comes about because of the total difference of language and the considerable difference of the general cultural background. In medieval India, on the other hand, monks following the earlier traditions and those who followed the Mahāyāna could live happily together in the same monastic settlement, and the difference between one temple and another was not so much "Hīnayāna" and "Mahāyāna" as simply a matter of period and date. The central object of worship was in the first instance the stūpa and then later as the anthropomorphic form of Śākyamuni was elaborated, the Buddha-image itself, either superimposed upon the stūpa or enthroned alone. In one form or another Śākyamuni, the Buddha of the present world-age, remains the center of Buddhist devotion. The images produced in the Gupta period are mostly a synthesis of the earlier images for which Mathurā, Gandhāra and thirdly the Andrā region of the south were famous. Thus the earliest images from Mathurā represent Śākyamuni baldheaded, as befits a monk, but with a kind of shell-like topknot, possibly suggesting the tuft of hair that was left when he first cut off his locks after fleeing from the palace (*Pls. 10, 88*). The Gandhāra images on the other hand, represent him with locks of hair, drawn up into a bun on the top of the head, while images from the South show the head covered with little curls, with what can only be a wisdom-lump, but of more modest proportions than the one suggested by the shell-like protruberance or the drawn up bun of hair. The suggestion that the protruberance, whichever of these various forms it may take, should be connected with the cutting-off of locks is an unnecessarily prosaic one. It is known as the *uṣṇīṣa*, a term that also means turban or headdress, and to be *uṣṇīṣa*-headed, whatever this may mean exactly, is one of the more prominent of the thirty-two main features of a "superman" (*mahāpuruṣa*).[12] In any event, the curly hair and a curl-covered wisdom-bump prevailed in northern India, passing thence to Nepal and later to Tibet as the iconographically correct kind of head for a Buddha. A variant form in the South was a flamelike headpiece and this can be seen on many images in Sri Lanka today. In the matter of dress a middle way was found between the heavy togalike drapery of the Gandhāra images and the light almost transparent

[11] See I-tsing, *A Record of the Buddhist Religion as Practised in India and the Malay Archipelago*, especially chapter XXIII.

[12] For further reference see *The Image of Buddha*, pp. 54, 76.

garment preferred at Mathurā. It was by such gradual accommodations that the "classical" Buddha image of the later Gupta period was evolved.

The most common hand-gesture of the earlier images represents the right hand raised as though in an act of blessing. This is known as the gesture of "fearlessness" (*abhaya*) presumably in the sense that the Buddha bestows a state of confidence. Other positions of the hands which gain in popularity are those of "meditation" (*samādhi*) with the hands placed together palms upward on the lap, and that of preaching or "turning the wheel of the doctrine" (*dharmacakra-pravartana*) with the hands in front of the chest, thumbs and forefingers touching and the other fingers turned round thus suggesting a circular motion (*Pls. 8, 14a*). It was inevitable that the last mentioned posture should become associated in particular with Sarnāth, where according to traditional accounts the first sermon had been preached, although this type of image seems to appear first in Gandhāra. Yet another typical Buddha-image represents Śākyamuni at the time of his enlightenment, touching the earth with the downward stretched fingers of his right hand, as he calls the Earth-Goddess to witness against the false assertions of Māra, the Evil One (*Pl. 16*). Being so much more specific than the other postures so far mentioned, it seems to have been cultivated especially at Bodhgayā and it is certain that numerous examples of this particular Buddha-image have been found in eastern India. In the period with which we are now dealing, approximately up to the seventh century, such Buddha images generally represent Śākyamuni himself. The exceptions are the occasional rows of previous Buddhas, while the special case of the future Śākyamuni before the previous Buddha Dīpaṅkara has already been mentioned. In the later tantric period these various hand-gestures become stereotyped as indicative of the Five Buddhas of the directions, but originally they are all aspects of Śākyamuni.

b. *Can There Be More Than One Buddha at One and the Same Time?*

As the main object of devotion after the stūpa, the anthropomorphic image received honor and worship quite as much from those who were content with the earlier scriptures as from those who now took pleasure in the recitation of Mahāyāna sūtras. All were agreed on the supramundane nature of a Buddha as realized in the person of Śākyamuni, although some might still refuse to accept as canonical those sūtras where the supramondane nature was described in so extravagant a style. This extravagance is expressed both in time and in space. There is nothing new in the time element as such, since the earliest known Buddhism takes for granted a series of Buddhas who have appeared in previous world-ages. However, time is now expressed as infinity. Thus Śākyamuni, anxious to impress upon his listeners the vast number of years ago that the Buddha Mahābhijñājñānābhibhū (Great Lord of Knowledge of Magical Powers) was living, explains the matter thus:

> "Suppose someone here were to reduce to powder the whole mass of the earth element as much as is to be found in this whole universe; that after taking one atom of dust from this world he might walk a thousand worlds farther in an

easternly direction to deposit that single atom; that after taking a second atom of dust and walking a thousand worlds farther he might deposit that second atom, and proceeding thus, he might at last have the whole of the earth element deposited in the eastern quarter. Now monks, what do you think? Is it possible by calculation to find the end or limit of these worlds?"

They answered: "Certainly not, Lord; certainly not, Blessed One."

The Lord said: "On the contrary, monks, some mathematician or master of arithmetic might, indeed, be able by calculation to find the end or limit of the worlds, both those where the atoms have been deposited and where they have not, but it is impossible by applying the rules of arithmetic to find the limit of those hundred thousands of myriads of aeons; so long, so inconceivable, so immense is the number of aeons which have elapsed since the expiration of that Lord, the Tathāgata Mahābhijñājñānābhibhū. Yet, monks, I perfectly remember that Tathāgata who has been extinct for so long a time, as if he had reached extinction today or yesterday, because of my possessing the mighty knowledge and insight of the Tathāgata."

Although expressed in more extravagant language, this quotation from the *Saddharmapuṇḍarīka* ("The Lotus of the True Law") asserts nothing with regard to Śākyamuni's powers that was not effectively claimed in the early accounts of his threefold knowledge as described above. However, a later chapter in this sūtra marks a clear advance in buddhological theory, when Śākyamuni explicitly identifies himself with all previous Buddhas:

I announce to you, O sons of good family, I declare to you, however numerous may be those worlds where such a man deposits the atoms of dust and where he does not, there are not in all those hundred thousand millions of myriads of worlds as many dust atoms as there are hundreds of thousands of millions of myriads of aeons since I have attained supreme and perfect enlightenment. . . .

Again, O sons of good family, the Tathāgata takes account of the variations in the vigor and strength of living beings who are yet to be born, and in each variety of case he reveals his name, he reveals the state of his final nirvāṇa, thus satisfying living beings with a variety of scriptures. So the Tathāgata tells living beings of differing dispositions, those whose basic merits are insignificant and who are greatly affected by their emotions: 'I am young, O monks, and having abandoned my paternity, I have recently achieved supreme and perfect enlightenment.' When however, the Tathāgata, who has remained fully enlightened for so long a time, declares that he is only recently enlightened, such scriptures are taught in order to mature living beings and bring them to a state of salvation. O sons of good family, all these scriptures have been taught by the Tathāgata for the guidance of living beings. Whatever words the Tathāgata uses for the guidance of living beings, whether speaking himself or under the appearance of another, whether on his own initiative or on the initiative of another, all that the Tathāgata says and all those scriptures taught by the Tathāgata are true and no false word pertains to him.[13]

[13] For the general context of these extracts one may refer to the translation of H. Kern, first

Aware perhaps that he is advancing the doctrine, here the preacher asserts the truth of the scriptures, even though the Lord is speaking through another. He is also addressing Bodhisattvas ("sons of good family") and not simple monks. However, such a doctrine may be seen as a logical development of what was already believed. In buddhahood there can be no distinctions of person and thus all Buddhas are essentially identical. But although such internal logic may be unanswerable, there is no doubt that such teaching represents a considerable advance on earlier views.

The infinity of space, as now applied to buddhahood, seems to represent an entirely new departure, coming into direct conflict with the earlier conviction that only one perfectly enlightened Buddha could appear at one time. The problem is discussed in an early apologetic work entitled "The Questions of Milinda" (*Milindapañha*) which emphasizes very well indeed the extent to which a foreign invader of the northwest (in this case the Greek King Menander who ruled in the second century B.C. from his capital Śākala, now Sialkot) might take in Buddhist teachings. This work consists of conversations between the king and the Buddhist monk Nāgasena concerning a wide range of Buddhist beliefs, and although it is a deliberate literary production it would be surprising if it did not have its inspiration in real discussions of just such a kind. As posed by the king, the following question certainly suggests that belief in the simultaneous existence of other Buddhas was already current in the area.[14]

> King Milinda said: "The Lord has said, Nāgasena, that it is a total impossibility for two perfectly enlightened Buddhas to appear at the same time within a single world-system. But, Nāgasena, all Buddhas always teach the same thirty-seven points which are conducive to enlightenment,[15] they explain the same four noble truths, the same three phases of training, and as they teach, they all inculcate zeal. If all the Buddhas propound the same teachings, the same doctrine and the same training, then why should two Buddhas not appear at the same time? The appearance of just one Buddha fills the world with light. If there were yet a second one, the world would be even more illuminated by the two of them. Also two Buddhas could instruct with much more ease, could admonish with more ease. Tell me therefore the reason for this saying of the Lord, so that my doubts may be at rest."
>
> Nāgasena replied: "This world-system of ten thousand worlds can bear just one single Buddha; it can bear the virtue of just one single Tathāgata. If a second Buddha were to arise, this world-system of ten thousand worlds could not bear him; it would shake and tremble, bend twist and disintegrate, become shattered, ruined and destroyed. It is just as with a boat that can carry only one man. . . . Here is another good reason why two Buddhas could not appear at the same time. If, O King, two Buddhas were to arise together, then

published in Oxford, 1884, now available from Dover Publications, pp. 153-4 and pp. 299-302. I have retranslated them from P. L. Vaidya's Sanskrit edition, p. 104, ll. 5ff. and p. 190, ll. 1ff.

14 For the context of the following excerpts, see T. W. Rhys Davids, *The Questions of King Milinda*, Part II, pp. 47-51.

15 These are the thirty-seven *bodhipakṣyā dharmāḥ*, for a detailed description of which one may refer to Har Dayal, *The Bodhisattva Doctrine*, pp. 80-164.

> disputes would arise between their followers, and with the word: 'Your Buddha. Our Buddha' they would divide into two parties just as would the followers of rival ministers. . . . Hear a further reason, O King, why two Buddhas could not appear at the same time. If that were so, then the scripture stating that the Buddha is the foremost would become false, that he takes precedence of all and that he is the best of all would be false. So all those passages where the Buddha is said to be the most excellent, the most exalted, the highest of all, the peerless one, without an equal, the matchless one, who has neither counterpart nor rival, all would be proved false. . . . But besides that, O King, this is a natural characteristic of the Buddhas, the Blessed Ones, that only one Buddha should arise in the world. And why? By reason of the greatness of virtue of the omniscient Buddhas. Of other things also whatever is mighty in the world is singular. The broad earth is great, O King, and it is only one. The ocean is mighty and it is only one. Sumeru, the king of mountains is great and is only one. Space is mighty and is only one. Śākya (King of the Gods) is great and is only one. Māra (the Evil One) is great and is only one. Great Brahmā is mighty and he is only one. A Tathāgata, a perfect and supreme Buddha is great and he is alone in the world. Wherever one such arises, there is no room for a second. Therefore, O King, only one Tathāgata, one perfect and supreme Buddha can appear at one time in the world."

It is made clear in this passage that those who held to the doctrine of one Buddha at a time in a single world-system were by no means diminishing the greatness of any particular Buddha, specifically Śākyamuni in this present world-age, and certainly not suggesting that as a "mere man" he was any the less worthy of worship and honor. Thus the cult of the Buddha-image has no immediate connection with Mahāyāna developments and there is no good reason for identifying any of the Buddha images produced in Mathurā or Gandhāra or even during the Gupta period as representing any Buddhas except mainly Śākyamuni and less often previous Buddhas, especially recognizable when they are arranged as sets. However, certain doubts may legitimately arise in one's mind when one contemplates a Gandhāran Buddha-image, seated in the posture of meditation and with flames issuing forth behind.[16] Do we have here the beginnings of the cult of the Buddha of Boundless Light (Amitābha), the Great Buddha of the West? Does he not originate in the inherited beliefs of some of those Greeks and Scythians and other peoples of the far northwest who before their conversion to Buddhism were already aware of another great religion centering on Ahura Mazda, the Supreme God of Light of Zoroastrian religion? Is it not possible that the idea of there being two Buddhas at once in our world has its origin in the eclecticism that was so typical of the Kushāna Empire? These are questions which cannot be answered with certainty, but so much is clear. By the third century A.D. an already well-established cult of this Buddha of the West had spread from the northwestern reaches of the Indian subcontinent across Central Asia to China. The fundamental text of this cult, a description of the

[16] References to this particular feature of the Buddha-image will be found in Maurizio Taddei's contribution to *The Image of the Buddha*, especially p. 184, with illustrations on pp. 186-7.

Land of the Blessed, for such is Amitābha's paradise in the West, was translated from Sanskrit into Chinese in the middle of the third century. It may fairly be regarded as a popular and unorthodox form of Buddhism in that its religious aspiration is directed primarily to rebirth in Amitābha's paradise and thus is largely unconcerned with the winning of nirvāṇa, the true goal of early Buddhist practitioners, or with cultivating the thought of enlightenment and leading the sacrificing life of a Bodhisattva as taught by other Mahāyāna sūtras. Amitābha becomes well known in later Indian and certainly in Nepalese and Tibetan Buddhism, but such an exaggerated cult of him seems to be little known. Thus here we have an extraneous influence upon buddhalogical theories in the far northwest of the subcontinent, which were only partially absorbed into the main stream of Indian Buddhist thought.

Whether or not these foreign contacts in the northwest were responsible for so greatly enlarging Buddhist notions of space, it is clear that the earliest Mahāyāna sūtras, which promulgate the Perfection of Wisdom teachings take as accepted the belief that there exist other Buddhas who are simultaneously preaching in countless other world-systems. They remain, however, mainly anonymous, except for the Imperturbable (Akṣobhya) Buddha of the East, who is mentioned as becoming visible thanks to the special vision of him vouchsafed by Śākyamuni.[17] The name "Imperturbable" may be related directly with Śākyamuni's composure when confronted at the time of his enlightenment at Bodhgayā by the forces of Māra, the Evil One. It is precisely the image of Śākyamuni, touching the earth with the fingers of his right hand as he calls the Earth-Goddess to witness against Māra, which is later identified iconographically as the Buddha Akṣobhya (*Pls. 16, 81*). While no such image is known to have existed with this particular posture at the time that the earliest Perfection of Wisdom texts were formulated, perhaps already in the first century B.C., this special Buddha name may have been associated by pilgrims with Bodhgayā, and regarded from the direction of Gandhāra, Bodhgayā is certainly in the East. It is significant that these two Buddha-names, Akṣobhya of the East and Amitābha of the West should come so much to the fore in these quite different contexts, Akṣobhya in the Perfection of Wisdom literature as the one clearly named Buddha in other world-systems, and Amitābha as the center of a special devotional cult, which spread from the northwest to China and was largely rejected in India. The position of Amitābha (also known as Amitāyus, "Boundless Life") as the primary Buddha of the western region came to be firmly accepted in Mahāyāna tradition. Thus if, as is likely, the Perfection of Wisdom literature originated in the northwest,[18] the specific naming of Akṣobhya as the Buddha of the East can be easily explained, and perhaps at that early time the name of Amitābha, even if it was already current, was associated with such a specialized cult, that it was deliberately not mentioned.

[17] See e.g., Edward Conze, *Aṣṭasāhasrikaprajñāpāramitā*, English translation, pp. 192-3; also *The Large Sūtra of Perfect Wisdom*, 464-5, 486-7.

[18] On this problem see Edward Conze, *The Prajñāpāramitā Literature*, pp. 3-4.

Names for no less than sixteen Buddhas of the directions are given in the *Saddharmapuṇḍarīka.*[19] Here they are rather curiously explained as all having once been the sons of the previous Buddha Mahābhijñājñānābhibhū before he took up the religious life so many thousands of myriads of aeons ago. They are said to have since progressed to the state of buddhahood and are teaching in the various directions simultaneously with Śākyamuni, who when telling the story lists himself as one of them. The only other two Buddha-names of later significance are precisely Akṣobhya in the East and Amitāyus in the West. We are thus still far from the time when sets of directional Buddhas become finally conventionalized. The whole matter of the orthodoxy of believing in the simultaneous existence of such Buddhas in other world-systems is represented as still being a matter of dispute between Sarvāstivādins and followers of the Mahāyāna by the anonymous author (probably of the fourth century A.D.) of a voluminous treatise, attributed to Nāgārjuna, which has been gradually translated from a surviving Chinese version by Étienne Lamotte. In this particular case of buddhalogical developments the arguments of the Mahāyānist are scarcely convincing when confronted by the clear dogmatic statements of the earlier scriptures.

> The Sarvāstivādin says: "The Buddha has said: 'Two Buddhas do not appear at the same time in the same world just as two Universal Monarchs do not appear at the same time in the same world.' Therefore it is not true that there are now other Buddhas besides Śākyamuni."
>
> The Mahāyānist replies: "Doubtless the Buddha has said this but you do not understand the meaning of his words. The Buddha means that two Buddhas do not appear at the same time in a trimyriad world-system; he does not say that there are not now Buddhas throughout the ten-directional universe. Thus two Universal Monarchs do not appear at the same time within the same four-continent world, since very powerful beings brook no rivals on their territory. Thus in the one same four-continent world there is only one Universal Monarch. Similarly two Buddhas would not appear at the same time in a trimyriad world-system. Here the sūtra compares Buddhas and Universal Monarchs. If you believe that there are other Universal Monarchs in other four-continent worlds, why do you not believe that there are Buddhas in other trimyriad world-systems? Furthermore a single Buddha cannot save all living beings. If a single Buddha could save all living beings there would be no need for other Buddhas and one and the same Buddha would appear. But the Buddha-*dharmas* which save those beings capable of salvation disappear as soon as they arise like a flame which is extinguished as soon as the torch is exhausted; indeed conditioned *dharmas* are impermanent and void of self-nature. Therefore for the present there must still be other Buddhas. Finally, living beings are innumerable and suffering is enormous. For this reason there must be magnanimous Bodhisattvas and innumerable Buddhas who appear in the world in order to save living beings.[20]

19 See H. Kern, *The Lotus of the True Law*, pp. 177-9.

20 É. Lamotte, *Le traitê de la grande vertu de sagesse*, vol. I (93b-c) pp. 302-4. (My translation.)

3. BODHISATTVAS

a. *Their Function as Quasi-Celestial Beneficent Beings*

It has been noted that some of the Buddha-images produced at Mathurā in the early centuries A.D. are inscribed as Bodhisattvas although they are in no way different from Buddha-images which were being produced at the same place and time. I have suggested that perhaps the human form was felt to be more suitable to Śākyamuni as Bodhisattva, thus active on behalf of living beings, rather than as a Buddha who had passed into nirvāṇa.[21] The title Bodhisattva would recall his self-sacrificing exertions throughout many previous lives, while the term Buddha would suggest an impersonal supramundane perfection. It is certain that some purists questioned the value of offering worship to the Buddha after his decease. This is one of the more difficult questions that King Milinda puts to the monk Nāgasena; "If he be entirely passed away, unattached to the world, escaped from all existence, then honours would not be offered to him. For he who is entirely set free accepts no honours, and any act done to one who does not accept it becomes empty and vain."[22]

Nāgasena's reply is a rather long and laborious one, but the gist of it is based upon the argument that merit accrues to those who make such offerings even though the offerings themselves are essentially empty of content. Perhaps the most cogent argument is the one that compares a Buddha with the earth, in which seeds are planted without the earth accepting them and yet they bear fruit: "As the broad earth, O King, is the Tathāgata, the Arhat, the Perfect Buddha. Like it he accepts nothing. Like the seeds which attain their development in it are the gods and men who by means of the treasures of those relics of the Tathāgata and of his wisdom—though he has passed away and gives no consent, being firmly rooted by the roots of their merits, become like trees casting a pleasant shade with the trunk of contemplation, the sap of true doctrine and the branches of righteousness."

However, the great majority of Śākyamuni's followers, whether monks or layfolk, in the earlier period as well as the later, continued to worship him spontaneously and not because such worship could be justified through argument. For the followers of the Mahāyāna worshipping was nothing new. They were merely spared the need for arguments of justification. If all persons and things are essentially void, a Buddha is assuredly no more "void" than any living being to whom something is given. In every case it is the action that counts. None the less the old dichotomy of Bodhisattva/Buddha, active and passive, persisted in the minds of the worshippers and thus there came about the spontaneous cult of Bodhisattvas who pair with Buddhas. The origin of this development, which is special to the Mahāyāna, is impossible to trace with any precision, as the new names suddenly make their appearance in certain Mahāyāna sūtras. A clear point of departure was the already existing cult of the

[21] See *The Image of Buddha*, pp. 52, 56-7.

[22] See T. W. Rhys Davids, *The Questions of King Milinda*, vol. I, pp. 144ff.

Bodhisattva Maitreya, the Buddha of the Future, but what was needed was a Bodhisattva who was already perfect in wisdom and who could therefore act fully on behalf of his presiding Buddha. Maitreya on the other hand was still progressing toward Buddhahood just as the Brahman boy Megha had in the past progressed toward becoming the Buddha of the Present, Śākyamuni. A noble princely figure was required, just as Śākyamuni had been a princely Bodhisattva in his last life on earth up to the time of his enlightenment. Thus we find Śākyamuni represented in certain early Mahāyāna sūtras by a Bodhisattva known as "Gentle Sound" (*Mañjughoṣa*) "in the form of a prince" (*kumārabhūta*). He is more usually known as *Mañjuśrī* ("Gentle Glory") and another early alternative name *Pañcaśikha* would seem clearly to relate him to Brahmā, who is also closely associated with divine sound. He is thus an adaptation, either spontaneous or deliberate, of the god Brahmā in the same manner that many other such "conversions" were later arranged (*Pls. 17, 30b, 83*). Subsequently he loses his dependence upon Śākyamuni, and enjoying a glorious advance, becomes in the later tantric period a form of the Supreme Being.[23]

While the Bodhisattva Mañjuśrī appears already well established as Śākyamuni's chief spokesman fairly early in the Mahāyāna tradition, certainly well by the second century A.D., the few other Bodhisattvas who are later to become famous come rather more slowly to the fore. We have already emphasized above that the Mahāyāna has its roots in a much earlier period, and this may be illustrated by reference to the *Aṣṭasāhasrikā Prajñāpāramitā* "Perfection of Wisdom Treatise in Eight Thousand Verses," which marks the formal beginning of the new movement both with its teaching of the "voidness" of all elemental particles and its praise of the career of the Bodhisattva. It is significant that here Śākyamuni is surrounded by his Early Disciples (*śrāvaka*), that no Bodhisattva is specifically named in the earlier part of the treatise, and that the speakers apart from the Lord himself are the disciples Subhūti and Śāriputra. Very occasional appeal is later made to Maitreya.[24] Later in the work certain Bodhisattvas are named in association with the Buddha Akṣobhya, whose special mention in the Perfection of Wisdom literature has already been noted, but no later great name is included.[25] It is interesting to observe that the greatest name, mentioned only in passing in this early Mahāyāna treatise, is that of Vajrapāṇi ("Thunderbolt-in-hand"), who is later to become one of the leading Bodhisattvas, if not indeed the chief one, in tantric Buddhism, but who here still occupies the lowly position

23 Already in the *Śūraṅgamasamādhisūtra*, composed at the latest by the second century A.D., curious legends concerning his past activities are in existence. According to one account he had been a Pratyekabuddha in a previous world age; according to another he had been a fully enlightened Buddha named Nāgavaṃśāgra. See É. Lamotte, *La Concentration de la marche héroïque*, pp. 242-5 and pp. 260-4. See also his article, "Mañjuśrī," *T'oung Pao*, vol. 48, pp. 1-96.

24 See E. Conze, *Aṣṭasāhasrikā Prajñāpāramitā*, pp. 104, 137-8.

25 See E. Conze, *op. cit.*, pp. 184 and 197. A certain Bodhisattva Śikhin is mentioned, thus suggesting an association with Mañjuśrī, one of whose names is Pañcaśikha (= Five-crested). Another Bodhisattva named Ratnaketu appears in later lists; he is raised to the rank of a presiding Buddha in the early tantric work, the *Mañjuśrīmūlakalpa*, and in the tantra entitled "Elimination of Evil Rebirths" he is named as one of the Five Cosmic Buddhas.

of a protecting divinity, qualified as a *yakṣa*[26] (*Pls. 4b, 47a*). It is in this capacity that he often appears on early sculptures from Gandhāra as the personal protector of Śākyamuni and thus it is no surprise to find him protecting Bodhisattvas who have reached the advanced stage of irreversibility: "Furthermore Vajrapāṇi, the great *yakṣa*, constantly follows the irreversible Bodhisattva, who is unassailable and cannot be defeated by men or ghostly beings." A Mathurā Buddha image of the second century A.D. is flanked by two attendant divinities, one holding a *vajra* (thunderbolt) and the other a lotus.[27] One is tempted to identify these as the Bodhisattvas Vajrapāṇi and Padmapāṇi, but although they may certainly anticipate later developments, a safer identification for this early period might be Indra and Brahmā, the two gods who in the earliest Buddhist literature as well as in the earliest scriptures appear as attendants on the Lord. Indra, the great Indian god of Vedic times, wields a thunderbolt, as does Vajrapāṇi, and as Indra's star goes into eclipse in Hinduism as well as in later Buddhism, so Vajrapāṇi's star begins to rise. However, further consideration of him is best left until we come to the tantric period.

The earlier Mahāyāna literature, while largely concerned with the cult of various Buddhas, conceived of as residing throughout an endless universe in different "pure lands," already takes for granted the existence of presiding Bodhisattvas, who preach and convert in accordance with the Buddha-Word. Thus the "Perfection of Wisdom in Eight Thousand Verses" ends with the story of the student-Bodhisattva Sadāprarudita ("Always Weeping"), who finally achieves his aspirations at the feet of the fully-endowed Bodhisattva Dharmodgata, whose happy land is in the eastern direction. To my knowledge this particular great Bodhisattva disappears from later tradition, but clearly the tradition of great Bodhisattvas, who preach, convert and save with all the powers of a Buddha, is already established as one of the main distinguishing marks of Mahāyāna Buddhism. Three of the later chapters of "The Lotus of the True Law" are concerned with the great activities of the Bodhisattvas Bhaiṣajyarāja, Gadgadasvara and Avalokiteśvara. In the later period the first of these becomes famous as the "Teacher of Medicine" (Bhaiṣajyaguru) with full Buddha rank. The second enjoys no such later cult, for despite his accomplishments, he appears in the chapter devoted to him as primarily concerned to show honor to Śākyamuni and Mañjuśrī. However, the third named, Avalokiteśvara, becomes the most popular of all the great Bodhisattvas of the Mahāyāna period, and apart from this one chapter in praise of his fantastic saving powers, a whole sūtra (the *Kāraṇḍavyūha*) is devoted to him. Since this work was translated into Chinese toward the end of the third century A.D., his cult was by then very well established. It extended across Central Asia and he became the popular Bodhisattva in Tibet, where his cult began to spread from the seventh century onward. The reason for his extraordinary popularity is obscure, but it may derive mainly from the meaning of his name, the "Lord who looks down" (in compassion); as

[26] Conze, *op. cit.*, p. 126 and also his *Large Sūtra on Perfect Wisdom*, p. 398.

[27] See *The Image of the Buddha*, p. 57, illustration no. 30.

the future Śākyamuni had looked down from the Tuṣita Heaven prior to his miraculous birth. Also by its mere sound it suggests an association with the Hindu god Śiva's title of Lokeśvara ("Lord of the World"), which later Buddhist tradition also applies to Avalokiteśvara (*Pls. 18a, 30c, 57*). He comes to be linked with the Buddha Amitābha in the same way that Mañjuśrī is linked to Śākyamuni. Once again this may have developed from the association of names, as the previous Buddha under whom the future Amitābha is said to have announced his aspiration to buddhahood, when he was the monk Dharmākara, is named as Lokeśvararāja. So many Bodhisattvas are listed in the later Mahāyāna sūtras and the few who become preeminent seem to owe their popularity to meanings, sometimes quite accidental, that came to be associated with their names. Apart from these few great ones who become the center of a cult in their own right, the main function of the many other celestial Bodhisattvas who are listed is to serve as the entourage of the presiding Buddha.

b. *The Career of a Bodhisattva as a Human Aspiration*

There are two aspects of the cult of Bodhisattvas, a devotional one for the generality of believers and a practical one for those who aspire to follow the Bodhisattva career themselves. It is with the latter category that the Perfection of Wisdom texts are primarily concerned, for it is clearly taught in these that the path toward eventual buddhahood is available to all gods and men who have inherited sufficient merit from their previous series of lives, and that such a career is infinitely superior to the aspirations of the Early Disciples (*śrāvaka*) of the Lord. To these he has taught a conception of nirvāṇa suitable to their merits and abilities, but when he next turned the Wheel of the Doctrine he revealed his own career of a Bodhisattva as a far more exalted alternative.

> Then the Venerable Śāriputra, contented, elated, overjoyed, filled with zest and gladness, stretched his joined hands towards the Lord, and looking upon the Lord, he said to the Lord: "I am astonished and amazed, O Lord! I exult at hearing such a call from the Lord. For before I had heard this Dharma from the Lord, I used to see other Bodhisattvas, and heard that in a future period they would bear the name of Buddhas. I then was exceedingly grieved and ashamed to think that I had strayed away from this range of cognition of the Tathāgata, and from the vision of this cognition . . . . I was constantly preoccupied with the ever-recurring thought: 'The entrance into the Realm of Dharma is surely the same for all. But we have been dismissed by the Lord with an inferior vehicle.' At the same time, however, it occurred to me that this was our fault, and not the Lord's. For if we had heeded the Lord at the time when he preached the lofty demonstration of Dharma concerning this supreme enlightenment, then we should have gone forth in these dharmas."[28]

This higher career is constantly contrasted with the "inferior vehicle" (*Hīnayāna*) of the Early Disciples (*śrāvaka*) and Lone Buddhas (*pratyekabuddha*) who

[28] The *Saddharmapuṇḍarīka*, Ch. 3. See H. Kern, *Lotus of the True Law*, pp. 60-1; also E. Conze, *Buddhist Scriptures*, pp. 120ff. For the Sanskrit see P. L. Vaidya's edition, p. 40.

have no concern with the salvation of others. Thus the Lord says:

> "For a Bodhisattva should not train himself in the same way in which persons belonging to the vehicle of the Disciples or Pratyekabuddhas are trained. How then are the Disciples and Pratyekabuddhas trained? They make up their minds that 'one single self we shall pacify; one single self we shall lead to final nirvāṇa.' Thus they undertake exercises which are intended to bring about wholesome roots for the sake of taming themselves, pacifying themselves, leading themselves to nirvāṇa. A Bodhisattva should certainly not train himself in such a way. On the contrary he should train himself thus: 'My own self I will place in Suchness, and so that all the world might be helped, I will place all beings in Suchness, and I will lead to nirvāṇa the whole immeasurable world of living beings.' With that intention should a Bodhisattva undertake all the exercises that bring about all the wholesome roots, but he should not boast about them. Imagine a man who unable to see an elephant, would try to determine his colour and shape. In the darkness he would touch and examine the foot of the elephant, and decide that the colour and shape of the elephant should be inferred from his foot. Would that be an intelligent thing to do?"

To Subhuti's reply in the negative, the Lord continues:

> "The same is true of those persons who belong to the vehicle of the Bodhisattvas, who do not understand this Perfection of Wisdom and ask no questions about it, but while desirous of full enlightenment, spurn it and prefer to look for the Sūtras which welcome the level of a Disciple or a Pratyekabuddha. Also this has been done to them by Māra. Just as if a person who desires jewels should not look for them in the great ocean, but in a puddle in a cow's foot-print, and would thus in effect equate the great ocean with the water in a cow's foot-print. Would he be a very intelligent person?"

This last quotation from the "Perfection of Wisdom in Eight Thousand Verses"[29] is one of the earlier texts, the first century B.C. and perhaps even earlier, to commend the career of the Bodhisattva as a higher path, and it may be of interest to note that in this passage as elsewhere in the work certain of those "who belong to the vehicle of the Bodhisattvas" are taken to task for their continuing regard for the earlier texts whose ideal remains that of the Arhat, the worthy disciple who experiences that state of nirvāṇa which is now regarded as incomplete. The Mahāyāna continued to be a movement within the already established Buddhist sects, especially the Sarvāstivādins and the Mahāsāṃghikas who predominated throughout the whole northwest of the Indian subcontinent. Thus for many centuries there was no division into separate communities and the only outward sign of difference of a monk who aspired to the career of a Bodhisattva was his predilection for Mahāyāna sūtras. All monks were bound by the same rules of monastic discipline, for those of Mahāyānist tendencies never disputed the validity of the Vināya, the first part of the early three-part canon. It is sometimes suggested that the Mahāyāna represents a more popular form of

[29] See E. Conze, *Aṣṭasāhasrikā Prajñāpāramitā*, pp. 84-5, Sanskrit, ed. Vaidya, p. 116, ll. 5ff.

Buddhism in which the attitudes and aspirations of the layfolk are accorded greater scope, but such a suggestion, while partly true, can also be quite misleading. There would seem to be no doubt that the real protagonists of the Mahāyāna were monks, and the new scriptures were compiled by monks, some of whom were renowned as masters of philosophy. Also the career of the Bodhisattva, as described in the texts, assumes that the life of a monk and at least a life of celibacy are essential conditions for his progress. It is indeed taught that throughout his long career through innumerable lives a Bodhisattva may well be born in any of the spheres of existence, but his aspirations should be directed toward joining the company of other Bodhisattvas in some Buddha-paradise. However popular amongst the layfolk the cult of the great celestial Bodhisattvas may be, there is no doubt that the teachings about the actual practice of the Bodhisattva career are directed primarily toward monks. Thus it comes about that wherever the Mahāyāna finally triumphed over the earlier sects, the monasteries remained as important as ever, and judging from what is known of the great monastic communities that flourished in eastern India up to the beginning of the thirteenth century as well as from the similar establishments that flourished in Tibet up to the mid-twentieth century, it is clear that Buddhism in these lands at least never developed as a popular lay movement. On the contrary, once the monasteries are destroyed, it is hard for Buddhism to survive. A more cogent question concerns the extent to which any monk who adopted Mahāyānist views, consciously strove to follow the exacting career of a Bodhisattva. It is taught again and again that it is only because of the accumulation of former merits that one meets with the Perfection of Wisdom teachings and so engenders the aspiration toward remote buddhahood. Thus the Lord says: "It is through the impetus of this former wholesome root that they will get this Perfection of Wisdom, even if they do not now hunt and search for it. Also the sūtras other than this one, which welcome just this Perfection of Wisdom, will come to them spontaneously. For it is a rule, Śāriputra, that if a Bodhisattva persistently hunts and searches for this Perfection of Wisdom, he will obtain it after one or two births, and also the other sūtras associated with Perfect Wisdom will also come to him spontaneously."[30] Surely it is one thing to embark upon a project that one may hope to finish within the course of one's present life, and quite another to consider embarking upon a project that one will not become fit to begin seriously until two or three more lives have been lived. One may well be amazed at the vastness of the project, and the whole while it is insisted that it is a project which essentially is no project at all. The philosophical aspect of the Bodhisattva's career will be considered below, and here it suffices for us to consider it according to its practical implications and ask how the daily life of a monk of Mahāyāna tendencies differed from that of one whose faith was fixed on the teachings of the earlier sūtras. Outwardly it can have differed hardly at all, and since both accepted the same monastic discipline, there need be no difficulty in their living together in the same community. The Chinese pilgrim-

[30] See E. Conze, *op. cit.*, p. 81, ed. Vaidya, p. 114, ll. 9ff.

scholar I-tsing, summarizing his experiences in Indian monasteries toward the end of the seventh century, describes the actual situation clearly enough:

> Those who worship the Bodhisattvas and read the Mahāyāna sūtras are called the Mahāyānists, while those who do not perform these are called the Hīnayānists (the Small). There are but two kinds of the so-called Mahāyāna. First, the Mādhyamika; second, the Yoga. The former profess that what is commonly called existence, is in reality non-existence, and every object is but an empty show, like an illusion, whereas the latter affirm that there exist no outward things *in reality*, but only inward thoughts, and all things exist only in the mind. These two systems are perfectly in accordance with the noble doctrine. Can we then say which of the two (Mahāyāna or Hīnayāna) is right? Both equally conform to the truth and lead us to nirvāṇa. Nor can we find out which is true or false. Both aim at the destruction of passion (*kleśa*) and the salvation of all beings. We must not, in trying to settle the comparative merits of these two, create great confusion and fall further into perplexity. For if we act conformably with any of these doctrines, we are enabled to attain the Other Shore (nirvāṇa), and if we turn away from them, we remain drowned, as it were, in the ocean of transmigration. The two systems are, in like manner, taught in India, for in essential points they do not differ from each other.[31]

It is interesting that I-tsing should inform us that both aim at the salvation of all beings, for it is precisely on this score that the followers of the Mahāyāna attacked the others so vigorously for their excessive introversion. But do we see any differences nowadays between the attitude to his fellow man of a Tibetan monk as a follower of the Mahāyāna and a monk from Sri Lanka, a Theravādin, to whom the disparaging term Hīnayānist has been unfairly applied? It is possible that the Mahāyānist philosophers literally preempted their own moral teachings with their doctrine of the "Void" (*śūnyatā*) and that the subsequent philosophical school, referred to as "Yoga" in the above passage, but perhaps better known as "Mind Only," reestablished the earlier emphasis on mental training. This point we shall take up below, for first we should attempt to clarify the differences which the early Mahāyānists clearly saw as distinguishing them from the followers of the earlier sūtras. In this respect I quote from a Mahāyāna sūtra entitled the *Śūraṅgamasamādhi* ("Concentration of Heroic Progress"), where the Lord, sometimes assisted by Mañjuśrī, discourses on various stages of perfection and powers achieved by a Bodhisattva who throughout his career is intent on the salvation of all beings.[32]

31 See I-tsing, *A Record of the Buddhist Religion*, pp. 14-15. I have added in brackets Mahāyāna or Hīnayāna, since from the whole context extending beyond the actual passage quoted here, it seems clear that these are the two he is equating, and not just the two philosophical schools of the Mahāyāna.

32 An invaluable study of this sūtra has been made by Étienne Lamotte, *La concentration de la marche héroïque* (MCB vol. XIII). My quoted passage corresponds to p. 253 of this work. See also R. E. Emmerick, *The Khotanese Śūraṅgamasamādhisūtra*, p. 45. I am grateful to this work for the careful edition of the Tibetan version (pp. 111-2), which is the basis for my present translation.

> Having heard this discourse, the gods were delighted and said: "Whoever enters the rarified realm of a Disciple or a Pratyekabuddha gets caught up and so fails in this Concentration of Heroic Progress. It is better to be one who is guilty of the five greatest sins and hearkens to this Concentration of Heroic Progress than to be the purest of those Worthy Ones (*arhats*) free of all foulness. If one challenges this, we reply that one who is guilty of the five greatest sins may yet raise his thoughts to perfect enlightenment, and although he may (first) fall into the hells as a result of the evil he has done, yet he may still embark upon this Concentration of Heroic Progress. But the worthy Disciple, so purified and learned, is not a suitable recipient, so how should he ever be able to perform this Concentration of Heroic Progress?"

It is made clear often enough that these teachings are primarily intended for gods and men, as far as possible excluding women, for the propounders of Mahāyāna teachings remained quite as attached to monkhood as the ideal life as were the early disciples of Śākyamuni. Thus describing the future Buddha-field of one of his foremost followers, the Lord Śākyamuni describes it as flat as the palm of the hand with wonderful buildings of the seven precious stones and peopled with gods and men. It will be free from all places of woe and from womenfolk, as all beings are born there by apparitional birth, etc.[33] The monk Dharmākara, when making his vow to become the Buddha Amitābha, makes one vow concerning women to the effect that they must become men:

> O Lord, if after obtaining enlightenment, those women in innumerable Buddha-fields in all directions who hear my name, may they have pure thoughts and aspire toward enlightenment, and if they, when reborn, are born again as women, then may I not obtain the highest enlightenment.[34]

Thus it is refreshing to note that the *Śūraṅgamasamādhi Sūtra* is capable of disposing of such a meaningless discrimination. Here the main spokesmen, the Bodhisattva Dṛḍhamati asks one of the gods, named Gopaka, by what good action had he become male, for on earth he had been the girl Gopakā. To this he replies:

> Those who are committed to the Mahāyāna do not see any difference between male and female. Why? Because omniscient thought has no application in the threefold world and male and female are just imaginative creations.[35]

Despite this clear assertion, the same sūtra remains sceptical concerning the suitability of feminine converts and special means may be necessary. Thus a certain Bodhisattva, suitably named Māragocarānupalipta (= Undefiled by Māra's Sphere) receives Śākyamuni's consent to go to Māra's world in an effort to convert him. His success might appear doubtful, because Māra eventually produces the thought of enlightenment with a false intention of trickery, but Śākyamuni prophesies that even this doubtful intention will eventually succeed,

[33] See H. Kern, *The Lotus of the True Law*, p. 194.

[34] See the *Sukhāvatīvyūha*, p. 390 (English translation), Sanskrit, p. 40 and Tibetan, p. 248.

[35] See É. Lamotte, *op. cit.*, p. 174. See also his *The Teaching of Vimalakīrti*, pp. 169-71.

such is the force of merely hearing of the *Śūraṅgamasamādhi.* In the course of the proceedings

> the Bodhisattva Māragocarānupalipta emitted a great radiance through his magical power, showing his most wonderful bodily form; the palaces of Māra were thus illuminated and Māra himself was eclipsed like a mass of lamp-black. Now there were in his entourage two hundred divine maidens who were greatly attached to the pleasures of sense, and seeing the perfection of beauty of the Bodhisattva they fell in love with him, saying: "If only this man would dally and make love to us, we would all be subservient to his orders." Then the Bodhisattva, knowing that they fulfilled the necessary preconditions for being saved, transformed himself into two hundred gods of a perfection of beauty like his own. He also created two hundred magnificent upper chambers superior to all the palaces of Māra. Seeing these magnificent upper chambers, each of the divine maidens thought that it was she who was enjoying herself with the Bodhisattva. When their desires were satisfied, their passion disappeared, and they made the great resolution and paid honor to the Bodhisattva. Then he preached to them in a suitable manner and all of them raised their thoughts toward supreme enlightenment.[36]

c. *An Evaluation of a Bodhisattva's Skill in Means* (upāyakauśalya)

There is an apparent contradiction in the teachings concerning a Bodhisattva's career, which runs right through Mahāyāna literature. On the one hand he is supposed to remain entirely pure from the world, and on the other he is supposed to make himself all things to all men. This contradiction is disposed of by the notion of "skill in means," according to which a Bodhisattva may indulge in any form of wantonness and even in great sin, such as murder, if only his ultimate intention remains pure and he does not separate himself from the thought of enlightenment. The Bodhisattva Vimalakīrti, after whom a whole sūtra is named, is shown as acting in just such a way. He asks the Great Bodhisattva Mañjuśrī to explain the situation in which he appears to operate, and he is told that those who truly belong to the Buddha's fold (*gotra*) are inevitably immersed in saṃsāra.

> Mañjuśrī replies: "Most noble youth, the fold of the Buddhas is the fold of transient things, the fold of ignorance, the fold of those who delight in life, the fold of passionate attachment and of anger, the fold of folly, the fold of the four kinds of wrong opinion, the fold of the five kinds of obscuration, the fold of the six spheres of consciousness and the seven operative kinds of consciousness. It is the fold of the eight wrong paths and of the nine kinds of annoyance and of the tenfold way of evil conduct. Most noble youth, such is the fold of the Buddhas. In short, the fold of the Buddhas is the fold of the sixty-two kinds of falsehood."
>
> "But what do you really mean, Mañjuśrī, when you say all that?"
>
> "Most noble youth, he who beholds the absolute, the nonconditioned (= nirvāṇa) and achieves fixity therein, becomes incapable of raising the

[36] See É. Lamotte, *La concentration de la marche héroïque*, pp. 196-202.

thought of the supreme and perfect enlightenment. But he who has not yet seen the truth and remains in the phenomenal world of conditioned things (saṃsāra), which is the place of afflictions (*kleśa*), such a one is capable of raising the thought of supreme and perfect enlightenment. . . . For example, seed does not sprout in the sky; it sprouts on earth. In the same way the true teachings of the Buddha do not manifest themselves in those who have achieved a state of fixity in the nonconditioned state. . . . Most noble youth, without diving into the great ocean you cannot bring up priceless pearls. Likewise without going down into the ocean of worldly turmoil you cannot raise the thought of omniscient buddhahood."[37]

This theoretical involvement of the Bodhisattva in all spheres of existence (saṃsāra) is a logical corollary of the Mahāyāna assertion of the essential identity of nirvāṇa and saṃsāra, which will be discussed in more detail below. However, it is justified in practical terms by the Bodhisattva's zeal on behalf of all living beings and his consequent need to assume forms and attitudes suitable to their conversion in varying circumstances. This "skill in means" (*upāyakauśalya*) is not one of the earlier set of Six Perfections, the practice of which is essential to a Bodhisattva's progress, namely: generosity, morality, patience, heroism, contemplation and wisdom, but it is soon added as the seventh perfection in the increased set of ten, namely skill in means, commitment, strength and knowledge.[38] We shall observe how in the tantric phase the Perfection of Wisdom and Skill in Means come to the fore as the two coefficients of Enlightenment, and it is interesting to find this development foreshadowed in such an early Mahāyāna sūtra as the *Vimalakīrtinirdeśa*.[39] Thus another Bodhisattva who visits Vimalakīrti aks him concerning the whereabouts of his father and mother, his sons and his wife, etc. Vimalakirti interprets all his relatives and associates in terms of Mahāyāna teachings with his parents heading the list:

For pure Bodhisattvas their mother is the Perfection of Wisdom and their father is Skill in Means; of such parents as these are the Leaders born.

The extent to which Bodhisattvas do in fact involve themselves in worldly affairs, let alone the sufferings of the hells, remains a rather subtle question. First one needs to identify these remarkable beings before one can investigate their actual practice. "The Teaching of Vimalakīrti" would seem to make it quite clear that all those who considered themselves followers of Śākyamuni were at least potentially Bodhisattvas and it was only necessary for them to respond to the call

[37] See É. Lamotte, *The Teaching of Vimalakīrti*, pp. 176-9. My translation is taken direct from the Tibetan version (TT vol. 34, 91-3-3ff.) and is abbreviated. Instead of the term *Tathāgata*, I have used Buddha as a synonym throughout the passage. The term *gotra* has a long history in Indian civilization and is often translated as "clan" or "lineage." Thus the Tibetans translate it as "lineage" or "class." It means originally a fold for animals, specifically cows, and it is quite legitimate to retain this sense in the present context. One may compare the NT use of the same term in John, 10, vv. 7 and 16.

[38] Concerning the Perfections (*pāramitā*) one may refer to Har Dayal, *The Bodhisattva Doctrine*, pp. 165ff.

[39] See É. Lamotte, *The Teaching of Vimalakīrti*, p. 180.

to raise their thoughts to perfect enlightenment and they could then already begin their higher career. The clear intention of those monks who read Mahāyāna sūtras with interest was to convert their religious brethren, often living as we have noted in the same community, but who were still content with the earlier sūtras. Thus in theory all those who were so converted were at the same time supposedly committed to the self-sacrificing career of a Bodhisattva, of which the more harrowing aspects might always be postponed until a future life. It is interesting to note that while legendary tales of self-sacrifice were eagerly recounted of the great Bodhisattvas, as they progressed toward buddhahood, especially of Śākyamuni himself in his former lives, it is difficult to locate acts of self-sacrifice in any historical context which have been acclaimed as the great acts of a Bodhisattva. In actual practice it might almost seem that such self-sacrifice is not expected and indeed scarcely understood when actually performed in this world.[40] The Buddhist religious ideal, as much for the Mahāyāna as for the Hīnayāna, remains in the first instance the celibate monk who withdraws from the world, achieving a state of inner tranquillity, and who subsequently guides others along the same path. It is religious teachers such as these who are acclaimed as Bodhisattvas in the biographies composed by their admiring disciples.[41] This is certainly the case in Tibetan tradition and one may fairly assume that the same was true in those Indian Buddhist communities where Mahāyāna teachings held sway. Similar conclusions may be drawn from the writings of the Indian monk Śāntideva, who lived in the seventh century A.D., the author of a famous work in verse entitled the *Bodhicaryāvatāra* ("Entering upon the Career toward Enlightenment"), which is studied and recited by Tibetan monks to this day. It certainly contains the usual admonitions toward self-sacrifice, as in Chapter III (vv. 10-13):

> My body and my possessions, my merits whenever acquired,
> I surrender all with no regrets for the welfare of living beings.
> Renouncing all, one gains nirvāṇa; on nirvāṇa my mind is set.
> Since everything must be surrendered, it's best surrendered to living beings.
> To all mankind I give my body to use as they please.
> Let them strike me, insult me, begrime me as they please.
> Let them make sport of me, mock me or laugh at me.
> To them I have surrendered my body, so to me it is all one and the same.

40 It is difficult to call to mind any historical biography of great Buddhist teachers, identified by their followers as Bodhisattvas, who are renowned for the sacrifice of their lives. One may note that no Dalai Lama or any other reincarnating lama, although unquestionably regarded as a Bodhisattva, is expected to sacrifice his life for his people. They are the more anxious that he should escape first to a place of safety. We have also noted that Tibetans, with whom we have discussed Christian parallels with Buddhist teachings, find the self-sacrifice of the Founder of Christianity on behalf of his followers not only incomprehensible, but actually distasteful, even though the doctrine of the resurrection parallels in some respects the glorified rebirth of a self-sacrificing Bodhisattva in Buddhist legends.

41 One may refer to my *Four Lamas of Dolpo* for such typical religious guides. Where a form of self-sacrifice is involved, as in the biographies of Nāropa (see H. Guenther in the Bibliography) or Mi-la Ras-pa (see Evans-Wentz) the motive is the proving of absolute faith in one's chosen teacher.

Yet the more general spirit that this work breathes is one of self-abnegation, strict self-control and even a deliberate withdrawal from the world:

When he realizes that his mind is disturbed by passion
or intent on useless exertion,
The Bodhisattva controls it firmly, applying a suitable antidote.
When he speaks, he must speak clearly, profitably and pleasantly,
free of attachment and aversion,
in all gentleness as suits the occasion.
When he looks at other living beings, he looks with candidness and kindness,
"It is by relying on them," he thinks, "that I shall gain buddhahood."
He is skilful and energetic, always doing things by himself,
In all his affairs careful not to depend upon others. (Ch. V, vv. 54, 79-82)

One chapter deals in particular with the merits of solitary meditation:

If one acts in the way of worldlings, one certainly comes to an evil state.
But one is not wanted if one fails to act in their way,
So what can be done in your dealings with them?
One moment your friends, the next moment your enemies,
Instead of being happy, they feel provoked.
The ordinary man is hard to please.
From keeping company with worldly folk sinfulness is bound to come,
Praise of self, contempt for others, the kind of talk in which the world delights.
Such company is detrimental to oneself and others,
So I go away alone, remaining happy with untroubled mind.
Keep away from foolish worldlings.
If one must meet them, make them happy with pleasing words,
As though meaning well in a way detached,
Thus not getting involved in close association.

When one acts freely without attachments, unbeholden to anyone,
Such is the joy and satisfaction one feels that even the chief of the gods might
hardly attain it.
Considering the advantages of isolation from the examples that have
been given,
One should quieten all disturbing thoughts and develop the Thought of
Enlightenment.
First of all one must make oneself realize that others are the same as oneself.
Since we are all the same in our joys and sorrows, we must do for others what
we do for ourselves.
Just as the whole body must be cared for although it consists of hands and
other separate parts,
Even so the whole world, while different in its parts,
is all the same in joys and sorrows.

If the sufferer of pain cares alone for the sufferer,
then a pain in the foot does not concern the hand,
So why should the hand protect it?

The bodhisattvas who understand such connections,
gladly accept the sufferings of others,
Plunging into the deepest hell (Avīci) like swans into
a lotus-covered lake.

(Ch. VIII, vv. 9-10, 13-15, 88-91, 99, 107-8)[42]

In reading such texts one senses that those teachings which involve dissociating oneself from the world are treated as applicable here and now, while those that recommend heroic self-sacrifice are more easily applicable to the lives of other Bodhisattvas in totally different spheres of existence.

The Bodhisattva who plunges into the deepest hell is preeminently the Great Bodhisattva Avalokiteśvara and so we are transported into an entirely mythological world. Thus the doubts expressed on the subject by an otherwise sympathetically disposed Christian scholar are surely justified.

> In the last resort is there any reality in the vow which the Bodhisattva makes to be reborn in wretched conditions, even down to the great Avīci hell so that he may save sinners there? It is certainly an heroic vow, the more so since according to at least one of the Mahāyāna schools of thought, the day will never come when there will be no longer the great Avīci hell and no longer any sufferers. But so great is the zeal which inspires such a vow, that the act of plunging into the Avīci hell becomes for the one who is so committed like a walk in a pleasure-park. It is useless to enquire whether the zeal really removes the suffering or whether it simply produces joy in suffering; in truth, in absolute truth, it is unlikely that our Bodhisattva will ever enter any such terrible place. For his resolve not to enter nirvāṇa so long as there remain sinners to be saved, does not prevent him from having always been in the state of nirvāṇa, precisely that nirvāṇa into which there is ultimately no entry, if only he is one day aware of all this. Can one truly enter into this Avīci hell, into which one is supposed to plunge, when one is all the time immersed in that state of nirvāṇa, into which there is ultimately no entry?[43]

The gentle mockery of the above quotation is in very much the same style as some Mahāyāna texts, since all the elements of existence, those of nirvāṇa quite as much as those of saṃsāra are ultimately revealed as fictitious. As Śākyamuni explains:

> What do you think? Subhūti, does it occur to the Buddha that he has saved sentient beings? Not so should one see it, Subhūti. But why? There is no being who has been saved by the Buddha. If there had been any such saved, then

[42] The best European translation of this whole work remains that of Louis de la Vallée Poussin, *Introduction à la pratique des futurs buddhas.* Here the interpretation is helped by the insertion of brief commentarial phrases. There is a recent English translation by Marion L. Matics, *Entering the Path of Englightenment*, but it does not attain to the standard of the French version. The Sanskrit and Tibetan versions from which my translation derives are available in a useful volume simply entitled *Bodhicaryāvatāra*, published by the Asiatic Society.

[43] See Henri de Lubac, *Aspects du Bouddhisme*, Paris, 1951, p. 35. His reference to the Avīci hell becoming like a pleasure-park derives from the first chapter of the *Kāraṇḍavyūha Sūtra* where Avalokiteśvara is described as plunging there to save the sufferers. A similar reference occurs in the eighth chapter (Verse 107) of the *Bodhicaryāvatāra*. See immediately above.

there would surely have been on the part of the Buddha an acceptance of the idea of a self, of a being, of a soul, of a person. "Acceptance of self," O Subhūti, has been taught as a nonacceptance by the Buddha, yet it is accepted by foolish worldlings. But "foolish wordlings" have been explained by the Buddha as no people at all. Therefore they are called "foolish worldlings."[44]

d. *Bodhisattvas in Paradise*

Concerning nirvāṇa itself one may quote a short passage from the *Sūraṅgama-samādhi Sūtra*, where the Bodhisattva Dṛḍhamati is conversing with one of the gods:[45]

Dṛḍhamati: The Buddhas, where do they go?

The god: The Buddhas, on account of their being "such a kind," do not go anywhere.

Dṛḍhamati: Do not the Buddhas go to nirvāṇa?

The god: All the elements are in a primordial state of nirvāṇa, and so Buddhas do not enter nirvāṇa. And why? Because of the very nature of nirvāṇa, one does not enter nirvāṇa.

Dṛḍhamati: All the Buddhas of the past, who are as numerous as the sands of the River Ganges, did they not go to nirvāṇa?

The god: All these Buddhas, as numerous as the Ganges, where were they born?

Dṛḍhamati: In fact the Buddha has said: "Buddhas as numerous as the sands of the Ganges, having been born, have entered nirvāṇa."[46]

The god: Noble son, did he not also say: "A single person born in the world is born for the benefit and happiness of many men, out of compassion for the world, for the benefit of ordinary folk, for the advantage and happiness of gods and men. This is the Tathāgata, the Arhat, the Perfectly Enlightened Buddha."[47] Now what do you think? Would the Buddha really be a person who is subject to birth and decease?

Dṛḍhamati: No, O heavenly being, for in truth the Buddha knows neither birth nor decease.

The god: Noble son, understand this: although the Buddha speaks of "a Buddha being born into the world," there is no real birth for a Buddha. Although the Buddha speaks of "a Buddha attaining nirvāṇa" there is no real decease for a Buddha.

It may not be surprising that the opponents of such teachings accused these early Mahāyānists of nihilism. But as is pointed out by Nāgārjuna, the chief exponent of Madhyamaka teachings, it is the others who are at fault, for if anyone believes that the Buddha really exists, then he must logically also believe

[44] See Edward Conze, *Vajracchedikā Prajñāpāramitā*, pp. 55-6 (Sanskrit text), p. 88 (English version).

[45] See É. Lamotte, *La concentration de la marche héroïque*, pp. 185-6.

[46] Compare H. Kern, *Lotus of the True Law*, p. 49, verse 70.

[47] I follow the Tibetan translation closely. The actual quotation is from an early scripture corresponding to the Theravādin version, *Aṅguttara-Nikāya* I, p. 22, 1-4. For further references see É. Lamotte, *op. cit.*, p. 186 fn.

that once he has entered nirvāṇa a Buddha ceases to exist.[48] It is precisely because a Buddha is free of birth and death that he transcends all such definitions as being and nonbeing. On the positive side, if indeed the word positive can be applied, are the numerous descriptions of Buddha-paradises which are to be found in incalculable numbers in all the directions of space. By their miraculous powers Bodhisattvas pass from one to another, visiting various Buddhas preaching to their separate assemblies, all equally vast in number. Again, the size of these wonderful beings is often immense and so special thrones have to be produced miraculously for them when they appear in assemblies of rather smaller dimensions, among which our own miserable world (*sahāloka*) is included. These Buddha-paradises are defined as pure or impure. In the former case the land is flat and all the buildings and even trees are made of precious stones, while the inhabitants are either gods or men, so that unhappy births are unknown. For the impure lands a description of our own world will suffice. This may be taken from the ninth chapter of the *Vimalakīrtinirdeśa Sūtra* where a story of a more unusual kind is also involved.

A vast gathering of Bodhisattvas has been discussing various points of doctrine in Vimalakīrti's house in Vaiśāli. As may be expected it is altogether a magical house thanks to Vimalakīrti's extraordinary powers, accommodating as many great beings as choose to visit him. Among them are the more renowned of Śākyamuni's earlier disciples, who can be relied upon to make rather naïve observations, as occasion demands. Thus Śāriputra has the sudden thought: "It is midday and these great Bodhisattvas are still not getting up. So when are we going to eat?"

Vimalakīrti knows of this thought without its even being expressed and so he says: "Honorable Śāriputra, the Buddha has expounded to the Disciples the subject of the eight kinds of salvation. You should be attentive and not listen to the Dharma with such preoccupation over material things. However, just wait a moment and you will enjoy such food as has never been enjoyed before." Then by means of his supernatural powers, Vimalakīrti revealed to the Bodhisattvas and Disciples another universe which can be reached in the direction of the zenith by traversing other universes as many in number as the grains of sand of forty-two River Ganges. This remote Buddha-paradise is named "Well Perfumed with All Perfumes" (*Sarvagandhasugandhā*). Here there are only Bodhisattvas, no Pratyekabuddhas or Disciples, and the tiered temples and palaces, the walks and the parks are all made of perfumes, and moreover the perfume of the food eaten by the Bodhisattvas there pervades innumerable universes. At the moment of the vision the presiding Buddha and all the resident Bodhisattvas were enjoying a meal. Vimalakīrti calls for a volunteer to go to this universe in order to fetch some food. Since no one is capable of this, he produces a specially created Bodhisattva of magnificent appearance and sends him all the way beyond the vast number of intervening paradises to the Paradise "Well Perfumed with All Perfumes." Here he pays Vimalakīrti's respects to the

48 See J. W. de Jong, *Cinq chapitres de la Prasannapadā*, p. 83.

presiding Buddha and begs for the remains of the meal. "With these remains," he explains, "Vimalakīrti will perform Buddha-works in the Sahā-world. Thus, beings with lowly aspirations will be moved to noble aspirations." The Bodhisattvas in this remote and delightful paradise have never heard of our wretched world, and a large party of them decide to accompany the specially created Bodhisattva on his way back with the bowl of remains from their meal. Their presiding Buddha lets them go with the following advice: "Since these beings will certainly become deranged and intoxicated by you, go there without your perfumes. Since the beings of this Sahā-world will fell jealousy toward you, conceal your beauty. Finally do not go around and arouse feelings of scorn and aversion. And why, noble sons? The real Buddha-paradise is a paradise of space, but in order to perfect living beings the Blessed Ones do not show them the Buddha-domain in its finality." Despite such advice, the whole town of Vaiśāli is pervaded with the wonderful perfume of the food and everyone gathers at Vimalakīrti's house. Some of the Disciples have the thought: "This food is very little. How will it suffice for so great an assembly?" They are soon put to shame by the specially created Bodhisattva and by the actual event of the meal, for the food in the bowl proves not only to be inexhaustible, but after all the various grades of beings from the Bodhisattvas downward have partaken of it, their bodies feel a happiness equal to that of the Bodhisattvas who live in another paradise named "Encompassed with Every Bliss" and the pores of their skin emit a perfume like that of the trees in the Buddha-paradise "Well Perfumed with All Perfumes." The conversation after the meal compares the form of instruction in this universe with the form of instruction in ours. There no words are necessary, for all spiritual advance is prompted by the perfumes of the trees. On the other hand in our wretched world where beings are so difficult to convert and where there are so many different locations of possible rebirth, instruction has to be varied and precise. To begin with, all physical misconduct and spiritual failings have to be dealt with in detail even before Śākyamuni can discourse on the conditions and rules for the religious life. The visiting Bodhisattvas are suitably edified. "The greatness of Śākyamuni is established," they say, "it is wonderful how he converts the lowly, the wretched and the unruly. Moreover the Bodhisattvas who are established in this mean Buddha-sphere must have inconceivable compassion." Vimalakīrti hastens to agree. "The Bodhisattvas born here," he says, "have a very stable compassion. In this world here in a single life they benefit more living beings than you do in the realm of "Well Perfumed with All Perfumes" during a hundred thousand world-ages." He then goes on to list ten good *dharmas* found in our world, which cannot be found elsewhere:

1. Converting the poor through generosity.
2. Converting the immoral through morality.
3. Converting the ill-tempered through patience.
4. Converting the lazy through heroic activity.
5. Converting the distracted through meditation.
6. Converting the foolish through wisdom.

7. Teaching those who have been reborn in unfavorable conditions to overcome these eight unfavorable conditions.
8. Teaching the Mahāyāna to those who follow lesser ways.
9. Converting through good roots (of merit) those beings who have not established good roots.
10. Perfecting beings continually through the four means of conversion (*saṃgrahavastu*).[49]

The term which I have translated as Buddha-paradise is more literally "Buddha-field (*Buddhakṣetra*), but those of them that are defined as "pure" can only properly be described as paradises. The "impure Buddha-fields," of which our world is the best known example, cannot normally be so described, but even in their case it is a matter of one's quality of vision. An ordinary person or a follower of the teachings of the Disciples will from ignorance continue to see the world as impure, but to a Bodhisattva who had purified his thought, any Buddha-field becomes spontaneously pure. Śāriputra, who is often taken to task in Mahāyāna circles for his naïvety, thinks to himself: "If the thought of a Bodhisattva must be pure in order for his Buddha-field to be pure, then when the Lord Śākyamuni followed the career of a Bodhisattva, his thought must have been impure, because today his Buddha-field appears to be so impure." For this thought he is immediately rebuked by Śākyamuni himself: "If beings cannot see the mass of good qualities of the Buddha-field of the Tathāgata, the fault lies with their ignorance; the fault is not the Tathāgata's. Śāriputra, my Buddha-field is pure, but you yourself cannot see it." The great god Brahmā then joins in the discussion against Śāriputra, maintaining that the Buddha-field of the Lord Śākyamuni is quite as splendid as one of the divine paradises. But Śāriputra persists in his ignorance and replies: "For my part, O Brahmā, I see this great land with hills and valleys, with thorns and precipices, with peaks and chasms, and all filled with filth." Brahmā replies: "If you see the Buddha-field as being so impure, it is because your mind goes uphill and downhill, O worthy Śāriputra, and because you have not purified your intention in the Buddha-knowledge. On the other hand, those who regard all beings with the sameness of mind and have purified their intention in the Buddha-knowledge, can see this Buddha-field as perfectly pure."[50]

The manifestations of Buddha-fields are generally conceived as deriving from the vows made by successful Bodhisattvas, but despite the earnestness of such vows, the eventual production is a mere mental creation. Thus all the splendid details, which arouse the faith of the simpleminded, are ultimately dissolved into nothingness. So the Lord Śākyamuni, referring as usual to himself as the Tathāgata, asks Subhūti: "What do you think, Subhūti, is there any *dharma* which was taken up by the Tathāgata when (as a Brahman youth) he was in the presence of Dīpaṅkara, the Tathāgata, the Arhat, the Perfectly Enlightened One?" Subhūti

[49] For this whole story of "The Obtaining of Food by the Imaginary Bodhisattva," see É. Lamotte, *The Teaching of Vimalakīrti*, pp. 204-218.

[50] See É. Lamotte, *op. cit.*, pp. 24-5.

rightly replies in the negative, and the Lord continues: "If any Bodhisattva should speak thus: 'I will establish a Buddha-field,' he would speak falsely. And why? The establishment of a Buddha-field, Subhūti, as nonestablishments have they been taught by the Tathāgata. Therefore they are called "field-establishments."[51]

In a similar way the whole long career of a Bodhisattva from the time when he first raises his thoughts toward Perfect Enlightenment up to the time when he presides over his Buddha-field, is firmly negated as ultimate reality despite the detailed descriptions of his envisaged progress. This is divided into various stages, first six corresponding more or less to the six great perfections, and then later extended to a set of ten.[52] This was later extended to twelve and even to thirteen. The first six stages came to be regarded later as open to a Disciple (*śrāvaka*) or a Pratyekabuddha, but thereafter their ways diverged, and having entered his seventh stage a Bodhisattva could no longer fall back, becoming what is frequently referred to in the texts as an "irreversible Bodhisattva." As such he could travel over the immense distances of myriads of universes listening to the teachings of innumerable Buddhas. The Mahāyānists certainly transformed earlier ideas of the universe, which according to the earliest teachings was a comparatively simple arrangement of a central sacred mountain with ever higher stages of divine residences rising up above it and then four continents to the four directions, of which ours named Jambudvīpa is the southern one. The whole complex was surrounded by rings of mountains and of oceans. Now there were supposed to be myriads of such universes in all directions, and while their number is never finally qualified as infinite (as this would in effect appear to limit the omniscience of Buddhas since it could be argued that there was always something else further beyond which they did not yet know), they are so exceedingly numerous that the usual way of suggesting their number is by referring to grains of sand of the River Ganges multiplied many times over. Like so much else which becomes typical of Mahāyāna thinking, this increase in the number of universes can be traced back into earlier scriptures, but the idea served the new teachings well because it could be used to justify the existence of innumerable Buddhas all existing at the same time. Not all universes need have a Buddha at any one time; those that are fortunate enough to have one become in effect Buddha-fields. Of these the pure Buddha-fields, such as the famous land of the Buddha Amitābha (*alias* Amitāyus) in the West or of Akṣobhya in the East, are clearly regarded by simple believers as paradises. They differ fundamentally from the heavenly abodes of the gods, for these belong to the "Wheel of Existence" as described above, section I.3.a and thus a fall, sooner or later, into less happy states is inevitable. The pure Buddha-fields on the other hand appear to offer unending bliss to those who are born there. One may quote from the vow of the Bodhisattva Dharmākara, which fixes the conditions of his Buddha-field when he becomes the Buddha Amitābha:

51 See E. Conze, *Vajracchedikā Prajñāpāramitā*, pp. 35 and 72.

52 See Har Dayal, *The Bodhisattva Doctrine*, pp. 270-91; N. Dutt, *Mahāyāna Buddhism*, 86-136.

O Lord, if those beings who have been born in that Buddha-land of mine, after I have won enlightenment, should not be all limited to one birth only leading to perfect enlightenment, except for those great beings the Bodhisattvas with their special vows who perform Bodhisattva-acts in all worlds . . . then may I not obtain the highest and perfect enlightenment!

O Lord, if after I have won enlightenment, those beings in inconceivable numbers of worlds who are brightened by my light should not be endowed with happiness exceeding that of gods and men, then may I not obtain the highest and perfect enlightenment![53]

e. *All Buddhas and Bodhisattvas Essentially One and the Same*

Aspirations such as these might suggest the existence of two main classes of beings, namely simple believers who by their faith and devotion merit rebirth in such a paradise, where they are content to remain, and Bodhisattvas who commit themselves to continual rebirths for the good of other living beings, even though they have won the right to final bliss themselves. To the latter group certainly belong the great celestial Bodhisattvas, such as Mañjuśrī, Avalokiteśvara, Samantabhadra and the rather exceptional human Bodhisattva Vimalakirti, to whom we have already referred. But who belongs to the first group if not simple layfolk and monks and nuns who have faith in Mahāyāna teachings? The earlier Mahāyāna texts, such as the "Perfection of Wisdom in Eight Thousand Verses," seem to expect little more of an "irreversible Bodhisattva" than was expected of a monk who remained content with the early canonical writings: he should realize the ultimate sameness (or "thusness") of all bases of activity, whether of the ordinary people, of the lesser religious ways (Disciples and Pratyekabuddhas) or of the career toward buddhahood. Once such an understanding is established, he does not imagine things or discriminate falsely.

He does not prattle away at whatever comes into his head. He speaks only when it is profitable and not when it profits nothing. He does not look down on what others have done or not done. Endowed with these attributes, tokens and signs, a Bodhisattva should be known as irreversible from perfect enlightenment. He does not pander to wandering religious (*śramaṇa*) and brahmans in other schools, telling them what they know is worth knowing and what they see is worth seeing. He pays no homage to other gods, offers them no flowers, incense and so on, and puts no trust in them. He is born no more in places of evil rebirth and he is never born again as a woman. Furthermore, an irreversible Bodhisattva undertakes to observe the ten moral rules of (1) not taking life, (2) not stealing, (3) not committing unchastity, (4) not lying, (5) not slandering, (6) not insulting, (7) not chattering, (8) not coveting, (9) not giving way to anger, (10) not holding wrong views. It is certain that an irreversible Bodhisattva observes these ten moral rules, that he instigates others to do so, incites and encourages them, and confirms others in them . . . Furthermore, when an irreversible Bodhisattva masters a text of Dharma, and offers it to others, he has in mind the happiness an welfare of all beings . . .

53 See the *Sukhāvatīvyūha*, pp. 387, 390 (English), pp. 32, 38 (Sanskrit), pp. 242, 248 (Tibetan).

He only says what is beneficial; he speaks gently and in moderation. He has but trifling idleness and torpor and he is free from evil tendencies. When he goes out and when he returns, his mind does not wander, for his mindfulness is well established. . . . His robe is free from lice, his habits are clean, he is rarely ill and rarely suffers. Moreover, the eighty thousand classes of worms which flourish in the bodies of other beings, flourish in no way whatsoever in his body. And why? The roots of his virtuous conduct spread over the whole world.[54]

Here we find an "irreversible Bodhisattva" depicted in rather more human terms and we may surely recognize in him the ideal monk who could be met in Mahāyāna communities in India and who can still be met in Tibetan communities living in foreign exile today.[55] Why then the need, one may ask, for the astronomical exaggerations, whether in space or time, in virtues, accomplishments and powers, which are continually met with in other Mahāyāna sūtras? They derive perhaps partly from that popular delight in marvels, in which the early scriptures also abound, but also, one must assume, from the deliberate intention of the more thoughtful compilers of these texts, to reduce the phenomenal and cosmological assertions of the earlier scholastic literature (*Abhidharma*) to total absurdity.

The conversations on duality that take place in Vimalakīrti's house before the specially produced Bodhisattva is sent to a remote Buddha-field in a quest for food, make nonsense of any such belief in any other Buddha-field and indeed in any definable nature of the one in which the discussion takes place. They make nonsense of the imagined paying of visits to other Buddhas since all Buddhas are essentially identical. In short they make nonsense of all concepts whatsoever. As the Bodhisattva Nārāyaṇa says: "To say 'this is worldly and this is supramundane' implies duality. In this world, empty by nature, there is absolutely no crossing, no entering, no moving, no stopping. Not crossing, not entering, not moving, not stopping, this is penetrating into nonduality." The final nonduality is the nonduality of the concepts of saṃsāra and nirvāṇa, the wretchedness of existence on any phenomenal level and the transcending of this wretchedness.

As we shall observe below, a theory of two orders of truth, absolute (*paramārtha*) and relative (*saṃvṛti*) makes it possible to deny the validity of all concepts relating to buddhahood or perfect enlightenment in one context and then in another to assert the identity or "universal sameness" of all Buddhas:

Ānanda, all the Buddhas are the same in the perfection of their Buddha-*dharmas*, namely their form, color, brilliance, body, characteristics, manner of birth, morality, concentration, wisdom, salvation, insight into the knowledge of salvation, powers, stances of confidence, deportment, practice, way,

[54] See E. Conze, ASPP, pp. 121-2. Some minor changes have been made in the translation; Sanskrit, ed. Vaidya, p. 161, ll. 10ff.

[55] One may see also another sūtra, *The Question of Rāṣṭrapāla*, translated and annotated by Jacob Ensink, Zwolle (Netherlands), 1952, especially pp. 12-37; this whole short work is concerned with describing the characteristics of good and bad Bodhisattvas, who are clearly regarded as monks. Bad Bodhisattvas are also described in the ASPP, pp. 83-92.

> length of life, teaching the Dharma, maturing living beings, saving living beings and purification of the Buddha-field.[56]

Thus Śākyamuni's identity with any other named Buddha may be freely asserted as occasion may require. In the sūtra named *Śūraṅgamasamādhi* the Bodhisattva Dṛḍhamati asks Śākyamuni how long his life will last.[57] With a kind of evasion the Lord replies:

> "Leaving this universe in the eastern direction and crossing over thirty-two thousand Buddha-fields one finds a universe named "Well Adorned." There resides there teaching the Dharma the Buddha named "Resplendent One, Adorned with Rays, Transformation-King' (*Vairocana-raśmipratimaṇḍita-vikurvaṇarāja*). . . . His length of life is just the same as mine."
>
> "How long is the life of this Buddha?" the Bodhisattva asks.
>
> "Go and ask him. He will tell you," the Buddha replies.

The Bodhisattva Dṛḍhamati travels there to ask this question and he is told:

> "My length of life is exactly the same as that of the Buddha Śākyamuni, and if you really want to know, the length of my life will be seven hundred incalculable world-ages, while that of the Buddha Śākyamuni is exactly the same."

The Bodhisattva returns with this information, and Ānanda, approaching Śākyamuni with the utmost respect, says:

> "In so far as I understand the words of the Lord, I would say that it is you, O Lord, who are in the universe named 'Well Adorned,' where with another name you work for the happiness and welfare of all living beings."
>
> Then the Buddha congratulated Ānanda and said to him: "Good indeed! It is by the power of the Buddha that you have understood this. That Buddha is myself with a different name, preaching the Dharma in that universe and saving living beings."

The supreme apotheosis of Śākyamuni occurs in chapter 15 of the *Saddharma-puṇḍarīka* where he discourses to a vast host of Bodhisattvas on the length of his life. His gaining of enlightenment at Bodhgayā was a mere display for the benefit of living beings in our world. In fact he has achieved enlightenment so many myriads of world-ages ago that they are totally incalculable. He ends this statement saying:

> So I am the world's father, the self-existent one, the healer, the protector
>   of all beings. Knowing them to be perverted, bemused and ignorant,
> I demonstrate nirvāṇa without being really in nirvāṇa.
> What is the reason for this continual demonstration of mine?
> Lacking in faith, foolish and ignorant, intent on sensual desires

56 See É. Lamotte, *The Teaching of Vimalakīrti*, p. 227.

57 See É. Lamotte, *La concentration de la marche héroïque*, pp. 267-70. I have chosen this particular quotation because of the early reference to this Buddha named "Resplendent One" (Vairocana) who becomes very important at the beginning of the tantric period.

> and out of their wits, because of their thoughtlessness they fall into evil rebirths.
>
> Knowing how this process goes on all the time, I tell living beings that I am so-and-so, so that I may incline them toward enlightenment and that they may be sharers in the Buddha-*dharmas*.[58]

It may be observed that there is no essential difference between such Buddha-actions and the saving efforts of Bodhisattvas, who having reached their final stage short of actual buddhahood, choose to continue appearing among living beings in order to assist and convert them. The identification of Buddha and Bodhisattva as the more passive and the more active aspects of enlightenment is confused in the single person of Śākyamuni, who is named on some of the very early Buddha-images, as noted above, indiscriminately as Bodhisattva or Buddha. It would seem clear that the extravagant theories of manifold Buddha-manifestations and the detailed elaborating of the Bodhisattva's career all derive from the earlier beliefs concerning Śākyamuni himself. Thus nothing essentially extraneous has produced these major features of the Mahāyāna.

Furthermore, in that the term Bodhisattva can be applied not only to the Great Beings, who do the work of Buddhas amongst living beings, but also to those who have only just embarked upon the long and arduous training toward buddhahood, all these, the leaders and the practitioners, are the more easily classed together as belonging to the "Buddha-fold." This leads directly to the further recognition that all beings and certainly those who belong to the "Buddha-fold" already possess the "essence of buddhahood" (*tathāgatagarbha*) and thus in the final analysis all distinctions disappear not only between Buddhas and the Great Bodhisattvas, but between Buddhas and all who merit the name of Bodhisattva, however modest their achievements. It is with this further identification, which will be treated in rather more detail below, that the Mahāyāna diverges from the earlier teachings. It is, however, an inevitable corollary of the assertion that between saṃsāra and nirvāṇa there is no essential difference.

4. THE THREE TURNINGS OF THE WHEEL OF THE DOCTRINE

We observed above that the early accounts of Śākyamuni's life have remained generally constant except for the contents of his doctrines, which were gradually extended in scope to accommodate the later teachings attributed to him. The technical term for a Buddha's act of teaching is "turning the wheel" of the doctrine. This expression was used in order to suggest that a Buddha is as mighty in the religious sphere as a Universal Monarch (*cakravartin*, literally a wheel-turner, interpreted as meaning "one whose chariot-wheels turn from one ocean-

[58] Compare H. Kern, *Lotus of the True Law*, pp. 309-10, Sanskrit text: Vaidya p. 195, ll. 13ff. and Kern, p. 326, where there are several doubtful readings, which I have checked against the Tibetan translation (TT vol. 30, p. 58-3-8), accepting the most likely interpretation.

shore to another") in the worldly sphere. Three such "turnings of the wheel" were recognized by the later followers of the Mahāyāna, one relating to the teachings received by the Early Disciples (*śrāvaka*), which have already been explained in some detail in the previous chapter, and the other two relating to the two main philosophical schools of the Mahāyāna itself. The tantras are generally excluded, for only a few of them can have been in circulation when this theory of the "three turnings" was first enunciated. The efforts of the later exponents of the tantras to establish some form of orthodoxy for their teachings will be explained in the next chapter. The doctrine of the "second turning" is represented primarily by the Perfection of Wisdom literature, to which many references have already been made in the present chapter. It consists largely of eulogies and descriptions of the career of a Bodhisattva and of a series of dogmatic assertions concerning the emptiness (*śūnyatā*) or vanity of all concepts whatsoever. The "third turning" is represented by such Mahāyāna sūtras as the *Laṅkāvatāra* ("Entry into Laṅka") and the *Sandhinirmocana* ("Resolving Enigmas") as well as by some Perfection of Wisdom sūtras, to which rather different interpretations were given. Little more needs to be written here about the "first turning" apart from explaining its relationship with the "second turning." So far as the teachings concerning the career of a Bodhisattva are concerned, the "second turning" has already been partly dealt with and thus it remains for us to explain the philosophical teachings of the Madhyamaka school, which represent its other important aspect. The "third turning of the wheel" relates to the theories of the Mind Only (*citta-mātra*) school, which brings together in a rather complicated synthesis the teachings associated with the previous two "turnings of the wheel."

For the expoundings of all these teachings two kinds of texts were employed, first the *sūtras*, dogmatic teachings regarded as the Buddha-Word, and scholastic treatises (*śāstra*) usually written by known authors for the purpose of elucidating meanings and for justifying their particular interpretations.

a. *The First Turning*

The followers of the Early Disciples (*śrāvaka*), now castigated as followers of an "inferior way" (*Hīnayāna*), appealed to the early sūtras ("threads of discourse") of Śākyamuni, some of which undoubtedly go back to the Master himself. Some of the early schools, notably the Theravādins and the Sarvāstivādins, developed scholastic works known as Abhidharma ("Further Dharma"), where the theory of elements (*dharmas*) as the ultimate "realities" is worked out in great detail. Other early schools rejected the Abhidharma literature as Buddha-Word and while they accepted the general theory of elements (*dharmas*) as the only form of reality underlying the phenomenal world, they often modified considerably the theories concerning their functioning. An interesting school so far as later developments are concerned is one known as Sautrāntika, meaning "Ending with the Sūtra" in the sense that they do not accept the Abhidharma as canonical. Although none of their scriptures survives they are known of from the views that are attributed to them by their opponents. Thus while the Sarvāstivādins believed that the elements of existence maintained a real existence in the past and the future as well as the present, the Sautrāntikas asserted that the elements only existed in any real sense as they manifested themselves momentarily in a continual transient present time. They also rejected the theory of nirvāṇa as being an element in its own right, for like space, they argued, it was physically nonexistent. Teachings such as this, which reduced physical existence to a bare minimum while leaving nirvāṇa free of any realistic designation, would appear to be halfway between what was later regarded as typical Hīnayāna and Mahāyāna opinions. In the earlier period there cannot have been such clear distinctions, as members of the same community and even those of the same sect might hold various opinions, if they chose to argue about these philosophical matters. When the Perfection of Wisdom teachings with their unmitigated attack on the reality of any *dharmas* whatsoever began to take shape, the first century B.C. at the latest perhaps, their main opponents were the Sarvāstivādins, who were particularly strong in the far northwest and whose theory of *dharmas* was one of the most extreme. The Theravādins, who survive in Sri Lanka to this day, held similar views, but already at this early period they seem to be scarcely involved in these philosophical battles, as though their links with the Indian mainland, certainly with the north, were already very tenuous.

b. *The Second Turning*

However, whether they were firmly asserted, hesitatingly asserted, denied altogether, or totally reinterpreted, the Buddhist doctrine of *dharmas* remains fundamental to all these philosophical schools. Thus the Perfection of Wisdom teachings of "emptiness" relates primarily to the "emptiness" of the whole *dharma*-theory. So when its protagonists insist that their teachings are not a form of nihilism, as some of their opponents claimed, they certainly deserve attention from other philosophers whose views are not limited to any such *dharma*-theory. The main protagonists are Nāgārjuna who probably lived some time between the mid-first century and mid-second century A.D. and his disciple and successor Āryadeva. The fundamental work elucidating the Perfection of Wisdom teachings is Nāgārjuna's *Mūlamadhyamakakārikā* ("Basic Verses on the Middle Way") which served as the basis for later commentarial works, of which the best known is that by another famous Buddhist philosopher, Candrakīrti, who lived some five centuries later.[59] The term "Middle" (*Madhyamaka*) has come to be used in a restricted sense of the school represented by Nāgārjuna, but the whole of Buddhism claims to be a "Middle Way" deriving from Śākyamuni's first announcement that his teaching avoids two extremes, that of laxity

59 This is his "Clear Commentary on the Mean" (*Prasannapadā Madhyamakavṛtti*), which was published by Louis de la Vallée Poussin at the beginning of this century in *Bibliotheca Buddhica* IV. The whole is now available in European translation, partly in English (see de Jong and Stcherbatsky in the Bibliography), partly in French (see J. May) and partly in German (see Schayer). Text referred to as MMK (*Mūlamadhyamakārikā*).

on the one hand and that of excessive hardship on the other. But such an assertion could also be applied to philosophical theory and especially to Śākyamuni's resolute refusal to allow himself to be committed by argument to asserting in any absolute sense the existence or nonexistence of a "self" (*ātman*) of the eternity or noneternity of the universal flux or whether a Buddha existed in the state of nirvāṇa or not.[60] All these noncommittal attitudes are fundamental to the Madhyamaka, but in one of Nāgārjuna's "Basic Verses" a special interpretation is given to the term after which his school is named.

> It is the (twelvefold) causal nexus that we declare to be the Void.
> It is a metaphorical name and it is this that is the Middle Path.[61]

Thus the twelvefold causal nexus remains a kind of dogmatic core for Buddhist philosophical theory, and it is as its author that Nāgārjuna salutes Śākyamuni in his opening verses:

> I salute the Perfect Buddha, the most worthy of worthy ones,
> who has proclaimed the peaceful Causal Nexus where all deliberations cease,
> where there is no extinction, no arising, no cessation, no permanence,
> no individuality, no generality, no coming and no going.

However, the Madhyamaka introduced a fundamental change in the interpretation of the Causal Nexus from one conceived of as a set of causal links in a time-process to one that insists upon the essential causality of the supposed process without reference to time. Since the elements (*dharmas*) of which the nexus is imagined to exist are mutually dependent and so mutually conditioned and contingent, they can have no real nature as the Sarvāstivādins and others claimed for them. Thus as Nāgārjuna asserts in his first verse:

> Nowhere are there any realities (*bhāvāḥ*) that come into being,
> either from themselves or from others, either from both or some other cause.

and again:

> There is no truth in realities which have no true reality (*niḥsvabhāva*),
> So it is inapt to say that one thing derives from another.
> If an element (*dharma*) does not appear as true (*sat*) or untrue (*asat*)
> or as both true and untrue,
> How in such a case can it be an effective cause?[62]

Thus the Twelvefold Causal Nexus, more literally translated as "Dependent Origination" (*pratītyasamutpāda*), is revealed as essentially a "nonarising" because the elements of which the process supposedly exist are themselves

[60] Concerning such undetermined questions, one may refer to E. J. Thomas, *History of Buddhist Thought*, pp. 124-32. Also see above, pp. 20-1 and 28.

[61] MMK XXIV, 18. See J. May, *Candrakīrti*, pp. 237-9 for further references, and N. Dutt, *Mahāyāna Buddhism*, pp. 264ff.

[62] MMK I, vv. 10 & 7. The whole chapter is translated by Stcherbatsky, *The Conception of Buddhist Nirvāṇa*, pp. 79-182.

mutually dependent, and whatever is dependent upon something for its existence cannot be truly existent. This basic lesson is repeated again and again.

> There is no independent existence of anything anywhere at any time,
> So there is nothing eternal anywhere at any time.
> Nothing exists without a cause and that which has a cause is not eternal.
> The wise man states that whatever is effected without a cause
> must be a noneffect.[63]

By showing the emptiness of all the elements of existence as accepted in varying degrees by other Buddhist philosophical schools, the Madhyamakas establish the essential emptiness of all phenomenal existence. Thus one might logically expect them to assert the reality of whatever exists without a cause, preeminently the state of nirvāṇa. However, Nāgārjuna asserts that nirvāṇa is equally empty (*śūnya*) of all conceptual being.[64]

> Grasping and mutually dependent, such is the state of coming and going
> (= birth and death). That which is free of grasping and mutual dependence
> is said to be nirvāṇa.
> The Teacher has taught the abandoning of being and nonbeing,
> and so it is not right to say that nirvāṇa is either real or unreal.
> It cannot be said that the Lord exists after his decease, or that
> he does not exist, nor that he both exists and does not exist,
> nor that neither case applies.
> It cannot be said that the Lord is actually existing or that he is not.
> Nor can it be said that both statements are true or that neither is true.
> There is no difference at all between saṃsāra and nirvāṇa,
> no difference at all between nirvāṇa and saṃsāra.
> The limit of nirvāṇa is the limit of saṃsāra.
> Not even the most subtle difference is found between the two.
> Opinions about an ultimate state after decease and so on, about
> eternity and so on, these derive from nirvāṇa as a prior and
> anterior ultimate.
> Since all *dharmas* are empty, why an infinite, why a finite?
> why both, why neither?
> Why just that? why something else? why eternal? why noneternal?
> why both noneternal and eternal? why neither?
> Peaceful is the quiescence of all conceptions, the quiescence of deliberations,
> No *dharma* was taught by the Buddha to anyone anywhere.

The term *dharma* in the last verse may be understood equally well as "element of existence" or as "religious doctrine." The idea that Śākyamuni, having achieved perfect enlightenment at Bodhgayā, never spoke another word, becomes quite a

[63] Āryadeva, *Catuḥśataka*, IX 2-3. See ed. V. Bhattacarya, pp. 32-4; ed. P. L. Vaidya, pp. 76-7 and 134. See also note 69 below.

[64] MMK XXV. The verses quoted are 3, 10, 17-24. See K. K. Inada, *Nāgārjuna*, pp. 154-9; Stcherbatsky, *The Conception of Buddhist Nirvāṇa*, pp. 193-212.

frequent one in Mahāyāna literature.[65] Thus Candrakīrti in his commentary on this verse quotes from the *Tathāgataguhyakasūtra*:

> The night on which the Tathāgata was enlightened in the final and perfect enlightenment up to the night on which he enters final nirvāṇa, the Tathāgata has not pronounced a single word; he has not spoken; he does not speak; he will not speak. But all living beings with their different humors and attitudes conceive of him giving different kinds of discourses in accordance with their aspirations. So they separately think: "The Lord is teaching us this *dharma*; we are listening to the Tathāgata's instruction in the *dharma*." But the Tathāgata does not compose and argue. The Tathāgata is free from all deliberations which are the latent effects (*vāsanā*) of a tangle of propositions and arguments.[66]

Such ideas need come as no surprise since the state of perfect enlightenment is just as clearly denied in the Perfection of Wisdom literature:

> Whoever would say, O Subhūti, that the Tathāgata, the Arhat, the Perfectly Enlightened Buddha has realized supreme and perfect enlightenment, such a one would speak falsely and misrepresent me by seizing upon an untruth. Why is that? There is no *dharma* that the Tathāgata has realized as supreme and perfect enlightenment, and any *dharma* that the Tathāgata has realized or taught, is neither true nor false. So the Tathāgata says: "All *dharmas* are Buddha-*dharmas*," and why? All *dharmas*, O Subhūti, have been explained by the Tathāgata as non-*dharmas*, and therefore all *dharmas* are said to be Buddha-*dharmas*.[67]

Elsewhere Śāriputra, representative of earlier views, but in that case having learned his lesson, replies to a question of Subhūti about where the Buddha takes his stand: "Nowehere did the Tathāgata stand, because his mind sought no support. He did not take his stand either in the sphere of the conditioned nor of the unconditioned, nor again did he emerge from them." Subhūti commends this saying, adding the corollary: "Even so should a Bodhisattva take his stand and train himself. Even thus should a Bodhisattva, a Great Being, be poised as he trains, never parted from the reflection that he abides in the Perfection of Wisdom."[68] The compilers of such texts were quite aware that they were composing conundrums, for we are informed that on this occasion

> The thought came to some of the gods in that assembly: "The *yakṣa*-words of *yakṣas* (local divinities), their *yakṣa*-cries, their *yakṣa*-syllables, their *yakṣa*-spells, their *yakṣa*-utterances, these are comprehensible when muttered, but that which has been spoken, announced and taught by the Elder Subhūti, cannot be comprehended." Then the Venerable Subhūti, knowing by the

65 Such a theory had been expressed much earlier by the Theravādins, in that Śākyamuni after his enlightenment must have been composed only of pure *dharmas* thus breaking contact with impure worldly *dharmas*. For references see Louis de la Vallée Poussin, *Bouddhisme*, pp. 251-5.

66 See MMK, ed. L. de la Vallée Poussin, p. 539.

67 See E. Conze, *Vajracchedikā Prajñāpāramitā*, p. 48 (Sanskrit), p. 83 (English).

68 See E. Conze, ASP, p. 17; P. L. Vaidya (Sanskrit text), p. 19, ll. 12ff.

power of his intellect the kind of doubts that those gods were harboring, advised them thus: "This is not to be comprehended, not to be comprehended, O gods. Here nothing is indicated and nothing is taught."

Despite their claim to tread a middle way, the Perfection of Wisdom scriptures quite as much as their philosophical interpreters appear to take some delight in bewildering or even scandalizing their opponents by the apparent negativity of many of their sayings:

Where worldly teachings prevail, there progress is extolled.
Where absolute truth is the subject, there discontinuance is lauded.
"What shall we do if nothing exists" you (worldly ones) say in your fear.
But if there were something to be done, this could not be reversed.
You are attached to your own circle; another circle is abhorrent to you.
Thus you will not obtain nirvāṇa; there is no peace for the contentious.
Nirvāṇa is for the nondoer; for the active there is continual rebirth.
By freedom from thought nirvāṇa is easily gained; there is no other way.[69]

Āryadeva's *Catuḥśataka* ("Four Hundred Verses") is perhaps one of the most negative of all Mahāyāna works, in that it commends continually total withdrawal from the world as though the goal were a kind of "individual nirvāṇa" without reference to the altruistic strivings of a Bodhisattva's career. The author presumably directs it toward those who are disposed to enter a closed religious life and its arguments in favor of this are surely of the least heroic kind:

Born that they may die, having the nature of conditioned being,
before them appears the notion of death, not that of life. (I.2)
Death is the common lot of all, as of a herd of cattle ready
to be slaughtered,
So how should you not fear death, even when it comes to others. (I.6)
If you act as though considering yourself eternal just because
the time of death is uncertain, at some certain time death
will come and afflict you. (I.7)

Since moments and other calculated time-periods are just like
enemies (which gradually rob you of your life),
You should never be attached to these malevolent ones. (I.21)
A man who fears to part with false opinions will never abandon
his worldly life.
What man of wisdom (he asks) will act so as to fail in just what
he ought to do. (I.22)

If you are thinking that having done such and such, you will really
enter the religious life,

69 Āryadeva, *Catuḥśataka*, VIII, vv. 8-11. See V. Bhattacharya, pp. 8-11; P. L. Vaidya, pp. 71-2 and 130-1. Both these editions contain the edited Sanskrit and Tibetan texts for chapters VIII-XVI only. The Sanskrit is missing for the earlier chapters and for quotations from these I refer direct to TT vol. 95, 131-1-1 onward (*Catuḥśataka* verses only) and TT vol. 98, 183-4-4 onward (Candrakīrti's commentary). Note also the article which gives references to Āryadeva's other works, "Le nirvāṇa d'après Āryadeva" by L. de la Vallée Poussin in *Mélanges chinois et bouddhiques*, I, pp. 127-135.

What is the virtue of having done it, if you must abandon whatever
you have done. (I.23)

But he who is convinced that he must die, how should he fear
death; he will have abandoned all attachments. (I.24)[70]

It comes as no surprise that women are firmly rejected in such stereotyped verses, which might scarcely seem to breathe the noble spirit so often attached to Mahāyāna teachings:

However long the time, there is no reaching the limit of the world
of desire. (III.1)
It is like the wrong medicine for your body, like effort without reward.
Just as one cannot destroy the attachment of a man to a particular
place to which he is devoted,
Even so it is with the expectation in the desires of men who are
attached to things. (III.2)

The commentary may be quoted here: "It is said: 'As fire by fuel and a river by floods, even so is men's expectation of desires increased by the enjoyment of desires.' But you reply: 'This teaching may perhaps be able to turn men away from ordinary women, but how can I turn my mind away from those who are beautiful in form and inviting to the touch, who are delightful in all their parts, pleasing to heart and eye, who give enticing glances and are of uncommon enjoyment, captivating the hearts of those who are inflamed like butter when it meets with fire?" In order to overcome your desire, it is said in the next verse:

In physical union with all women, there is not the slightest difference;
As this exterior form is also enjoyed by others, what is the gain
to you from such a special woman. (III.3)
The man to whom any such one is pleasing, boasts of his good fortune
because of her.
But as it is all the same to dogs and others, why do you cling here
with your false ideas? (III.4)[71]

Having thus inculcated in the earlier chapters a total aversion to the world, Āryadeva proceeds to the demolishing of all thought constructions conceived of as "elements of existence" (*dharmas*), preaching the same doctrine of "universal emptiness" as does his teacher Nāgārjuna.

In Chapter XXIV of his "Verses" Nāgārjuna anticipates the objections of his opponents and in his reply confirms his adherence to conventional teachings despite the seeming negativity of his assertions:

[70] *Catuḥśataka*, I, vv. 2, 6-7, 21-4. The commentary (see n. 69 above) explains the reference in verse 22 "what he ought to do" thus: "Again you say, although everything should certainly be abandoned, nevertheless I must produce a son, and when he has come of age, get him a wife and hand over the house to him, and when everything is finished that has to be done, I will set forth." The typical Hindu householder is intended, delaying his setting forth to the religious life until his latter years.

[71] *Ibid.*, III, vv. 1-4.

If all this is void, there is no appearing and no disappearing,
and logically the Four Noble Truths must be unreal.
Because of the nonreality of the Four Noble Truths there can be
no knowledge or self-discipline, no contemplative practice and
no realization (of any truth).
Since these are unreal, the four grades of achievement cannot exist.
As these are unreal there can be none who achieve them and none
who aspire to do so.
If the eight categories of religious practitioners (those in the four
grades of achievement and the four corresponding grades of aspiration)[72]
do not exist, then there is no Order of Buddhists.
Because of the nonreality of the Four Noble Truths there is no
Buddhist Religion.
If there is no Religion (*Dharma*) and no Order (*Saṅgha*) how will
there be a Buddha?
Thus speaking as you do, you destroy the Three Jewels.
With your Void you destroy the actual reality of any attainment,
equally bad conduct and good conduct and all expressions relative
to our world.

Nāgārjuna replies:

Here we state that you do not understand the use of the Void
or the Void itself or the meaning of Void; therefore you
resist in this way.
Religion as taught by the Buddhas is based on Two Truths,
the conventional truth of the world and the absolute truth.
Those who do not understand the distinction between the Two Truths
fail to understand the profound quiddity (*tattva*) in a Buddha's teaching.
One cannot indicate the Absolute without reliance on expressions relative
to our world.
Without such an approach to the Absolute nirvāṇa cannot be achieved.
Wrongly envisaged the Void destroys a person of feeble mental powers.
It is like mishandling a snake or mismanaging a spell.
Thus the Sage was (at first) adverse to teaching his Religion,[73]
considering the difficulty of the feeble-minded in penetrating it.
Everything is applicable where the Void is applicable.
Nothing is applicable of which the Void is not applicable.
Projecting your own faults upon us,
You are unmindful of the very horse on which you have mounted.
If you envisage a true reality of real things because of their innate reality,
then that being so you conceive of them as uncaused and independent.
Thus you reject the effect and the cause, the one who acts, the instrument
and the action, the coming into existence, the extinction and any result.
It is this causal nexus that we (too) declare to be void.
It is a metaphorical name and it is this that is the Middle Path.[74]

72 Literally "the eight persons of men" (*puruṣapudgalāḥ*).
73 Concerning this well-known tradition see E. J. Thomas, *Life of Buddha*, pp. 81-2.
74 MMK, XXIV, vv. 1-18.

This quotation brings us again to our point of departure in the discussion of the Madhyamikas, but here we draw attention to the theory of two aspects of truth, the acceptance of which exonerated them (at least in their own view) from the accusation of being nihilists. However, in fairness to their opponents it may be pointed out that the term *saṃvṛti* which we have translated as "relative" truth, might more suitably be translated as "deceiving" for in reality it is no truth at all. It is in this sense that it was explained to the early Tibetan translators who coined the Tibetan term *kun-rdzob* ("altogether spurious") for it. The Sanskrit term means literally to wrap around and hence to obscure, as Candrakīrti's commentary on this particular verse asserts unequivocally:

> *Saṃvṛti* means "completely obscuring." It is called "completely obscuring" because it refers to that absence of knowledge which conceals completely the "quiddity" (*tattva*) of things. It also has the meaning of "mutually dependent" in that the mutually dependent (= the causal nexus) is completely obscuring. It also means "sign" in the sense of those designations in ordinary use. Thus it characterizes the act of saying and what is said, the act of knowing and what is known.[75]

We have quoted above from Śāntideva's work *Bodhicaryāvatāra* and thus one may also refer to his interpretation, which opens the ninth and last chapter on the Perfection of Wisdom itself.

> The Sage has taught this collection (of perfections) with Wisdom in view.
> So he who wants the elimination of misery should arouse wisdom.
> Truth is accepted as twofold, as "relative" and as "absolute."
> The range of the intellect does not encompass the "absolute."
> The intellect is said to be "relative."
> In this world there are two kinds of person, the yogin and the ordinary man, and the ordinary world is rejected by the yogin's world.
> Yogins too, according to their intellectual power, reject (the views beneath them) in ever higher gradations, without there being any doubt concerning the final objective because of the (differing) views to which both (the higher and the lower) adhere.
> Worldly persons conceive of visible things as real, and not as illusion, so the world and the yogin are in disagreement. (Ch. IX, 1-5)

I shall continue to use the term "relative," although it must be emphasized that relative truth is essentially no truth at all, even though it includes not only the causal nexus, but also the whole doctrine and practice of Buddhism, the stages toward arhatship of the early disciples, the stages toward enlightenment of a Bodhisattva, and even buddhahood itself when expressed in conceptual terms.[76] The extent to which "absolute truth" might be tacitly acknowledged as

[75] See L. de la Vallée Poussin, MMK, pp. 492-4; J. May, *Candrakırti*, p. 432.

[76] One may contrast the meaning of this term (*saṃvṛti*) which is usually translated as "relative," but is scarcely relative at all, with another term (*paratantra*) as used by the Mind Only school, which really does mean "relative" (literally "dependent upon another") in a genuine sense. See further below.

real depended upon later interpretations, and here was a major source of doctrinal disagreement between some Mādhyamikas and those of the Mind Only school of thought, which we shall be considering immediately. Devastating as their teachings appeared to their opponents, Candrakīrti and Śāntideva both belonged to the moderate Madhyamaka tradition, claiming that they represented the true Buddha Word avoiding affirmation on the one side and negation on the other. Thus, commenting on Nāgārjuna's verse:

> Although a self is designated, a nonself is also taught.
> In fact neither self nor nonself has been taught by the Buddhas.

Candrakīrti argues that Śākyamuni has used such terms as self and nonself depending upon the various wrong views held by those whom he was teaching, but for those who already adhered to the true doctrine he taught neither self nor nonself. In support of this view, he then quotes from the *Ratnakūṭa* ("Gem Peak") *Sūtra*:

> O Kāśyapa, it is one extreme view to assert a self; it is another extreme view to assert a nonself. That which comes between these two extreme views, namely that which is formless, undemonstrable, unsupported, nonmanifesting, without designation and situation, that O Kāśyapa is the Middle Way, the true understanding of the elements (*dharmas*).[77]

Despite their claim to truly represent the Middle Way, the Mādhyamikas tended to exceed in their use of the *via negativa*, and they were certainly regarded by their opponents, Buddhist as well as non-Buddhist, as all but nihilists. The theory of two aspects of truth that they invoke in their defence scarcely preserves them from such criticism, since their relative truth is manifestly an altogether spurious nonentity even in its loftiest ranges. Thus Nāgārjuna's verses continue:

> When the range of thought is checked, then the conceit itself is checked.
> The "nature of dharmas" (*dharmatā*) is like nirvāṇa, which never appears
> and never disappears.
> Everything is so (*tathyam*) or not so, and both so and not so at once,
> and neither so or not so; this is the Buddha's teaching.
> Independent of anything else, tranquil, never propounded with propositions,
> inconceivable, nondiversified, this is the character of quiddity.[78]

Candrakīrti's commentary on the last verse deserves to be quoted as he refers to the simile of defective vision, which is often used in Mahāyāna literature in order to illustrate the nature of relative truth.[79]

> "Independent of anything else" means that one cannot understand by means of others' teaching, but one understands by oneself. It is like people suffering from an eye-disease who see nonexistent things such as hairs, midges or flies. Although they may be told by people with normal sight that one must

77 MMK; XVIII, v. 6 (pp. 355-8); de Jong, *Cinq Chapitres*, pp. 15-18. The *Ratnakūṭa* quotation is from the *Kāśyapaparivarta Sūtra*, ed. von Staël-Holstein, para. 57 (p. 87).

78 MMK, XVIII, vv. 7-9.

79 MMK, ed. L. de la Vallée Poussin, p. 373. See also de Jong, *Cinq Chapitres*, pp. 29-30.

understand the true nature of these hairs etc. simply by not seeing them, yet in their situation they cannot understand this. And why? They merely understand as false whatever the persons of normal vision tell them. But if they wash their eyes with a medicament that removes the defect and their vision becomes normal, then they will understand the true nature of the hairs, etc. simply in that they do not see them. In the same way although eminent men may explain quiddity by means of suggestive teachings, ordinary people do not understand the true meaning, but if they wash the eye of their mind with the defect-removing medicament of the true vision of the Void so that the understanding of quiddity arises, then they will understand the true nature of things in that they do not conceive of any quiddity at all.

For the Mādhyamikas everything that pertains to a human approach of whatever spiritual level falls within the fateful category of relative or spurious truth. They therefore demolish any value that may be attached to the career of a Bodhisattva with his practice of the perfections of generosity, morality, patience, heroism, contemplation and wisdom, except perhaps for the last two. The ideal of a would-be Buddha who strives throughout myriads of lives for the benefit of all other living beings may seem a fantastic ideal, but the earlier Mahāyāna sūtras surely preach this ideal in all seriousness. Thus a Bodhisattva must expect to be immersed in the world and he should not necessarily seek refuge from it. The doctrine of the "void" or "emptiness" of all the elements of existence (*dharmas*), which is inculcated at the same time, aims at destroying utterly the very last element of self-seeking. However, the combination of these two teachings, the Bodhisattva ideal and the emptiness of all concepts, has probably come about in these texts quite fortuitously without any immediate awareness of the effect that so extreme a philosophical view might have upon what is probably the highest of moral aspiration to be found anywhere in this imperfect world. Thus when Āryadeva says

Nirvāṇa is for the nondoer; for the active there is continual rebirth.
By freedom from thought nirvāṇa is easily gained; there is no other way,

he is drawing the logical conclusion from the philosophical views to which he adheres. His religious ideal may seem to resemble rather the Arhat or Early Disciple (*śrāvaka*) than the Bodhisattva, whose cause his fellow Mahāyānists were so anxious to promote, and the fifth chapter on the Bodhisattva's career in his "Four Hundred Verses" certainly lacks in enthusiasm. This becomes inevitable when the difference between the two ideals is presented as one of theory rather than of practice. The stages of a Bodhisattva's career then become meditative stages which take him from the very first stage quite out of this world, and it is in such a context as this that the *via negativa* of the Mādhyamikas is logically applied. It is not so much a philosophy as a therapeutic, or more aptly a strong medicine, which while curing the strong, may be deadly to the weak. Āryadeva is quite explicit on this score:

Generosity is preached to the lowly; morality to those of medium strength;
Tranquillity is taught to the foremost ones, so always do as the foremost.

In the first case unrighteousness is disposed of, and in the next
case the notion of a self.
In the last case all false notions are overcome, and he who knows
this is wise.
A viewer of one thing is a viewer of all things.
The void of one thing is the void of all things.
Attachment to the elements of existence (*dharmas*)
is taught by the Buddhas to those who seek heaven.
Precisely this is detrimental to those who seek release,
and why commend the other way?
One who seeks righteousness should never pronounce on the Void.
Cannot medicine turn into poison when wrongly applied?[80]

This is an argument which will be met with again in the tantras and it is interesting to find it used so early in the Mahāyāna period. Already we find generosity, morality, patience and heroism, and eventually contemplation as well, becoming in effect lesser perfections, while the sixth perfection, the Perfection of Wisdom, becomes all in all as the final vanity of all conceptual truth. One may well ask what is the difference between Madhyamaka teachings and those of the nihilists (*nāstika*) with whom their opponents identified them. As Nāgārjuna claims, it is precisely in their allowing a form of relative truth and hence a therapeutic value to the more practical aspects of a Bodhisattva's career. Thus the twelvefold causal nexus as an explanation of the continual process of rebirth, whether rebirth in wretched states as a result of unrighteous acts or rebirth in relatively happy states as a reward for righteous acts, all this is accepted as a kind of relative truth, however spurious it may be in terms of absolute truth. A nihilist on the other hand gives no such provisional adherence to any of this and thus he falls from one evil rebirth to another until he is touched, if ever, by some saving grace.[81] There may be a lack of logic in the Madhyamaka position, but as it is claimed throughout that any stance is essentially a nonstance, they can scarcely be judged by logical considerations. L. de la Vallée Poussin made some shrewd observations over fifty years ago:[82]

> The Madhyamaka affirms as relative truth the existence of the world and of suffering, of the way and of salvation from suffering. This is the ancient immortal creed of Buddhists. This creed the Madhyamaka denies as absolute truth. He teaches that relative truth or the truth of experience is the truth of an illusory and nonexistent world. I suspect that the Madhyamaka does not know himself very well. He affirms experience provisionally, namely the *pratītyasamutpāda*, the causal production of ephemeral things, and the egress from such experience, namely nirvāṇa. This is what he names as relative truth; in fact it is the real truth, for his absolute truth is nothing but a

80 *Catuḥśataka*, VIII, vv. 14-18. For texts see V. Bhattacarya, pp. 14-22.

81 Those who never attain salvation are known as *icchāntika* ("willful"). See e.g., Suzuki, *Laṅkāvatāra Sūtra*, pp. 58-9. See section II.4.e.

82 See "Réflections sur le Madhyamaka" in *Mélanges chinois et bouddhiques*, II (1933), pp. 1-59. I have translated two short extracts from pp. 54 and 58-9.

methodical truth; his negation of relative truth—negation of the extremes of existence and nonexistence as well as of the middle position, viz. total nonexistence—is a methodical negation.

Insisting that in real truth appearances do not exist even as mere appearance, a candidate for nirvāṇa must accept this forced proposition if he wants to detach himself from appearances. The followers of the Lesser Vehicle, who are certainly not fools, have given a name to such erroneous opinions, to these auto-suggestions which are produced by force of recollection with purification as the intended result; these are the *adhimuktimanaskāra* ("aspiring reflections"). Thus, it is all too true that there are such things as women; the ascetic applies himself to the reflection that women are nothing but emaciated skeletons; he makes of such a reflection a kind of real truth and thereby extinguishes all desire. Nāgārjuna's method is quite similar; the ascetic persuades himself that in real truth misery and pleasure, the I and the you, etc. are all void of misery and pleasure, of I and of you.

In the Perfection of Wisdom sūtras, that is to say in the canonical texts that claim to be Buddha Word, the teachings about the emptiness of all concepts are to some extent balanced by recommendation given to the career of a Bodhisattva, and as we have already noted above, these teachings are primarily directed to ordinary monks and to some extent layfolk as well. There would appear to be no intention of relegating for instance the perfection of generosity to the status of a practice suitable for those of inferior capacity. Rather, this and all the other perfections should be performed within the spirit of the perfection of wisdom. Thus we are told:

A Bodhisattva should not give a gift with the fixation of anything given or of anywhere (that it is given). He is not to give a gift with a fixation relating to form or sound or smell or taste or touch. He must give gifts without being fixed in any indicating concept.[83]

Generosity remains an essential perfection for a Bodhisattva, and here he is being told with the prolixity which is typical of these texts precisely what has been said with a rather different figure of speech in another religious tradition, namely: "When you give alms, do not let your left hand know what your right hand is doing."[84]

However, as Subhūti realizes, the doctrine of the emptiness of all concepts threatens the validity of the practice of the perfections, and he asks the Lord a very cogent question: "Can there be increase or decrease of something that is ineffable?" The Lord replies that there is not, and Subhūti presses his next question:

"If there can be no increase or decrease of something ineffable, there can be no increase or decrease in the perfection of generosity, nor of morality or of patience, or of heroism, or of meditation or of wisdom. If that is so, Lord, how by the force of the ever-increasing six perfections can a Bodhisattva realize

[83] *Vajracchedikā*, ed. E. Conze, pp. 29 and 67.

[84] Matthew VI, v.3.

final and perfect enlightenment?"

The Lord replies: "Indeed there is no increase or decrease in the substance of a perfection, so a Bodhisattva who is skilled in means and who practices the perfection of generosity does not reflect: 'This perfection of generosity is on the increase' or 'This perfection of generosity is on the decrease.' On the contrary he reflects that 'perfection of generosity' is a mere form of words, and as he gives his gift he lets all reflections, all thoughts that arise find their own maturation as roots of merit in supreme and perfect enlightenment, so that supreme and perfect enlightenment effects the maturation. It is the same process for the other perfections of morality, patience, heroism, meditation and wisdom."[85]

In the noncanonical treatises, from which several quotations have been drawn, the whole career of the Bodhisattva like everything else is reduced to such emptiness that it tends to lose all significance except perhaps as a meditational exercise. Nāgārjuna states that there is not the most subtle difference between saṃsāra and nirvāṇa, and Āryadeva shocks his readers by saying that there is nothing to be done, for if there were anything to be done, saṃsāra could never be stopped. On occasions the canonical texts themselves use similar language, when to the bewilderment of the gods at his discourse, Subhūti replies that nothing at all has been explained. This is by no means the same as saying that there is indeed a great deal of religious practice of various kinds to be performed but that all must be done in a spirit of total self-abnegation. Such is surely the intention of much of the Perfection of Wisdom teaching, but it tends to be subverted by another interpretation, which treats the realization of enlightenment as a purely mental process, with the result that Buddhist religious practice remains what it appears to have been from the start, a highly disciplined training in thoughts, words and actions with the main emphasis placed on meditational techniques backed by an interpretation of the physical world which reduce it to a transient and illusory state. In terms of such practice the perfections of generosity, morality, patience and heroism have no more play than the ten rules of good conduct prescribed for the Early Disciples, and concern for others need amount to no more than the earlier practice of the so-called "pure abodes" (*brahmavihāra*) of love, compassion, sympathetic joy and equanimity. In many respects the Perfection of Wisdom literature presents itself as much ado about nothing that was not realizable already.[86] It may be of interest to quote a description of Madhyamaka practice as interpreted by a renowned Tibetan scholar who lived over the turn of the nineteenth to twentieth century:

85 From the ASP, Sanskrit text ed. Vaidya, pp. 181-2, much abbreviated. Compare E. Conze, ASP (translation), p. 133.

86 Discussing the problems of the existence or nonexistence of a Buddha, Professor Lamotte observes that when one examines the matter deeply, the Mādhyamika remains very close to early Buddhism, but that he transfers to an ontological level arguments that the earlier schools have based on the historical plane. See *Concentration de la marche hēroïque*, pp. 53-6. Similarly the doctrine of "no self" which is based upon a theory of quasireal elements in the earlier schools is transferred to the maybe improved basis (which is defined as no-basis) of quasiunreal elements. To the religious practitioner the theoretical shift can make little difference.

> The Path is, ordinarily, the practice of the six perfections, and, ultimately, the meditation on the unity of radiant light and transcendent awareness. The method of the practice of concentration is to sit cross-legged and first to take refuge and to develop an enlightened attitude; then, with a mind utterly relaxed to remain, without the fluctuations of mentation, in a steady radiant brilliancy, in a realm into which no dichotomic thought enters as there is no thinking of and about anything whatsoever, such activity having been cut off, as it were, by the vision of reality; when thereby all referential perceptual situations have faded away because there is neither affirmation nor negation in a mind engaged in meditation devoid of external objects and of the projects before a mind and acts of projection, then perceptiveness, internally freed from judgmental activity due to the cessation of the operations of the phenomenal mind and its mental events, becomes the contemplation of radiancy as individual intrinsic perception. In the post-concentrative stage one engages in the accumulation of the merits on behalf of the beings who are like an apparition, without attachment or involvement.[87]

The fantastic number of lives, albeit essentially unreal, through which a Bodhisattva must progress, need not be daunting to a would-be practitioner, for it may be safely assumed that if he is conscious of so strong an aspiration toward the religious life, this is precisely because of the vast stores of merit, albeit essentially unreal stores of merit, that he has accumulated already through numerous previous lives, essentially unreal as they may be.

c. *The Third Turning*

We now come to the third turning of the Wheel of the Doctrine, which represents for those who subscribe to these particular teachings the indisputable truth in its final form. In his account of the threefold event the Tibetan historian Bu-ston (1290-1364), who is able to draw on all the later Indian traditions, quotes from the *Sandhinirmocana Sūtra* ("Resolving Enigmas"), which is an especially favoured work of the Mind Only school.

> The Lord first turned the Wheel of the Doctrine at Vānānasi in the Deer Park, where sages hold forth, for the benefit of those who follow the Interior Way, and teaching the Four Noble Truths he turned the Wheel in a wonderful way such as no one, god or man, has ever turned it in this world in relation to the Doctrine. But this teaching could be surpassed, as it befitted an occasion and the meaning requires interpretation so that it becomes a basis for argument. Then the Lord turned the Wheel of the Doctrine a second time for those who follow the Great Way, beginning with the nonsubstantiality of the elements, their nonarising and noncessation, their primordial state of rest, their natural state of total nirvāṇa, and with this kind of teaching of the Void he turned the Wheel in a most wonderful way. But this teaching too could be surpassed, as it befitted an occasion and the meaning requires interpretation so that it

[87] H. V. Guenther, *Buddhist Philosophy in Theory and Practice*, p. 153. Extracts from a work of the rNying-ma-pa Lama Mi-pham 'Jam-dbyangs rnam-rgyal rgya-mtsho are presented.

becomes a basis for argument. Then the Lord turned the Wheel of the Doctrine a third time for all Buddhists, beginning with the nonsubstantiality of the elements, their nonarising and noncessation, their primordial state of rest, their natural state of total nirvāṇa, and he turned it in a wonderful way with precise definitions. Thus this turning of the Wheel is unsurpassable, for the meaning is sure, providing no basis for argument.[88]

As Bu-ston observes in a subsequent comment the Mādhyamikas were by no means willing to admit that their teachings, as represented by the second turning of the Wheel, were not the ultimate truth, and thus argument did in fact continue, since for them the theories of the Mind Only school pertained to relative truth and thus required interpretation. The above translation obscures for us the use of two important technical terms, namely "derivable meaning" (*neyārtha*), i.e., requiring interpretation, and "sure meaning" (*nītartha*), i.e., intended literally. By applying these terms, it was possible to accept in a provisional manner not only some of the statements of otherwise opposing schools of thought but also to reinterpret to one's own satisfaction canonical statements, which all agreed were the Buddha Word. As a disinterested listener to the various claims to represent the most valid interpretation of the sum total of Buddhist doctrine, one is likely to favor those who subscribed to the teachings of the third turning of the Wheel. Coming last in time they were able to produce a remarkable synthesis of the two previous interpretations of the Doctrine, which from their point of view were either excessively positive or misleadingly negative. They agree with the Mādhyamikas in adopting the general Mahāyāna thesis concerning the essentially unreal nature of the elements of existence (*dharmas*), but at the same time they attribute to the whole *dharma*-theory a psychological importance based upon painstaking and precise analysis. Thus they elaborate a form of relative truth of a higher order than merely spurious truth. For them the whole of existence, as conceived by the earlier schools as the sum total of conditioned and unconditioned elements, has three modes of manifestation:

an imagined one (*parikalpita*) referring to normal worldly experience where persons and things have apparent separate nameable identity;
a relative one ("depending one upon another," *paratantra*) as applied to the elements when analyzed in terms of the Causal Nexus ("mutually dependent origination," *pratītyasamutpāda*);
a perfected one (*parinispanna*), which is the true nature of things such as a Bodhisattva aspires to and finally realizes as the Suchness (*tathatā*) of things.[89]

It is thus not possible to assert unequivocally that saṃsāra is identical with nirvāṇa, for the difference exists as between an enlightened or an unenlightened mind. As the Lord explains:

[88] See Bu-ston, *History of Buddhism*, vol. I, pp. 52-4. I have taken the quotation direct from the *Sandhinirmocana Sūtra*, ed. É. Lamotte, p. 85 (Tibetan text), with French translation on pp. 206-7.

[89] As detailed in the *Sandhinirmocana Sūtra*, ed. É. Lamotte, pp. 59-65 and 188-191.

> If the character of the elemental impulses (*saṃskāra*) is not different from the character of the absolute (*paramārtha*), then all ordinary simple people will be beholders of the truth; they will have obtained the success and the happiness of the high state of nirvāṇa and they will have realized supreme and perfect enlightenment. But if the character of the elemental impulses is different from the character of the absolute, then the beholders of the truth will not be parted from the character of elemental impulses, and so they will not be free from those bonds of such a character and thus not free from the bonds of potential evil. If they are not free from these two kinds of bonds then they are not beholders of the truth, they have not obtained the success and happiness of the high state of nirvāṇa and they have not realized supreme and perfect enlightenment. . . . If the character of the elemental impulses is not different from the character of the absolute, then just as the character of the elemental impulses is identified with the character of the afflictions (*kleśa*) so the absolute would be similarly identified. But if the character of the elemental impulses is different from the character of the absolute, then the character of the absolute will not be the general character of the elemental impulses, . . . so it is unsuitable to say that the character of the elemental impulses is not different from the character of the absolute, and it is also unsuitable to say that it is different from it.[90]

Thus the term conditioned (*saṃskṛta*) as applied to saṃsāra and the term unconditioned (*asaṃskṛta*) as applied to nirvāṇa are mere appellations devised by those who know better in order to assist others. The true state of the elements (*dharmatā*) remains the ineffable Suchness (*tathatā*) which is only realized in the state of perfect enlightenment. It is this "true state" which is at the same time the general character of all the elemental impulses and it is in this latter sense that nirvāṇa cannot be said to be different from saṃsāra. The relationship between the two is illustrated by a simile that occurs again and again not only in Sanskrit works but was also continually used later by Tibetan seers:

> O noble son, it is as though a magician or a clever magician's disciple stationed himself at a crossroads and collected there some grass or leaves or twigs or pebbles or potsherds, and then produced a (magical) display of a group of elephants or horses or chariots or foot-soldiers, and of gems or pearls or lapis lazuli or conch shell or crystal or coral, or of money or grain or treasure or deposited wealth. Then ordinary simple folk in their ignorance and defective knowledge, knowing nothing of the grass and leaves and so on and according to what they saw and heard, would think: "This group of elephants is real. This group of horses is real," and so on for all the other things. Depending upon what they see and hear, they cleave to it and hold to it, saying: "This is true. Anything else is false." They apply to everything an everyday name, and so afterwards they will need to investigate carefully. . . .In the same way ordinary simple folk who have not attained to that exalted supramundane wisdom, fail to understand the ineffable elemental state (*dharmatā*) of all the

[90] *Ibid.*, pp. 43, 44-5 and 175-6. The passage has to be much abbreviated because of the usual prolixity of Mahāyāna sūtras.

dharmas, and in accordance with what they see or hear in the matter of conditioned and unconditioned things they think: "This really is conditioned or this really is unconditioned just as we see and hear it." Thus they cleave to it and hold to it, saying: "This is true. Anything else is false." They apply to everything an everyday name, and so afterwards they will need to investigate carefully.[91]

The basis of existence, both conditioned and unconditioned, of saṃsāra and nirvāṇa, which is referred to unambiguously as the absolute state of Just So or Suchness (*tathatā*), is also named by the Mind Only school as Mind (*citta*) used in the absolute sense of Mind Only (*cittamātra*)—free from the dichotomy of subject and object. Their school is also known as Consciousness Only (*Vijñānamātra*), where consciousness must be understood in the same exalted sense. It is also known as Nomenclature Only (*Vijñaptimātra*) in that all determining factors are mere names. Finally and perhaps more usually it is known as Practice of Yoga (*Yogācāra*), a name which, like the name Madhymaka, as applied to the other main Mahāyāna school, is equally applicable to all Buddhists of whatever persuasion. As used by the Mind Only school (alias *Yogācāra*) it suggests that only by the practice of suitable yoga can Mind which is impure in its conditioned or worldly state be realized as essentially pure in the final state of enlightenment. It will be observed then that this school, representing the third turning of the Wheel, tends to posit an overall state of reality whereas the Mādhyamikas continue to speak noncommittally of the Void (*śūnyatā*). At the same time neither of these main Mahāyāna schools represents a single unified tradition with the result that each of them embraces a varying range of affirmation or denial.[92] Thus a later Mādhyamika named Bhāvaviveka, who also wrote a commentary on Nāgārjuna's "Basic Verses," adopting an extreme negative interpretation of reality, castigates the followers of the Mind Only school as introducing the heretical notion of a "self" (*ātman*) under another name.

If you say that *tathatā* (Suchness), although beyond words, is a real thing, then this is the *ātman* of the heretics which you designate with the different name of *tathatā*. Your *tathatā* is a real thing, and yet from the viewpoint of absolute truth it does not belong to the categories of being or nonbeing; but such is the *ātman*. The heretics also believe that the *ātman*, a real thing, is omnipresent, eternal, acting, feeling, and yet beyond all categories and concepts (*nirvikalpa*). Because it does not pertain to the sphere of words, because it presents no object to the discursive intellect (*vikalpa-buddhi*), it is said to be beyond categories. The teaching of the heretics says: "Words do not reach there; thought (*manas-citta*) does not present itself; this is why it is called *ātman*."

Although such is the character of the *ātman*, you say none the less: "Knowledge that relies on *tathatā* (*tathatālambana-jñāna*) produces salvation, but knowledge that relies on the *ātman* does not." But what is the difference between your *tathatā* and the *ātman*, since both of them are ineffable and yet

91 *Sandhinirmocana Sūtra*, pp. 36-7 and 170-1.

92 They remain however vigorously opposed to one another. See Stcherbatsky's brief introductory comments to the *Discourse on Discrimination between the Middle and Extremes*, pp. 3-7.

> possess real self-nature? It is only out of a partisan spirit that you speak as you do. Therefore I cannot accept this *tathatā*, the same as the *ātman*, real yet nonexisting.[93]

In fairness to the Mind Only school it may be pointed out that such an argument can only be pressed by taking *ātman* in a purified Vedānta sense and dissociating it from all notion of a personal sense. To their credit, at least from the orthodox Buddhist standpoint, this school does little effectively to solve the perennial Buddhist problem of individual continuity from one birth to another. This problem cannot be really solved without incurring the inevitable charge of heterodoxy, so firmly is the dogma of "no self" (*anātman*) rooted in Buddhist doctrine. However, the Mind Only school certainly elaborates a complex theory of a Basic Consciousness (*ālayavijñāna*), which represents a vast stream of elements (*dharmas*) much as the early schools envisaged them. The essential difference from them consists in their denial of any essential difference between such a stream of unpurified elements (= saṃsāra) and the same stream when purified (= nirvāṇa). Since personality in any form is relegated to the order of an imagined character (*parikalpita*) of the whole, the problem of differentiating individual streams of consciousness from the universal stream need not arise. It is sufficient for their purposes to analyze the stream according to its relative character (*paratantra*) and in doing this, use is freely made of the earlier *dharma*-theories.

> This consciousness is known as the "apprehending consciousness" in that it grasps at and comprehends this bodily form. It is also called "basic consciousness in that it adheres and clings to this bodily form with a single sense of security. It is also called "mind" in that it is an accumulation and aggregation of appearances, sounds, smells, tastes, sensations of touch and of thoughts.[94]

Perhaps one of the best descriptions of this Basic Consciousness given in any European work is the one that occurs in a footnote in Th. Stcherbatsky's translation of the "Discourse on Discriminations between Middle and Extremes."[95]

> The fundamental change which Asanga has introduced into Buddhism or, what is the same, into the *anātma* = *dharma* theory, was, according to his own confession, the establishment of a "common foundation" for all the Elements of Existence (the *dharmas*). It is called *ālayavijñāna*, which means "all-conserving Mind" or a "Magazine of ideas," a "Mind-Store." Its implication is first of all the denial of the external world which is replaced by ideas. It is also a step towards the reintroduction of the dethroned Soul. Uddyotakara

93 See L. de la Vallée Poussin, "Madhyamaka," in *Mélanges chinois et bouddhiques*, vol. II (1933), pp. 115-6.

94 *Sandhinirmocana Sūtra*, pp. 55 and 184-5.

95 This is the *Madhyānta-vibhaṅga*, one of the works ascribed to the Bodhisattva Maitreya, as interpreted by Asaṅga and supplied with commentaries by Vasubandhu and Sthiramati. Stcherbatsky's translation was first published as vol. XXX of the Bibliotheca Buddhica, Moscow-Leningrad, 1936, reprinted in Calcutta, 1971 in the series Indian Studies Past and Present, of which see p. 119 for the above quotation. This work is the best available "textbook" in English concerning the Mind Only school. See also D. L. Friedman in the Bibliography.

> and Vācaspatimiśra reject it as a poor substitute for their substantial Soul. . . . This sacrifice Buddhism could not make. The *anātma-vāda* could not become *ātma-vāda*. The whole system of *dharmas* has been retained, the number even was enlarged from seventy-five to one hundred and the *ālaya* received a place in it. Buddhism continued to be a pluralistic *dharma*-theory, but a monistic subway has been added to it. The theory of the *ālaya* is very elaborate . . .; it is beginningless (*anādi*) and everlasting (*dhruva*, not *nitya*) through all incarnations up to Nirvāṇa. It is the source of all ideas and the receptacle of all past experience, hence the source of memory. It replaces both the external (*nimitta-bhāga*) and the internal (*darśana-bhāga*) worlds. But it is not a substance; it is a process; it runs underground of actual experience. Since we have no word in European languages, no adequate term for a running Soul, we must either leave the term *ālaya* untranslated (like the terms nirvāṇa and *karma*) or resort to the term Psyche which is not yet engaged in Buddhist philosophy. We must of course keep in mind its difference not only from the Greek psyche but also from the Vedic *ātman* (which was likened to the Greek psyche by Prof. H. Jacobi), from the Vedāntic *jīva*, from the transmigrating *liṅga-śarīra* of Sānkhya, not to mention the *ātman* of Nyāya-Vaiśesika. But that it is a substitute for an individual's surviving Soul is clear from the words of Uddyotakara and Vācaspati.

The eighteen sense-spheres (*dhātu*) of the early schools are retained with rather more emphasis on the rôle of consciousness throughout. The earlier scheme assumed the existence of elements (*dharmas*) representing the power of sense on the one hand, the object of the particular sense on the other and consciousness as a mental element linking the two thus:

1. sight	7. appearances	13. visual consciousness
2. hearing	8. sounds	14. auditory consciousness
3. sense of smell	9. smells	15. olfactory consciousness
4. sense of taste	10. tastes	16. gustatory consciousness
5. sense of touch	11. touchables	17. tactile consciousness
6. power of thought	12. thoughts	18. mental consciousness

When mentioning these sense-spheres (*dhātu*), the canonical texts may at the same time refer to the sense-pairs (*āyatana*) which include the first twelve items as listed above conceived of simply as subject and object. These two sets of six are also intended in the writings of the Mind Only school by the terms "apprehender" (*grahaka*) and "apprehended" (*grāhya*) as produced by the corresponding forms of consciousness, which is thus spilt into an imagined duality of subject and object.

They also make use of the set of Five Aggregates (*skandha*) into which personality was dissolved by the earlier schools, but the terminology may be slightly changed in order to remove the suggestion of external form as implied by the term "body" (*rūpa*) and in order to free "consciousness" (*vijñāna*) for its more specialized use. Thus we have: touch (*sparśa*), feelings (*vedanā*), perceptions (*saṃjñā*), mental activity (*manaskāra*) and will (*cetanā*).[96]

96 See Sylvain Lévi, *Vijñaptimātratāsiddhi*, pp. 19-20 (viz. verse 3 of Vasubandhu's *Triṃśikā*).

Having listed these "elements" which according to the Mind Only school represent a relative truth useful for analyzing the wholly imagined idea of a "self," we may quote from another favorite sūtra of this school, using the available English translation of Professor Suzuki:

> What is meant by egolessness of persons? . . . In the collection of Skandhas, Dhātus and Āyatanas there is no ego-substance, nor anything belonging to it; the Vijñāna is originated by ignorance, deed and desire, and keeps up its function by grasping objects by means of the sense-organs, such as the eye etc. and by clinging to them as real; while a world of objects and bodies is manifested owing to the discrimination that takes place in the world which is of Mind itself, that is in the Ālayavijñāna (Basic Consciousness). By reason of the habit-energy (*vāsanā*) stored up by false imagination since beginningless time, this world (*viṣaya*) is subject to change and destruction from moment to moment; it is like a river, a seed, a lamp, wind, a cloud; [while the Vijñāna itself is] like a monkey who is always restless, like a fly who is ever in search of unclean things and defiled places, like a fire that is never satisfied. Again it is like a water-drawing wheel or a machine; it goes on rolling the wheel of transmigration, carrying varieties of bodies and forms, resuscitating the dead like the demon Vetāla, causing the wooden figures to move about as a magician moves them.[97]

A notion which is essential to the operation as thus described is *vāsanā*, which Suzuki translates as "habit-energy." The Sanskrit term is usually derived from *vāsa* in the sense of "perfume," so that *vāsanā* suggests a perfuming agent, for which an aerosol spray might perhaps serve as a modern example. An accurate interpretation may be: "the impression unconsciously left on the mind by past good or bad actions, which therefore produces pleasure or pain."[98] The word "seed" (*bīja*) , which has many other applications, is often used as a synonym, in that good or bad actions are thought of as sowing seeds in the Basic Consciousness, which inevitably bear fruit when other circumstances are suitable. The early Tibetan translators who were very careful in fixing upon a suitable translation for such technical terms, coined the word *bag-chags*, which they invented by combining *bag* (probably in its sense of "minute") and *chags* (in the sense of "clinging"). There is clearly no word available in any European language to give the full meaning of such a term ("latency" is perhaps the best available), just as originally there was no word available in Tibetan. It was translated into Chinese by a term meaning "force of habit,"[99] which accounts for Suzuki's rendering, although with his term "habit-energy" he presumably means a kind of residual element that produces its effect on the analogy of what we may understand as a habit. Clearly a habit is something that occurs again and again, whereas a *vāsanā* may produce its effect in the stream of consciousness once

French translation available in *idem*, *Matériaux pour l'étude du système vijnaptimātra*, p. 74.

97 See D. T. Suzuki, *The Laṅkāvatāra Sūtra*, p. 61; Sanskrit text, ed P. L. Vaidya, p. 29, ll. 21-8.

98 See V. S. Apte, *Sanskrit Dictionary*, p. 963.

99 See Soothill and Hodous, *A Dictionary of Chinese Buddhist Terms*, p. 362 (last item).

only. I have discussed this term at some length, as it typifies perhaps to an unusual degree the difficulty of finding a suitable word in any other language for a technical term such as this. It is thus best to retain the original term, just as we have come to accept the term *karma* in the special meaning of the moral effect of one's acts. It will be noticed at once that *vāsanā* is similar in meaning to *karma*, but the implications of *karma* are far wider in that it is used to explain (in so far as it does explain) the continual unfolding of the phenomenal world on the one hand and the advance toward perfection on the other. The seeds (*bīja*) whose pervasive effect (*vāsanā*) continue to produce ever more seeds, pure or impure as the case may be, seemingly exist since beginningless time. They provide no solution for the origin of the whole phenomenal process and in effect no solution is required since according to fundamental Buddhist teaching the whole process is without beginning or end. Furthermore both the main Mahāyāna schools, Madhyamaka as well as the Mind Only school, regard the phenomenal process (saṃsāra) as mere illusion, with the result that in absolute truth no intellectual problem of beginning or end can have any meaning.

In such a brief account as this one is bound to attempt to simplify, but the scholars who attempted to systematize the various teachings that are given in such canonical works as the *Sandhinirmocana Sūtra* and the *Laṅkāvatāra* had to find room for so much earlier traditional material that continued to be incorporated with the later, often clearer, concepts, and all had to be worked into a satisfactory framework, unless one were to follow an extreme Madhyamaka way, reducing all teachings whatsoever to the status of "spurious truth." The Mind Only school had a far more difficult task in elaborating an order of truth based upon the mutually dependent (*paratantra*) character of reality. Thus I quote once more from one of the above sūtras:

> The beings which are born in whichever realm of the Wheel of Six Realms, whether they are born from eggs or from wombs or from heat and moisture or miraculously, appear in the manifestation of a bodily form. Now in the first instance they are dependent upon two kinds of appropriation, the assuming of sense-organs and what they depend on together with a body, and the assuming of *vāsanās* with their prolixity relating to the appellations of characteristics, names and discriminations, and so mind with all these seeds (*bīja*) matures and progresses, spreads and extends. Thus in the spheres where bodily form is involved there are these two appropriations, but in the sphere of no bodily form there are not two.[100]

In this short passage reference is made to the Wheel of Existence with its six realms as well as to the ancient notion of a threefold world, consisting of a Sphere of Desire (*kāmadhātu*) where all six realms are placed, the Sphere of Form (*rūpadhātu*), the abode of lower ranking celestial beings, and the Sphere of No Form (*arūpadhātu*) where the higher celestial beings manifest themselves. These last are the "radiant = gods" (Skr. *ābhāsvara*, Pāli *ābhassara*) who consist

[100] *Sandhinirmocana Sūtra*, pp. 55 and 184.

of thought, are self-evident and subsist on joy. According to the earlier concepion of nirvāṇa as a tranquil state beyond the highest heaven, these exalted spheres correspond with the higher states of trance leading to nirvāṇa. All such earlier mythology has to be reinterpreted in accordance with later philosophical theory and the task was no easy one.

Just as two greatly renowned scholars, Nāgārjuna and Āryadeva appear in the second century A.D. as the main exponents of Madhyamaka teachings, so two other renowned scholars, Asaṅga and Vasubandhu, appear in the fifth century as the leading exponents of the Mind Only teachings. Their literary output was truly enormous, especially if all that later tradition attributes to them was really their work. Asaṅga is represented as having a special relationship with the Bodhisattva Maitreya, who is said to have revealed to him the basic verses of some of his works and even to have appeared on earth in order to continue his dictations.[101] This tradition has inevitably endowed these works with considerable prestige, although they do not qualify as canonical (viz. Buddha Word). Reference was made above to the distinction between sūtra, inspired discourse accepted as canonical, and *śāstra*, a learned treatise elucidating the sūtras. The origins of *śāstra* may be fixed with some semblance of historical exactitude, although attributions of authorship at a time when relationships between religious master and pupil were so strong may often be suspect to modern scholarship, the more so when there is no fixed tradition available. Nowadays, authors are often all too anxious to claim credit for their work, however much they have benefited from the labors and ideas of their predecessors. By contrast, in any well established religious tradition one prefers to attribute one's literary productions to a more famous teacher, both out of respect for him and also to give greater prestige to the teachings one is reproducing. For one must also bear in mind that much of the vast literary output of these Buddhist scholars was largely repetitive, and the Tibetans in their turn continued this tradition of restatement and elaboration. The origin of the sūtras as declared Buddha Word is far more obscure. There need be no doubt that some of the earliest sūtras, as preserved for instance by the Theravādins and the Sarvāstivādins, derive originally from some of the actual teachings of the Buddha Śākyamuni, but being for the first few centuries an entirely oral tradition, they underwent elaboration and extension as occasion required.[102]

It is this tendency to elaborate and even to restate earlier teachings by teachers in the monastic compounds that led to the evolving of the Mahāyāna sūtras.

[101] A suggestion that Maitreya represented an actual human teacher is given currency in E. J. Thomas, *History of Buddhist Thought*, p. 238, but it should be dismissed. For a more recent survey of this matter one may refer to D. S. Ruegg, *Le théorie du Tathāgatagarbha*, pp. 50-5. For the larger problem of the actual authorship of works attributed to Asaṅga see also *ibid.*, pp. 39ff.

[102] Readers may be reminded that whereas the early sūtras as accumulated by the Theravādins are preserved in the Pāli canon, those of the Sarvāstivādins and the other early sects that flourished in India largely perished with the destruction of Indian Buddhism. Their extent, however, is known by later reference and quotation.

Although the art of writing was already well established in India before the Christian era, teaching and especially religious teaching continued to be mainly oral. Thus, teachings learned by rote with the inevitable repetitions that this required, passed from religious master to pupil, acquiring the prestige and eventually formal recognition as Buddha Word. Most of the Mahāyāna sūtras, as subsequently recorded in writing, are compilations of such teachings, which more or less fit together in composite wholes. Also a process of continual enlargement by the incorporation of extra teachings can be proved by the existence of earlier and later translations of the same work into Chinese and Tibetan. In fact the only means available for dating a particular sūtra in a certain state of formation is provided by its Chinese translation. This remains a rather rough and ready guide, as can well be imagined, for every sūtra, as soon as it acquired a manuscript form, was not immediately translated into Chinese, and these translations date only from the second century A.D. onward. This however covers the Mahāyāna period fairly well; Tibetan translations, although far more accurate linguistically because of the remarkable care that was taken in fixing an adequate technical vocabulary, are of far less use for dating purposes, because the serious work of translation into Tibetan did not begin until the eighth century, while most of it was done between the tenth and the thirteenth, by when the sūtras as well as the tantras had assumed a final form.[103] As an example of the value of the Chinese datings, we may note that the three sūtras from which we have quoted above in discussing Madhyamaka teachings, namely the "Perfection of Wisdom in Eight Thousand Verses," the *Vimalakīrtinirdeśa* and the *Śūraṅgamasamādhi*, were all translated into Chinese before the end of the second century A.D., whereas the two sūtras used in discussion of Mind Only teachings, namely the *Sandhinirmocana* and the *Laṅkāvatāra*, were not translated into Chinese until the fifth century A.D. It may be readily assumed that they already existed in India in manuscript form up to as much as a century earlier, and a dating such as this is in conformity with what is known of Asaṅga and his brother Vasubandhu.

The three turnings of the Wheel of the Doctrine thus represent a perfectly valid historical development of Buddhist teachings, and the origins of all of them are firmly rooted in what goes before. Hence the date of formulation of the various phases of teaching cannot represent their actual origin as Buddha Word. We observed above that even the earliest known Buddha Word is closely related to religious and philosophical beliefs which were current in India of the fifth century B.C., especially the belief in continual rebirth, the doctrine of no self (*anātman*), which only has meaning in terms of the then prevalent notions of a self (*ātman*), as well as the theory of real elements of existence. Thereafter, just as the Madhyamaka insistence on the essential nonreality of these supposed "real elements" can only be understood in terms of the earlier theories, so now the

[103] A notable example of the considerable differences that can exist between two Tibetan translations is that of the *Sarvadurgatipariśodhana Tantra* (see T. Skorupski in the Bibliography), which was translated first toward the end of the eighth century and then again in the thirteenth.

Mind Only school can only be understood as a thoughtful reverse move, which had the effect of restoring the whole *dharma*-theory, albeit in a modified form, to its earlier plausibility. Thus although the two later turnings of the wheel come one after another in time, each of them has a just claim in different ways to represent the true Buddha Word in that earlier exaggerated tendencies, excessive positivity in the first case, excessive negativity in the second, were being corrected.

For the followers of the Mind Only school the state of enlightenment is represented by the Basic Consciousness (*ālayavijñāna*) in its purified or perfected form. This Basic Consciousness operates as the total sphere of the elements of existence (*dharmadhātu*), and as we have already observed above these are analyzed in accordance with the *dharma*-theories of the earlier schools. The essential difference in interpretation derives from the general Mahāyāna conviction that there is no essential difference between nirvāṇa and saṃsāra, analyzed as they were by the earlier schools into nonconditioned and conditioned elements. The apparent difference between the two is now envisaged as a matter of the impurity or purity, as the case may be, of Consciousness (*vijñāna*) or Mind (*citta*), both these terms being used as synonyms in the absolute sense. The basis for Consciousness in this absolute sense is the continuing stream of *dharmas*, of which an imagined person with his body and organs of sense, and an imagined outer world with its objects of sense is the everyday experience. This so-called Basic Consciousness (*ālayavijñāna*) thus corresponds as a later concept to the earlier concept of the person as a mere continuance (*santāna*) of a stream of *dharmas* from one birth to the next.[104] The purpose of religious practice of those Early Disciples (*śrāvaka*) was to stop the *dharmas* manifesting themselves, so that the "blank" of nirvāṇa might become manifest. By contrast, the practice of those who follow the Mahāyāna schools aims at a fundamental change in the mind. Thus it can be said that essentially there is nothing to be done, for as Āryadeva exclaims: "If there were anything to be done, this world could never be stopped." There is essentially nothing to be stopped, as the *dharmas*, which the earlier schools endowed with varying degress of reality, are essentially non-existent. The general difference between the two main Mahāyāna schools is to be found in a certain willingness or a certain unwillingness, as the case may be, to interpret the absolute reality, as realized by a Bodhisattva at the end of his career, in positive terms. We have seen that by attempting to do so, the followers of the Mind Only school lay themselves open to a possible charge of reintroducing a self (*ātman*) under another name. However, if the attempt is not made, how is the career of a Bodhisattva to be usefully and helpfully analyzed? The analysis is characterized as "relative" (*paratantra*), for once the goal is reached the whole apparatus disappears. Mind Only remains free of the duality of an

[104] The concept of such a Basic Consciousness was not an invention of the Mind Only schools. Like so many concepts that receive prominence in later teachings, it can be traced back to some of the earlier schools. See L. de la Vallée Poussin, *Siddhi*, pp. 178ff. For my previous references to *santāna* see the Index.

imagined subject and object, which have their basis in consciousness in its condition as sixfold, listed just above as items 13 to 18 of the eighteen *dhātus*. As coordinator of these six aspects of consciousness, a seventh known as Mentation (*manas*) is also posited, although there is some discussion of its precise relationship to "mental consciousness" (*manovijñāna*, item 18). This is but one of the complications in a very complex systematization. However, this seventh coordinating "consciousness" is identifiable as the basis of the false idea of a self. It is inevitably associated with four afflictions (*kleśa*)—the illusion of selfhood, the actual concept of a self, the pride of self and the love of self—and it operates through the Five Aggregates (*skandha*), now known as touch, feelings, perceptions, mental activity and will.[105] One suspects that these are introduced into the system, albeit in a modified form, as venerable concepts of the earlier period, which cannot be lightly dismissed. Thus they may appear to introduce complications that are unnecessary to the scheme of eight forms of consciousness, which may be listed accordingly:

Basic Consciousness (*ālayavijñāna*) when impure gives rise to:
Agitated Mentation (*kliṣṭa-manas*) with its idea of a self and an exterior world, as experienced through
Mental Consciousness,
Tactile Consciousness,
Gustatory Consciousness,
Olfactory Consciousness,
Auditive Consciousness,
Visual Consciousness.

The Basic Consciousness in its impure state serves as the operative basis for all the other types of consciousness. Continuing like a stream from a beginningless past it contains all the latent "seeds" which mature when attendant conditions are suitable. In some respects it may be compared with our idea of a subconsciousness accepted as the basis of our whole psychological life. But it is more than this, because it contains within itself not only our subjective life, but also the whole objective world which we apprehend through our senses.[106] Thus it produces both the body with its sense-organs and the corresponding manifestations of the objects of sense. However, all is a mere mental fabrication. The Basic Consciousness itself is never stable, for it consists of a succession of *dharmas* which manifest themselves momentarily. Continuity is maintained by the theory of *vāsanās*, the latent after-effects that every manifestation of any *dharma* leave, as it were, in store until conditions for its remanifestation produce the inevitable effect. These "seeds" can remain latent for indefinite periods and there is no limit to their continuing accumulation. Conceived of as a personal

105 See L. de la Vallée Poussin, *Siddhi*, pp. 257ff., and for a full discussion of the seventh consciousness, pp. 225ff.

106 There are different theories on the extent to which the outer world may materialize. See L. de la Vallée Poussin, "Note sur l'Ālayavijñāna" in *Mélanges chinois et bouddhiques* vol. III, pp. 145ff., which precedes an important translated excerpt by É. Lamotte (see Bibliography).

stream of consciousness, this store of latent seeds will produce only those which suit actual circumstances. Thus one born as a human being will see a human world, while in a subsequent rebirth in the animal world only those seeds will mature that are suited to the experience of a dog or a pig or whichever animal it may be. The theory takes for granted the earlier Buddhist teaching that the interminable process of rebirths has gone on for so long that everyone has been born at some time in relationship to everyone else in all the possible spheres of rebirth. The resulting teaching is a curious mingling of mythology and psychological insight, inevitably circumscribed by what was taught in the sūtras as Buddha Word. The most precise statement of the whole theory is given by Vasubandhu in a short work of thirty verses (*Triṃśikā*) with interspersed commentary. It is sufficient for present purposes to quote one verse (no. 15) together with the following explanation and supporting quotation:

> In accordance with circumstances the five kinds of consciousness
> Arise in the Basic Consciousness, whether together or not, like waves from
> water.
>
> *Commentary*: "The five" are the consciousness of sight and so on together with the consciousness of thought, which accompanies them. The consciousness in which they fuse together (*layavijñāna*) is called the Basic Consciousness because it is the bed for the seeds of the five, the consciousness of the eye and the rest and because there is a grasping for (re)birth as the seeds spring up from it. The springing up occurs in all certainty of whatever is ordained by attendant circumstances, and so the idea of a self exists. "Together or not" means simultaneously or in succession, that is to say, like waves on water. It is an illustration of the arising, whether simultaneously or not, of the kinds of consciousness proceeding from the Basic Consciousness. As it is said (in the *Sandhinirmocana Sūtra*): "O Sthiramati, as in the case of a great flood of water, if the circumstances exist for the arising of a single wave, then just a single wave arises; if the circumstances exist for two or three or more waves to arise, then so many more waves arise. Nor is there interruption or cessation of this moving flood of water. It is even so, O Viśamati. If the circumstances exist for the arising of a single state of consciousness, embedded in, depending upon the Basic Consciousness, which is like the flood of water, then just the consciousness of sight (or any of the others singly) will arise. If circumstances exist for the arising of two or three of five states of consciousness, then at once up to five such states will arise.
>
> The Receiving Consciousness is profound and subtle, carrying all seeds
> like a flood,
> Simple folk in their delusion might conceive of it as a Self,
> so it is not taught to them.[107]

This Basic Consciousness (also referred to in the above quotation as fusing consciousness and receiving consciousness) is neither the same nor different from

107 See Sylvain Lévi, *Matériaux*, pp. 103-4, and for the Sanskrit text his *Vijñaptimātratāsiddhi*, pp. 33-4. The quotation used in the commentary will be found in a shorter version in the *Sandhinirmocana Sūtra*, ed. Lamotte, p. 185.

the perfect state of enlightenment as known to the Buddhas and realized by Bodhisattvas on the final stage of their long career. In general the Mind Only school subscribes to the view that a vast series of lives is necessary in order to attain to the truth, but it is doubtless assumed that those who adopt their teachings are already well advanced on this arduous path. The process of enlightenment may be expressed in the simplest of terms as freedom from the duality of the lower states of consciousness, as expressed in subject (apprehender = *grahaka*) and object (apprehended = *grāhya*), resulting in the tranquilizing the Basic Consciousness which is then manifest as Mind Only or Consciousness Only. It is simply a matter of knowing.

> There is no difference whatsoever in any true sense between tranquility
> and the process of rebirth here.
> Yet it is stated that the achievement of tranquility by those of virtuous
> deeds derives from the cessation of rebirth.
>
> *Commentary*: This means that there is no distinguishing at all in an absolute sense between saṃsāra and nirvāṇa. Yet it is said that the attainment of salvation comes from the cessation of rebirth for those of virtuous deeds who practice on the way to salvation. Circumventing wrong views, there are now four verses concerning knowledge in an absolute sense as a counteraction against them:
>
> When a Bodhisattva has accumulated an unlimited stock of knowledge
> and merit,
> As the result of his precision of thought regarding the *dharmas*, he
> penetrates their meaning as consequent upon verbalized reflection.
> Having recognized that their meanings are mere verbalized reflections,
> he is established, as it were, in Mind Only.
> Realizing in his wisdom that there is nothing but Mind, he then advances
> to the nonexistence of Mind.
> Having realized the nonexistence of duality (subject and object),
> the wise one is established in the Dharma-Sphere, where there is no such.
> By the force of his nondiscriminating knowledge, which is always and
> everywhere associated with sameness, their support, that dense evil mass, is
> expelled by the wise one, as poison by its antidote.

These excerpts are taken from one of the main works usually attributed to Asaṅga supported by Maitreya's inspiration. Entitled *Mahāyānasūtrālaṃkāra* ("Adornment of Mahāyāna Sūtras"), it consists of verses interspersed with commentary, suggesting a relationship of master and pupil. A pious fiction attributes the verses to the Bodhisattva Maitreya and the commentary to Asaṅga, but such a format may well be a literary device of a single author. A short section of commentary follows the first of the verses quoted above. The next four are followed by further commentary, not quoted here, but drawn on for the interpretation of the extremely succinct verses.[108] The theme of the whole

[108] Sanskrit edition by Sylvain Lévi, pp. 23-4 (= Ch. VI, vv. 5-9). His French translation (see Bibliography) may be difficult for any reader who does not first familiarize himself with the fixed terminology for technical terms used strictly throughout.

work is the preparation for and the career of a Bodhisattva as practiced in accordance with Mind Only teachings. Allowing for the difference in scope between the career of a Bodhisattva toward Buddhahood and that of an Early Disciple (*śrāvaka*) toward Arhatship, one may note considerable similarity between a Mahāyāna work such as this and any guide to the religious life based on the earlier Buddhist teachings.[109] The Mind Only school was just as much preoccupied with Abhidharma as were ther early sects, and in fact another of Asaṅga's attributed works is a "Compendium of Abhidharma,"[110] which is a considerable collection of well-ordered terminological definitions in the traditional question and answer format. Discriminating knowledge certainly plays a preponderate part in their teachings, although the final aim is the cessation of all discriminating thought.

> For when consciousness is unaware of anything on which to depend,
> Then one abides in Consciousness Only since there is no apprehender
> (subject) in the absence of anything apprehended (object).
> This is Non-Mind, Non-Dependance, Knowledge which is supramundane,
> The Reversal of the Basis now freed of its twofold evil.
> It is the ineffable sphere, unpolluted, firm and good,
> Proclaimed by the Great Sage as blissful, as Salvation-Body, Dharma-Body.

These are the final verses of Vasubandhu's short work of thirty verses (*Triṃśikā*) with interspersed commentary, from which we may perhaps usefully quote concerning the "Reversal of the Basis," as this may help to explain the difference (which is essentially no difference) between saṃsāra and nirvāṇa.

> The Basis is the Basic Consciousness (*ālayavijñāna*) with all the seeds, and as for its Reversal, there comes about a cessation because of the absence of those evil maturing *vāsanā* of duality and thus a reversal because of the presence of competence and the nondual knowledge of the Dharma-Body. But this Reversal of the Basis is obtained by the elimination of what? In reply he says: "freed of its twofold evil," and the two are the evil of the "obstruction from the emotions" (*kleśāvārana*) and the evil of the "obstruction of knowables" (*jñeyā-vāraṇa*). The evil relates to the absence of competence in the Basis, and this again is the seed of the two obstructions of the emotions and knowables.[111]

This quotation introduces two or more technical terms that are constantly met with in this literature and thus are equally common in related Tibetan works. The two kinds of obstruction are in effect the reverse of the two kinds of "stocks" which a Bodhisattva must accumulate, namely stocks of merit and stocks of knowledge. His progress is clearly hindered by nonmeritorious obstructions, desires, passions, annoyances, emotional disturbance of all kinds, as well as by

109 An outstanding work of this kind is Buddhaghosa's *Path of Purification* (*Visuddhimagga*), available in English translation by Bhikkhu Ñāṇamoli.

110 Available in French translation as *Le Compendium de la Super-Doctrine* (*Abhidharma-samuccaya*) *d'Asaṅga*, by Walpola Rahula.

111 See Sylvain Lévi, *Vijñaptimātratāsiddhi*, pp. 43-4 (= *Triṃśikā* vv. 28-30 with excerpts from the commentary). For the French translation, see his *Matériaux*, pp. 121-2.

obstruction relating to matters that should be known and known accurately. Difficulty in fixing suitable terms in English for these two kinds of obstruction is caused by the word *kleśa*, which means literally "anguish" or "distress," but which in Buddhist usage comes to mean whatever is morally distressful and thus in effect "sinful emotions." It is often translated as "passion" but this word tends to be overused, as it provides a ready translation for other Sanskrit words. Because of its special difficulty the early Tibetan translators invented a special term for it (as in the case of *vāsanā*), namely *nyon-mongs*, which is presumably a compound of a word meaning "crazed" (*nyon* = *smyon*) and another meaning "obscured" or "stultified" (*mongs* = *rmongs*). This term simply corresponds in meaning to *kleśa* and has no other use in the Tibetan language. Although quite sure that it comes close enough to the actual meaning of this difficult term, I have tried to avoid the translation "sin" out of deference to a new generation of westernized Buddhists, who react very quickly against the introduction into Buddhist texts of terms with a specialized Christian application. "Affliction" may be regarded as a tolerable translation in that it can refer to anything that upsets the equanimity of the mind, although it misses the moral aspect of the disturbance, which must be understood as also included. The term "sinful" (for *upasaṃkliṣṭa*) becomes essential in some contexts.

d. *The Theory of Buddha-folds*

Despite their differences in the interpretation of the absolute state of buddhahood, more or less negative, more or less positive as the case might be, the two main Mahāyāna schools, the Madhyamaka and the Mind Only agreed that theirs was the superior "way" or "Vehicle" (*yāna*) as distinct from those of the earlier schools, namely the "way of the Disciples" (*śrāvaka*) and the "way of the Lone Buddha" (*pratyekabuddha*), regularly classed together as an "inferior way" (*Hīnayāna*). The Lone Buddha continues to figure in all lists of the various accepted grades of practicing Buddhists, but he has little or no historical significance for the development of the Doctrine. Unlike the Early Disciple who achieves nirvāṇa (thus receiving the title of Arhat or "Worthy") with the help of Śākyamuni's teaching as expounded at the first turning of the Wheel of the Doctrine, a Lone Buddha achieves enlightenment independently and he is not expected to preach the doctrine.[112] The concept was probably an early concession to the fact that enlightened beings could exist outside the Buddhist fold, as constituted by Śākyamuni's early following, but once approved of, the Lone Buddha continued to be referred to as belonging inside the fold. Like earlier mythological concepts, referred to above, the later schools continue to take for granted his existence as a special type of Buddhist practitioner, just as they continued to operate within the same kind of mythology. Among the followers of the Mahāyāna, opinions varied concerning the situation of those

112 It is recounted concerning Mañjuśrī that he appeared as a Pratyekabuddha precisely in order to convert living beings in a previous world age when the Good Law (*saddharma*) was eclipsed for a time, but this may be regarded as an exceptional occurrence. See É. Lamotte, *La concentration de la marche héroïque*, p. 243.

who followed the lesser vehicles. The *Saddharmapuṇḍarīka* insists that there is in reality only one "way" or "vehicle," namely the way leading to the perfect nirvāṇa of a Buddha. Thus there is only one final stage of nirvāṇa for all beings, and Śākyamuni has only taught what appeared as "inferior ways" in order to lead those of lesser accomplishments more gradually into the one and only way of a Bodhisattva. However, we have already noticed in a quotation from the *Vimalakīrtinirdeśasūtra* that a clear distinction is drawn between the "fold of the Buddhas," which is fully involved in the world for the good of living beings, and those "who have achieved a state of fixity in the nonconditioned state," viz. the Arhats. Following such an argument, these last cannot advance toward final enlightement from their inferior state of nirvāṇa, and thus must retrace their steps and follow the one and only way of the Bodhisattva, if they are ever to reach final enlightenment.

That there can be only one final state of nirvāṇa is asserted unequivocally by the *Sandhinirmocanasūtra*, but living beings are graded into different "folds." Having described the process toward final salvation, the Lord continues:

> Even those beings who are of the fold of the *Śrāvakayāna* obtain supreme nirvāṇa with its achievements and happiness by means of this way and this practice; likewise beings who are of the fold of the *Pratyekabuddhayāna* and those who are of the fold of the *Tathāgatas* obtain supreme nirvāṇa with its achievements and happiness by means of this way and this practice. So this is the one pure way, the one purification of Disciples, Lone Buddhas and Bodhisattvas, and there is no other one. But while I teach with such an intention that there is a single way (*yāna*), this does not mean that there do not exist in the (various) realms of living beings, depending on their natures, beings of dull faculties, of medium faculties and of acute faculties. Someone belonging to the fold of the Disciples, who is intent on tranquility alone, even if he possessed the zeal of all Buddhas, is incapable of taking his place on the throne of enlightenment and realizing supreme and perfect enlightenment. If you ask why, it is because he belongs to an inferior fold on account of the smallness of his compassion and his fear of suffering. His compassion being small, he is not at all disposed to further the welfare of living beings. His fear of suffering being great, he is not at all disposed to involve himself in the phenomenal world (literally: in all the contingent activity of elemental impulses, *saṃskāra*). I have not taught that one who is not disposed to further the welfare of living beings or to involve himself in the phenomenal world, can take his place on the throne of enlightenment and realize supreme and perfect enlightenment. But a Disciple who is receptive to enlightenment, him I declare to be a Bodhisattva by integration, because once released from the obstruction of the afflictions and if encouraged by the Buddha, his mind will be freed from the obstructions relating to all that should be known.[113]

The *Laṅkāvatārasūtra* describes no less than five folds, those of Disciples, of Lone Buddhas, of the Tathāgata (i.e., for Bodhisattvas), of uncertain people, and of those who never desire salvation. This last interesting group is said to

113 See the *Sandhinirmocana Sūtra*, pp. 73-4 and p. 198.

consist of two kinds of living beings, those who have given up all accumulating of merit and are thus damned (except for the mercy of the Buddhas) and those Bodhisattvas who have vowed never to enter nirvāṇa on the assumption that there will always be living beings who require their administrations. This sūtra allows for the possibility of a Disciple transferring from his fold to that of the Tathāgata,[114] as also does the *Sandhinirmocana Sūtra*. These appear to be the only two classes of living beings who can aspire to final enlightenment. It is likely that we are concerned here with the practical proposition of the actual conversion of monks who followed the teachings of the earlier sūtras, to the Bodhisattva path, as proclaimed in the Mahāyāna sūtras, for as we noted above Hīnayāna and Mahāyāna monks often lived within the same monastic compound. The third group may well refer to a large number of Buddhist monks who were committed to neither vehicle. There is no clear teaching on such a moot point as this.[115]

e. *The Theory of the Buddha-embryo*

This term *gotra*, which we have translated as "fold" and which is more often translated as "lineage" or "clan," undergoes a remarkable semantic change which may be fairly simply explained. Only those born within the fold of the Buddhas or who succeed in transferring to it, can aspire toward enlightenment or to use the traditional phrase "raise the thought of enlightenment." Thus *gotra* comes to mean the inherent nature of buddhahood that needs to be developed into maturity by the training which a Bodhisattva undergoes on his long career. It thus comes to be identified in another sūtra as the essence of buddhahood, with the result that it can no longer represent categories of any kind:

> As for this *gotra* of the noble ones, there is no action (*karma*) there, no involvement in action, nor is any action performed there by body, speech or mind. This *gotra* cannot be ordered as inferior, as medium or as inferior, and why? It has no distinction because of the single savour of all the *dharmas*. It is void, in that it is void of body and mind, and so it accords with nirvāṇa. It is pure in that it is free of the impurity of all afflictions (*kleśa*). It is never "mine" because it is free from the sameness of existence and nonexistence. It is true in the sense of absolute truth. . . .[116]

Several Mahāyāna sūtras associated with the third turning of the Wheel of the Doctrine contain teachings of a similar kind, according to which the essence of buddhahood exists in living beings in a defiled form like a fragment of gold or a jewel that has fallen into filth and which only needs to be cleaned and polished

114 See the *Laṅkāvatāra Sūtra*, Vaidya's text p. 29, ll. 19ff., and Suzuki's translation, pp. 58-60.

115 The matter is treated in more detail in the *Ratnagotravibhāga* (see below). See Takasaki's translation, pp. 201-7 and again pp. 222-4. The term *gotra* is not used in this work in the meaning of "fold" or even of "lineage," as it assumes the special meaning that will be explained immediately. Thus, these different categories of people are no longer categorized as *gotra*.

116 Translated from the *Kāśyapaparivarta Sūtra*, ed. von Staël-Holstein, 103-4 (p. 151f.).

for its pristine brightness to shine forth.[117] An authoritative scholastic work on the subject is a treatise consisting of verses and interspersed commentary attributed like several other works already mentioned above, to the Bodhisattva Maitreya and his devotee Asaṅga and entitled *Ratnagotravibhāga* ("A Study of the Jewel Enclosure").[118] It differs from the other works attributed to this illustrious pair in that it is not concerned with theories of a Basic Consciousness and the other derivative aspects of consciousness, which have been described above. Whereas these are predominantly investigations into the nature of phenomenal existence, this last study proclaims the nature of the very essence of buddhahood, which is the goal of this whole class of literature. In that the essence of buddhahood is recognized as Mind in its pure pristine state, there exists a fundamental connection between all these works, which are associated with the third turning of the Wheel, however justified may be the doubts that are expressed concerning the attribution of authorship to the various treatises. Here we must content ourselves with a clarification of the main terms and a few quotations in illustration of the actual teaching.

The term *gotra*, translated earlier as "fold," is perhaps suitably translated in the changed context as "enclosure," since this English word has the useful double meaning of both that which encloses, as does a fold, and that which is enclosed. A similar shift in meaning may well explain the use of *gotra* as now synonymous with the essence of buddhahood. The Sanskrit term used for "essence" in this particular sense is *garbha*, which normally means "womb" or "embryo." Both these words provide tolerable translations in suitable contexts, but "essence" (Tibetan: *snying-po*) is a satisfactory translation. For the equation of these various terms we may now quote from the *Ratnagotravibhāga*:

> With regard to Suchness (*tathatā*) in its defiled state it has been said that "All beings are of the essence of buddhahood," but what can this mean?
> Because of the inclusion of the host of living beings in the Buddha-Knowledge,
> Because of the nonduality of their (defilement and) nondefilement primordially,
> Because of the identification of the fruit (of their practice) in the Buddha-enclosure,
> All embodied beings are said to be of the essence of buddhahood.
> Because of the nondifferentiation of Suchness and the consequent amplitude of the Buddha-body, also because of the Buddha-enclosure,
> All embodied beings are always of the essence of buddhahood.

[117] Two major works on this whole subject have appeared in recent years, both by D. S. Ruegg: *La théorie du Tathāgatagarbha et du Gotra*, and *Le traité du Tathāgatagarbha de Bu-ston Rin-po-che*. The introduction to the latter work (pp. 7-18) discusses the various Mahāyāna sūtras, mainly as known from quotations, used in justification of these teachings.

[118] The Sanskrit text was published by E. H. Johnstone in Patna, 1950. An English translation by Jikido Takasaki, published in the Rome Oriental Series no. XXIII is also available. See also E. Obermiller in the Bibliography. The Tibetan title of the work corresponds to a Sanskrit title of *Uttara-tantra-śāstra* ("Treatise on Higher Tantra").

> In short it is said by the Lord by means of a threefold argument that "All beings are of the essence of buddhahood": because of the amplitude of the Dharma-body of the Buddha in all living beings, because of the nondifferentiation of Suchness of the Buddha and because of existence of the Buddha-enclosure.[119]

Elsewhere it is shown how the Buddha-enclosure provides the basis for the religious life, and we may note that the term Buddha-sphere (*Buddha-dhātu*) is used with identical meaning:

> If there were no Buddha-sphere, there would be no aversion to the misery (of saṃsāra),
> So there would be no wish, no desire, no aspiration for nirvāṇa.
> So it is said: "If there were no Buddha-essence, O Lord, there would be no aversion to suffering or wish for nirvāṇa or any such desire or aspiration." In short it is stated that even for those beings who are committed to wrong views the Buddha-sphere, the Pure Enclosure, is the basis for a twofold necessity; it produces aversion to saṃsāra based on insight into the evil of its misery and it arouses the desire for nirvāṇa based on insight into the gloriousness of bliss.[120]

From the last passage it would seem clear that the Buddha-enclosure (*gotra*), which is synonymous with the Buddha-essence (or embryo = *garbha*), also known as the Buddha-sphere (*dhātu*), provides the essential basis for "raising the thought toward enlightenment" and so embarking upon a Bodhisattva's career, the sole means of achieving buddhahood. If one proclaims, as some now proclaim, that all living beings are capable eventually of attaining buddhahood, then logically the Buddha-essence must be present in all living beings, however much covered and obscured it may be.

> Like the Buddha in a wretched lotus-flower, or honey in its comb,
> like grain in the husk, or gold in the dirt,
> like treasure in the ground, or a green shoot (dormant) in a seed,
> like the Buddha-nature in the ragged garment (of an ascetic),
> like a king-to-be in a foul female womb,
> like a precious image in its clay mould,
> even so is the Buddha-sphere to be found in living beings,
> obscured with the dirt of accidental afflictions.[121]

In so far as all the terms just listed refer to the quiddity (*tattva*) of perfect enlightenment, so often referred to as Suchness (*tathātā*) in order to avoid more compromising terminology, it follows that Suchness itself is not only pure but also involved in impurity. This accords entirely with the Maḥāyāna view that

119 *Ratnagotravibhāga*, ed. Johnston, p. 25, ll. 18ff., Takasaki, pp. 197-8.

120 *Ibid.*, p. 35, ll. 18ff., Takasaki, pp. 221-2. My translation differs from his especially in the translation of terms previously analyzed.

121 *Ibid.*, p. 59, ll. 16ff., Takasaki, pp. 268-9. According to the Commentary the "Buddha-nature in a ragged garment" refers to a Buddha-image wrapped up in a filthy cloth. It may equally well be the Buddha-nature concealed within a rag-clad ascetic.

there is no essential difference between nirvāṇa and saṃsāra.

As Suchness may be polluted, so it is also pure, and as pure
it possesses the Qualities of a Buddha, the Actions of a Conqueror.
Being the realm of the seers of absolute truth and the source
of the immaculate Three Jewels (Buddha, Doctrine and Community).
What is clarified by this?
The Enclosure of these Three Jewels is the realm of the seers of the absolute;
It is unimaginable from four points of view in accordance with four
kinds of reasoning.

Here polluted Suchness refers to the Enclosure unreleased from its cover of afflictions, being the Buddha-essence, while pure Suchness is characterized by the Reversal of the Basis in the Buddha-stage, being the Dharma-body of the Tathāgata. Pure Buddha-qualities refer to the supramundane Buddha-*dharmas*, the Ten Powers (of a Buddha) and so on, occurring in the Dharma-body of a Tathāgata as characterized by the Reversal of the Basis. The Actions of a Conqueror refer to that supreme spontaneous activity of the Buddha-*dharmas*, viz., the Ten Powers etc., which consists in the uninterrupted recounting of announcements about Bodhisattvas, unchanging, unceasing, unending. This is said to be the realm of the omniscient ones because once again these four points, as listed, are unimaginable in accordance with four kinds of reasoning. With which four?

Because of the pairing of purity and the sinful state,
Because of defilement of the totally sinless state,
Because there is nowhere that (Buddha-)*dharmas* are not inherent,
Because of their spontaneous and undiscriminating character.[122]

A long commentarial passage elucidates all these reasonings, the gist of which is to argue the immanence of the essence of Buddhahood in all realms of phenomenal existence. Thus (1) saṃsāra and nirvāṇa are effectively paired; (2) the pure Buddha-essence is obscured in the afflicted (= sinful) state of ordinary living beings; (3) yet the Buddha-qualities are everywhere available; and (4) the Actions of a Buddha despite their apparent multiplicity in accordance with the needs of living beings transcend all notions of discrimination. In short what is finally unimaginable is the pairing of transcendence and immanence, and Buddhists are not the only ones who have wrestled with what is, in effect, a theological problem, even if one avoids, as they do, the assertion of supreme being.

The dichotomy of transcendence and immanence is expressed in terms of Mind as "pristine purity" (*prakṛtiviśuddhi*) and Mind pervaded by "accident defilement" (*āgantuka-mala*) usually defined as the two kinds of obstructions, those relating to the afflictions (*kleśa*) and those relating to what should be known (*jñeya*). Defiled Mind thus corresponds to the Basic Consciousness (*ālaya-vijñāna*) as described above, while pure translucent Mind corresponds to the Reversal of the Basis in the stage of buddhahood. Thus it is by no means illogical

122 *Ibid.*, p. 21, ll. 3ff., Takasaki, pp. 186-8. On the use of "sin" for *kleśa* see p. 109 above.

that certain passages in the *Laṅkāvatārasūtra* should identify the Buddha-essence (*Tathāgata-garbha*) with Basic Consciousness itself.[123] On the one hand the Buddha-essence must be identified with Pure Mind, albeit involved in defilement, and on the other hand it is Basic Consciousness in its reversal which is identified with the supreme enlightenment of buddhahood. Thus an overall identification is inevitable, while the "unimaginable character" of the identifying of purity and impurity, nirvāṇa and saṃsāra, remains. Its unimaginable character corresponds to the undetermined character of certain basic questions in the earlier teachings.[124]

f. *The Theory of Buddha-bodies*

Before bringing to an end this survey of doctrine relating to the third turning of the Wheel, there remains one other important formulation that may be described rather briefly, although the development of these particular teachings was gradual and fairly complex. The early followers of Śākyamuni soon began to formulate theories of two conceivable Buddha-bodies. There was the Body of Form or Maturation (*rūpakāya* or *vipākakāya*), referring to any kind of body assumed by a Buddha in the phenomenal world, and there was the Dharma-Body, representing from one point of view the sum total of the Buddha-Doctrine and from another the absolute supramundane state into which a Buddha passed on entering final nirvāṇa. According to early Buddhist scholasticism this consisted of pure Buddha-*dharmas* (in the sense of "elements" or "impulses"), and this theory was retained in the Mind Only school since they retained, in a rather changed form as already noted, the whole theory of *dharmas*. Correspondingly, our last quotation refers to supramundane Buddha-*dharmas*, the Ten Powers and so on.[125]

Early Perfection of Wisdom teachings and other early Mahāyāna sūtras require no development in the doctrine of Buddha-bodies, because here everything that is not demonstrable as absolute truth falls within the category of relative or spurious truth and it is here that all kinds of Buddha-manifestations belong without the need for the drawing of distinctions. At the same time there were already in existence even from the earliest times notions of other possible Buddha-bodies, even if scholastic definition was lacking.[126] Thus according to early legends Śākyamuni visited his mother in the heavens, assuming for this purpose a "mind-made" (*manomaya*) body. Also the various magical powers with which not only he himself but also any Early Disciple who had achieved nirvāṇa (thus becoming an Arhat) were credited included the ability to produce replicas of one's bodily form at will. Furthermore, we have already noted that some early Mahāyāna sūtras identified all the many Buddhas who taught in

123 *Laṅkāvatāra sūtra*, Suzuki's translation, pp. 190, 193, 203-4, etc.

124 See "undetermined matters" in the Index.

125 For a brief account of the Buddha-*dharmas*, see Har Dayal, *Bodhisattva Doctrine*, pp. 19-29.

126 On this subject, see L. de la Vallée Poussin, *Siddhi*, pp. 762ff. for appendix on "Les corps du Bouddha." One may also refer to N. Dutt, *Mahāyāna Buddhism*, ch. V, pp. 141ff.

myriads of Buddha-fields with a one and only Buddha, envisaged as Śākyamuni himself. Thus scholarly speculation and eventual formulation of these various ideas became inevitable. In some sūtras, such as the *Laṅkāvatāra*, ideas on the subject seem to be very confused, but in such cases we are dealing with composite works, where different popular traditions exist side by side.[127] A fairly precise formulation was finally evolved by scholars of the Mind Only school, and since their most important treatises are usually attributed to Asaṅga, the scheme of three main types of Buddha-body may be credited to him:

1. Dharma-body or Self-Existent (*svabhāvika*) Body (*kāya*)
2. Glorious Body (*saṃbhoga-kāya*)
3. Transformation Body (*nirmāṇa-kāya*).

Briefly stated, the Dharma-Body is the Body of the Dharma-sphere (*dharma-dhātu*) in the traditional sense of the totality of purified elements (*dharmas*) and the sum-total of the Buddha-Word. It is beyond diversity and is the same for all Buddhas. The Glorious Body is manifold in manifestation and represents the form in which Buddhas teach in pure Buddha-fields. The Transformation Body is the one assumed in any realm of phenomenal existence for the purpose of instructing and saving living beings. It also includes Buddha-images as supports for faith in the Doctrine.[128] One may note the existence of parallel sets of four Buddha-Bodies, usually involving two types of "Glorious Body," a "self-enjoyment-body" (*svasaṃbhoga-kāya*) and an "enjoyment-body for others" (*parasaṃbhoga-kāya*). The term "enjoyment body," which is here interpreted as "Glorious Body," derives from the idea of enjoying the benefits of the practice of the Perfections on the way toward buddhahood.[129] Its acquisition is one of the fruits of such practice, and this kind of Body is in fact assumed by Bodhisattvas in their final stage. At a later stage the Self-Existent Body comes to be distinguished from the Dharma-body in that it is regarded as absolutely transcendent, thus resulting in a different set of four Buddha-bodies, which is often met with in tantric works (see pp. 250-1).

[127] See the *Laṅkāvatāra Sūtra*, Suzuki's translation, pp. 51-2, 118-9, 256.

[128] For Asaṅga's definition see the *Mahāyāna-Sūtralaṃkāra*, ed. Sylvain Lévi, pp. 44-5 (IX, vv. 59-66), and the French translation, pp. 86-8. See also Takasaki, *Ratnagotravibhāga*, pp. 288-90.

[129] E.g., see the *Sandhinirmocana Sūtra*, ed. Lamotte, pp. 136 and 247. This sūtra remains generally content with the older formulation of two Buddha-bodies, referred to as Dharma-body and Transformation Body (*nirmāṇa-kāya*). See pp. 162-3 and 268-9, where it is taught that only a Buddha (not a *śrāvaka* or *pratyekabuddha*) can send forth such "transformation bodies."

III
TANTRIC BUDDHISM

1. CONNECTIONS WITH THE CONVENTIONAL MAHĀYĀNA

With the effective canonization of a vast variety of works of ritual and yoga-practice, known as *tantras*, we enter upon the final astounding phase in the history of Buddhism. It is astounding for two reasons, doctrinal and moral, and by explaining these we shall be able to show how extraordinary a *tour de force* was involved in the conversion of tantric rituals to orthodox Buddhist use. That they were so converted, there can be no doubt, for generations of serious Tibetan scholars, translators and commentators, not to mention devout men of religion, bear witness to this fact. At the same time it must be fairly recognized that very few scholars outside the Indo-Tibetan tradition of interpretation have felt able to accept this last Buddhist phase in its entirety. Certainly Chinese and Japanese Buddhists have found much canonical tantric material objectionable, and have either employed evasive translations or have treated whole texts as later corruptions.[1] More recently, Western and modern Indian scholars have freely attributed to tantric developments the gradual decline of Buddhism in India from the eighth to the thirteenth centuries A.D., as though it had allowed itself to be submerged indistinguishably into forms of popular Hinduism. There is considerable evidence against such a view. While it is true that Buddhism remained throughout its whole history in the land of its origin dependent upon other Indian religious movements (and in tracing the origins of tantric Buddhism we shall deal with this point in more detail), it clearly remained self-consciously distinct right up to its very last days. This is proved by the existence of its great monasteries and smaller religious centers that continued to flourish as specifically Buddhist establishments until they were destroyed in one region after another, as Moslem conquerors steadily advanced eastward. It is proved more than anything else by the vast Buddhist literature that was being produced in these centers of learning up to the last days and of which so much has been preserved in Tibetan translations. Whatever features they have in common,

[1] R. Tajima in his *Étude sur le Mahāvairocana-Sūtra*, observes: "Esoteric teachings were introduced into Tibet after their establishment in China. As for their links, we have historical proofs that they derived principally from Vikramaśīla as their center. On the one hand research work done on the Tibetan versions of the scriptures are valuable for the texts themselves; but one notes that the strange esoteric teachings of Lamaist religion are in fact rather far from the Buddha's teachings. Thus one should never lose sight of the considerable distance separating Chinese esotericism, from which derives the whole of Japanese Shingon, from that of Tibet" (p. 7). For a further quotation from R. Tajima see section III.6.b below.

Buddhist tantras are quite distinct from Hindu tantras, and there was never any confusion in their transmission. It is an extraordinary fact that Buddhism has absorbed tantric theories and practices, however scandalous some of them may appear outwardly, strangely enriching itself thereby. This was recognized long ago by one of the greatest of Western Buddhist scholars, namely Louis de la Vallée Poussin. After summarizing the contradictions of earlier orthodox teachings that these texts seem to imply, he continues:

> One point seems to me free of doubt: the virtue of the ceremonies is not properly speaking thaumaturgical; it resides entirely in the spiritual state which the faithful practitioner realizes (*utpādayati*) under the influence of the dogma that is meditated or by the exterior excitation of the ritual. The mystique of our tantras can easily be reduced to the fundamental principles of the Mind Only school or of the Madhyamakas. The axis of religious thought is not displaced: tantrism has become Buddhist; without denying essential dogma Buddhism has annexed a whole new province. We shall understand one day the secret of the long elaboration which removed the original antagonism of so many factors of the Tantra-yāna. The theologians, making use of all the finds of doctrinal thought, have constituted a scholarly theory of popular religion; they were able to exteriorize this theory and render it full of life by miracles of the boldest symbolism, filling space with divine and hallucinatory visions.[2]

The Tibetans, who were the full inheritors of the whole Indian Buddhist tradition in the various forms in which it existed in India up to the thirteenth century, followed their Indian masters in treating the tantras, to which they were introduced, as authoritative Buddhist works, canonically valid as Buddha Word just as much as were the Mahāyāna sūtras. When they finalized the contents of their own canon in the thirteenth century, they strictly excluded from the Tantra section certain tantras for the existence of which no direct Indian authority in the form of a Sanskrit original or other acceptable Indian original could be proved. It is likely that these canonical tantras were quite as much studied in the great Indian Buddhist monasteries as were the sūtras, and thus the Tibetans took as granted what was then already an Indian Buddhist assumption, that there were in general two approaches toward buddhahood, the slower but surer way as taught in the Mahāyāna sūtras, i.e., the way of the Bodhisattva, as described above, and the risky way as taught in the tantras, which could result in buddhahood in this very life, but which employed methods which only those of strong faculties should dare to use. So the Mahāyāna could be classified as twofold, as the System of Perfections (*Pāramitānaya*) and the System of Formulas (*Mantranaya*), the latter seemingly being the primary name under which the tantras were grouped. Its followers claim that "It is superior because of freedom from confusion due to singleness of meaning, because of its many methods, because it is not difficult to do and because of its suitability for those

[2] L. de la Vallée Poussin, *Bouddhisme, études et matériaux*, pp. 174-5.

with keen senses."[3] However, despite its general acceptance by later Buddhists, Indian, Nepalese and Tibetan, and to quite a considerable extent by the Chinese and Japanese as well as by many Buddhist groups throughout Southeast Asia, the whole tantric system was not only a latecomer, but also hard to accommodate formally with the rest of the teachings, traditionally attributed to Śākyamuni Buddha.

It has been related in some detail in the previous chapter how the scriptures of later Indian Buddhism were arranged as a series of three turnings of the Wheel of the Doctrine by Śākyamuni himself, and it may be noteowrthy that the Tibetan historian Bu-ston (1290-1364) who completed the great work of compiling the contents of the Tibetan Buddhist Canon with its enormous collection of tantras, all supposedly Buddha Word, nevertheless limits his account of Śākyamuni's teaching, as given in his history, to the sūtras that were traditionally promulgated with the three turnings of the Wheel.[4] Since Tibetan historians would normally reproduce Indian historical and legendary material, when treating of such matters, this suggests that the tantras were never formally incorporated into any Indian Buddhist canonical groupings, and it was left to the compilers and promulgators of these works to give some apparent proof of authority. Efforts were certainly made to arrange the vast variety of tantras into convenient categories, of which the four main ones came to be accepted as:

Action Tantras (*kriyā-tantra*)
Performance Tantras (*caryā-tantra*)
Yoga Tantras (*yoga-tantra*)
Supreme Yoga Tantras (*anuttarayoga-tantra*).[5]

Those of the first two categories, in so far as they are concerned with the correct recitation of magical formulas for the warding off of various ills and for the gaining of merit especially from the worship of relics and the building and repair of stūpas, are easily attributed to Śākyamuni during the course of his last life on earth, especially as this included his visit to the Heaven of the Thirty-three Gods. His own miraculous powers were an accepted part of the earliest traditions concerning his teaching and thus there need be nothing incongruous in his giving instructions in magical incantations of a beneficial kind to his lay converts, although he might be expected to discourage the exhibition of such

[3] From Advayavajra's *Tattvaratnāvalī* as published in the *Advayavajrasaṃgraha*, p. 21, ll. 12-13.

[4] A more popular tradition as reflected in the *Padma Thang-yig* (see Toussaint's translation, pp. 124-5) clearly refers to the third turning as the last *'khor-lo tha-ma* (f.63a[6] of Tibetan block-print), but then adds a fourth turning devoted to "exoteric tantras and magical rites" (*phyi-rgyud kriyā'i chos*). In the list that is given of such texts mainly taught "in the Willow Grove and on the Thunderbolt-Peak in Malaya," the Yoga Tantras are named separately as having been taught by the Nairañjana River and in the Highest Heaven (thus in agreement with an Indian tradition reproduced immediately below). As for the "esoteric supreme Vajrayāna" (*nang-pa bla-med rdo-rje-theg-pa*) Śākyamuni is said to have announced formally: "Vajrapāṇi, you teach!" and then to have not said a word.

[5] For the convenience of readers who are already acquainted with it, it seems best to accept provisionally this conventional fourfold arrangement, leaving its rather arbitrary nature to be clarified later. See the Index under Tantras, various classifications.

powers by monks who were supposed to be intent on a more serious objective. The distinction between mundane and supramundane achievements is a very old one in Buddhism and both continue to be practiced throughout the whole history of the doctrine at all stages of its development.

In the case of the third category of tantras there was an apparent difficulty in attributing these to Śākyamuni unless it could be shown at the same time that he had himself realized at the time of his enlightenment the type of ritual yoga with which these works are primarily concerned. No one would dispute that he had taught sūtras suitable to the Early Disciples (the first turning of the Wheel), and the followers of the Mahāyāna, as represented by the Perfection of Wisdom literature, could claim with justification that the Madhyamaka teachings (the second turning) and the Mind Only teachings (the third turning) represented the essence of his teaching as realized by him throughout his long career of a Bodhisattva and in his absolute state of perfect buddhahood. However, the Yoga Tantras taught that buddhahood could be achieved through a highly ritualized series of consecrations, and there was no traditional authority for this in the case of Śākyamuni's enlightenment. Thus it had to be deliberately supplied by what can only be described as a *tour de force*. The main tantra of this class, entitled *Sarva-tathāgata-tattva-saṃgraha* ("Symposium of Truth of All the Buddhas"), is supposedly promulgated by Śākyamuni, also referred to as "Resplendent" (Vairocana), in the palace of the king of gods in the Highest Heaven understood to be on the summit of Mount Meru. It opens with a description of Śākyamuni's enlightenment achieved through consecrations (see section III.13.f below); it is reenacted at the end through the agency of Vajrapāṇi, of whom more will be said below; then the text relates:

> As soon as he was fully enlightened in the adamantine state (*vajra*) of Body, Speech and Mind of all Buddhas, knowing himself as embodying all Buddhas, he came from the summit of Mount Meru to the Place of Enlightenment and in order to conform to the way of the world he took some dry grass (and seated himself) under the Tree of Enlightenment, saying:
>
> Oho! the best of teachings for oneself and for the good of living beings
> that they may remain firm from their conversion against false doctrine!
> O may one win the Buddha state for the sake of purifying with the light
> of knowledge the world that cannot be converted else with its blindness
> of false views.[6]

Śākyamuni's situation is also elaborated by the commentaries.[7] His final progress toward buddhahood is marked in the traditional accounts by four ever higher stages of "inner composure" (*samādhi*), but now to suit this later theory the process is interrupted at this point by the Buddhas of the Ten Directions, who

6 Yamada's edition of the Sanskrit text of the *Sarva-tathāgata-tattva-saṃgraha*, p. 531. Because of the rather cumbersome nature of this title we shall refer to it hereafter in footnotes as STTS and in the main text as the "Symposium of Truth."

7 E.g., see mKhas-grub-rje's *Fundamentals of the Buddhist Tantras*, ed. Lessing and Wayman, pp. 28-35.

arouse him from his composure by snapping their fingers and announcing: "You cannot become a perfected Buddha just by this inner composure." Then leaving his physical body on the banks of the Nairañjana River, they conducted his mind-made body to the Highest Heaven, where they bestowed upon him the preliminary consecrations, followed by the five stages of Perfect Enlightenment (*abhisaṃbodhi*) as marked by five formulas of self-consecration.[8] Thus he became the perfected Buddha, the Great Vairocana, and having taught the Yoga Tantras on the summit of Mount Meru, he descended to the everyday world, took possession of his physical body, defeated Māra, the Evil One, and so the earlier traditional account of his ministry follows.

If it was possible by such a manipulation of the earlier tradition to fit the third category of tantras into Śākyamuni's curriculum, the fourth category of Supreme Yoga Tantras (*anuttarayoga-tantra*) might appear at first sight to be altogether unadaptable. These are the tantras where the four main consecrations consist of ritualized performance of the sexual act of union, and as for the place of their promulgation, it is usually announced in the opening verse: "Thus have I heard: at one time the Lord reposed in the vaginas of the *Vajra*-maidens—the heart of the Body, Speech and Mind of all Buddhas."[9] It may be fair to observe that in this fourth category the Lord is seldom named specifically as Śākyamuni, but the connection exists in so far as he embodies all Buddhas, in this case through his hypostasis as the Buddha Imperturbable (*Akṣobhya*), with whom such great tantric Lords as Heruka, Hevajra and Caṇḍamahāroṣaṇa are identified. But while it need not be disputed that Śākyamuni had taught strict celibacy, certainly in his first turning of the Wheel, it could be argued that his own activities as a Bodhisattva, not least of all his life in the harem and his marriage, prepared him for the act of renunciation leading to final enlightenment.[10] Commentators on Supreme Yoga Tantras have devised a modified version of the account of his enlightenment, as described in the Yoga Tantra "Symposium of Truth" and elsewhere, introducing a feminine partner on the scene in the form of "the daughter of the gods Tilottamā," thus justifying in his name the use of sexual yoga.[11] But there appears to be no authority for this in the actual tantras of that class, and whereas the whole setting of the Yoga Tantras accords with their story, the setting of Supreme Yoga Tantras scarcely accords at all.

Such haphazard attempts at bringing the tantras inside the Buddhist tradition, which had continued to center around Śākyamuni Buddha, however many other Buddha- and Bodhisattva-names had been introduced during the more conventional Mahāyāna period, tend to emphasize the extraneous nature of much tantric teaching. However, in so far as this last Indian Buddhist phase is

8 For the physical body (*vipākakāya*) and the mind-made body (*manomayakāya*) see p. 115.

9 Thus begin both the *Guhyasamāja* and the *Hevajra Tantras*, both available in their Buddhist Sanskrit editions. In my translation of the *Hevajra Tantra* I have tended to gloss over such imagery, as indeed so often do the Tibetans.

10 See L. de la Vallée Poussin, *Bouddhisme, études et matériaux*, pp. 143-5.

11 See mKhas-grub-rje, *op. cit.*, pp. 36-9.

known as the System of Formulas (*Mantranaya*) and is envisaged together with the System of Perfections (*Pāramitānaya*) as an acceptable part of Mahāyāna practice, there need be no break in the Buddhist tradition, which as we have noted before, continued to develop against a more general Indian (Hindu) background of religious beliefs and practices. As protective formulas or talismanic words, mantras occur in the Theravādin canon, where their appearance has probably been reduced to a minimum. It is likely that the Mahāsāṃghikas who separated from the Theravādins at an early date, included in their collection of scriptures a special section devoted to formulas of one kind or another.[12] There is no lack of them in Mahāyāna sūtras, where they are usually bestowed upon the faithful by well-disposed divinities as protective spells. The *Karuṇāpuṇḍarīka Sūtra* contains as its second chapter a whole collection of such formulas listed as "bases for confidence" (*adhimuktipadaṃ*) in the acquisition of the various accomplishments demanded of a Bodhisattva, the four applications of mindfulness, the four determined efforts, the four magical powers, etc.[13] They are known in this text as *dhāraṇī*, which should properly refer to a short mnemonic string of words, holding (the term derives from a Sanskrit root meaning "to hold") the meaning succinctly of an intention which in normal speech would need to be much more prolix. *Mantra* is a more general term, comprising a vast range of ejaculations of a fixed traditional form, achieving their powerful effect within the context of a strictly controlled ritual usage.[14] Those easiest to explain are those which are clearly translatable, such as OṂ VAJRATMAKO 'HAM = "I am verily adamantine," but it must be conceded that even when the words themselves are normally intelligible, such a mantra can have no essential meaning outside the prescribed ritual. Thus normal intelligibility is of secondary concern. What is primary is the spontaneous significance of a particular mantra to those who have been initiated into its proper use. Thus not only can the various stages of a ritual be induced to occur actually by those taking part in accordance with the appropriate mantras, but one who knows the mantras can enact the same ritual mentally, usually to the accompaniment of traditionally fixed hand-gestures (*mudrā*).[15]

We have already mentioned the distinction that is drawn between mundane and supramundane powers, viz. those concerned with protection or personal benefit of one kind or another in this world, and those concerned with the progress toward enlightenment. The use of mantras for both purposes is very ancient in India, going back to Vedic times, but while Śākyamuni and his early followers may well have accepted their use for the benefit of the faithful in this life, their use for a higher religious purpose would have been contrary to the

[12] See L. de la Vallée Poussin, *op. cit.*, pp. 58, 67.

[13] See Yamada's edition, London, 1968, pp. 14-50, and also the Appendix to his Volume I.

[14] One should refer to the excellent chapter on "Mantras" in Agehananda Bharati's *The Tantric Tradition*, pp. 101-63.

[15] Examples of mantras and *mudrās* conveniently arranged in parallel will be found in Stephan Beyer, *The Cult of Tārā*, pp. 143ff., and also in Jeffrey Hopkin's *The Yoga of Tibet*, pp. 77ff.

whole tenor of Buddhist doctrine, in so far as its practice was based upon a strict moral code (*śīla*), mental composure (*samādhi*) and wisdom (*prajñā*), involving a kind of analytical knowledge of the whole nature of existence according to the theory of elements (*dharmas*). This rationalizing approach toward the solution of the mysteries of existence (saṃsāra) was continued right through the Mahāyāna period by the followers of the Mind Only school, who elaborated, as we have already seen, an even more complex theory of elements, while accepting the main thesis repeated interminably in the Perfection of Wisdom literature and elaborated by Nāgārjuna and his school, that there is no essential difference between saṃsāra and nirvāṇa, in that both are void (*śūnya*) in their self-nature, which becomes therefore an absence of self-nature. We have already commented upon the remarkable fact that this thesis, which reduces everything to a state of universal relativity, was accompanied by a doctrine that promoted the long career of the self-sacrificing Bodhisattva, who strives over aeons of time through innumerable rebirths toward the state of final buddhahood, which the best of his sort never enter in so far as they continue to preoccupy themselves with helping others toward the objective, which is equally well described as a nonobjective. The career of the Bodhisattva remains certainly one of the noblest religious aspirations of mankind. It was vociferously proclaimed as such, as well as taken up in all seriousness by those later followers of Śākyamuni in whom the Thought of Enlightenment (*bodhicitta*) became active. At the same time it is easily understandable that such a doctrine of universal relativity should open the way to less arduous methods of achieving enlightenment. The question may well be posed, what is the essential difference between achieving enlightenment in the present life and that of achieving it after innumerable rebirths, all of which in their self-nature are essentially void? The whole notion of progress in the religious life is entirely relative to any result achieved, and progressive methods may be quick or slow, depending upon the aptitude of the practitioner. Moreover, since there is no difference between saṃsāra and nirvāṇa in any ultimate sense, between the state of ignorance and the state of knowledge, where lies the difference except in the conviction of enlightenment achieved by a kind of psychophysical switch applied to one's whole being? It was never doubted that the training of the whole person, envisaged under the traditional trilogy of body, speech and mind, was necessary in order to achieve the desired state of enlightenment or "release" or whatever term might be used in yogic circles, but the kind of training to be used was by now an open question these thousand years and more after Śākyamuni had first preached his doctrine. It was already agreed by the majority of those who considered themselves his faithful followers that he had taught various doctrines to suit the aptitudes of potential converts by turning the Wheel of the Doctrine three times, and were there not other theories and practices which might with equal justification be acceptable, if they were only proved valid by the results achieved? There was at the same time no need for Buddhists to invent new theories and experiment with new practices, as these were already available in the general Indian (Hindu) religious life, in which Śākyamuni's first teachings had their origins and where the Buddhist Doctrine had continued to develop and enrich itself. It separated itself from the religious life around only in so far as its followers might hold fast to certain essential teachings and practices, e.g., the doctrine of "no self," of rebirth and of salvation from rebirth, the practice of celibacy and a regulated monastic discipline, and the continuance of a doctrinal tradition that would clarify the essential differences between Buddhism as a self-contained religion and the many other forms of religion in India going under the more or less general name of Hinduism.

All these distinctive features continue, and Buddhism in India clearly remains a separate religion right up to its last days in the land of its origin, but this does not mean that it was not at the same time open all the time to influences from the more general Hindu religious world. The Mahāyāna teachings concerning the career of the Bodhisattva continued to uphold the desirability of monastic life under the traditional forms of religious discipline (*vinaya*), and it is significant that it is precisely this traditional form of Buddhism that became the basis of the new religion in Tibet and indeed of the whole of Tibetan society until the mid-twentieth century. At the same time the Mahāyāna clearly taught that layfolk were no longer to be regarded at best as the meritorious supporters of the monks, thereby merely gaining for themselves a better state of rebirth in another life. It was recognized that they could be the equal of the monks in their religious striving toward enlightenment, and it was largely a matter of personal decision based upon the circumstances of life whether one might be layman or monk. The practice of yoga was an essential part of Indian religious life, accepted as a matter of course by all Buddhists, and much of it could be practiced as well by married laymen as by celibate monks. So much has been written about yoga, that a short quotation should be sufficient to assist any reader who remains vague about what is meant by the term.

> Yoga finds its classical expression in the Sūtras of Patañjali, written somewhere between A.D. 300 and 500. The author was a compiler, a systematizer, rather than an original thinker. While the *Sūtras may* be interested in speculation as such, still, they are based upon methods of *action*, disciplined actions, with their concomitant supernatural powers associated with self-hypnotism and the like. The superior powers of the Yogī are simply those of attaining the highest goal, release; such powers *as such* being viewed as unworthy of the struggle.
>
> The aims of Yoga, in Patañjali's sense, may be spoken of as controls of various kinds, a graded series of disciplines, directed towards steadying the mind; gradually advancing stages of rigid control of body and mind; the stoppage of all movement and all thought—that the soul be absorbed in itself, loosing the sense of duality, of subject and object; immediate perception; ultimately, prolonged, fixed attention to the point where the mental processes are stopped absolutely.
>
> But there is ancillary to the mental discipline, a long period of preparatory action, organized according to a well-developed, progressive plan. In the preliminary stages of the preparation for the fixing of the attention, there are

purifying processes to be carried out, first with stress laid upon external means, then, after these have been mastered, with recourse to the internal controls.[16]

It is not without significance that whereas the early Buddhist literature refers to serious practitioners as *bhikṣus* or *arhats* and the Mahāyāna literature refers to them as *bodhisattvas*, already in the later Mahāyāna literature the term *yogin* makes its appearance, and from now on is used ever more frequently, embracing, as it does, monks as well as laymen. We find it already in the *Ratnagotravibhāga*, from which quotations have been taken in the previous chapter:

Without beginning, middle or end, indivisible, nondual,
Thrice liberated (from emotional disturbance, defective knowledge and faulty meditation), pure and nondiscriminating,
Such is the self-nature of the *dharma*-sphere as yogins see it, who are self-collectedly intent upon it.
It is the pure sphere of the Buddhas, replete with inconceivable and peerless virtues, more numerous than the sands of innumerable Ganges Rivers, and where all pollution and evil are removed.[17]

The alternative name "Yoga-Practice" (*Yogācāra*) used for the Mind Only school emphasizes the fact that it was only by the practice of suitable yoga that the necessary "reversal" could be achieved, and thus defiled mind be recognized for what it essentially is, namely mind in its pure state. Also as we have already noted, a necessary corollary of this is the assertion that all living beings are essentially of Buddha-nature, if only they know it. These perfectly orthodox Buddhist teachings provide the philosophical basis for all tantric theory and practice; on this point the *Hevajra Tantra* is quite explicit.

The six faculties of sense, their six spheres of operation, the five *skandhas* and the five elements are pure in essence, but they are obstructed by ignorance and emotional disturbance (*kleśa*). Their purification consists in self-experience, and by no other means of purification may one be released. This self-experiencing, this supreme bliss, arises from the pure condition of the sense-spheres. Form and so on, and whatever other sense-spheres there are, all these appear to the yogin in their purified condition, for of Buddha-nature is this world.

Such is the basic theory as found in Mind Only teachings and throughout the tantras. But there is also agreement about the basic theory on which the actual religious practice must be based. This too is stated clearly in the *Hevajra Tantra*:

Those things by which evil men are bound, others turn into means and gain thereby release from the bonds of existence. By passion the world is bound, by

[16] One of the best brief descriptions of yoga that I have come upon is to be found in G. W. Briggs, *Gorakhnath and the Kanphata Yogis*, pp. 258-74. The passage quoted here is taken from p. 265.

[17] Sanskrit text, ed. by E. H. Johnston, p. 85, ll. 12ff. In his translation (p. 325) Takasaki translates *yoginah* as "Saints." For its use by Śāntideva, see p. 88 above.

passion too it is released, but by heretical Buddhists this practice of reversals is not known.[18]

It is seldom realized that precisely the same doctrine has already been asserted in Asaṅga's *Mahāyānasūtrālaṃkāra* ("Adornment of Mahāyāna Sūtras"), from which quotations were drawn in the last chapter to illustrate Mind Only teachings.

Now come three verses concerning extrication from the emotions (*kleśa*) by means of the emotions:
There is no element (*dharma*) apart from the elemental sphere (*dharma-dhātu*),
So passion, etc. (viz., wrath and delusion) serve as their own extrication in the opinion of the Buddhas.

Commentary: As the Lord has said: "I say that there is no extrication from passion other than by means of passion." It is the same in the case of wrath and delusion. Here he reveals the actual meaning (*abhisaṃdhi*). As there is no element apart from the elemental sphere, so there is no essential truth (or elemental essence, *dharmatā*) apart from the elements. Therefore the essential truth of passion, etc. (which is their purification) receives the connotation of passion, etc., and it is this which serves as the extrication from passion etc.

There is no element apart from the elemental sphere; such is the actual meaning accepted by the wise concerning emotional disturbance (*saṃkleśa*).

Commentary: As has been taught: "Delusion and enlightenment are one and the same. So the actual meaning is the same in the matter of emotional disturbance on the assumption that delusion is the essential truth of enlightenment.

In that one has recourse to them, passion and the rest, at the source (*yoniśaḥ*)
One is released by their means; thus they are their own extrication.

Commentary: Having recourse to them, passion and the others, at the source, they are thereby recognized and this is their release. Such is the actual meaning.[19]

This text, of which the verses are supposedly dictated by the Bodhisattva Maitreya and the prose commentary, which seldom adds much to the meaning, is the work of Asaṅga, is by no means easy of interpretation. Thus one could debate the meanings to be given to the terms *dharma*, *dharma-dhātu* (*dharma*-sphere) and *dharmatā* (essential truth) in the present context, but even so the intended meaning would seem to remain quite clear. The word translated as "source" in the last of the three verses is properly the word for "vagina," which may well be an intentional second meaning. The renowned Indian scholar, Benyotosh Bhattacharyya, to whom all of us who write about tantras must remain indebted, asserts in his introduction to the *Guhyasamāja Tantra*

[18] H.T. I.ix.2-3 and II.ii.50-1.

[19] Ch. XIII, vv. 11-13 with commentary; Sanskrit text p. 87; French translation pp. 156-7.

(published at the Oriental Institute, Baroda in 1931) that its author is no less a person than Asaṅga, whom he dates to the third century, thus making the formal appearance of tantric teachings much earlier than others would accept. The attribution to Asaṅga of this particular text is rash, as is also his assertion that it is the first tantra to appear, but his intuition may not go far astray. It is by no means improbable that already by the fifth century when Asaṅga was writing, these techniques of sexual yoga were being used in reputable Buddhist circles, and that Asaṅga himself accepted such a practice as valid. The natural power of the breath, inhaling and exhaling, was certainly accepted as an essential force to be controlled in Buddhist as well as Hindu yoga. Why therefore not the natural power of the sexual force? There need be nothing surprising about this at all. Sexual relationship had long since been ritualized (see the *Bṛhad-āraṇyaka Upaniṣad*, VI.4) as a form of yoga, and within the terms of Mahāyāna theories, there need be no objection to it by Buddhist yogins. That it was unsuitable for celibate monks goes without saying, but Asaṅga was not writing only for these. There happens to be a passage in Asaṅga's *Mahāyāna-sūtrālaṃkāra*, which refers specifically to copulation (*maithuna*) in a list of "reversals," and within this context it can scarcely refer otherwise than to the deliberate retension of *semen virile*, for this was certainly accepted Buddhist tantric practice.[20] Since it may be misleading to quote one verse out of context, I give in translation the whole set of verses dealing with the subject of reversal (*parāvṛtti*).[21] Once it is established that sexual yoga was already regarded by Asaṅga as an acceptable yogic practice, it becomes far easier to understand how tantric treatises, despite their apparent contradiction of previous Buddhist teachings, were so readily canonized in the following centuries.

The self-control of the Early Disciples surpasses that of a worldly person,
but this disposition of an Early Disciple is surpassed by the Lone
Buddhas. [38]
However this does not approach even fractionally the self-control of a
Bodhisattva. It does not approach even fractionally the self-control
of the Tathāgatas. [39]
The self-control of the Buddhas is said to be immeasurable and inconceivable
with regard to the person involved, the place, the manner and the
occasion. [40]
Supreme self-control is achieved in the reversal of the five sense-organs
with regard to the universal operation of all of them, associated with
the manifestation of twelve hundred good qualities. [41]
Supreme self-control is achieved in the reversal of mental activity
with the consequent self-control with regard to knowledge which is

[20] Shashibhusan Dasgupta refers to this passage in his *Obscure Religious Cults*, pp. 17-18 and 231, accepting it in its obvious sense, as I do. It is strange that Bhattacharyya himself in his "Notes on the *Guhyasamāja-Tantra* and the age of the Tantras," *Indian Historical Quarterly*, vol. IX (1933), pp. 1-10, attempts to circumvent the true meaning. However, in this article he retreats from the rash views about the authorship of the *Guhyasamāja Tantra* referred to above.

[21] Concerning reversal in a more general philosophical sense, see section II.4.c and Index.

free of discriminating thought and thus totally immaculate. [42]
Supreme self-control is achieved in the reversal of appearances and
their (imagined) significance in a (Buddha-)realm that is thus purified
for the blissful vision just as desired. [43]
Supreme self-control is achieved in the reversal of discriminating thought
resulting in the nonobstruction at all times of all knowledge and acts. [44]
Supreme self-control is obtained in the reversal of substrata
resulting in that imperturbable state of the Buddhas, nirvāṇa without
any substratum. [45]
Supreme self-control is obtained in the reversal of sexual intercourse
in the blissful Buddha-poise and the untrammeled vision of one's
spouse. [46]
Supreme self-control is obtained in the reversal of spatial perceptions
resulting in the supernatural production of thought-forms and in
material manifestation in phenomenal spheres (*gati*). [47]
(In the matter of self-control in the reversal of spatial perceptions
the results are two: the supernatural production of thought-forms
whereby one becomes of the very essence of space (*gaganagarbha*) and
material manifestations in phenomenal spheres because one moves as
one pleases and because of one's control over space.)
Thus with regard to this immeasurable and supreme (power of) reversal
this self-control is said to be immeasurable in the immaculate state
of the Buddhas since (great) acts are performed spontaneously (lit.
without mental reflection). [48][22]

There need be little doubt over the meaning of these verses. The return to the phenomenal world (verse 47) after experiencing the "blissful Buddha-poise" (verse 46) corresponds with the arrangement of the tantric states of Symbols and Joys, which is explained on p. 266 below.

2. THE VAJRAYĀNA AS A NEW AND DISTINCT "WAY"

Buddhist tantric scholars are aware of a seeming similarity between the goal of the Void (*śūnyatā*), recognized as an "adamantine state" (*vajra*), and the goal of Hindu yogins, which is the nonmanifest (*avyakta*) state of Brahman, but for them the essential difference would seem to exist precisely in the manifestation of the Buddha-form.[23] Whether many of the tantric yogins who pursued their practice within what they might claim as a Buddhist context were always aware of such a distinction may perhaps be doubted. When they used non-Buddhist vocabulary, many must have operated in non-Buddhist thought-forms. In the

[22] For the Sanskrit text see Sylvain Lévi's edition of Asaṅga's *Mahāyānasūtrālamkāra*, IX, 38-48 (pp. 40-2) and for his French translation see vol. II, pp. 80-2. I have translated only the actual verses except for verse 47, where the commentary is also included. Elsewhere the commentary merely repeats the contexts of the verses and scarcely assists with elucidating the meaning.

[23] A short work entitled *Sekanirṇaya* (*Advayavajrasaṃgraha*, pp. 28-31) deals with this matter, using as argument several quotations from non-Buddhist sources. Also see p. 200.

Hevajra Tantra the state of enlightenment is acclaimed in Hindu as well as Buddhist terms: "Brahmā because one is quenched and enlightened, Viṣṇu because one is all-pervading, Śiva because one is always propitious, Sarva (Universal) because one abides in everything, Tattva (Quiddity) on account of the real bliss, and Vibuddha (Fully Awake) because of the awareness of such happiness."[24] In one passage in the *Guhyasamāja Tantra* the Hindu trinity of Brahmā, Śiva (= Rudra) and Viṣṇu is equated with the triple Vajra of Body, Speech and Mind and represented as the "purifiers" of the three basic evils—Delusion, Passion, Wrath.[25]

> Then Vajrapāṇi, Lord of all the Buddhas, brought forth the Pledge (*samaya*) of Brahmā from his own Vajra Body, Speech and Mind:
> Whatever actions one performs, fearful and terrible, in the way of Delusion, being conducive to the enlightenment of a Buddha, it is essentially Vajra-Body.
> Then he brought forth likewise the Pledge of Rudra:
> One should make love to all women in their various modes of existence, regarded as the triple Vajra, throughout the threefold world.
> This is the most wonderful pledge (relative to Passion).
> Then he brought forth likewise the Pledge of Viṣṇu (relative to Wrath):
> All those conceived as living beings, existing indistinguishably in the Three Bodies,
> And even the Vajra space-sphere itself, one should slay with the Vajra of meditation.
> Then he brought forth likewise from his own Vajra Body, Speech and Mind this Pledge of the Triple Vajra:
> The Vajra of Body is Brahmā. The Vajra of Speech is Maheśvara (Śiva).
> The Holder of the Vajra of Mind, the King, is Viṣṇu of great magical power.[26]

We have noticed above that the followers of the Mind Only school were sometimes accused of being Buddhist Brahmins, and it might appear that this process is carried even further in some tantric circles, despite the continuing appeal to the notion of the Void (*śūnyatā*).

However, it is with the adoption of the term *vajra* (adamantine) for the absolute state, as explained above, that tantric Buddhism becomes a separate "Way" (*yāna*), as distinguishable from the Mahāyāna as this is distinguishable from the so-called Hīnayāna. Mantrayāna, the earlier alternative name for Vajrayāna, continues to suggest closer links with traditional Mahāyāna practice than fits the case, as the term Vajrayāna comes into use, for both the goal (although some might dispute this)[27] and certainly the means employed to reach

24 H.T. I.13-14.

25 As will be noted below in section III.11, these three "evils" belong to the developed set of five.

26 G. S. T. Bhattacharyya's ed., p. 129, ll. 3ff. On "perverse teachings," see this term in the Index.

27 See Tsong-kha-pa, *Tantra in Tibet*, translated and edited by Jeffrey Hopkins, 1977, for such a refutation, although it is conceded that: "In some scriptures Buddhahood and Vajradharahood seem to be different, and thus some have thought that the fruits of the two vehicles must be different and that Vajradharahood is higher than Buddhahood." This "unresolved matter" could only be settled

it, are no longer the same. The followers of the Mahāyāna had advanced from the earlier goal of nirvāṇa as achieved by an Arhat to the goal of enlightenment as achieved by a Buddha. The followers of the Vajrayāna in their turn direct their energies toward a state of enlightenment (for this term is still used) which is also referred to as Great Bliss (*mahāsukha*) and as the sphere of Vajrasattva ("Adamantine Being"), while those who achieve it are known as "great adepts" (*mahāsiddha*). Although it may be shown that many of the roots of the Vajrayāna were already present in the Mahāyāna, just as those of the Mahāyāna were in the Hīnayāna, the differences between the Vajrayāna and the earlier forms of Buddhism are extreme. The main difference derives from the Vajrayāna use of incantation and ritual as means toward the ultimate goal, whereas in the earlier phases of Buddhism their use was largely peripheral. By their means one gains power over beings in other spheres of existence, either dominating them, so that they may do one's will, or identifying oneself with them, so that one may enjoy their higher states of existence. It is unfortunate that Sanskrit and Tibetan terminology used of such practices often has no adequate equivalent in modern European languages, thus making the task of writing about them especially difficult. The word "adept" (from Latin *adeptus*, "attained") translates fairly well the Sanskrit term *siddha*, which is the perfect participle of the root *sidh*, meaning "to succeed" or "to be accomplished." However, it has several other derivatives, which are not so easily equated in English. Thus the particular success that is achieved is known as a *siddhi*, and in our present context this must be understood as a supramundane or a magical power. "Success" or "accomplishment," which might otherwise be legitimate translations, are quite inadequate for us. Also connected with the root *sidh* is the term *sādhana*, meaning the act or the means of being successful, and this comes to mean in our context the ritual of incantation or evocation, or whatever particular means may be employed to win over the chosen divinity. Whatever form of translation is used, one inevitably influences an unwary reader into a particular understanding of the term that is only partially valid, and there is no solution to this problem. The problem is made even more difficult because we now have with us a young generation of Western Buddhists, much attracted by the Tibetan form of this great religion, who object to the most natural translations because they suggest the kinds of superstitious and magical practices such as were prevalent in our own "unenlightened" Middle Ages. Yet the resemblance between much of that superstition and magic with tantric rites aiming at magical powers of a mundane kind cannot be denied. Wherein then lies the difference? The difference is well illustrated by the formal proscribing by the Christian Church of all such practices as contrasted with the general Indian acceptance of them as means

experimentally by one who had achieved enlightenment by the conventional methods of the Mahāyāna (viz., pursuing the career of a Bodhisattva through aeons of time) and as a separate exercise by tantric methods in a single lifetime, and who is then available to accept the evidence? One appreciates, however, that the identity of the two goals must be asserted dogmatically in order to maintain the unity of the whole Mahāyāna tradition.

that might be used to a higher purpose.[28] However, the higher purpose still involved the same kind of religious and certainly credulous (if not superstitious) disposition on the part of the practitioner. It would be useless to invoke any form of divinity, higher or lower, without believing in such a being. The high point of any such rite is the descent of the actual divinity (known as the "wisdom-being" or *jñānasattva*) into the symbol of the divinity (the "sacramental being" or *samayasattva*), which has been prepared for this mystical (or magical) conjunction. The practitioner is certainly taught that the divine forms are also emanations of his own mind, but they are not arbitrary imaginings and they are far more real than his own transitory personality, which is a mere flow, as we have seen, of nonsubstantial elements. In learning to produce mentally such higher forms of emanation and eventually identifying himself with them, the practitioner gradually transforms his evanescent personality into that higher state of being. Thus belief in them is essential; otherwise the means by which one would progress dissolve before the desired "success" (*siddhi*) is achieved.

The highest state of all, in which all Buddha-emanations ultimately dissolve and yet continually reemerge, is the Adamantine Being (*Vajrasattva*) and thus it is defined as *Vajra*, meaning diamond or thunderbolt. As the weapon of the Vedic god, Indra, transferred to the *yakṣa* (local divinity) who acts as escort to Śākyamuni in the earlier Buddhist period, "thunderbolt" might suggest itself as a convenient translation. Precisely as the wielder of this weapon this chief of *yakṣas*, known as Vajrapāṇi (Thunderbolt-in-Hand), appears as chief of Bodhisattvas in several tantras, for he has become the holder of the supreme symbol of this whole latter phase of Buddhism. Thus, as we shall see, he is also referred to as *Vajradhara* (Thunderbolt-Holder) and with this name becomes the supreme Buddha of tantric traditions. He may also be acclaimed as *Vajrasattva* (Thunderbolt-Being), but this is more logically understood as a general appellation of the highest state of tantric being, a term formed on the analogy of *Bodhisattva* (Enlightenment Being). However, despite the association with Indra's thunderbolt, and the same instrument that Vajrapāṇi as chief of *yakṣas* does not hesitate to use against the enemies of the doctrine, the term "diamond" (derived from Greek *adamas*, "unyielding," hence the adjective "adamantine"), referring to the hardest, most precious and translucent of minerals, is probably the most suitable translation. The Tibetans translated *vajra* as *rDo-rje*, meaning literally "lord of stones," a deliberately invented term, so that they used neither their term for thunderbolt (*gnam-lcags*, literally "sky-iron") nor diamond (*pha-lam*). It is by the use of such specially coined terms that the precise Buddhist meaning of the Sanskrit word is so accurately rendered in their translations. The best alternative for us is to use the Sanskrit term, in order to avoid ambiguity of meaning. The vajra as an instrument plays an essential part in all Vajrayāna ritual, where it is used in conjunction with a bell, of which the handle

[28] Interesting parallels can be drawn between the more traditional Mahāyāna practice and certain Christian forms of devotion. A particularly good example of a "mantra" as a prayer formula may be found in *A Treasury of Russian Spirituality*, ed. by G. P. Fedotov (London, 1952), pp. 280-345.

is a half-vajra (*Pl. 20b*). Treated thus as a form of duality, the vajra represents the active principle, the means toward enlightenment and the means of conversion, thus the actual Buddha-manifestation, while the bell represents the Perfection of Wisdom, known as the Void (*śūnyatā*). In the state of union, however, the vajra comprehends both these coefficients of enlightenment (*bodhi*), the means and the wisdom. We have here the Buddhist version of the Indian conception of manifest and unmanifest Brahman, as expressed in the Hindu tantras in the forms of Śiva and Śakti, but as is now generally realized, the male and female roles are reversed.[29] For the Buddhists wisdom, rather like Sancta Sophia in Christian tradition, is regarded as feminine, and the active saving principle is male. In Hinduism the feminine Śakti inherits the age-old Indian tradition of a productive mother of all creatures, and thus the corresponding role of blissful quiescence devolves upon Śiva as the lord of yogins. Despite the reversal of roles the use of sexual symbolism is developed in Buddhist tantras quite as much as in Hindu ones. Thus vajra refers also to the male organ, and bell (as well as lotus-flower) to the female one. Continuing the analogy of the sexual act, the drop (*bindu*) of *semen virile* with which the disciple is consecrated in the Secret Consecration (*guhyābhiṣeka*) represents the Thought of Enlightenment. Consecrations will be described in more detail below, but it may be of interest to quote from the opening chapter of the tantra which is known precisely as the "Secret Union" (*Guhyasamāja*). Such opening chapters regularly set the stage, as it were, for the following discourses, with a description of the entourage of the presiding Buddha and a demonstration by him of his universal miraculous powers.

> Then the Lord Buddha, Vajra Thought of Enlightenment, relapsed into that state of composure known as Vajra Subjugation of All Buddhas, and immediately the Lord, foremost (*adhipati*) of All Buddhas, was thus composed, the whole realm of space became established in the Vajra nature of All Buddhas, and all living beings throughout the whole realm of space experienced the bliss and the happiness of All Buddhas as a result of their empowerment (*adhiṣṭhāna*) in Vajra-Being (*vajrasattva*).
>
> Then the Lord Buddha, Vajra Thought of Enlightenment, relapsing into that state of composure known as Vajra Source of the Sacramental Pledge (*samaya*) of the Vajra of Body, Speech and Mind of All the Buddhas, bestowed the divine favor of the mantra of All Buddhas, which embodies these persons of great miraculous power. As soon as he thus bestowed it, he himself, the Lord Buddha, Vajra Thought of Enlightenment, was seen by all the Buddhas as possessed of three faces, while the Buddha Imperturbable (Akṣobhya) and the other Buddhas (of the maṇḍala) emerged from the heart of the Great Resplendent One (Mahāvairocana) intoning this verse.

[29] Following the Hindu terminology for the feminine partner, some writers, often including those responsible for the identification of Buddhist images in our museums, continue to refer to the Buddhist feminine partner as *śakti*. The normal Buddhist term is *prajñā* (= wisdom), but in English "female partner" is an adequate rendering.

Oho! this emerging of the Thought of Enlightenment of All Buddhas,
This All Tathāgata Secret, inexpressible and groundless.

Then all the Lord Buddhas united as one and, worshipping the Lord Thought of Enlightenment with showers (literally: clouds) of gems, being the quiddity (*tattva*) of the out-spreading sacramental pledge (*samaya*) of All Buddha worship, they approached him and said:

O Lord! Tell us of that quiddity comprised of the Vajra essence,
The All Tathāgata Secret, that Unity of secret origin.[30]

Every such extract from these texts requires commentarial exegesis in order to be fully comprehensible, but in so far as our main purpose at present is to illustrate the term *vajra* as representing the Buddhist tantric absolute, we can make do here with a minimum. The primary emanation of cosmic Buddhas (referred to in the requisite mantra as "persons of great miraculous power")[31] takes the usual fivefold form, which will be described later on, but they are all subsumed in this Tantra by a single unity of buddhahood, referred to as Vajra-Being (*vajrasattva*), as Great Resplendent One and as Vajra Thought of Enlightenment. These are titles rather than names that can be applied iconographically, but more will be said concerning the Resplendent One (Vairocana) in due course.

The symbolic significance of the vajra as an instrument is described in a short exegetic work of Advayavajra:[32]

The vajra is twelve finger-spans in length because it eliminates the twelvefold causal nexus. The syllable HŪṂ on the rounded middle-part indicates the unsurpassable essential truth (*dharmatā*): H representing freedom from causality (*hetu*), Ū representing freedom from argumentation (*ūha*) and Ṃ the groundlessness of all *dharmas*. The five points that emerge (at each end of the vajra) from the lotus-flower source of existence (its middle part) represent the Sages (*muni*) as fivefold since by emerging in bodily form they eliminate the five aggregates of personality. Four of them face in toward the center one, indicating that body and the rest (viz., feelings, perceptions and impulses) depend upon consciousness. Furthermore, they all have four sides in order to indicate their universality. Then men of wisdom who understand the Vajra-dharma, having attained to the fivefold form of salvation, spread out in a form that causes the syllable HŪṂ to resound.[33] On all sides there are trifoliate patterns indicating Voidness, Signlessness and Effortlessness. That such is the nature of the Five Wisdoms, namely Mirrorlike Wisdom, the Wisdom of

30 *Guhyasamāja Tantra*, ed. B. Bhattacharyya, p. 3, ll. 15ff. I am grateful to Francesca Fremantle for allowing me to make use of her greatly improved edition of the Sanskrit text, produced with an edition of the Tibetan translation and a provisional English version. The actual beginning of this tantra leading into the passage here quoted will be found in section III.12 below.

31 The Sanskrit term is *mahāvidyapuruṣa*, and there need be no doubt of its application here.

32 *Advayavajrasaṃgraha*, p. 37, ll. 1ff. The Tibetan translation is in T.T. vol. 68, p. 280-1-7ff.

33 The reference is presumably to eight small looped protrusions that spread out from the rounded middle of the vajra toward the five-pointed head at each end. Some vajras have a nine-pointed head, thus continuing the eightfold pattern, still with a single point right at the top, to the head of the vajra.

Sameness, Discriminating Wisdom, Active Wisdom amd the Wisdom of the Pure Absolute, all this must be learned from one's preceptor. Indicating the indivisibility of wisdom we have this concise statement:

Firm, substantial and solid, of uncuttable and unbreakable character,
Unburnable, indestructible, the Void is said to be Vajra.

In the *Hevajra Tantra* (I.1.4) the vajra is said to be unbreakable. The bestowal of the Vajra Consecration gives, as it were, an infusion of the seed which grows into this unbreakable wisdom.[34]

The preeminence of the vajra in the last phase of Indian Buddhism, which thus gives us the term *Vajrayāna*, certainly indicates the great difference between this and the earlier phases, which the term *Mantrayāna* does not. It has no place in early Buddhist symbolism beside the major symbols of the sacred tree, the wheel and the lotus flower, and as already observed, it appears first in Buddhist iconography as the weapon of the chief of *yakṣas* in his role of Śākyamuni's personal protector. In Mahāyāna texts the term *vajra* occurs as a spontaneous symbol of hardness without any specifically Buddhist association. Thus the monk Dharmākara, when making his vow to become the Buddha Amitābha, states as one of his self-imposed conditions:

O Lord, if after obtaining enlightenment, those Bodhisattvas who are born in that Buddha-field of mine, do not possess bodily strength as solid as Nārāyaṇa's vajra, then may I not obtain the highest enlightenment.[35]

Here it is identified with the staff or sceptre of Viṣṇu (= Nārāyaṇa) and its connection with the yakṣa Vajrapāṇi who appears quite frequently in Mahāyāna sūtras still in the role of personal guardian, is apparently overlooked.

3. VAJRAPĀṆI (ALIAS VAJRADHARA) BECOMES PREEMINENT

As for Vajrapāṇi himself, there are so many references to him as a mere guardian that one or two may suffice as illustration of his extraordinary rise from so lowly a position to one of absolute preeminence. I confess to finding him by far the most interesting divine being throughout the whole history of Buddhism, for he has a personal history and considerable personal character. In his lowlier state he is mentioned incidentally in the sūtra "Perfection of Wisdom in Eight Thousand Verses": "Furthermore Vajrapāṇi, the great yakṣa, constantly follows behind the irreversible Bodhisattva."[36] In the "Sūtra of Golden Light" he is referred to as "great general of the yakṣas," where he is one among several, or

[34] The translation follows the Tibetan version, wherever the Sanskrit is defective. "Solid" translates Sanskrit *asauśīrya*, lit. "without holes," which the Tibetan renders as having a nonvoid interior (*khong-stong-med*).

[35] See the *Sukhāvatīvyūha*, pp. 388-9 (English translation), Sanskrit p. 36, already quoted more fully in section II.3.b.

[36] See Edward Conze, *Aṣṭasāhasrikā*, p. 126 and *The Large Sūtra of Perfect Wisdom*, p. 398.

again as "lord of the yakṣas." Together with the Four Kings of the Quarters or with Brahmā, acclaimed in this particular context as lord of the heaven of the thirty-three gods, he honors the Buddhist religion and protects its supporters.[37] He receives a rather higher position in *Saddharmapuṇḍarīka*, where he is listed as one of the bodily forms that the Great Bodhisattva Avalokiteśvara may adopt in order to convert living beings, such as another Bodhisattva or a Lone Buddha (*pratyekabuddha*), as Brahmā or Indra or a Gandharva (a heavenly musician), as Maheśvara (= Śiva), as a universal monarch, as god of wealth (Kubera), as a military chief, as a brahman or as Vajrapāṇi. Despite the rather mixed company, his status is clearly improved.[38] He succeeds in coming to the fore as leader of one of the two families, those of the Lotus and the Vajra, which are ranged on either side of Śākyamuni in the maṇḍala described in the second chapter of an early tantra entitled "The Fundamental Ordinance of Mañjuśrī." Here he is described as "The Noble Vajrapāṇi, of dark hue like that of a blue lotus flower, of gracious appearance, adorned with all his jewelry, waving a chowry in his right hand, while with his left hand he makes the wrathful gesture of the Vajra-Fist. He has as entourage (the goddesses) Vajra-Hook, Vajra-Chain, Strong-Armed, Vajra-Army and all the mighty ones of magical power, both male and female, all with suitable dress, accouterments, postures and thrones."[39] Elsewhere in this voluminous text he is known both as Bodhisattva and as chief of *yakṣas* (or rather *guhyakas*, a similar class of local divinities used here synonymously). Another term used in that quotation needs mention in passing and that is *vidyā*, translated here as "magical power." *Vidyā* means knowledge, sacred lore and hence power in the sense of magical power. Thus we have the compound term "holders of magical power" (*vidyādhara*) and "mighty ones of magical power" (*vidyārāja*), as in the last quotation. These can be human or supramundane beings, just as Bodhisattvas can be either. Thus the term can be a synonym for *mahāsiddha*, "great adept" in the sense of highly perfect yogin, or it can refer to powerful divinities of the kind that one might expect to find in Vajrapāṇi's following.[40] In an earlier quotation from the *Guhyasamāja Tantra* the five cosmic Buddhas are referred to as "persons of great magical power" (*mahāvidyāpuruṣa*), being merely an extension of the term "great person" or "great man" (*mahāpuruṣa*) as applied to Śākyamuni himself.

Having thus made his mark as leader of the Vajra Family, Vajrapāṇi predominates entirely in the great tantra "Symposium of Truth," where the

[37] See R. E. Emmerick, *The Sūtra of Golden Light*, pp. 33, 37, 66.

[38] See H. Kern, *The Lotus of the True Law*, p. 411.

[39] See Ariane Macdonald, *Le maṇḍala du Mañjuśrīmūlakalpa*, p. 109. My translation differs slightly from hers, but this is a difficult text. Vajrapāṇi appears to have an entourage of four goddesses. The names are feminine in Tibetan, as Mme Macdonald points out, and three are feminine in Sanskrit, so one may assume the fourth should be as well. Corruptions are rife in this text. See below under section III.11 for a larger quotation comprising the whole context in which these divinities appear.

[40] See J. Przyluski, "Les Vidyārāja," in BEFEO 1923, pp. 301-18.

main maṇḍala consists of the circle of divinities of the Vajra-sphere (*vajra-dhātu*). More will be written below about Buddha-families, but it may already be observed that the great interest shown by tantric yogins in gaining magical powers, whether aiming at the possession of "enlightenment" (*bodhi*) or rather more mundane successes (*siddhi*), results in the predominance of the vajra symbol, the naming of the whole tantric Buddhist phase as Vajrayāna, and the creation of a large number of divinities with Vajra names, of whom Vajrapāṇi *alias* Vajradhara (Vajra-in-Hand or Vajra-Holder, the meaning is the same) is inevitably regarded as chief (*Pls. 19, 20a*).[41] Vajrapāṇi's personal triumph as a "mere *yakṣa*" who is recognized as a Bodhisattva, then as the most powerful of all Bodhisattvas in that he wields the vajra, and finally his identity as Vajra-Being (*vajrasattva*) when he becomes the expression of perfect enlightenment, as conceived in tantric tradition, is pleasantly illustrated in this particular tantra, from which I quote a long passage. Part II opens with an invocation of the "Lord of the Maṇḍala," acclaimed as Great Resplendent One (Mahā-Vairocana), Vajradhara, Vajrapāṇi, altogether one hundred and eight sacred names. But Vajrapāni himself hesitates to subscribe to it.

> Placing his vajra on his heart, he said to all the Buddhas: "O all you Lord-Tathāgatas, I do not comply." They said: "O why?," and he replied: "O Lords, there are evil beings, Maheśvara (Śiva) and others, who have not been converted by all of you Tathāgatas. How am I to deal with them?" In response the Resplendent One (Vairocana) relapsed into the state of composure known as Wrathful Pledge-Vajra, the great compassionate means of all the Tathāgatas, and enunciated the syllable HŪṂ. At once there emerged from the vajra at the heart of Vajrapāṇi the Lord Vajradhara who manifested a variety of fearful Vajrapāni-forms, reciting this verse:
>
> Oho! I am the means of conversion, possessed of all great means.
> Spotless, they assume a wrathful appearance so that beings may be
> converted by these means.

After a further fearful manifestation of Vajrapāni, the Lord (Vairocana) utters the spell HŪṂ ṬAKKIJJAḤ, which has the effect of bringing Maheśvara and the other gods of the threefold world to his presence. There now follows an interesting altercation between Vajrapāṇi and Śiva (Maheśvara).[42]

> Then Vajrapāṇi raised his vajra away from his heart and waving it, he surveyed the whole circle of the threefold world to its limits. He spoke: "Come, my friends, to the teaching of all the Tathāgatas. Obey my command!" They replied: "How should we come?" Vajrapāṇi said: "Having sought protection with the Buddha, the Dharma, the Community, approach, O friends, so that

[41] One should note that in later tantric tradition as received by the Tibetans Vajrapāṇi (as Bodhisattva) and Vajradhara (as Supreme Buddha) come to be clearly distinguished iconographically, but at this earlier state there is no such distinction and Vajrapāṇi is frequently referred to as a Tathāgata (viz., Buddha).

[42] Throughout the following passage Śiva is referred to as Maheśvara (= Great Lord, viz. *Mahā-īśvara*), as Īśvara alone, used as his name, and as Mahādeva (= Great God).

you may gain the knowledge of the Omniscient One."

Then Mahādeva (Śiva), the Lord of the whole threefold world in this worldly sphere, proud of his overlordship of the whole threefold world, appeared very wrathful and said: "Listen you *yakṣa*, I am Iśvara, Lord of the threefold world, Creator, Destroyer, Lord of all Spirits, God of Gods, Mighty God. So how should I carry out the order of a *yakṣa*?"

Then Vajrapāṇi waved his vajra once more and gave the command: "Listen, you evil being, quickly enter the maṇḍala and hold to my pledge!"

Then Mahādeva, the god, addressed the Lord (Vairocana): "Who is this creature of such a kind who gives orders to me, Īśvara?"

Then the Lord said to Maheśvara and the whole host of gods of the threefold world: "Friends, enter upon the vow of the pledge of the triple protection, lest Vajrapāṇi, this so-called *yakṣa*, the Great Bodhisattva, wrathful, terrifying and fearful, should destroy the whole threefold world with his blazing vajra."

Then Maheśvara by the power of his overlordship of the threefold world and of his own knowledge, together with his whole company, manifested a fearful and wrathful and greatly terrifying form with great flames shooting forth and with a terrible laugh for the purpose of causing fear to the Lord Vajrapāṇi. He then said: "I am the Lord of the threefold world, and you would give me orders!"

Then Vajrapāṇi, waving his vajra and laughing, said: "Approach, you eater of corpses and human flesh, you who use the ashes of funeral pyres as your food, as your couch, as your clothing, and obey my command!"

Then Maheśvara, lording it over the whole world which was pervaded by his great wrath, said: "You obey my command and take upon yourself my vow!"

Then Vajrapāṇi, the greatly wrathful king, said to the Lord: "Because of pride in the power of his own knowledge and because of his overlordship as Maheśvara, this Great God, O Lord, does not submit to the teaching of all the Tathāgatas. How is one to deal with him?"

Then the Lord recalled the great vajra-pledge which has its origin in the heart of all the Tathāgatas: OṂ NIŚUMBHA VAJRA HŪṂ PHAṬ![43]

Then Vajrapāṇi pronounced his own vajra-syllable: HŪṂ! As soon as he pronounced this, all the great gods who belong to the threefold world, fell down on their faces, emitting miserable cries, and they went to Vajrapāni for protection. The Great God himself remained motionless on the ground, quite dead.

All except Maheśvara are raised up and converted. Only thereafter at Vairocana's behest does Vajrapāṇi bring Maheśvara back to life, for as Vairocana remarks: "If he is not raised up. his life will be wasted to no purpose, while if he is brought back to life, he will become a good man." However, when he is restored, Maheśvara still refuses to submit. "I can bear death," he says, "but I will not obey your command." There follows a further short battle, in which Vajrapāṇi triumphs by means of his spells, and treads down Maheśvara with his left foot, and Umā, Maheśvara's consort, with his right.

[43] For an interpretation of *niśumbha* and *ṭakkijja* see section 4 on "Magical Formulas" below.

Then the Lord felt great compassion for Mahādeva and pronounced this spell, comprising the compassion of All Buddhas:

OṂ BUDDHA MAITRĪ VAJRA RAKṢA HŪṂ! (= OṂ Buddha Kindness Vajra Protection HŪṂ)

As soon as he said this, the suffering that Mahādeva experienced was allayed and from the contact with the sole of Vajrapāṇi's foot he became the recipient of consecrations, powers of meditation, salvation, mnemonics, faculties of knowledge and magical powers, all of the highest perfection, tending even to buddhahood. So Mahādeva from contact with the Lord's foot experienced the joys of salvation through the powers of meditation and the spells of all the Tathāgatas, and his body having thus fallen at the feet of Vajrapāṇi, he became the Tathāgata Bhasmeśvaranirghoṣa (Soundless Lord of Ashes) in the realm known as Bhasmacchatra (Umbrella of Ashes), which exists down below, over and beyond worldly realms equal in number to the atoms of worldly realms which are as numerous as the grains of sand contained in thirty-two River Ganges. Then from the body of Mahādeva (Śiva) this verse gained utterance.

Oho! the peerless wisdom of all the Buddhas!
Falling at the feet of a *yakṣa*, one is established in nirvāṇa!

Then Vajrapāṇi, the Great Bodhisattva, said to those other lords of the threefold world, Nārāyaṇa and the others: "Enter, friends, into this great Vajra-Pledge maṇḍala of all the Buddhas, and having entered, hold to the pledge of all the Buddhas." They replied: "We do as you command us." Then calling them, he said: "Once again, friends, accept this vow of the pledge with its teaching of the triple taking of refuge, and be constant in this pledge of mine." They replied: "Let it be so, we enter into this pledge of yours." Then Vajrapāṇi announced the self-imposed vow:

Having raised the excellent Thought of Enlightenment in due course
Strive composedly with all your might with enlightenment your goal!

Then Vajrapāṇi, the Great Bodhisattva, making the gesture-bond of the great pledge of entry for those gods, bound them with this quintessence of the great pledge-gesture:

OṂ take the vajra-pledge, bind the pledge,
Bear in mind the pledge of All Buddhas.
You are the pledge of All Buddhas.
Be firm in me! Be stable in me!
Be all-pervasive of me! Be inseparable from me!
In all my actions make for felicity of thought!
HA HA HA HA HŪṂ

With the mere recitation of this the *Terintiti* gesture of Vajra-Wrath was formed in the two hands of each one of those who belonged to the threefold world and he was made firm in the bond.

Then bringing them in correctly, Vajrapāṇi showed them the great maṇḍala in the regular way, and having consecrated them with the gem-consecration and having given into their hands the vajra-accouterments, he consecrated them with the name-consecration and established them in the cause of the welfare of living beings in the way of all Buddhas.[44]

Before commenting on this passage, I quote further from the beginning of a later chapter in Part II of this tantra, which goes back on the story just told, assuming that Śiva is still under Vajrapāṇi's foot:

Then all the Lord Tathāgatas came together as one and said to Vajrapāṇi the Great Bodhisattva: "Attend to the command of all the Buddhas so as to release Maheśvara's body from under the sole of you foot. Vajrapāṇi replied: "I have been consecrated by you Lords as the wrathful suppressor of all evil ones. This one has been defeated by me, so how should I release him?" Then all the Buddhas produced from their hearts that "quintessence" which draws in the consciousness of a dead person so as to restore the life in the corpse of Maheśvara, lord of the threefold world: OṂ VAJRASATTVA HŪṂ JJAḤ. The making of the hand-gesture is this:

Making firmly the secret hook-gesture one extends the ends equally.[45]
One places this on the head of the dead man and he will again receive his life-force.

As soon as the spell was pronounced the Lord Buddha "Soundless Lord of Ashes" of the realm "Umbrella of Ashes" entered the body of Maheśvara and he pronounced this verse:

Oho! the peerless wisdom of all the Buddhas.
Even a body which is dead returns to the sphere of the living!

Then Vajrapāṇi the Great Bodhisattva uttered this "quintessence" named "Coming forth from the foot": OṂ VAJRA MUḤ. The making of the hand-gesture is this:

Making in an upward direction the finger-gesture of Vajra-Wrath, one puts the tips together.
Then turning these vajra(-gestures) round, one protrudes them from below.

As soon as he pronounced the spell, Mahādeva was released and came to life again. Then the Buddhas consecrated Maheśvara's body as fully alive and established him a vice-regent in that particular realm for the benefit of all living beings and for the conversion of evil-doers.

Then from the sole of Vajrapāṇi's foot there was produced this Symbol (*mudrā*) of the Thought of Enlightenment of All Buddhas, known as "Moon-Foot."[46]

[44] From our STTS MS fo. 91, l. 7 onward, already translated by me in the introduction to our facsimile edition, pp. 39ff., but I have continued the translation a little further for the present work in order to include the reference to consecrations.

[45] The descriptions of hand-gestures are some of the most difficult passages in these tantric texts. They were written in concise form as mere guidance and it is clear from the problems that the Tibetan translators had in understanding them, that in some cases at least they were not clear in meaning even to them and thus also to the Indian pundits who assisted them. This is a doubtful translation, but it follows the Tibetan version well enough.

[46] *Mudrā* (refer to Index) is also used, as will be seen below, with reference to the partner of a divinity, usually feminine, but masculine in this case. The name "Moon-Foot" has a feminine ending in grammatical agreement with *mudrā*, but the divinity is male, as will be apparent from the passage immediately following.

OṂ Most Excellent Moon, Light-Ray of Samantabhadra,[47]
Great Adamantine One HŪṂ

This is the hand-gesture:

Making firmly the vajra-binding, one places together the little fingers and thumbs.
When they are extended together, this is known as "Moon Radiance."

As soon as the spell was pronounced, the Buddha Most Excellent Moon came forth from his foot, and having settled in the form of a lunar crescent on the head of Maheśvara, who was trodden on by Vajrapāṇi's foot, he took up his position on Vajrapāṇi's left side. Then all the Buddhas gave a vajra-mace into the hand of Vajrapāṇi's friend, and he was consecrated with the name-consecration, "Excellent Magical Power of the Vajra" (*Vajravidyottama*). Then the Great Being, the Bodhisattva "Excellent Magical Power of the Vajra," waved his vajra-mace like a blazing firebrand, and worshipping with dancing and oblations, he enunciated this verse:

Oho! the peerless wisdom of all the Buddhas,
That one should gain buddhahood by the mere touch of this foot.

Then Vajrapāṇi the Great Bodhisattva rose from his Vajra-Wrath composure, and said this to the Lord: "I have been given in my hands the vajra by all the Buddhas and I have been consecrated as "Vajra-in-Hand" (Vajrapāṇi). Now I will fix a place in this Great Maṇḍala of Victory over the Threefold World for these gods who are outside the Vajra-Family, so that these beings should not be back-sliders in the matter of supreme and perfect enlightenment."[48]

Apart from the interesting characterization of Vajrapāṇi found in these selected passages, I have chosen them also in illustration of the roundabout means that were employed in order to incorporate non-Buddhist traditions into their changed Buddhist setting. It was not just a matter of giving converted Hindu divinities new names, but also of explaining their attributes within the terms of a Buddhist context. Thus the Great Lord (Maheśvara) Śiva is revitalized as a Buddha named "Soundless Lord of Ashes," a curious name it may seem, unless one recalls that Śiva, as lord of yogins, frequents cemeteries as a naked ascetic, covered in matted hair and besmeared with ashes. Thus Vajrapāṇi mocks him as "you eater of corpses and human flesh, you who use the ashes of funeral pyres as your food, as your couch, as your clothing." Also the curious rite of extracting the lunar disk from Vajrapāṇi's foot and its settling on the head of Śiva was presumably suggested by the presence of just such a lunar crescent resting on Śiva's head in already existing Hindu tradition. The moon also corresponds to the male element in tantric sexual symbolism, representing the Thought of Enlightenment. Complications such as these result in the inevitable

[47] Samantabhadra (All Good) is yet one more name for supreme buddhahood, also identified with Vajrapāni. These acclamations are all feminine vocatives (see below section III.11).

[48] MS fo. 145, ll. 4ff., already partly translated in the facsimile edition, p. 47. See Yamada's edition, pp. 253ff.

equations of names, making such a text even more difficult to follow intelligibly. In this tantra sufficient Hindu divinities, male and female, are given names to make up the Maṇḍala of Victory over the Threefold World, which Vajrapāṇi is intent on producing. We thus have a deliberate incorporating of non-Buddhist divinities into the Buddhist fold, and as well as being given new Vajra names, they are also worked into an entirely Buddhist setting.

4. MAGICAL FORMULAS

The last quotation provides several examples of the use of magical formulas, often associated with the appropriate hand-gestures (*mudrā*), and here again we meet with problems of terminology. We have already discussed the term *mantra* as the most general word in use for such formulas, and we have also taken note of the term *dhāraṇī*, which is used in much the same sense, although properly it seems to refer to a kind of mnemonic. We now have yet another term, the Sanksrit word *hṛdaya*, meaning "heart," used in these texts in such a variety of ways that it becomes yet one more alternative for *mantra*. In their translations the Tibetans use for it the term *snying-po*, which may be rendered in English as "quintessence." It has often been translated as "seed-syllable" referring to single syllable sound, conceived of as comprehending the essence of a particular divinity. For this, however, the correct term is *bīja* (Tibetan *sa-bon*), which means literally "seed." While *hṛdaya* may be used in this sense, it is not at all difficult to find examples where the more general term *mantra* is used instead. It is, however, certainly frequently used of the personal "spell" of a divinity even when this consists of several syllables, and examples of this can be given immediately following upon the last quotation, when Vajrapāṇi introduces his Maṇḍala of Victory over the Threefold World. It will also be noted from this short further quotation that the term *vidyā*, which we have translated above as "magical power," is also used as an alternative. Thus we have at least four terms all meaning very much the same, although one can doubtfully argue for a special application of them by carefully selecting examples. As the list of these converted Hindu divinities has been given elsewhere in full, it suffices to list just a few here.[49] As may be expected, Vajrapāṇi controls the maṇḍala himself in a fourfold manifestation, involving a duplication of his own name. The reason for this will be clear, when we discuss below the arrangement of families in a maṇḍala.

> Then the Bodhisattva Vajrapāṇi, the Great Being, enunciated his own most excellent *vidyā*: OṂ NIŚUMBHA VAJRA HŪṂ PHAT.
>
> Then again Vajrapāṇi enunciated this "quintessence" from his heart: OṂ ṬAKKIJJAḤ.[50]

[49] See the STTS, facsimile edition, my introduction, pp. 49 and 50; Yamada's ed., pp. 259ff.

[50] The two spells attributed here to Vajrapāṇi were used just above by the presiding Buddha, with whom Vajrapāṇi comes to be identified, as already observed. *Niśumbha* and *śumbha*, which occur just below, are the names of two titans famous in Hindu tradition for their prolonged austerities and

Then the Bodhisattva Vajragarbha, the Great Being, expressed his most excellent *vidyā*: OṂ VAJRA-RATNOTTAMA JVĀLAYA HŪṂ PHAṬ (O blaze! Most excellent vajra-gem).

Then the Bodhisattva Vajranetra, the Great Being, expressed his most excellent *vidyā*: OṂ SVABHĀVAŚUDDHA VAJRA-PADMA ŚODHAYA SARVAṂ VIDYOTTAMA HŪṂ PHAṬ (O purify all, Vajra-lotus, naturally pure, supreme magical power!).

Then the Bodhisattva Vajraviśva, the Great Being, expressed his most excellent *vidyā*: OṂ VAJRA-KARMOTTAMA VAJRADHARASAMAYAM ANUSMARA ŚUMBHA NIŚUMBHA-ĀKARṢAYA PRAVEŚAYA-ĀVEŚAYA BANDHAYA SAMAYAṂ GRAHAYA SARVAKARMĀṆI ME KURU MAHĀSATTVA HŪṂ PHAṬ (O vajra-action, most excellent, bear in mind the pledge of Vajradhara. *Śumbha niśumbha* —coerce, induce, prevail, bind, hold to the pledge, affect all actions for me, O Vajrasattva).

Then the Bodhisattva Vajravidyottama, the Great Being, brought forth his "quintessence" as fit for honoring the Bodhisattva Vajrapāṇi: OṂ ŚUMBHA NIŚUMBHA VAJRAVIDYOTTAMA HŪṂ PHAṬ (Most excellent magical power of the vajra).

Then the Vidyārāja Krodharāja (the new name of the vanquished Śiva = King of Magical Power, Vajra Wrath), falling at the feet of the Lord, gave his "quintessence": OṂ VAJRAŚŪLA (Vajra-mace!).

Then the Vidyārāja Māyāvajra (the new name of the vanquished Nārāyaṇa = King of Magical Power, Illusion Vajra), pronounced his "quintessence": OṂ VAJRA-MĀYA VIDARŚAYA SARVAṂ HŪṂ PHAṬ (O vajra-illusion, destroy all!).

Then the Vidyārāja Vajraghaṇṭa (the new name of the vanquished Sanatkumāra = King of Magical Power, Vajra Bell) gave his "quintessence": OM VAJRA-GHAṆṬA RAṆA RAṆA HŪṂ PHAṬ (O vajra-bell, tinkle tinkle!).

Then the Vidyārāja Maunavajra (the new name of the vanquished Brahmā = King of Magical Power, Sagelike Vajra) gave his "quintessence": OṂ VAJRA-MAUNA MAHĀVRATA HŪṂ PHAṬ (O Vajra-Sage of mighty vows!).

Then the Vidyārāja Vajrāyudha (the new name of the vanquished Indra = King of Magical Power, Vajra Weapon) gave his "quintessence": OM VAJRĀYUDHA DĀMAKA HŪṂ PHAṬ (O Vajra-weapon, subdue!).

In the above example we have the words *vidyā* (magical lore or power) and *hṛdaya* (quintessence) used with the same meaning. Elsewhere in the same tantra (the beginning of Chapter 13) the term *samaya*, which we have translated provisionally as "pledge" is used with the same meaning as the other two. Thus the divinities, one after another, state the *samaya*, and we have mantras just like all the others. Elsewhere again (the beginning of Chapter 20) the divinities state the *mudrā*, a term which we have translated so far as "hand-gesture," but here again it refers to their individual spells. All these terms refer to the "expression" of the divinity, verbal or otherwise, and the reader is advised that this can make translation of these texts unusually ambiguous. Thus, both *vidyā* and *mudrā*, as

magical powers. Thus the application of such names to Śiva is quite suitable. *Niśumbha* also means "slaughter," and thus it may have come into use as a destructive spell with Śaivite associations. *Ṭakka* seems to have been applied to certain aborigines, hence gaining the meaning of "wild." *Ṭakkijjaḥ* would thus mean "savage-born." *Ṭakkara* is an epithet of Śiva.

the expression of the divinity, refer also to the feminine partner, which the divinity may be envisaged as embracing, and thus are freely used for *prajñā* (wisdom) in this particular meaning.[51] So far as the verbal expression is concerned, the most suitable English word to be used for all these Sanskrit terms is undoubtedly "spell." One attracts by a spell, one binds by a spell, one releases by a spell, exactly as has been done in so many other ritual settings quite apart from the Indian ones we are now considering. I am aware that present-day Western Buddhists, specifically those who are followers of the Tibetan tradition, dislike this English word used for mantra and the rest because of its association with vulgar magic. One need only reply that whether one likes it or not, the greater part of the tantras are concerned precisely with vulgar magic, because this is what most people were interested in then, just as they are interested chiefly nowadays in scientific achievements and technological inventions. Most of us are made this way and only a minority show a sincere interest in higher religious exertion. When exactly the same terms are used throughout a particular religious tradition, by the majority who are interested in magic and by the minority who are interested in higher states of spiritualized realization, it is very difficult to separate the two, especially when so many of the more famous practitioners seem to have been interested in both mundane as well as supramundane "successes" (*siddhi*). A spell is an enunciation of certain syllables, which should have a spontaneous (viz., magical) effect, when correctly pronounced by someone who is initiated into its use. In translating all these many tantric texts, the Tibetans did not normally translate the actual spells, because the change of enunciation might threaten their efficacy.[52] They merely transliterated them into Tibetan script, as I have done into English script with the more intractable ones. The early Tibetan commentators usually understood the Sanskrit terminology, but except for a minority of serious practitioners who have studied under competent teachers, the recitation of these "spells" has all too often become a form of gibberish, a term that has been applied rather more unfairly to the use of spells by whomever they are recited under whatever circumstances.

In studying any science it is essential to understand the precise meanings of the terminology employed by its practitioners, and in modern science an exact terminology is demanded. The tantras certainly represent a "science" of a kind. In so far as the ritual should be followed exactly if the desired results are to be achieved, it may even be called an "exact science," but it can scarcely be said to

[51] Again in passing one may note that to fix the meanings rigidly of the Sanskrit terms *jñāna*, knowledge or wisdom, and *prajñā*, wisdom or insight or knowledge, is in practice impossible, as the meaning varies in both cases depending upon the context in which these terms are used. One can argue endlessly about which suits where. The Tibetans solved the problem easily by inventing compounds based on their word to know: *ye-shes*, "primordial knowledge" for *jñāna* and *shes-rab*, "plenitude of knowledge" for *prajñā*. We cannot solve the matter so satisfactorily. For an attempt at elucidation see A. Wayman, "Notes on the Sanskrit Term *jñāna*."

[52] Translations may sometimes be added in small lettering underneath the main text, thus leaving the Sanskrit predominant. Mr. Larry Mermelstein kindly draws my attention to this in the case of a Cakrasaṃvara-sādhana that he has been translating. See "translation rules", pp. 441-3 below.

possess a scientific vocabulary, and in writing about it "scientifically" as one may well be expected to do in a book such as this, one has either to forge one's own vocabulary, or else continue to use Sanskrit terms, having first analyzed the range of their possible meanings. For the writer the second course is certainly the easiest, for it places the onus of understanding the most suitable meaning upon the reader, but this seems unfair unless he has been initiated into the whole context of the particular text or ritual. It is interesting to observe that Tibetan lamas refuse to believe that someone who has not received the initiation into a particular text can possibly understand its meaning. This meant originally an initiation (Sanskrit *āgama*) into the whole meaning of the text by a competent teacher to a worthy disciple and in this sense it was absolutely necessary, since the Tibetan translations use stereotyped terms (hence their extraordinary faithfulness to the original Sanskrit) and the meaning of these terms varies according to the context in the way we are describing. Nowadays the initiation into a text has all too often become a kind of magical rite, in which at best the text in question may be read through rapidly, but even this is seldom done. So important is this now considered that a good lama will insist on performing such a ceremony before going through the text in a more comprehensible manner.

By developing a fixed vocabulary as consistently as possible one can give what appears to be a more intelligible version of the text than even the Sanskrit original can provide, for as we have observed in the matter of the various words used for "spell," the subject-matter might be clearer if terms were carefully distinguished in usage, but often they are not. Also the spells themselves are of very unequal content, as though invented on the spur of the moment. Indeed this is probably how they were formed on a particular occasion by a certain tantric master, then becoming more or less fixed according to the tradition of his teaching.

5. THE VOTARIES OF THE TANTRAS

Many of the tantras, that is to say the main texts that were regarded as canonical, tend to be haphazard in content and formation, and this state of affairs provides a good clue to their origins. For clearer expositions one can turn to commentaries and exegetical works, which are often brilliantly written. But it is clear from the disagreements that continued to exist in the categorizing of tantras, and the forced interpretations of unwelcome passages, that the material was already found to be intractable long before Western scholars began to take any interest in it. The inevitable uncertainties concerning the categories to which tantras might be assigned is well illustrated in mKhas-grub-rje's *Fundamentals of the Buddhist Tantras*.[53] The same work also provides us with an example of the ease with which an unwelcome statement in a tantra might be disposed of. The matter in question concerns who may receive the benefits of

[53] Lessing and Wayman's edition, pp. 250-69.

entering the maṇḍala, and the "Symposium of Truth" is quite explicit on this.

> Now the way in which a Vajra-pupil enters the Great Maṇḍala of the Vajra-sphere is explained. In the first place this entry is for saving the whole sphere of living beings without exception and without reminder, for effecting their well-being, their supreme happiness and their success. So in the matter of entering the Great Maṇḍala one should make no distinction between who is a worthy recipient and who is not. And why is this? It is because living beings who have committed great evil, having seen the Great Maṇḍala of the Vajra-sphere and entered it, will be saved from all evil rebirths. Those beings who are greedy for all kinds of things, food and drink and sensual pleasures, who hate the pledge (*samaya*) and are not proficient in the preliminaries and so on, even in their case when they enter for the purpose of effecting their desires, all their hopes will be fulfilled. There are living beings, who because of their pleasure in dancing and song, in laughter and love-play and dallying and because of their ignorance of the essential truth which is the Mahāyāna lore of All the Tathāgatas, enter the maṇḍalas of the families of other gods, and being afraid of the bases of training do not enter the maṇḍalas of the family of All the Tathāgatas, which are productive of supreme pleasure, happiness and joy; even they, finding themselves facing the entry into maṇḍalas of woe, should enter the Great Maṇḍala of the Vajra-Sphere for the sake of experiencing all pleasure, joy, the highest success, happiness and bliss and so as to avoid the paths that lead to all evil destinies. Then there are those righteous beings who are seeking the enlightenment of the Buddhas by means of supreme success in the morality, mental composure and wisdom of all Buddhas, and in their striving, are exhausted with the various stages of meditation and salvation, by the mere entry into the Great Maṇḍala of the Vajra-Sphere universal buddhahood will not be difficult for them to obtain, let alone other kinds of success.[54]

Surely the point of this passage, now quoted complete, is that this particular ritual is available to all without exception, and it must be assumed that they all accept the necessary training. As will be clear as we proceed, tantric practice offers success (*siddhi*) to all and sundry, if only their senses are keen enough and they are prepared to submit to the discipline imposed by their preceptor. mKhas-grub-rje in his *Fundamentals of the Buddhist Tantras* quibbles about this, arguing that all may enter the maṇḍala, but that only the worthy ones should receive consecration.[55] In a sense this is true, but the point being made is that no one should be refused in the first instance because of moral unworthiness. In fact the need of such a one is even greater, and the argument that unworthy ones may enter the maṇḍala, but not receive consecration, is surely a

[54] STTS, Yamada's edition, pp. 66-7. An almost identical passage occurs in the *Sarvadurgatipariśodhana Tantra* (SDPS), see Skorupski's translation, p. 100. Here the meaning is made even more explicit, viz., "There are some living beings who commit great sins but they are (potentially) worthy Tathāgatas. On seeing and entering this mandala of Vajra-Hūṃkara (= Vajrapāṇi), they will become free from every evil destiny."

[55] See Lessing and Wayman's edition, pp. 144-5.

forced one. If he is unworthy at this stage, he will not even see the maṇḍala. Our tantra is quite explicit about this in another passage:

> There are living beings of wrong views, of evil actions, lacking fortitude, devoid of application, ignorant of the various acts. Because of their poor fortitude, they are not to enter the great maṇḍalas of the Family of All the Tathāgatas, the maṇḍala of the Vajra-Sphere, and the others. . . . You are never to break faith with the secrets of the Pledge-Symbols of the Family of All the Tathāgatas, lest you are born in the hells, or the realms of tormented spirits, or meet with misfortune and die an untimely death." So saying, he (the preceptor) removes the face-cloth and reveals the maṇḍala to the pupil.[56]

It should be noted that the pupil is led to the maṇḍala blindfolded, and thus to see the maṇḍala in any constructive sense would be difficult when one takes into account the secrecy which is continually enjoined in these tantras. One may observe at the same time that such secrecy must have been limited to certain consecration rites, and that there were many others that by their nature were made public. Thus this same ritual of calling upon a particular set of divinities to take possession of their symbolic representation or "pledge" (*samaya*), provides the main subject of much liturgy that is still performed publicly in Tibetan monasteries today.[57] Having thus manifested themselves and received their due praise and the conventional sets of offerings, they bestow their "empowerment" (*adhiṣṭhāna*) in return.[58] Such ceremonies are certainly not a Tibetan invention, and the question of how soon their use developed in Indian monasteries is yet another one that affects any attempt to understand the beginnings of tantric Buddhism and its more general acceptance. The "Symposium of Truth" from which we have quoted just above can scarcely be taking account of yet another unquestionable fact, namely that the bestowal of consecrations upon all and sundry has become a function expected, even demanded, of any well-known Tibetan lama. This is just as true of earlier times, as biographies of such lamas show,[59] as it is of famous lamas who go on tour in India or the Western world, or wherever else in these unhappier days, when Tibetan religion is driven into exile. The effect of such general ceremonies is to produce the sort of spiritual uplift, which is experienced in all religious communities, not only Buddhist, and it can induce some of those present to a more serious practice of their professed beliefs, although the majority continue afterward in their old ways, such being the hold of saṃsāra.

Although the tantras were capable of a popular application and were peopled with higher beings of the celestial kind already met with in the Mahāyāna sūtras as well as with Hindu divinities who presumably possessed already a considerable

56 MS fo. 85, ll. 3-8; Yamada's edition, pp. 144-5.

57 Concerning the term *samaya* in this context, see section III.13.b and also refer to the Index.

58 For such praises and lists of offerings see my *Buddhist Himālaya*, pp. 254-6, and in far more detail, Stephan Bayer, *The Cult of Tārā*, pp. 148ff.

59 See for instance my *Four Lamas of Dolpo*, pp. 151ff.

popular following, they can scarcely be described as a popularizing form of Buddhist literature. They were clearly composed for the use of those who were accepted for properly prepared initiation into the rites that were believed to produce special effects, and thus they can only have been composed by the religious teachers and yogins who conducted such rites. In that the religious master, any such religious master who had been accepted in faith and devotion by his pupils, represented for them the lord of the maṇḍala, thus identified with the supreme adamantine state, his words were inevitably Buddha-words. Once codified and transmitted through a succession of masters and pupils, such a corpus of teachings and instructions might easily gain acceptance as "canonical." Canonization of religious literature, whether in the Buddhist or the Christian sense, means no more in the first instance than the gradual acceptance by an ever widening circle of believers of certain oral and textual traditions as valid doctrine relatable to earlier traditional teachings which have been already accepted as true. The mere fact of this wider acceptance results in their increased circulation, which assists in stabilizing their contents, although at the same time there is an increase in minor textual variants, usually caused by errors in copying, which may later be rectified slightly differently from the original. However, the work becomes established, and when collections are later made by some recognized authority, it is judged as worthy of inclusion, while the works of others may be rejected. It thus becomes in effect "canonical" and is fairly certain of finding a place in all later collections that are made. While there is no evidence of any vast canon of Mahāyāna sūtras and tantras ever having been produced in India itself, some works were certainly grouped together as particularly significant, and the accounts of Śākyamuni's three turnings of the Wheel of the Doctrine represent a clear attempt to relate much of this later teaching with the one master whose authority must remain unquestioned by all who call themselves Buddhists. We have already drawn attention to the methods that were employed by their promoters to link the tantras as far as possible with the person of Śākyamuni himself.

6. VARIOUS KINDS OF TANTRAS

a. *Tantras Relatable to Mahāyāna Sūtras*

To give a date to a particular tantra is a difficult, indeed an impossible task, unless one is content to date it from the time that it became sufficiently accepted in scholarly Buddhist circles for commentaries to be written upon it. The problem is then transferred to finding approximate dates for the commentators. The actual origins, for the reasons just explained above, must go back several generations earlier into restricted religious circles, of whom nothing was yet known. Whether they were deliberately secret and eventually achieved their renown as the result of the magical powers they achieved may not have been true in every case, as the Tibetan historian Tāranātha (born 1575) asserts, but he is surely correct in assuming that their origins were unknown, simply because no one else outside a limited circle knew anything about them.

> Because in the early stages these men were very careful and guarded the secret, no one knew that they were practicing the secret mantras, until they actually became possessed of magical powers (*vidyādhara*). But when they had these powers, traveling in the sky or becoming invisible, then it was known conclusively that they were practitioners of mantras. On account of this there is very little (traceable) handing down of traditional teachings from master to pupil, and although there had been much study devoted to the Action Tantras (*kriyā-tantra*) and the Performance Tantras (*caryā-tantra*) from the time when the Mahāyāna began to spread, as they were practiced very much in secret, no one knew who was studying them except for those actually engaged in these secret mantras.[60]

Tāranātha suggests that the earliest tantras to take shape were those which were subsequently classed as the two lower grades of tantras, in so far as they are concerned with the acquisition of certain magical powers, some of which may appear frivolous, while others were concerned with the curing of disease and demonical assault, the staving off of death, the avoidance of evil rebirths, as well as consecration of those considered fit to be potential Buddhas. We have already noted the presence of similar materials in some of the Mahāyāna sūtras, and indeed some of the works that were subsequently cataloged by the Tibetans as tantras are referred to in their titles as sūtras. Thus there is a slight overlapping between these two classes of Buddhist literature, although clear distinctions of content can be drawn between them.

The kind of tantra where such overlapping takes place would appear to have its origins in the same sort of religious circles as the later Mahāyāna sūtras, namely in established monastic centers, where traditions were already wholeheartedly Buddhist. This means that the Buddha and Bodhisattva manifestations who people the maṇḍalas have names that are already clearly acceptable in Buddhist Mahāyāna tradition. Examples of this kind are the "Sūtra of Golden Light," classed subsequently as a tantra because of its presentation of buddhahood as fivefold (thus potentially as a maṇḍala) and the many chapters devoted to protective divinities together with their spells, or again the "Fundamental Ordinance of Mañjuśrī," of which the main maṇḍala has been admirably described by Mme Macdonald, or again the "Symposium of Truth," a work in which I have had a special interest for many years. Listed thus, these three works serve to illustrate that progressive tantric development, which eventually distinguishes sūtras from tantras. There is clearly nothing secret or restricted about the "Sūtra of Golden Light."[61] It contains some basic teaching on the Void, prayers and confessions, especially praises of the Buddhas,

[60] Tāranātha's *History of Buddhism*, edited by Schiefner, Tibetan text, p. 82, ll. 15ff. This passage has already been published by me with comments in my edition of the *Hevajra Tantra*, vol. I, pp. 11-12.

[61] One may refer to R. E. Emmerick's excellent English translation of this sūtra.

vows befitting a Bodhisattva who follows a regular path toward enlightenment, and chapters devoted to certain divinities, female as well as male, who have offered to protect those who practice Buddhist teachings and especially those who are devoted to the "Sūtra of Golden Light." Even earlier associations are suggested by the inclusion of *jātaka* (earlier birth) stories of Śākyamuni. The nearest this work comes to suggesting any form of consecration is the shower of manifold blessings that the kings of the four quarters promise to bestow upon any king who promotes the cause of this particular sūtra. With the "Fundamental Ordinance of Mañjuśrī" we find far more that is typical of tantric Buddhism, spells and demonstrations of magical powers, a well ordered maṇḍala, which however has not yet assumed the typical fourfold manifestation of the central divinity to the four quarters, and a detailed description of consecration rites according to a regal pattern. This is a most voluminous work, certainly compiled over several centuries, but many of its pronouncements, especially those concerning Buddha-families and consecrations, would seem to place parts of it at least in the early formative period of tantric developments.[62] More will be said about this below. The "Symposium of Truth" is referred to as a sūtra in its Sanskrit MS colophon, but this may refer only to the last of the five parts in which this tantra is divided. The other parts are known as *kalpa*, a term often used of tantric texts presumably with the meaning of "that which lays down the ritual and prescribed rules for ceremonial and sacrificial acts" (Apte's *Sanskrit Dictionary*, p. 388). In this work, as in other related Yoga Tantras, the pattern of the maṇḍala with a central divinity manifested to the four directions, is the norm, although there is still some hesitancy over the final number of Buddha-families. They are five so far as the arrangement of the maṇḍalas is concerned, but only four when the sets of rituals are arranged according to families, thus resulting in just four *kalpas*. Selected aspects of these and other related tantras will be dealt with below, for now it may be interesting to consider what these classes of tantra have in common with Mahāyāna sūtras.

They continue the process, which goes right back into the earliest period, of introducing Indian (Hindu) divinities into the Buddhist fold, and they continue to keep them entirely subservient to the Buddhas and great Bodhisattvas. The Mahāyāna sūtras had already increased to infinity the number of Buddhas and Bodhisattvas, all provided with acceptable Buddhist names, and there is no overt suggestion that they were converted to the doctrine from outside. Even the exceptional Vajrapāṇi, whose rise to greatness we have traced, is never regarded as a convert, but rather as belonging to the Buddhist fold by some kind of natural right. The same applies to the other great Bodhisattvas, Mañjuśrī and Avalokiteśvara, whatever their non-Buddhist antecedents may have been. Other Bodhisattvas appear in leading roles in certain sūtras, but even those who appear with some kind of character (e.g., Vimalakīrti or even Padmākara) scarcely achieve the universal greatness which these three achieve, and most of the many

62 For general references to this tantra see *Mañjuśrīmūlakalpa* in the Bibliography. See especially section III.11 below.

other Bodhisattavs appear as mere names. The great gods of Hinduism were explained as emanations or deliberate manifestations of certain Bodhisattvas, especially of Avalokiteśvara, but it was also satisfactory to represent them as converts to the doctrine, who are forced into its service. Our quotation (section III.3) from the "Symposium of Truth" well illustrates such an act of conversion, and in this way all the classes of minor Indian divinities, both male and female, were gradually brought into the Buddhist orbit. The related tantra entitled the *Sarvadurgatipariśodhana* ("Elimination of All Evil Rebirths") contains several subsidiary maṇḍalas—of the Four Kings of the Quarters, of the guardian divinities of the ten directions (four quarters, intermediate quarters, zenith and nadir), of the eight great planets, of the eight great serpents (*nāgas*), of Bhairava (The Terrible) with his eight subsidiary terrible manifestations, all accompanied by equally terrible female partners.[63] Bhairava is merely the fierce manifestation of Śiva, and we shall note in the next section how these same divinities, who appear in Yoga Tantras in lowly status, gain acceptance in Supreme Yoga Tantras as the embodiment of supreme buddhahood. It would appear that in the tantras classed as Action (*kriyā*), Performance (*caryā*) and Yoga, feminine spouses are regarded as suitable only for those divinities of non-Buddhist origin who appear in a subsidiary role. However, it is not considered unsuitable to provide the great Buddhist divinities with what may best be described as handmaidens. These are goddesses who have been discreetly received into the Buddhist fold, so discreetly that it is often impossible to guess at their origins. Thus in the maṇḍala described in Chapter Two of the *Mañjuśrīmūlakalpa* ("Fundamental Ordinance of Mañjuśrī") Avalokiteśvara has around him several such goddesses, Pāṇḍaravāsinī, Tārā and Bhrukuṭi, as well as Prajñāpāramitā, Locanā and Uṣṇīṣarājā, while Vajrapāṇi has four more, provided with suitable Vajra names (see section III.11). Both these great Bodhisattvas remain celibate, and one may assume that it was considered suitable to provide them with such a feminine entourage, because it was the custom for princely figures to appear thus in real life. There is no indication of any goddess receiving high Buddhist status before the beginning of these tantric developments which we are now attempting to unravel. Prajñāpāramitā, being the Perfection of Wisdom herself, was the most easily personified, but there is as yet no cult of her as a great goddess in Mahāyāna sūtras. The first goddess to find a niche in Buddhist monasteries was Hāritī, the goddess of plenty, and her cult together with that of the guardian god Mahākāla, certainly belonged to traditional everyday Mahāyāna practice[64] (*Pls. 21a & b, 86*). Whereas these were essentially non-Buddhist in origin like so many of the later tantric divinities, the goddesses who surround Avalokiteśvara and who later receive an honorable place within the group of the Five Buddhas, are probably imaginative Buddhist creations. Pāṇḍaravāsinī simply means the "one with the white garment" and it

[63] See T. Skorupski, SDPS Tantra, pp. 49ff.

[64] This particular cult is well attested by the Chinese pilgrim-scholar I-tsing. See his *A Record of the Buddhist Religion*, pp. 37-8.

is thus that she is described in the present context. She holds a lotus in her left hand and with the right she is making a gesture of salutation in the direction of Śākyamuni. Both she and Tārā, whose name means the "one who saves" may be regarded in origin as hypostases of Avalokiteśvara himself, since the act of holding a lotus flower and the will to save all beings are his two chief attributes. The other names all relate to essential parts of a Buddha's head. Bhrukuṭi is thus the goddess of the eyebrows, between which reposes the *ūrṇā* or circle of white hair, one of the thirty-two marks of a Buddha. Light rays shoot forth from this spot in many Mahāyāna sūtras, and this may have suggested the idea of such a goddess. Locanā is the goddess of the all-seeing Buddha-eye, and the *uṣṇīṣa* or wisdom-bump, which is the primary mark of a Buddha, provides a whole set of Buddha-emanations apart from the "uṣṇīṣa-queen" who appears in the present context. The goddesses around Vajrapāṇi have self-explanatory names.

Of the six high ranking goddesses around Avalokiteśvara three are later attached to the set of Five Buddhas, namely Locanā, Pāṇḍaravāsinī and Tārā. Since they are placed at the intermediate points of the compass, four such goddesses are needed, their number being made up with Māmakī, whose name means "my own" and concerning whose origin I have so far no suggestion to make. Of the others Prajñāpāramitā remains a great goddess in her own right, continuing to symbolize the Perfection of Wisdom, but she attracts no great cult in the tantric period. This privilege comes to Tārā in relationship with the other Buddha-goddesses of the intermediate points of the compass, and as a White Tārā, when she manifests herself as a Great Goddess, indeed as the greatest of all Buddhist Goddesses, in her own right (*Pls. 22a, 31b*). In effect she assumes the primacy which belonged to Pāṇḍaravāsinī, "the white clad one," in Avalokiteśvara's entourage in the mandala to which we have just referred. She becomes a feminine version of Avalokiteśvara rather than his partner in that both of them remain major celibate divinities. Tārā also tends to replace Prajñāpāramitā in that she comes to be regarded as the Mother of all Buddhas. Her remarkable success appears to be an exclusively Buddhist development for which no convincing Hindu parallel can be found.[65] Her cult and to some extent her significance correspond in a marked way to the Christian Orthodox veneration of Mary as Mother of God, and it is not impossible that the conception of such a supreme feminine divinity should have taken place in Buddhist minds as a result of cultural contacts through northwestern India. It is more likely however that the cult developed of its own accord in India with the concept of the Perfection of Wisdom as a goddess leading the way. The remaining one of the six listed above, Bhrukuṭi, has no very brilliant future. Her name comes to suggest a wrinkled forehead and thus she finds herself regarded as an ill-humored

65 For examples of the faith and confidence she inspires one may turn to Stephen Beyer, *The Cult of Tārā*, pp. 229ff. The Hindu goddess Durgā also delivers her supplicants from distress, but she is conceived of as a terrible bloodthirsty divinity. Tārā for all her power remains benign and is always represented thus. Concerning the worship of Tārā with examples of hymns intoned in her honor see Beyer, *op. cit.*, pp. 201ff.

manifestation of the far more popular Tārā.

The main point being made throughout so much incidental discussion is that the leading figures, Buddhas, Bodhisattvas and high ranking feminine divinities can make a fair claim to a Buddhist pedigree in those classes of tantras that we have been considering.

b. *Tantras with Non-Buddhist Associations*

In certain other tantras, especially those which were later placed in a Supreme Yoga class, the chief divinities have no affinity with those other Great Beings, the Buddhas and Bodhisattvas of the Mahāyāna sūtras and most tantras of the other three classes, of which we have considered some examples. Also the whole setting, the background to the play as it were, is entirely different.[66] Thus we find ourselves in circumstances much changed from the conventional Buddhist world with its glorious palaces and paradises. Such scenes are normally set in the opening chapter. Thus the Lord Śākyamuni/Vairocana preaches the "Symposium of Truth" in the palace of the king of gods in the Highest Heaven. He teaches the *Sarvadurgatipariśodhana Tantra* in a heavenly park adorned with flowers and trees of all kinds, resounding with the warbling of birds, etc. He teaches the *Mañjuśrīmūlakalpa* in the high heaven known as the Pure Abode. He teaches the *Mahā-Vairocana Tantra* (also referred to as a sūtra) in the magnificent palace of the Vajra Dharma-sphere. By violent contrast these other tantras, to which we now refer in some detail, open with the words: "Thus I have heard: at one time the Lord reposed in the vagina of the Lady of the Vajra-sphere—the heart of the Body, Speech and Mind of all Buddhas" or some very similar phrase and we are given no immediate description of the actual physical conditions under which the tantra is proclaimed. Even without the help of the commentaries we would be very naïve indeed if we took such an opening statement literally, and it is probably superfluous to explain to any informed reader that what is here suggested is the union of the practicing yogin with the absolute state of buddhahood.[67] Thus is is claimed that the tantra in question should be

[66] R. Tajima in his *Étude sur le Mahāvairocana-Sūtra* draws a distinction between those tantras which were "a development of Mahāyānist thought," thus "an orthodox esoterism founded on the Vinaya" with Nālandā as their center, and those "formed in a rather popular mould toward the end of the eighth century and declining into the esoterism of the left." These he centers at Vikramaśīla. I would be doubtful about so clear a division and certainly about the precise place of origin, but some rather more general distinctions can probably be drawn. See also first footnote in section III.1.

[67] It may be of interest to quote a short extract from Indrabhūti's *Jñānasiddhi*, Chapter Fifteen (see Bhattacharyya, *Two Vajrayāna Works*, p. 81), where he comments briefly on this opening gambit, bringing it into direct relationship with the opening passage in the STTS, which describes the process of final enlightenemnt of a perfected Buddha (still with Śākyamuni in mind) according to the tantric notion of spontaneous realization.

> At one time Bhagavan (the Lord or Blessed One) so called because he is possessed of good qualities such as lordship and so on, was reposing in the "heart," viz., wisdom, which is referred to as "vajra-maiden" because it has the nature of unbreakable knowledge (*prajñā*), and again as *bhaga* ("vagina," although the Sanskrit word is here deliberately equated with *bhanga*, "breaking" or "destroying") because it destroys all the afflictions (*kleśa*). So it is in these *bhaga* of the vajra-maidens—the heart of the Body, Speech and Mind of all the Buddhas that he reposes. It is taught

regarded as a statement of absolute truth, albeit in relative, viz., symbolic or suggestive terms. Moreover the Lord (Bhagavan) is no longer Śākyamuni in any of his recognizable hypostases, but a fearful being with the name of Śambara, Vajraḍāka, Heruka, Hevajra or Caṇḍamahāroṣaṇa ("Fierce and Greatly Wrathful"). The terms *ḍāka* (male) and *ḍākinī* (female) refer to the fiendish flesh-eating followers of Durgā, often simply known as Devī ("the Goddess"), spouse of Śiva. By association they also refer to the yogins and yoginīs who follow Śaivite rites. The names of Heruka, Caṇḍamahāroṣaṇa, as well as Bhairava ("the Terrible One"), already mentioned above, are all associated with Śiva. These names alone would be enough to suggest that those tantras, where such a being is the Lord, originated amongst groups of yogins, whose practices brought them into close relationship with Śaivite communities. A description of one such Lord may be helpful.

Since a description of Hevajra is already available in English translation,[68] I choose one of Śambara, also known as Cakrasaṃvara, whose cycle of tantric texts became very popular in Tibet (*Pls. 24, 26*). *Śambara* and *saṃvara* represent the same name in Sanskrit with slightly variant spellings, but the second spelling happens to be indentical with the word meaning a vow or a bond. Thus the Tibetans translated them differently: Śambara as *bDe-mchog*, "Supreme Bliss," which is how they interpret this name, whatever the spelling, and Saṃvara as *sDom-pa*, understood as "binding" or "union." The compound name, Cakrasaṃvara, is therefore interpreted as the "union of the wheel of the elements" explained in various ways, but suggesting in every case the blissful state of perfect wisdom. Thus the point may be made at once that the investigation of origins of the materials used in the formation of the tantras and the interpretation that Buddhist tradition places upon these materials are two very different things indeed. *Śamba* means in Sanskrit blessed or fortunate, similar in meaning therefore to Śiva. A similar word *Śambhu* with the same meaning is used as a name of Śiva. Śambara, like Ṭakkara (see section III.4) and Śumbha were used as demonic names in the Śaivite circle just as were Heruka and Bhairava. Thus in their original use all these names suggest no more than a fierce manifestation of divinity, to be placated on occasions by such epithets as "fortunate," precisely as Śiva ("fortunate") was earlier applied to the god Rudra ("Wild"). In translating Śambara as "Supreme Bliss" the early Tibetan translators, presumably following the advice of their Indian masters, were

thus: that the wisdom (*jñāna*) of the yogin penetrates the wisdoms of All Buddhas and these are mutually pervading and pervasive. Reposing in this state totally means that one does not repose in all the wisdoms by degrees, but that one reposes in them spontaneously (Sanskrit *yugapad*, Tibetan *cig-car*). [The Sanskrit text, p. 81, l. 15 must be corrected in accordance with the Tibetan text, TT vol. 68, p. 249-3-2, by inserting a negative particle *a-* before *sthitam* and incorporating the additional words which Bhattacharyya relegates to a footnote.]

Indrabhūti then illustrates this by a quotation from the STTS (translated below in scetion III.13.f). For its explicit application to the Buddha Śākyamuni, see Lessing and Wayman, *Fundamentals of the Buddhist Tantras*, pp. 28-35.

68 See my edition of the *Hevajra Tantra*, beginning of II.5.

deliberately interpreting it in a very special tantric sense, which detaches it from its "pagan" origins. We now see how this fierce manifestation is described:

> Within the divine abode (the maṇḍala) in the center of the circle on a solar disk resting on an eight-petalled lotus is Cakrasaṃvara himself. He has four faces, the front one dark blue, the left one green, the back one red and the right one yellow. These symbolize the four material elements (earth, water, fire and air), the four infinitudes (= "pure abodes", *brahmavihāra*), the four releases and the four ritual acts.[69] His body is blue, indicating that he does not diverge from the (celestial) Dharma-sphere. Each face has three eyes, indicating that he sees the (whole) threefold world and that he knows the substance of the three times (past, present and future). He has twelve arms, indicating that he comprehends the evolution and reversal of the twelvefold causal nexus and eliminates these twelve stages of transmigration. With his first pair of hands, which hold a vajra and bell, he embraces his spouse, symbolizing the union of Wisdom and Means. With his next pair of hands (he holds aloft) a raw elephant hide made into a garment, thus rending the elephant of illusion.
>
> With the third (right) hand he holds a drum, for his voice resounds joyously.
> With the fourth an axe, since he cuts off birth and death at the roots.
> With the fifth a sacrificial knife, since he cuts off the six defects, pride and the rest.
> With the sixth a trident, since he overcomes the evil of the threefold world.
> With his third left hand he holds a *khaṭvāṅga* (scepter adorned with superimposed skulls), since he is possessed of the blissful Thought of Enlightenment.
> With the fourth he holds a skull filled with blood, since he has cut away discrimination between existence and nonexistence.
> With his fifth he holds a vajra noose, since he binds pure wisdom in the life-series of living beings.
> With the sixth he holds the (severed) four-faced head of Brahmā, since he avoids all illusion.
>
> Indicating that through his great compassion he remains in the realm of living beings, with his outstretched right foot he treads on the supine figure of the Night of Time (who represents) the extremity of nirvāṇa.[70] She is red and emaciated and holds a sacrificial knife and a skull cup. Indicating that through his great wisdom he holds neither to the idea of a person nor of any real element, with his left foot which is drawn back he treads face-downward the figure of Bhairava (who represents) the extremity of saṃsāra. He is black with four hands and in the right ones he holds a drum and a sacrificial knife and in the left ones a *khaṭvānga* and a skull cup.
>
> Since he (Cakrasaṃvara) is replete with accumulations (of merits and

[69] The four releases (*vimokṣa*) are that of the Void (*śūnyatāvimokṣa*), of Signlessness (*animitta-*), Effortlessness (*apranihita-*) and the totally nonconditioned (*anabhisaṃskāra-*). The four ritual acts are explained below in section III.13.e.

[70] "Night of Time" (Tibetan Dus-mtshan-ma, corresponding to Sanskrit Kālarātrī) is conceived of as a goddess. Thus like a good Mādhyamika he avoids the two extremes of nirvāṇa (understood as final destruction) and saṃsāra, symbolized by the bloodthirsty Bhairava.

knowledge), the tip of his matted hair, which is bound up on the top of his head, is adorned with a precious wish-granting gem, for he bestows all desirable things in accordance with one's wishes. Since the Thought of Enlightenment is ever on the increase, there is a lunar crescent on the left side, while on the top of his massed hair there is a crossed double vajra (*viśvavajra*), indicating that he operates through different kinds of action for the good of living beings. There is a crown made of five desiccated human heads surmounting each of his four faces, indicating the fully developed quality of the five Wisdoms. He has a garland of fifty freshly severed heads representing the purity of the fifty vowels and consonants (of the Sanskrit alphabet). Indicating that he has vanquished the Evil One (Māra) and false teachings he makes a grimace and his teeth are fanglike. His ear ornaments symbolize (the perfection of) patience, his necklace generosity, his bracelets morality, his girdle effort, and the coronet of bones meditation; the funeral-pyre ashes with which he is smeared represent wisdom, thus completing the Six Perfections as represented by these six adornments.

Heroically subjugating the Evil One and avoiding the concepts of subject and object, he has a loose lower garment of tiger skin. He possesses the fully developed qualities of Body, Speech and Mind and is skilful in coming to the aid of those potential followers who are distressed by the emotions. Thus he is flamboyant, heroic, unlovely, wild, fearful, terrible, compassionate, dignified and serene. Such are the nine modes of his dance.[71]

Despite the symbolic interpretation in exclusively Buddhist terms, the origin of this divinity must surely be clear. The naked ascetic smeared in ashes with piled

71 A shorter "canonical" description of this divinity, viz., without interpretations, will be found in Shinichi Tsuda's excellent edition of selected chapters from the *Saṃvarodaya Tantra*, pp. 283-4.

My extract is taken from a Tibetan ritual text entitled: "Clarifying the order of the rite (*sādhana*) of the circle of the maṇḍala of Srī Cakrasaṃvara" as published with Dawa Samdup's English translation by Arthur Avalon (John Woodroffe) in his *Tantric Texts*, vol. VII. The volume is misleadingly entitled *Shrīchakrasambhāra Tantra, A Buddhist Tantra*, as though it contained the basic tantra, which it does not. Arthur Avalon is well known for his work on Śaivite tantras, and in this volume he finds himself in unfamiliar territory, as is at once clear from his introduction. Kazi Dawa Samdup was a quite remarkable Sikkimese lama, whose abilities were made use of by others in a manner that would scarcely be possible nowadays. He is responsible for all the difficult work of translation in three of the volumes of Tibetan texts, edited by W. Y. Evans-Wentz, who imposed his personal interpretations upon them in his long introductions. Thus Kazi Dawa Samdup never received the kind of assistance which he deserved, such as encouragement in the editing of his texts before translation. In the present case the Tibetan text is simply reproduced as he found it on his block print. Thus my translation presumes the need for certain emendations.

The extract will be found on p. 11, l. 7 to p. 13, l. 4 of his reproduced text. Many such *sādhanas* are available, but for convenience I have checked it against Tsong-kha-pa's "Clarification of the blissful method of Cakrasaṃvara according to the Great Yogin Luipa" as rendered into Italian by Professor Tucci in *Indo-Tibetica*, III.2, pp. 22-6. The description is practically identical but the assimilations are slightly differently ordered. One should refer to this work for a detailed description of the whole maṇḍala. One may add that Kazi Dawa Samdup's translation is rendered rather tedious to follow because of his use of invented phonetic spellings for the vast number of divinities who appear before us, although in many cases accurate Sanskrit equivalents are given in his footnotes. Other notes are not so successful and indeed could not be given in the conditions under which he worked. He deserves acclamation as the most heroic (and self-effacing) translator from Tibetan into English who has ever appeared in our scholarly world. He produced singlehanded the first *English-Tibetan Dictionary* (Calcutta, 1919), inventing ingenious Tibetan interpretations for English terms (e.g., balloon, buffer, etc.) for which there was no straight equivalent.

up matted hair, adorned with a lunar crescent, wearing skins of elephant and tiger, garlanded with skulls, holding trident, drum and *khaṭvāṅga*, all these attributes indicate Śiva as lord of yogins, the very one whom Vajrapāṇi is presumed in another context to have reduced to abject submission. Thus the same Indian divinity, who already possesses several aspects in Hindu devotion, enters the Buddhist pantheon at varying levels of acceptance, and no contradiction whatsoever manifests itself, as this spontaneous appropriation of religious figures (and some not so religious figures) proceeds. All the divinities listed above together with Śambara are of Śaivite type and the only name amongst them which is a Buddhist invention is Hevajra, derived from the salutation of He Vajra ("Hail Vajra!"), with which a master acclaims his pupil after the relevant consecration (see the extract from STTS in section III.13.a). The representatives of supreme enlightenment as interpreted by tantric yogins, they are all said to be fierce forms of Akṣobhya, the Imperturbable Buddha of the East, whose name is duplicated as *Acala* (also meaning imperturbable, immovable) within this context of fierce divinities. As will become clear below, when we deal specifically with Buddha-families, Akṣobhya's family is the family of wrath. However, it seems to have been in eastern India in the central and lower Ganges valley, where Bodhgayā as the actual site of the winning of enlightenment was certainly the chief place of traditional Buddhist pilgrimage, that the tantras which center on these divinities who are identified with Akṣobhya originate or at least first come to light. As was observed in section II.2.a above, the image which fixes symbolically the winning of enlightenment is that one where Śākyamuni is represented as touching the earth with the fingers of his right hand in order to call the Earth-Goddess to witness, thus showing him as imperturbable (*akṣobhya*) in his resistance to the onslaughts of Māra, the Evil One. It is in this conception that Akṣobhya appears as the primary Buddha of the eastern quarter, and so for this reason too, his association with the tantras that arose later in this region need not be surprising. Their geographical origin would seem to be certain for two reasons. Many of the famous yogins, who first promulgated these tantras, some of them writing commentaries that are preserved in the Tibetan canon, are also well known as the authors of religious songs relating precisely to the same tantric teachings, and surviving in a Middle Indian dialect, which has been variously referred to as Old Bengali, Old Bihari, Old Mithili and Old Oriya.[72] They may well relate in some way to all the modern languages of India which go under these names, but there is no doubt that they all belong to eastern India. They may be dated at the latest to the twelfth century, but many of them are likely to be several centuries earlier. Datings according to the authorships attributed depend upon the dates one attempts to give to these tantric yogins, and with very few exceptions, for example Nāropa (probably A.D. 956-1040), uncertainty prevails. It may even be doubted whether the same name means the same author, as names are so often duplicated. None

72 For a definitive edition of them see Per Kværne, *An Anthology of Buddhist Tantric Songs*. For examples see below.

of these problems, however, affect our present arguments, for the geographical area in which their activities are centered remains unquestionable. A second reason for certainty derives from the fact that these yogins, who are conventionally numbered as eighty-four "Great Adepts" (*mahāsiddha*) are also known of in Śaivite tradition, being associated with the practice of tantric cults in the same general area, which continued to be practiced long after Buddhism had ceased to be in any sense an established religion in eastern India (*Pl. 23*). It is interesting to note that two of these great yogins are associated with the founding of a form of yoga, closely related to that which is described in the Buddhist tantras now under consideration, which has survived to this day in a Śaivite setting, and has been accurately and sympathetically described.[73]

What may be fairly deduced so far from these rather general observations so far as the origins of these Buddhist tantras are concerned? Between the eighth and the twelfth centuries certain Buddhists began to take a special interest in forms of "violent yoga" (*haṭhayoga*) which were then in vogue in eastern India. Thus they frequented the places of retreat where such practices could be learned. Most of these yogins, as will immediately be seen from our further discussion, lived deliberately as "outcastes" from society, rejecting its conventions and norms. However, while they were not "Hindu" in any strict Brahmanical sense, they were inevitably affected by the whole religious environment of their upbringing. Thus those who met together as masters and pupils would certainly not be all operating at the level where all distinctions are merged into a "single flavor" and all divine forms are resolved into the person of the practicing yogin. There can hardly be any religious practice anywhere, even that which relies upon the mental and physical cult of yoga, which dispenses altogether with outward forms of worship of a chosen divinity. This may have been attempted in the earliest Buddhist period, when Śākyamuni himself was present as a center of devotion, but we have observed already how rapidly the cult of the stūpa developed, followed by that of his images, gradually coming to represent a plurality of Buddha-names.

If we seek to know what kind of worship was practiced by these later yogins of eastern India or at least by their less advanced followers, the answer is clearly available in the relevant tantric texts at our disposal. They worshipped a divinity in terrible form, whether male or female, identifiable in Hindu tradition as a fierce form of Śiva or of his spouse the Great Goddess (Devī), using a variety of names, such as were adopted by the Buddhist practitioners who were associated with these groups. The Śaivite identification represented the continuing Indian tendency to bring all locally indigenous manifestations of religion into the Hindu fold, mainly by means of cross-identification of divinities, and thus in origin such fearful gods, being no more Hindu than Buddhist, could be interpreted in accordance with differing philosophical and religious traditions.

All these high ranking fierce divinities are essentially the same and the various traditions that developed concerning their names, attributes, feminine partners

[73] G. W. Briggs, *Gorakhnāth and the Kanphata Yogis*, to which I make detailed references below.

and personal entourage, depended upon whatever became fixed in a particular circle where the cult was established. These tantric circles drew upon similar source materials, as is clear from the texts, which were gradually accumulated, usually in a rather haphazard method. Even the names of the chief divinities are to some extent interchangeable; thus Hevajra's partner, who is usually Nairātmyā (the Selfless One—a good Buddhist name), may also be Vajravārāhī (the Sow-Headed Goddess, usually associated with Śambara) or the less known Vajraśṛṅkhalā (the Goddess with the Chain), depending upon his various manifestations (*Pls. 26, 27*). According to the texts the possible combinations could be infinite because the distinctions have no real significance in themselves. In the matter of the entourage there is far greater stability, because the divinities, male or female as the case may be, of which it was composed, fixed in effect the description of the maṇḍala and it was always important that this should be laid out correctly. The great tantric divinities are usually surrounded by females, as may be expected, and probably Hevajra's circle is the most carefully formulated:

> Envisaging in the sky that Lord, who is vajra-born and of great compassion, one should worship him in the company of eight goddesses who are all wearing their adornments. Gaurī (the Blond) holds the moon, Caurī (the Thief) the sun-vessel, Vetālī (the Vampire) holds water, Ghasmarī (the Rapacious) holds medicament, Pukkasī (the Outcaste) holds a vajra, Śavarī (the Hill-woman) holds ambrosia and Caṇḍālī (the Half-caste) sounds a drum. By these the Lord is worshipped, with Ḍombī (the Washerwoman) clinging to his neck and impassioned with great passion.[74]

The items being offered by these goddesses are concealed by the use of the so-called "enigmatic language" (*sandhābhāṣa*). They comprise semen and blood, urine and excrement, seldom referred to explicitly in the *Hevajra Tantra*, but frequently listed elsewhere, especially in the *Guhyasamāja*, which is not so much concerned about secrecy.[75]

Ḍombī, the Washerwoman, who is identified in the above passage with Nairātmyā, is probably the most favored partner, and Kṛṣṇa (Kāṇha) who wrote a commentary on the *Hevajra Tantra* constantly sings her praises.

> Outside the town, O Ḍombī, is your hut.
> The shaven headed (brahmin boy) goes constantly touching you.
> Ho Ḍombī! I shall associate with you,
> I, Kāṇha, a kāpāli-yogin, shameless and naked.
> One is the lotus, sixty-four its petals.
> Having mounted on it, the poor Ḍombī dances.
> Ho Ḍombī! I ask you earnestly:

[74] H.T. I.iii.8-10. These eight "goddesses" are also the companions of his partner, Nairātmyā.

[75] They may be interpreted in the *Hevajra Tantra* by making use of Kāṇha's commentary (vol. II, p. 114) and the list of equations on pp. 99-100. As for the *Guhyasamāja Tantra*, see e.g., Chapter Fifteen (Bhattacharyya, p. 64, l. 5, p. 65, l. 13, etc.). This chapter also commends the Ḍombī as the ideal partner. A good discussion of "enigmatic language" will be found in Agehananda Bharati, *The Tantric Tradition*, pp. 164-84. A useful list of examples occurs in the *Hevajra Tantra*, as interpreted by me in vol. I, pp. 99-100.

In whose boat, O Ḍombī, do you come and go?
Strings you sell, O Ḍombī, and also baskets.
For your sake I have abandoned the actor's box.
Ho! You are a Ḍombī, I a kāpāli.
For your sake I have put on the garland of bones.
Troubling the pond, the Ḍombī eats lotus roots.
I kill you, O Ḍombī, I take your life!

Or again:

In the middle between Ganges and Jumna there flows a river.
The outcaste woman effortlessly ferries across the yogin who is sunk there.
Steer on, Ḍombī, steer on, O Ḍombī.
It became twilight on the way; (yet) by the grace of the feet
of the True Guru I shall go again to the City of the Jinas.
Five oars are plied at the stern, the rope is tied behind.
With the pail of the sky saturate (the boat so that)
water does not enter through the joints.
Sun and Moon are the two wheels for raising and lowering the mast.
Ignoring the left course and the right, steer on at will.
She does not take pennies, she takes not farthings—
she ferries across at her own will.
But whoever enters transport unable to control it, sinks down
on either bank.[76]

The companions of the other great tantric figures may not be so colorful. Thus Śambara, whose spouse is the Sow-Headed Goddess, has four other female companions, who are named as Ḍākinī ("Enchantress"), Lāmā ("Paramour"), Khandarohā (?"Arising from Fragments" according to the Tibetan form of the name, viz., *Dum-skyes-ma*) and Rūpiṇī ("Beauty"). They are all referred to as *kāpālinīs*, companions of kāpāli-yogins and seem to be distinguished only by equations that are made between them and the four classes into which Indian erotic literature divides women as objects of enjoyment.[77] The *Caṇḍamahāroṣaṇa Tantra*, which delights more than any other in the joys of copulation, provides its chief divinity, the "Fierce and Greatly Wrathful One" with an entourage which is manifestly an entirely Buddhist creation. His partner is the

[76] See Per Kværne, *An Anthology of Buddhist Tantric Songs*, pp. 113ff. and 131ff. for a detailed exposition. One may refer also to S. Dasgupta, *Obscure Religious Cults*, pp. 103-6. We are concerned here with yoga and thus what is being described in the internal process with the yogin's body; see section III.15.c. *Kāpālin*, meaning "associated with skulls," is an adjective formed from *kāpāla*, and refers to the class of yogin with whom we are now dealing. This type of yogin in a Śaivite context is described by D. N. Lorenzen in *The Kāpālikas and Kālāmukhas*; he touches upon similar groups of Buddhist yogins but refers to little relevant material in this respect. On pp. 69-70 he quotes some of Kānha's verses, but lacking Per Kværne's authoritative versions (published five years later) of this very difficult linguistic material, he provides a rather unsatisfactory translation. Following upon G. W. Briggs and S. B. Dasgupta (see the Bibliography) his work is an invaluable contribution in this little known subject, otherwise vitiated by the prejudices of ignorance.

[77] See S. Tasuda, *Samvarodaya Tantra*, XIII, 25-7 and XXI, 1-16. The four classes are "lotus-like" (*padminī*), "elephantlike" (*hastinī*), "conchlike" (*śankhinī*) and "variegated" (*citriṇī*). They are all defined in Apte's *Sanskrit Dictionary*, which quotes in each case from the *Ratimañjarī*.

"Lady of the Vajra-sphere" (*Vajradhātvīśvarī*) and they have eight companions, four male and four female. The male ones are all known as Acala ("Immovable") synonymous with Akṣobhya, as we noted above, and they are distinguished only by their colors as appropriate to the four quarters, namely white, yellow, red and dark green.[78] The female ones are all Vajrayoginīs named after four of the Five Evils: Delusion, Desire, Malignity and Envy. Wrath is omitted as this coalesces with the "Lady" at the center.

7. TANTRIC FEASTS

The reader of tantric texts soon becomes aware that they range from the preaching of strict living to extreme licentiousness, the former applying quite explicitly to the pupil who is undergoing training, and the latter to the perfected yogin, who is not only free from all social conventions but who has also learned the secret of the absence of passion by means of the passions. There is a tendency nowadays, much promoted by Tibetan lamas who teach in the Western world, to treat references to sexual union and to forms of worship carried out with "impure substances" (referred to usually as the "five nectars") as symbolic. There is some justification for this, but it is only part of the truth. Thus when Kāṇha serenades his washerwoman as the source of his bliss, he is referring to internal practices of yoga. Likewise the *Hevajra Tantra* is often quite explicit in its reference to esoteric meanings. But when modern apologists use the term "symbolic" as though to suggest that the external practices were never taken in any literal sense, they mislead us. Central to tantric pracice is the refusal to distinguish between the everyday world (saṃsāra) and the experience of nirvāṇa. The outer practices were certainly performed in the centers where the materials of which such tantras consist were recited and eventually committed to writing, even if the Tibetans have since ceased to perform most of them. Indeed many of them were so much part of the Indian scene, that their transference to Tibet was possible only in a partial form. I observed earlier that the setting of these tantras is totally different from that of the Mahāyāna sūtras and those other tantras (mainly *kriyā-*, *caryā-* and *yoga-*) that continued the tradition of attributing their teachings to Śākyamuni in one of his more recognizable forms in a park or palace or some such idyllic place. The typical setting of these tantras which center on the cult of Heruka and similar fierce manifestations is quite well described for us and the sites are even methodically listed.

> Placing the *linga* in the *bhaga* and kissing her again and again, so producing the experience of Great Bliss, the Adamantine One talked about feasting. Now listen, Goddess of wide open eyes, to the matter of feasting in the company-circle, where having feasted, there is such fulfillment (*siddhi*) which

[78] See C. S. George, *The Caṇḍamahāroṣaṇa Tantra*, pp. 18 and 44. In a footnote (p. 18) he seems to relate the name *Acala* to the name of the eighth stage of Bodhisattva. It is indeed the same word, but there is no direct association in the present case.

> fulfills the substance of all one's desires. One should set about this feasting in a cemetery or a mountain cave, in a resort of nonhuman beings or in a deserted place. One should arrange seats there, reckoned as nine, in the form of corpses or tiger skins or shrouds from a cemetery. The one who embodies Hevajra should be placed in the center of the yoginīs, whose places are known, as taught before, in the main directions and intermediate points. Then seated upon one's tiger skin, one should eat the "spiced food" of the sacrament, enjoying it, and one should eat with eagerness the "kingly rice." When one has eaten and eaten again, one should honor the mother-goddesses there and they may be mother or sister or niece or mother-in-law. One should honor them to a high degree and gain fulfillment in their company. The chief lady should offer to the master an unmarred sacred skull filled with liquor, and having made obeisance to him, she should drink it herself. She should hold it in her hands in a lotus-gesture, and present it with the same gesture. Again and again they make obeisance, those winners of fulfillment.[79]

The "spiced food" of the sacrament refers to a concoction of the flesh of a human being, a cow, an elephant, a horse and a dog. The "kingly rice" refers to specially selected human flesh, that of a man who has been hanged, a warrior killed in battle or a man of irreproachable conduct who has returned seven times to a good human state.[80] There need be no doubt that these items were sought after and used according to their availability. We are also informed by Kāṇha's commentary that the "special skull" means one of a brahmin. The tantra itself is explicit enough: "One should mark out a 'seven-timer' with the characteristics recounted in *Hevajra*. In the seventh birth there comes about that perfection which is typical of the 'Joy of Cessation.' He has a fair-sounding voice, beautiful eyes and a sweet-smelling body of great splendor and he possesses seven shadows. When he sees such a one the yogin should mark him out. By the mere act of eating him, one will gain at that moment the power of an aerial being." (I.xi.9-11). A commentary by a certain Dharmakīrti explains the magical rite by which the seven shadows may be seen, but there was probably no need to proceed so far once the more obvious characteristics were noted. Did one track him down and wait for him to die or did one hasten the process? All these tantras give so many fierce rites with the object of slaying, that the second alternative might not seem unlikely, and indeed there can be no doubt that the followers of the Great Goddess (Devī or Durgā as she may be known) sought out suitable sacrificial victims, a practice still attested in British days. Such a fate almost befell the most famous of Buddhist Chinese pilgrim-scholars, who toured all over northern India in the seventh century. It is not without interest to quote from his travelog:

> The Master of Dharma left the kingdom of Ayodhyā, having paid reverence to

79 *The Hevajra Tantra*, II.vii.5-13. I have amended my earlier translation.

80 The terms are interpreted in accordance with the fixed "enigmatic language" as confirmed by commentators. Kānha used the code *go-ku-da-ha-na* for the five kinds of flesh (my vol. II, p. 155, l. 24). For the interpretation of the code see H.T. I.xi.5-9. Concerning the one who returns seven times, see H.T. I.xi.9-11 as well as I.vii.21 with the relevant footnotes.

> the sacred traces, and following the course of the River Ganges, proceeded eastward, being on board a vessel with about eighty other fellow passengers. He wished to reach the kingdom of 'O-ye-mu-khi (Hayamukha). After going about a hundred *li*, both banks of the river were shrouded by the thick foliage of an *aśoka* forest, and amidst these trees on either bank were concealed some ten pirate boats. Then these boats, propelled by oars, all at once burst forth into the midstream. Some of those in the ship, terrified at the sight, cast themselves into the river, whilst the pirates, taking the ship in tow, forced it to the bank. They then ordered the men to take off their clothes, and searched them in quest of jewels and precious stones. Now these pirates pay worship to the Goddess Durgā and every year during the autumn, they look out for a man of good form and comely features, whom they kill, and offer his flesh and blood in sacrifice to their divinity, to procure good fortune. Seeing that the Master of Dharma was suitable for their purpose, both in respect of his distinguished bearing and his bodily strength and appearance, they exchanged joyful glances and said: "We were letting the season for sacrificing to our goddess pass by, because we could not find a suitable person for it, but now this monk is of noble form and pleasing features—let us kill him as a sacrifice and we shall gain good fortune." The Master of Dharma replied: "If this poor and defiled body of mine is indeed suitable for the purpose of the sacrifice you propose, I, in truth, dare not grudge (the offering), but as my intention in coming from a distance was to pay reverence to the image of Bodhi (= Bodhgayā) and the Gṛdhrakūṭa (the Vulture Peak), and to enquire as to the character of the Sacred Books and the Law, and as this purpose has not yet been accomplished, if you, my noble benefactors, kill this body of mine, I fear it will bring you misfortune."[81]

The "pirates" refused to relent and while the sacrificial altar was prepared, Hsüan-tsang composed himself by meditating upon Maitreya, becoming so ravished by the joys of Maitreya's paradise, that he was totally unaware of what was happening around him. A most terrible storm suddenly arose from the four quarters, smiting down trees, throwing up clouds of sand and lashing great waves from the river. The "pirates" were terrified at such an omen, and so renounced their intention. Hsüan-tsang, meanwhile awoken from his trance, accepted their change of heart with compassion and preached to them on the evils of their way of living.

Allowing for the quite proper literary embellishments, we have here a valid account of how a suitable victim might be found. If we are indeed dealing with "pirates," then they might well pass on a portion of such valuable flesh to related groups of yogins, who could use it for their own special purposes. Flesh was certainly required at these festivals, and one reason is given implicitly in the short passage quoted concerning the "seven-timer." By eating his flesh, one

[81] See *The Life of Hiuen-Tsiang* by Shaman Hwui Li and Samuel Beal, first published in London, 1884, available now from Academica Asiatica, Delhi, 1973, pp. 86-90 for the whole story. Concerning Ayodhyā (modern Ajodhya) and Hayamukha, one may refer to Samuel Beal, *Buddhist Records of the Western World*, pp. 224-34. Slight amendments have been made in the translation with the help of Dr. Katherine Whitaker.

appropriates to oneself his exalted nature, which is said to typify the last of the four stages of joy (see pp. 245-6, 264-6). The "power of an aerial being" is interpreted in Saroruha's commentary as meaning the universal power of a Vidyādhara. The partakers can scarcely have expected such an immediate effect, but they may well have believed that the sacrificial flesh would fortify them "spiritually" on the way toward the powers they sought.[82] Thus any kind of flesh, once consecrated sacramentally, would serve the required purpose, and if meat could not be obtained any suitable substitute, worked on with the imaginative power of mental concentration, would do. The *Guhyasamāja Tantra* teaches quite openly on these matters without the constant use of "enigmatic language," in which the *Hevajra Tantra* excels.

> With the preeminent sacrament of human flesh one attains to the supreme threefold Vajra (= the Body, Speech and Mind in the ultimate Vajra sense).
> With the preeminent sacrament of faeces and urine one becomes a lord of magical power (*vidyādhara*).
> With the sacramental flesh of the elephant one gains the five magical accomplishments (*abhijñā*).
> With the sacramental flesh of the horse one masters the art of becoming invisible.
> With the sacrificial flesh of the dog one achieves all ritual successes (*siddhi*).
> With the sacrificial flesh of the cow the Vajra power of invoking (*ākarṣaṇa* = conjuring up, drawing into one's presence) works best.
> If all these kinds of flesh are not available, one should envisage them all by meditating. With this vajra-yoga one becomes empowered by all the Buddhas.[83]

The twelfth chapter from which this is taken emphasizes the importance of visualizing in the performance of the various rites, and thus the above list is intended merely as a general statement on the uses of different kinds of flesh. The fifteenth chapter prescribes the actual course of the rites, such as gaining enlightenment, gaining power over others, slaying, becoming invisible, poisoning, removing poison, etc. and the use of the different kinds of flesh is there carefully specified. That substitutes were often used, there need be no doubt, and this has become the norm in the fierce Tibetan rites which have their origin in precisely such beliefs as these. When yogins and yoginīs assembled in their meeting-places for the festivals which are so clearly described, flesh was certainly required. Equally important was the use of spirituous liquor. Thus the twenty-eighth chapter of the *Saṃvarodaya Tantra* contains recipes for the making of suitable liquors, which it resumes with the general statement:

> One knows the different kinds of liquor as a matter relating to the particular

[82] See D. N. Lorenzen, *op. cit.*, pp. 87-95 for such sacrificial needs in their Shaivite context.

[83] Bhattacharyya's ed., p. 55, ll. 17ff. One may note also p. 128, ll. 1-16, which is quite explicit concerning the use of human flesh, faeces and urine, blood and semen. Moreover a true practitioner should envisage whatever food he eats as faeces, urine and meat as befits the ritual, p. 140, last lines.

region, and this distinction between liquors is made known in the tantras and related works. Without the drinking of liquor there can be no worship, just as there can be no burnt offering (*homa*) without butter, no religion without a good guru, and no salvation without religion. Without the production of liquor there can be no sacrament, and such is obtained by force of one's own merit thanks to a satisfied guru.[84]

The eighth chapter of this same tantra deals in some detail with the ordering of such sacramental ceremonies, and in order to stress the serious nature of such a gathering I reproduce the first few verses:

Now I shall explain carefully the sacraments in due order,
by the mere knowledge of which fulfillment is quickly achieved.
In one's own house or in a secret spot or a pleasant unfrequented place,
in mountain-cave or thicket, on the shore of a great sea,
in a temple of mother-goddesses, in a cemetery or between two rivers at
their confluence,
the one who wants the very best results should draw the maṇḍala.
The donor, great in faith, should invite the master with the yoginīs
and yogins and all the divinities who come from sacred sites (*pīṭha*),
born of the mantras of their locations.
For a layman or a novice a monk may be master (of ceremonies),
or the master may sometimes be a monk who lives by a layman's rules,
or it can be done by any accomplished man who has acquired the proper skills.
The faithful donor should choose the best available from such as these,
and with the master in first place, the glorious maṇḍala should be arranged.
So one should make as master of the offerings a leader of good qualities,
who has received the consecrations and who avoiding the ten evil acts
has no ill reputation.

Having insisted that everyone who is unworthy should be excluded, the text continues:

One should always perform the worship correctly by making a separation between the elders and the juniors, using flowers and incense, lamps and perfume especially that of sandalwood. Having prepared the sacrificial offering (*bali*) which is decorated with banners and a parasol the master (of ceremonies) should pay honor to it thus propitiating the divinities. Then he should ask the donor what ritual he has in mind, whether one for pacifying (*śānti*) or one for prosperity (*puṣṭi*); for the purpose of fulfillment and in accordance with the rite decided, he should carry through the ritual. Liquor made from honey or molasses or grain, such as is obtainable, is offered. Pure and mentally reposed, confident, free from desire and delusion, knowing the essential sameness of all things, the adamantine master of the rite should make his dispositions. The donor should place in front of the maṇḍala the food and drink as well as water, betel-nut and his donation. Afterward, the expert adamantine master should distribute the things. First he distributes the sacrament (*samaya*), which is joined together with a hook. With this all

84 See S. Tsuda's edition, XXVI, 50-2.

completed the master (of ceremonies) should invoke a blessing: "O You Heroic Lady Goddesses who dwell in sacred sites (*pīṭha*) and related sites (*upapīṭha*), in sacred localities (*kṣetra*), places of pilgrimage (*mela*) and cemeteries (*śmāsana*), I bow before you with devotion. You goddesses are our surety. The sacrament is our surety. The proclamation so made is our greatest surety. Through this truth may these goddesses be a cause of succour to me!"[85]

Probably one should distinguish between a ceremony performed for a specific purpose, categorized as the four rites of pacifying, prospering, overpowering or subduing, and destroying, instituted by a donor, who may be a layman, a monk or even a whole community, and general religious feasts held at particular religious sites on auspicious days. The first kind is still performed in Tibetan monasteries and its origins presumably go back precisely to the kind of ceremony referred to in our immediately quoted extract.

In translating I have often used the word "sacrament," and this requires some explanation. The Sanskrit term is *samaya*, which means literally "coming together." In ordinary classical Sanskrit usage it means an occasion, a suitable time, a compact, a convention, etc. In Buddhist tantric usage it becomes a crucial term in that it signifies the "coming together" of transcendent being and immanent being.[86] Thus an image of any kind as prescribed by tradition, once properly consecrated (or empowered) is possessed by the divinity, and for this kind of "coming together" *samaya* is used. To call such an empowered image a "symbol" of the divinity is scarcely adequate, but sometimes one has to make do with such an interpretation. The ultimate aim of tantric yoga is the self-identification of the practicing yogin with the divinity he is invoking and whose powers he then appropriates. This form of "coming together" is also known as *samaya*, when the word "union" might suggest itself as a tolerable translation. Similarly in the ceremonies we are now reviewing the sacrificial offering (Sanskrit *bali*, Tibetan *gtor-ma*) is consecrated to the divinity who is being invoked, and thus comes to represent the divinity. For the fierce divinities who are central to so many tantric rituals, the best offerings, as we have noted, are flesh and blood and other bodily substances. By partaking of these consecrated items, one absorbs the nature of the divinity, and for this use of *samaya*, "sacrament" suggests itself as a fit translation. We have already observed above in the case of the "seven-timer" that by eating his flesh, one absorbed his good qualities. Thus once the sacrificial items are "consubstantiated" with the chosen divinity one partakes of his even higher qualities. The association of ideas between this meaning and the Christian understanding of sacrament scarcely

[85] The *Saṃvarodaya Tantra*, VIII, 1-7 and 18-26. My translation differs in many details from that of Shiníci Tsuda (see pp. 263ff. of his edition) but no unfriendly criticism is implied. Because of the uncertainty of grammatical endings, interpretations are often doubtful, e.g., in verse 23 I take *dānapati* as subject, while he had chosen an accusative ending from conflicting MSS and translated accordingly. I recognize that it is one thing (by far the harder task) to make known a text by publishing one's work, and another thing to make use of this text and improve upon interpretations, once the hard "spade-work" has been done.

[86] Since consecration (*abhiṣeka*) implies empowerment (*adhiṣṭhāna*), these terms become practically synonymous. I normally distinguish them in translation; see Empowerment in the Index.

requires further elaboration.[87] In the Buddhist tantric understanding the *samaya* becomes a "pledge" of a "coming together" of the divinity with the image that represents him, the sacrificial offering that "embodies" him, or with the yogin or even the faithful worshipper who is one-pointedly intent upon him. "Pledge" is probably the best word in English to cover the whole range of interpretations, and it is thus that the Tibetans translated the term (*samaya* = *dam-tshig*), but it would scarcely convey the intended meaning to an uninitiated reader. Using different English words to translate the same Sanskrit word has the disadvantage of giving the impression that this word has a variety of meanings. This may be argued in certain cases, e.g., where this word means "occasion," but in the present case *samaya* in its Buddhist tantric sense has one meaning embracing all the interpretations, which I have just attempted to give. It is thus a highly mystical term, used in its own right as a powerful mantra.

As a religious offering (*bali* = *gtor-ma*) consecrated to the divinity, the sacrament consists of those items sanctified by traditional usage. While there need be no doubt that the actual bloody items named in these texts were used in Indian tantric circles where some of our texts originated, it is equally certain that substitutes in the form of sacrificial cakes were used in other tantric communities, where flesh and blood were not so easily available, or where their use met with disapproval (*Pl. 80b*). This was probably the case in those established Buddhist communities, the great monasteries of eastern India, where the cult of fierce divinities was gradually introduced. Apart from the liturgies preserved in Tibetan translations, we have little knowledge of these, but it is certain that the Tibetans did not invent themselves the many rituals of such a kind, which are performed in their temples and monasteries (now all in exile) down to the present day. The sacrificial cake (*gtor-ma*) which they mold out of roasted

[87] Since writing this I have come across by chance a relevant passage in Gregory Dix, *Jew and Greek* (London, 1953, reprinted 1955, 1967), p. 93, where he is distinguishing between magic and sacraments.

> I am old enough to remember professors trained in all the assumptions of the nineteenth century talking easily of the formative influences of "Mithraism" on S. Paul (the disciple of Gamaliel!) and using the interesting word "magic." It is a pity that they never thought of consulting with practising magicians. They would soon have discovered that (whatever we may think of the efficacy of either in its own sphere) "magic" and "sacraments" operate in different worlds of thought, the world of natural science and the world of religion. (I remember a leading Ju-ju man of Kumawu among the beautiful Ashanti mountains in West Africa explaining to me the difference clearly and simply. He had all the *aplomb* and that touch of courteous condescension which always mark the man of science explaining to the theologian.) True, both magic and sacraments seek to operate by means of an external action; it is their only similarity. The effect of magic is attributed to *the performance of the rite* itself; this is conceived of as a "scientific" procedure, effective by an entirely natural causation. The effect of a sacrament is attributed directly *to the Will of God* Who has explicitly commended that action to bring about that effect; it is conceived of as an act of worshipping obedience, effective by an entirely *super-natural* causation.

Gregory Dix makes his definitions within an exclusively Christian context, but very little change is needed in his wording in order to accommodate Buddhist as well as Christian usage, e.g., "The effect of a sacrament is attributed directly to divine intervention as prescribed by tradition; it is conceived of as an act of worshipping obedience, effective by *super-natural* causation." Thus magic and sacraments can be distinguished quite as clearly in Buddhism as in Christianity.

barley-flour (tsamba), water and butter, is modelled to a conventional pattern to represent a particular divinity, and not only are such sacraments used during the rituals, but they are also sometimes placed in a case as a kind of "reserved sacrament" representing the divinity. Subsidiary offerings often represent in gruesome details the bodily parts after which they are named. It may be added that in some circumstances a discreet use of actual flesh (even human flesh when available) is also sanctioned.

This rather long digression from the subject immediately under consideration, namely the circles in which some of the tantric traditions originated in India, is justified by the need to see the whole subject in as wide a context as possible. It is certain that sooner or later substitutes were found for sacrificial items, which a modern spectator as well as many earlier ones might consider repulsive. It is equally certain that the references to ritualized copulation were interpreted by certain practiced yogins, such as Kāṇha, whose verses have been quoted, as applying to processes of internal yoga. But all such terminology was used in this "symbolic" way precisely because the practices to which they clearly refer were prevalent in the circles where these deliberate substitutions were made.

We have noticed some of the distinguishing features of ceremonies performed for specific purposes of the kind which continue in use in Tibetan communities. Something more needs to be said about the general religious feasts held at particular "holy places," for in a strange esoteric sense these have even greater importance. The full title of the *Hevajra Tantra* is "Union of the Assemblage (literally, web or net) of *Ḍākinīs* of the Glorious Hevajra" (*Śrī-Hevajra-ḍākinī-jāla-saṃvara*) and its meaning is effectively the same as that of the related tantra from which we have been quoting, namely the *Cakrasaṃvara*, interpretable as "Union of the Wheel or Circle" of divinities (or *ḍākiṇīs*) in the central divinity Heruka/Hevajra. Such an interpretation of these titles marks such tantras as primarily concerned with processes of internal yoga, in which the physical attributes, which are brought under control, are identified with various sets of divinities, whose union represents the perfect integration of the expert yogin. Various sets of divinities were used for this purpose, but one set derives directly from the divinities who were believed to preside over certain sacred places, where the very rites, interpreted as stages of internal yoga, were performed as externalized ritual. They are referred to at the end of our last quotation, and although there is a certain vagueness concerning some of them, such places clearly existed. They are listed with their actual geographical names in Part I, Chapter Seven of the *Hevajra Tantra*, being quite widely dispersed over the Indian subcontinent, although the actual sites may be no longer identifiable.[88] In this respect one may note the existence of certain yoginī-shrines, the most impressive of which, precisely in the form of a circle, can still be visited near Hirapur (*Pls. 29a & b*), some twelve miles from the town of Bhubaneshwar in

[88] See also the *Saṃvarodaya Tantra*, IX, which contains similar material, noting also what S. Tsuda writes on the subject in his introduction, pp. 54ff.

Orissa.[89] This particular shrine is datable to about the tenth century, the period with which we are now concerned. Places such as these with their cults of presiding divinities provide the cultural background to much of the teaching in these tantras. In these resorts female partners were available to wandering yogins, who might use secret signs in order to identify suitable yoginīs (*Pl. 28*). Thus, commenting on a whole series of such signs, listed in the *Hevajra Tantra*, a certain Vajragarbha explains the reasons for their use.

> Yogins and yoginīs who practice the Hevajra yoga must make effort to remember these signs of body and speech, so that in the company of malicious outsiders and male and female go-betweens (*dūta*) from other groups (Lit. families) one need not converse in the terms of ordinary speech, but if we refer to that great secret by means of signs, malicious people and go-betweens who are outside our circle will be bewildered.
>
> Practicing yogins who visit the sacred sites (*pīṭha*) and places (*kṣetra*) looking for proficient yoginīs, should use these signs so that they may know which among the yoginīs are in possession of the necessary tenets which accord with their own, so that they may arouse in them a condition of mutual responsiveness.[90]

Just as nowadays, sacred places were open to all and sundry, and it is interesting to note how the practitioners of Hevajra yoga are referred to as one group among several such schools of yoga. While it was doubtless easy to remain separate from other equally well-constituted groups, they would inevitably come into contact with the hangers-on of such groups, who may have been looking out for suitable contacts and supporters.[91] In such a setting as this, we are as near to the origins of the *Hevajra Tantra* and similar tantras as we can ever hope to get. That they also had their own organized gatherings is clear from the extract quoted above. These must have been colorful and carefree events. "If in joy songs are sung, then let them be excellent vajra-songs, and if one dances when joy has arisen, let it be done with release as its object. Then the yogin, self-collected, performs the dance in the place of Hevajra. Song represents mantra, dance represents meditation, so singing and dancing the yogin always acts."[92] The Lord is asked to explain this and he replies in the form of a song which is included in the tantra in one of those dialects of eastern India, in which Kāṇha's verses, quoted above, are likewise preserved.

[89] For a description see Charles Fabri, *History of the Art of Orissa*, pp. 74ff. For an account of the meetings of yogins at similar "sacred places" up to present times, see G. W. Briggs, *Gorakhnāth and the Kanphata Yogis*, ch. 5.

[90] See my edition of the *Hevajra Tantra*, vol. I, p. 66 n. 1.

[91] It may be of interest to note that when Vajrapāṇi makes up the maṇḍala of "Victory over the Threefold World," composed of converted heretics, he groups them as "leaders of the group" (*gaṇapati*), "go-betweens" (*dūta*) and "servants" (*ceṭa*). Such terms may have been used to indicate grades amongst the yogins, but such a theory requires confirmation. See STTS, *Facsimile Edition*, p. 49.

[92] *Hevajra Tantra*, I.vi.10 & 13. This whole chapter describes very well how a practitioner of Hevajra yoga should conduct himself.

The yogin is from Kollagiri, the yoginī from Munmuni.
Loudly the drum resounds; love is our business and not dissension.
Meat is eaten there zestfully and liquor is drunk.
Hey there! Worthy are we who are present; the unworthy are kept away.
Fragrant ointment and musk, frankincense and camphor are taken.
Spiced food and special rice are eaten with relish.
We come and go (in the dance) with no thought of pure or impure.
Limbs adorned with bone ornaments and the corpse duly present,
Intercourse occurs at the meeting, where the untouchable is not kept away.[93]

The commentaries give to this song a literal interpretation, explaining the "enigmatic language" accordingly, and a parabolic interpretation according to which a process of internal yoga is indicated.[94] While the latter may be quite valid in its own right, in no way does it cast doubt upon the actuality that is described in the song, the meaning of which is deliberately obscured to some extent by the use of the "enigmatic" terms. Their use is quite superfluous so far as the parabolic interpretation is concerned. Thus the items listed in the fifth and sixth lines are interpreted as the Five Aggregates (*skandhas*) of personality, namely bodily form, feelings, perceptions, consciousness and impulses (in this word-for-word order) and the last item "special rice" as the false notion of a self to which they all give rise. All these are consumed. The "going this way and that" refers to the Thought of Enlightenment which rises producing the effect of Great Bliss and then returns pervading the whole body. "With no thought of pure and impure" means with no thought of existence or nonexistence. "Limbs adorned etc." refers to the pervading of all the lesser veins throughout the body by the sensation of bliss, and the "corpse" refers to Nairātmyā, the partner of Hevajra with whom union is symbolically effected, and she as the untouchable (= *Prajñā* in its double meaning of feminine partner and Wisdom) is not absent. Now all this and more can be better explained, as indeed it is in exegetical works, without recourse to such labored equations. The real meaning of the song is however entirely relevant to our enquiry into the background where such works as the *Hevajra Tantra* originated, for the summary that it gives of such ritualized gatherings confirms other similar descriptions. Moreover the whole purpose of the "enigmatic language," which is so strictly used in this particular tantra, is to obscure the meaning for the uninitiated while declaring it for the initiates. Thus the items listed in lines five and six mean faeces and urine, blood and semen, a concoction containing five kinds of flesh (spiced food) and finally the special human flesh, as explained above. "Adorned with bone ornaments" means the same as naked. The corpse means the place of repose. The untouchable is Ḍombī, whose praises have already been sung. Kollagiri is a "sacred site" (*pīṭha*) according to the commentary and Munmuni is listed as a sacred

[93] *Hevajra Tantra*, II.iv.6-8.

[94] Both are taken from Kāṇha's commentary. See notes to my edition of the tantra, vol. I, pp. 101-2, and vol. II, pp. 145-6 for the actual commentary.

place (*kṣetra*) elsewhere in the tantra.[95] Places such as these, whether listed as twenty-four or thirty-two represented in a real sense the whole world for these wandering yogins, and thus they could be arranged symbolically around a maṇḍala in order to express its universality in all directions.[96] Furthermore, since the external world (macrocosm) comes to be identified in tantric theory with the body of the practicing yogin (microcosm), all these places are identified with "veins" related to the various "lotus-centers" (see section III.15.c) up and down the spinal cord. A full list of these equations is available in the *Saṃvarodaya Tantra*, chapter 7, and nothing is gained by listing them here. Despite these "symbolic" interpretations, the actuality of these "sacred sites and places" and the rites performed there links this class of tantric literature, at least in their origins, with fraternities of yogins who were very well acquainted with them. Moreover, similar fraternities of yogins have continued to exist in India and their practices, found as abhorrent by modern observers, correspond in very many details with those referred to in Buddhist tantras.[97]

8. THE ARGUMENT FOR IMPLICIT INTERPRETATIONS

I have referred above to this last phase of Buddhism as astounding, using this word advisedly, for we are informed in the *Guhyasamāja Tantra* (in chapters 5 and 9), that "right-thinking" Bodhisattvas were not only astounded but also fainted with fear at the teachings propounded.

> Then the King Holder of the Vajra (*Vajradhara*) of the Body, Speech and Mind of All Buddhas, Supreme One, Lord of the World, discoursed on the character of the practice which has as its object that Dharma which is the best of all practices:
>
> Those belonging to the families of Passion, Wrath and Delusion, being well versed in the meaning of nondiscrimination, achieve the very best success (*siddhi*) in the supreme (*anuttara*) and highest way. Half-castes, basket-weavers and suchlike, those who resort to killing and are intent on personal gain, succeed in this excellent way, the supreme Mahāyāna. Even those who have committed the five worst sins and other evils succeed in the vastness (lit. great ocean) of the Vajrayāna, this excellent way. Those who speak ill of their teacher never succeed despite their practice, but those who take life, who take

95 H.T. I.vii.10-14. See also the *Saṃvarodaya Tantra*, all chapter vii and ix.13 to end. These "places of pilgrimage" are carefully divided into categories, of which the "sites" (*pīṭha*) and "places" (*kṣetra*) are but two. The others are *chandoha*, *melāpaka* and *śmāsana* (cemetery). S. Dasgupta (*Obscure Religious Cults*, p. 197) lists *Sandoha* (meaning "assemblage") instead of *Chandoha*, which has no easy interpretation. *Melāpaka* is clearly connected with *mela*, a term still in use in India for a great religious gathering. These categories are duplicated by the use of the prefix *upa-*, which can give the meaning of "near by" or "subsidiary." A list of ten such categories is artificially equated with the ten stages of a Bodhisattva in the *Saṃvarodaya Tantra*, ix.22-4. Such equations seem to be made quite casually.

96 For a description of such a maṇḍala see G. Tucci, *Indo-Tibetica*, III.2, pp. 38ff.

97 See for example G. W. Briggs, *Gorakhnāth and the Kanphata Yogis*, pp. 172-5.

pleasure in lying, who always covet the wealth of others, who enjoy making love, who purposely consume faeces and urine, these are worthy ones for the practice. The yogin who makes love to his mother, sister or daughter achieves enormous success in the supreme truth (*dharmatā*) of the Mahāyāna. Making love to the mother of the Lord Buddha he is not defiled, for it is thus that the wise man who does not discriminate achieves buddhahood."

Then all the Bodhisattvas led by Sarvanivaraṇaviṣkambhin (Preventer of All Obstructions) were overcome with wonder and astonishment, saying: "How comes it that the Lord, the Chief of all the Buddhas should pronounce such evil words in the midst of this assembled circle of all the Buddhas!" Then All the Buddhas hearing what was said by Sarvanivaraṇaviṣkambhin and the other Bodhisattvas, spoke thus: "Enough! Do not speak thus, O sons of good family. This is the pure truth (*dharmatā*) of those enlightened ones who know the essence of things (*sāra*). Such is the basis for the practice of enlightenment consisting in this essence as the meaning of Dharma."

Then those Bodhisattvas who were as numerous as the atoms which go to make up the number of holy mountains (*Sumeru*) in the innumerable and yet more than innumerable Buddha-paradises, were frightened, were terrified and fell into a swoon. Then all the Lord Buddhas seeing those Bodhisattvas in a swoon said to the Lord who is the Chief of the Body, Speech and Mind of All the Buddhas: "We beg you to resuscitate these Great Beings the Bodhisattvas."

Then the Lord Buddha who is the Vajra of the Body, Speech and Mind of All Buddhas relapsed into the state of mental composure known as Nondual Vajra of the Sameness of Space, and as soon as they were touched by his radiance, all those Great Beings, the Bodhisattvas, were seated again in their right places.[98]

While it may be urged that such "perverse" teachings are a form of hyperbole intended to emphasize the doctrine of universal sameness as realized by a perfected yogin, they are taught, it may be noted, in the same tantra (chapter 9) as a meditational practice.

Then the King Holder of the Vajra (*Vajradhara*), the great unchanging one of universal space, supreme in the practice of all consecration, all-comprehending, lord supreme, discoursed on the maṇḍala of the triple vajra, that enjoyment of Body, Speech and Mind, which is the supreme and delightful secret of those who possess Buddha-knowledge:

"One should envisage a Buddha-maṇḍala in the middle of space. Then one produces from it Akṣobhya-Vajra and envisages him with a vajra in his hand. It blazes in a mass of sparks and is replete with rays of five colors. Meditating upon the Buddhas of past, present and future, one should crush them to powder there with that vajra. One should practice this best of meditations, where the enjoyment of Body, Speech and Mind is destroyed and crushed with the vajra, as it conduces to fulfillment (*siddhi*) of Mind. With that secret vajra one should slay all living beings, so that they may be born as Buddha-sons (= Bodhisattvas) in the Buddha-paradise of Akṣobhya-Vajra. This is the Pledge (*samaya*) of the quiddity (*tattva*) of the Family of Wrath in the

98 *Guhyasamāja Tantra*, Bhattacharyya's ed., pp. 20-1.

universal family flood."

Then the King Holder of the Vajra who effects true salvation through ignorance (*ajñāna*), pure and immaculate in his true nature, teacher of the practice of enlightenment, explained the Pledge, that quiddity which produces the enlightenment of a Buddha.

"One should envisage a Wheel-maṇḍala in the middle of space, and having produced Vairocana (Resplendent One) from this, one should envisage all the Buddhas. One conceives of them in vajra-form with the universal use of gems. Then one imagines the robbery of all these things by means of the triple vajra. Replete with this vast quantity of things, which are like a wish-granting gem, they (?living beings) become sons of all the Buddhas, truly herolike sages. This is the Pledge of the quiddity of the Family of Illusion in the universal family flood."

Then the King Holder of the Vajra who effects salvation through passion, inconceivable in his secret purity, explained this maṇḍala. "In the middle of space one should envisage a Lotus-Maṇḍala, and having produced Amitāyus (Boundless Light) from this, one should fill it all with Buddhas. One should envisage them all in union with feminine figures with the yoga of the fourfold Pledge. Such is the supreme Vajra method. Joining the two sexual organs together, one should enjoy them all. This is the meditation on the invisible triple body of all Buddhas. This is the Pledge of the Family of Passion which is to be meditated upon."

Then the King Holder of the Vajra who fulfills the intention of Vajra-mantras, who is selfless in his wisdom-nature, spoke these words: "In the middle of space one should conceive of all these forms as the vajra-basis of falsehood, and so one should deceive all Buddhas and all (beings in the) Buddha-abodes. This is the pure skylike Speech of all Buddhas, known as the fulfillment of mantras and the secret of those who are possessed of wisdom. This is the Pledge of the quiddity of the Family of Pledge-Fictionalization[99] and it should be practiced in accordance with different intentions."

Then the King Holder of the Vajra, source of the Buddhas of the indestructible triple vajra, the teacher of vajra-fulfillment, spoke these words: "In the middle of space one should envisage a Pledge-maṇḍala, and having produced from it Ratnaketu, one should fill it with all (Buddha-)forms. Then treating them with words of abuse and so on, one obtains wisdom. Thus spoke the Lord, The Vajra-Multitude of All Buddhas."

Then all the Bodhisattvas led by Sarvatathāgatasamayavajraketu (Vajra Banner Pledge of All Buddhas) were overcome with wonder and astonishment, and said these vajra-words: "Why has the Lord, Chief of All Buddhas, who transcends the threefold world and all phenomenal spheres, pronounced in the midst of the assembly of all Buddhas and Bodhisattvas, such vajra-words of untrue import?"[100]

I have quoted this passage in full in order to illustrate how the deliberately

99 "Fictionalization" translates Sanskrit *ākarṣaṇa*, which means to draw to one's presence, to conjure up a person or thing. Thus one makes a "fiction" of the person or the thing so that it may be worked upon during the ritual.

100 GST, Bhattacharyya, pp. 35-6.

perverse teachings of some of these yogins came to be elaborated in a Buddhist context. Here the set is arranged, perhaps rather casually, to accord with a set of Five Buddhas and in this context I have need to refer back to this particular quotation (see p. 207). Elsewhere more direct interpretations are given. Thus in the *Hevajra Tantra* we read:

> You should slay living beings; you should speak lying words; you should take what is not given; you should frequent others' wives. To practice singleness of thought is the taking of life, for thought is life. Saying "I will save the world" is interpreted as lying speech. Semen from women is what is not given, and another's wife is as fair as one's own.[101]

A well-known Western writer on tantric Buddhism has written: "It is customary in certain Western circles and among those in the East who have come under Western philosophical and Christian influence, or who are anxious to commend the East to the West by establishing an identity between Eastern and Western doctrines, to consider Tantrism as a medley of ritual acts, yoga techniques, and other practices, mostly of an "objectionable" type, and therefore as a degenerate lapse into a world of superstition and magic. . . . Nothing of what is thus fancied about Tantrism is borne out by the original texts. Although this crude and yet highly cherished dogma has been challenged recently, the question 'what does Tantra mean?' has remained unanswered." He then goes on to explain in a footnote that it is the present author who has challenged that "highly cherished dogma" in the introduction to his edition of *The Hevajra Tantra*, but immediately complains that I do not say "what Tantra means" and deal with it merely as a literary document.[102] One's knowledge being limited, one can never satisfy all readers, but we must urge the value of literary interpretations.

Western readers may sometimes be confused by the use of the word Tantra to refer to tantric developments as a whole. A *tantra* in the singular can normally refer only to a particular tantra, just as the word *sūtra* can only refer to a particular sūtra, Mahāyāna or otherwise. No one has yet thought of using the word *sūtra* in a Buddhist context as a general term for non-Tantric Buddhism, for we are well aware of the great variety of literature that is covered by the term. The same applies to the tantras, which contain a vast variety of teachings, which may fairly be described as "a medley of ritual acts, yoga techniques and other practices." Many of its propositions had been found objectionable in India long before Western influences began to affect ideas of public and private morality, and even if not considered objectionable, they would appear to be unnecessary, if the only intention is indeed the inculcating of a higher mystical understanding.[103] Study of the tantras is quite properly a literary interest, if one wants

101 H.T. II.iii.29-30. Concerning the withdrawal of *semen virile*, to which there is a presumed reference, see section III.14.d.

102 See Herbert V. Guenther, *The Life and Teaching of Nāropa*, p. 114, a book which is to be commended and to which further reference will be made.

103 Thus chapter 6 of the *Caṇḍamahāroṣaṇa Tantra* lists a considerable variety of postures for sexual intercourse, and the following chapter gives advice on the regaining of strength to counteract

to know anything of the origins of this phase of Buddhism, just as literary exegesis in biblical studies, despite earlier protests from those in higher authority, has gradually transformed our understanding of Christian origins. It is now generally agreed that there is a perfectly valid literal and historical meaning in many Old Testament passages, which were deliberately interpreted in a prophetic or allegorical manner (and often quite reasonably so) by the early Christian Church. The same arguments apply in any effort we make to understand the history of Buddhist thought despite the protests of those whose faith is so narrowly based that everything must be explainable according to a single unified tradition, where uncomfortable pronouncements are simply ignored if they cannot be reinterpreted suitably.

The freedom to kill, to rob, to live with total sexual licence, to lie, which is proclaimed in so many Buddhist tantras (with varying forms of interpretation) is clearly a deliberate reversal of the first four of the set of ten moral rules imposed upon any convert to Buddhism. In origin it may be understood as a form of hyperbole, which proclaims the perfected yogin's total freedom of action.

> The true yogin should never think of things as eatable or not eatable, as enforced or not enforced, as suitable or as unsuitable. He should not conceive of merit or of evil, of heaven or salvation. He should remain composed in the single-state of Innate Bliss. Thus if a yogin, constant in yoga, is perfect in meditational practice, through the union which he thus effects with the Fierce Wrathful One (Caṇḍaroṣaṇa) he becomes the Self Incarnate.[104] Even if he should slay a hundred brahmins, he is not touched by evil. So he should meditate upon the Lord Fierce and Wrathful in precisely this manner. By the same evil acts that bring people into hell, the one who uses the right means gains salvation, there's no doubt. All evil and virtue are said to have thought as their basis. One's state of rebirth, one's actual condition and so on, all such distinctions are forms of thought-construction.[105]

The same tantra teaches the regular moral rules as binding upon the neophyte before he should be granted any consecration, and thus a contrast is drawn between what is suitable for the beginner and what is permitted to the one whose "perfection" (*siddhi*) transports him above all distinctions of whatsoever kind. However, elsewhere the "perverse" actions are rationalized in accordance with earlier Mahāyāna teachings, which allow a Bodhisattva to commit wrong actions (and willingly pay the penalty for them by a temporary sojourn in one of the hellish abodes), if only it is for the good of living beings. This kind of interpre-

the inevitable physical exhaustion. However, it may not be impossible for a "purist" to find a suitable symbolic interpretation for all this.

104 Literally "the bearer of the notion of selfhood" (Skr. *ahamkāradhārin*). Such a term as this might seem to suggest the negation of the fundamental Buddhist doctrine of "no self" (*anātman*), but it can easily be paralleled with similar expressions. Thus in the *Hevajra Tantra* (I.x.10-12), the absolute state is labeled *inter alia* as supreme person and lord, as "self" (*ātman*), "soul" (*jīva*), "being" (*sattva*) etc.

105 *Caṇḍamahāroṣaṇa Tantra*, ed. C. S. George, Sanskrit text, p. 32, ll. 1-12. Similar ideas will be found in H.T. I.vi.18-24.

tation seems to be found in those tantras, whose origins may be more closely linked with Mahāyāna sūtras. Thus in the *Sarvadurgatipariśodhana Tantra* the rules that a pupil must observe are given in at least three places, and the exceptions that are allowed are also once clearly stated:

> He should not abandon the Three Jewels (Buddha, Doctrine, Community), the Thought of Enlightenment and his Good Teacher. He should not kill living beings or take what has not been given him. He should not speak ill of his teacher or step on his shadow. He should not cleave to one who is not his teacher, and the name of his teacher is not to be used. He must never speak ill of the mantras, the symbols (*mudrās*) and the divinities. If ever in his folly he does so, he will certainly die of disease. He must never place his feet across the shadows of the immaculate divinities and the symbols, marked out with seed-syllables, whether relating to (the gods of) this world or the world beyond.
>
> As for those who are confused about the Buddhist teachings, hating the Three Jewels and intent on speaking ill of religious teachers, the thoughtful slay them. Out of compassion the one skilled in mantras should slay by means of mantras those nonreligious people who delight in evil, hate our sacraments and are always harming living beings. Seizing the possessions of the miserly, he should give them to suffering creatures. Also in order to honor one's teacher or to complete a sacramental offering (*samaya*), for making a maṇḍala, for the general benefit of those who adhere to the sacrament (*samayin*) or for worshipping the Bodhisattvas one should take things if they are the possessions of miserly people. One who is intent on the good of living beings should always speak falsehoods for the purpose of protecting sacramental items, one's teacher's possessions and the life of living creatures. For the purpose of impassioning the Buddhas and for cherishing the sacrament, the one skilled in mantras should resort to another's wife for the sake of fulfillment. Abiding in the state of Vajra-Being, one does everything, enjoys everything. He succeeds, yet he does no wrong, and how the more so, if he is endowed with compassion.[106]

Similar ideas, perhaps rather more neatly expressed, are found throughout another tantra, from which quotations have been drawn, namely the "Symposium of Truth." I give one which links with a previous quotation toward the end of section III.3.

> Then Vajrapāṇi, knowing that he had established all those who belong to the Vajra family at the stage where there could be no back-sliding for the good of all living beings, said to the Lord: "I have been consecrated by all the Buddhas, the Lords, as the repository of secrecy (*guhyadhāritvaṃ*). Pronounce that secret of the Buddhas!"
>
> Then arising from that state of composure known as Secret Vajra of All Buddhas, the Lord pronounced this secret of All Buddhas:
>
> "Since all beings must be converted according to their various natures,
> So it is for the good of living beings that purity is effected through
> passion and the rest (viz., delusion and wrath)."

106 *SDPS Tantra*, ed. T. Skorupski, Sanskrit MS fos. 60-1 and his translation pp. 100-1.

Then Vajrapāṇi said his own secret verse:
"If for the good of all living beings or on account of the Buddha's teaching, one should slay living beings, one is untouched by sin."

Then Vajragarbha said his own secret Gem verse:
"If for the good of living beings or from attachment to the Buddha's interest, one seizes the wealth of others, one is not touched by sin."

Then Vajranetra said his own secret Dharma verse:
"There is no bliss like passion for offering to the Buddhas.
So one gains merit by resorting to another man's wife for the good of others."

Then Vajraviśva said his secret Karma verse:
"Performing all one's actions for the good of living beings and on account of the Buddha's teaching, one gains enormous merit."[107]

Here the "perverse" teachings have been arranged to fit in with the fivefold scheme of buddhahood and in accordance with the more general Mahāyāna willingness to countenance evil acts if they are committed for an ultimate good. It may be difficult to explain how the act of resorting to the wife of another can serve the good of living beings, but with special pleading even this might be justified. It is however likely, as suggested above, that the original notion was the total freedom of the perfected yogin from all social restraint, even such universally acknowledged evils as sexual relations with another's wife, not to mention one's mother, sister, daughter and so on. To my knowledge these last extremes of license are not justified by appeal to a Bodhisattva's willingness to sacrifice his own personal destiny, which is something quite different from being in a state which is "beyond good and evil." Yet as we have seen from the quotation from the *Durgatipariśodhana Tantra*, even these two quite different notions can be linked.

9. THE IMPORTANCE OF ONE'S CHOSEN TEACHER

We must now deal with one injunction which can never be transgressed as it is the basis of all tantric practice, namely that of the absolute necessity of total devotion to one's chosen teacher or master (Sanskrit: guru; Tibetan: lama). Here no exception whatsoever is permitted, and it may be noted how in the midst of so many "evils," which are acceptable in given circumstances, this one is specifically listed as allowing of no reservations. It is noteworthy that it receives in the tantras, especially in those of the Supreme Yoga class, where secrecy is also strictly enjoined, a central importance, which it never had in the early history of Buddhism. One may fairly state that it takes the place of all the great perfections

[107] STTS MS fos. 167^{6}-168^{5}, Yamada's ed., pp. 311ff. This chapter (14b) completes the section of Vajrapāṇi's maṇḍala for the converted divinities. See above, pp. 136-42. For the names of the Family-Bodhisattvas used here, see p. 242 n. below.

that are taught in the Mahāyāna sūtras. Here the advantage of having "good friends" (*kalyāṇamitra*) as opposed to evil ones (*pāpamitra*) is certainly urged, and to have a good friend as one's teacher is highly recommended and it is proper that one should trust him, but for all his virtues he is but a means toward final enlightenment. One quotation from the "Perfection of Wisdom in Eight Thousand Verses" should be sufficient to illustrate the difference between the traditional concept of a religious teacher and the peculiarly high state to which he is elevated in some tantras:

> Son of good family, you should strive for the Perfection of Wisdom by developing the conviction that all *dharmas* (elements) are void, signless and effortless. You must practice abandoning signs, existence and the false view of any being. You must avoid bad friends. You must honor, love and stay close to good friends. These are they who teach the Dharma saying: "All *dharmas* are void, signless, effortless, nonarisen, unborn, unobstructed, nonexistent." Progressing thus, my son, you will before long be able to study the Perfection of Wisdom either as found in a book or in the person of a monk who preaches the Dharma. You should invest with the name of Teacher (*śāstṛ*) the one from whom you learn about the Perfection of Wisdom. You should be grateful and appreciative, thinking: "This is my good friend from whom I am learning the Perfection of Wisdom, and learning this I shall become irreversible in regard to supreme and perfect enlightenment, I shall be near to those Tathāgatas, Arhats, Fully Enlightened Buddhas, I shall find myself in Buddha-paradises where there is no lack of Tathāgatas, I shall avoid unfortunate conditions and enjoy propitious conditions." Weighing up these advantages, you should invest this monk who preaches thus the Dharma with the name of Teacher. You should not be attached to this monk who preaches the Dharma with thoughts that are affected by ideas of worldly gain. You should be attached to him in your quest for the Dharma because of your respect for the Dharma.[108]

In contrast to this passage we may take a quotation from the *Guhyasamāja Tantra*:

> Then Maitreya the Bodhisattva, the Great Being, bowed before all the Buddhas and said: "How should the Lord the Vajra-Teacher consecrated in the hidden Secret Union of the Vajra of the Body, Speech and Mind of all the Tathāgatas be regarded by all Buddhas and all Bodhisattvas?"
>
> All the Buddhas replied: "Son of good family, he is to be regarded by all Buddhas and all Bodhisattvas as the Vajra of the Thought of Enlightenment. And why so? The Teacher and the Thought of Enlightenment are the same and inseparable. We will just explain briefly. All the Buddhas and Bodhisattvas who dwell, who hold and maintain places in all the ten directions throughout the past, present and future, worship the Teacher with the worship of All Buddhas, and then returning to their Buddha-paradises make this pronouncement of vajra-words: 'He is the father of all us Buddhas, the mother of all us Buddhas, in that he is the Teacher of all us Buddhas." Furthermore, O son of good family, the merit of a single pore of the Teacher

108 *Aṣṭasāhasrikā*, ASP, Vaidya, p. 238, ll. 25ff.; Conze, pp. 201-2.

is worth more than the heap of merit of the Vajra Body, Speech and Mind of all the Lords the Buddhas of the ten directions. And why so? The Thought of Enlightenment is the very essence of All Buddha-Wisdoms, and being the source it is the repository of omniscient wisdom."

Then the Bodhisattva Maitreya, the Great Being, was frightened, was terrified and so remained silent.

Then the Buddha Akṣobhya, the Buddha Ratnaketu, the Buddha Amitābha, the Buddha Amoghasiddhi and the Buddha Vairocana relapsed into the state of composure known as Sustaining Vajra of the Sacramental Fulfillment of All Vajra-Holders, and then they instructed all the Bodhisattva's thus: "Listen, Lord Bodhisattvas, all the Lord Buddhas in the ten directions, who are born of the Vajra-Wisdom of past, present and future, come to the Teacher of the Secret Union (*Guhyasamāja*), worship him and bow before him. And why so? He is the Teacher of all Bodhisattvas and all Buddhas. He is the Lord, the Great Holder of the Vajra, the Chief of all Buddha-Wisdom."

Then all the Bodhisattvas said to all the Buddhas: "Where, O Lords, are to be found the fulfillments (*siddhi*) of the Body, Speech and Mind of All Buddhas?"

They replied: "They exist in the Body, Speech and Mind of the Vajra Teacher who is the Body, Speech and Mind of the Secret Triple Body."

The Bodhisattvas questioned further: "Where is this Secret Vajra of Body, Speech and Mind?"

The reply was: "Nowhere." Then all those great Bodhisattvas were overcome with wonder and astonishment and so they remained silent.[109]

The astonishment of the Bodhisattvas, like the alarm shown by Maitreya, who had been brought up in the older school of devotion to a single Buddha (see section II.2.b), may be presumed to arise not from the teaching of "nothingness" in which they should be well versed already,[110] but from the preeminent position that is given to the Teacher. In tantric Buddhism this becomes so central that it is not enough to explain it as the natural development of earlier Buddhist practice. In all religions teachers are essential and in this respect they play an equally essential part in early Buddhism and throughout the whole Mahāyāna period. The teacher is thus a quite proper means to an end which transcends him as much as it transcends the pupil. In certain forms of tantric Buddhism he is not only the essential means but also effectively the end, and thus in keeping with the Mahāyāna "dogma" of the Perfection of Wisdom, he is identified with the Void (*śūnyatā*) out of which he becomes, in a certain sense, manifest to his pupil.[111] This last piece of elaboration is entirely Buddhist, but the cult of the

[109] GST, Bhattacharyya's ed., p. 137, ll. 15ff.

[110] The *Guhyasamāja Tantra* contains quite a few passages that conform to the regular Perfection of Wisdom teaching of the Void (*śūnyatā*). See e.g., all of chapter 2, the end of chapter 15 (Bhattacharyya p. 107, ll. 13ff, specifically on the dreamlike nature of existence, and part of chapter 17 (p. 133 l. 2 to p. 135 l. 8) on the "voidness" of Body, Speech and Mind.

[111] A good example of this notion is provided by Nāropa's search for his Guru Tilopa. See H. V. Guenther, *The Life and Teaching of Nāropa*, pp. 24ff.

Guru was also central to the religious movements outside organized Buddhism that were now penetrating and transforming it. On the significance of the Guru in Indian religion generally one cannot do better than quote from Shashibhusan Dasgupta:

> It will be seen that in a sense all the systems of Indian philosophy and religion are mystic, for according to all the systems truth always transcends intellectual apprehension or discursive speculation—it is to be intuited within through the help of the preceptor, who has already realized it. Truth is transmitted from the preceptor to the pupil just as light from one lamp to the other. The only way of knowing the truth is, therefore, to ask the grace of the Guru, who, and who alone, can make a man realize the Supreme Reality. It is believed that the true preceptor in his non-dual state identifies himself with the disciple and performs from within the disciple all that is necessary for the latter's spiritual uplift. The true disciple becomes an instrument in the hands of the true preceptor. It is for this reason that in Indian religions the Guru is held in the highest esteem. Sometimes the Guru is a substitute even for God, or at least God is to be realized through the medium of the person of the Guru, who stands as living proof for the existence of God.[112]

In the rites, of which something will be said below, the Teacher is clearly identified with the particular god of the maṇḍala, be it Heruka or whoever is chosen, and the god is but an envisaged emanation from the Void, to whose substantial being worship is conventionally offered, just as to the Teacher himself. Identified with the Void, he is the end result or the so-called "fruit." His central importance is related to the need for a series of ever higher consecrations, some of which are treated as secret, and which only he can bestow. However he is equally important for the practice of internal yoga, and to this the enigmatic songs of tantric yogins bear full witness.

> High and lofty is the mountain; there dwells the girl of the hill-folk (*Śavarī*).
> A peacock's tail-feather she wears on her body and she has a necklace
> of gunja-berries.
> O drunken hillman, excited hillman, make no noise or complaint.
> Your wife is named Fair Lady of the Joy Innate.
> Various trees are in bloom and their branches reach to the sky.
> Alone the hill-girl roams the forest, wearing earrings and vajra.
> The couch of the Three Realms is prepared and the bed of Great Bliss
> made ready.
> The hillman is a lover who gives delight, increasing the pleasure of
> his paramour, and night becomes dawn.
> Eating the betel-nut of Thought and the camphor of Great Bliss,
> She gives delight as she clings to his neck. increasing his joy in Great Bliss,
> and night becomes dawn.
> With your Guru's word as your bow
> Hit the target with the arrow of your mind.

112 See S. Dasgupta, *Obscure Religious Cults*, pp. 87-8.

Apply just one shaft and pierce, O pierce, supreme nirvāṇa![113]

Or one may quote more explicitly from Saraha's songs:

Those who do not readily drink the ambrosia of their master's instructions,
Die of thirst in the desert of multitudinous treatises.
Abandon thought and thinking and be just as a child.
Be devoted to your master's teaching and the Innate will become manifest.[114]

10. THE LATER AMALGAMATING AND PROMULGATION OF TANTRIC TEACHINGS

Our excerpts serve to illustrate the difference in styles between those tantras which are more easily relatable to Mahāyāna sūtras and those whose background is represented by places sacred to wandering yogins. It should be stressed, however, that only some tantras may be allocated with confidence to either category, and little is gained by following those earlier Buddhist scholars, Indian and Tibetan, in attempts to prescribe exact categories for these elusive works. Typical of our first category is the Tantra *Sarvatathāgata-tattva-saṃgraha* ("Symposium of Truth of All the Buddhas") and the main features are the following:

1. A conventional Mahāyāna setting where the Lord Buddha, identifiable as Śākyamuni, presides over a gathering of Bodhisattvas and other celestial beings.

2. An arrangement of Buddha-families, five in number, although traces of an earlier threefold arrangement appear in the material.

3. The work is written in the same kind of Buddhist Sanskrit with which one is familiar from Mahāyāna sūtras.

4. Non-Buddhist divinities are clearly recognized as such by those who composed the work, and their rôle tends to be subsidiary.

Typical of the second category is the *Hevajra Tantra*, and the distinguishing features are the following:

1. There is no full introductory scene, and the presiding "Lord" in the embrace of his feminine partner is scarcely identifiable as Śākyamuni or any other Buddha-manifestation known in Mahāyāna sūtras.

2. Reference to Buddha-families is incidental to the material and scarcely affects the arrangement of the maṇḍala and the presentation of the teaching. Thus, there should be no need for the neophyte to throw a flower or a tooth-pick to decide an appropriate family, for the tantra in question presumes only one

113 For a detailed analysis of these difficult verses, see Per Kværne, *An Anthology of Buddhist Tantric Songs*, pp. 181-8. My translation is not quite as literal as his, and I have used the Tibetan version rather more readily, for example, instead of "bow" (third line from end) the original Indian text has "tail-feather." Concerning the term *sahaja*, rendered here as "Innate," see Index for references.

114 See *Buddhist Texts through the Ages*, ed. E. Conze, p. 231, and for the original text M. Shahidullah, *Les Chants Mystiques de Kāṇha et Saraha*, pp. 145-6 (vv. 57-8).

family, that of the presiding Lord, whether Hevajra, Heruka, Caṇḍamahā-roṣaṇa, or whoever it may be.

3. The work is written in clumsy, often seemingly ungrammatical, Buddhist Sanskrit, as though it were a sanscritization of a local dialect.[115] Also, the materials are presented in a haphazard order, sometimes as though they have come out of a "notebook."

4. No distinction is made between names already accepted within the Mahāyāna tradition and the names of Hindu divinities, and *ḍākinīs* and low-caste women are raised to the rank of leading goddesses.

It would seem that tantric Buddhism took shape simultaneously in both settings, those that were strictly Buddhist but which willingly accepted the new theories of meditational and yogic practice, and those that were primarily interested in the yogic practices, whether interpreted within the terms of a Buddhist or Hindu terminology. It is likely that the teachings recorded in properly Buddhist settings were the first to gain more general acceptance, and while there may have been some hesitancy about accepting works which were less specifically Buddhist, it would have been difficult to refuse them in so far as their basic theories and practices were essentially the same. Those aspects of tantric practice which are often found to be "objectionable" by outsiders and which modern supporters of tantric theories, including many Tibetan lamas, explain away as "symbolic" (thus conceding in effect their otherwise objectionable nature), are not the special preserve of the tantras produced in those circles of yogins and yoginīs illustrated above. There are, for example, constant references to them in the "Symposium of Truth," of which one example has been translated already. It must also be clearly stated that many exegetical works explain these various practices as actual ones, although they may also be treated, once one is expert in them, as an imaginative process. This is so generally the case that illustrative quotations may seem superfluous. However, one or two may be helpful, if only to emphasize the seriousness with which they were treated:

> At all times respectful to his lord, his glorious adamantine teacher, the valiant man who has done all that ought to be done, should apply himself to the secret practice.
> Possessing total freedom of action, having turned away from all attachments, he proceeds in all ways lionlike, intent on final reality.
> Knowing things for just what they are, established in right views, firm in thought and self-reliant, he is concerned to save the world.

115 In making this observation one recalls that some of the early Mahāyāna sūtras appear to be sanskritized versions of earlier recitations in dialect, since the adoption of Sanskrit from about the first century A.D. onward by Buddhists was a gradual process. However, by the seventh century when the tantras began to become part of an accepted Buddhist tradition, Sanskrit was well established and in regular use. Thus, any tantras that developed within an exclusively Buddhist community would be composed in the normal Buddhist Sanskrit idiom. By contrast, those which were first recorded by teachers and pupils in the circles of yogins, whom we have been characterizing as well as might be, would be written first in local dialects, which one may safely presume to have been the same as those in which the songs, of which examples have been given, are preserved. At least one tantra, the *Ḍākārṇava* (ed. N. N. Chaudhuri, Calcutta, 1935) is preserved whole in such a dialect.

He abandons altogether repining thoughts, sloth and torpor, the pleasures and companionships of ordinary life, thus all the eight worldly *dharmas*.[116]

He is always imperturbable, singleminded and resolved, intent on achieving buddhahood by application to the Six Perfections.

He is entirely devoted to the welfare of living beings while having no false ideas concerning them.

Thus raising his thought to enlightenment, he holds to the true course.

Personally united (*suyuktātmā*) with Wisdom and Means, turning away from all attachments, and intent upon his practice of the truth (*tattva*), he succeeds in this very life.

Enthused in his self-consecration by means of yoga as appropriate to his thought, he follows the whole sacramental course as prescribed on the Mantra Path.

He has recourse to the Five Ambrosias in order to pacify Māra and suchlike destructive forces, and this supreme protection consists of urine, faeces and the rest.

Fever, sickness, poison and disease, the attacks of *ḍākinīs* and constellations, Māras and evil spirits are eliminated thereby.

The knowing man eats with enthusiasm these five, human flesh and horse, camel and elephant as well as dog.

With the other sacred sacraments which elevate the mind he gratifies his adamantine thought so as to tranquilize the turbulence of breath.

The Perfection of Wisdom should be worshipped in all ways by those who desire release; she who is pure in an absolute sense, while possessing a body in terms of relative truth. Indeed she exists everywhere in feminine form, and thus it has been taught by the Vajra Lord that she is manifest in this exterior sense.

So the yogin (*sādhaka*) quickly succeeds by means of this true yoga as he makes love to this Symbol (*mudrā*), whether she comes of Brahman caste or of low degree, whether she is immoral, another's wife, deformed or maimed, whether she is one's mother, sister, daughter or niece.

With the sounds of flutes and other instruments which delight the mind, with the physical means who are the external Symbols performing the various modes of love, with the five kinds of sensual pleasure, he should worship himself for the sake of the happiness of his own jewellike thought by means of that yoga where he himself is the divinity.

He should have no doubts of any kind concerning suitability or unsuitability, for everything may be enjoyed by means of the yoga where everything appears as illusion.[117]

Like most of the "Great Adepts" (*mahāsiddha*), the date of the author of this well-composed work remains quite uncertain, although the eighth to ninth

[116] These are gain and loss, fame and ill-repute, praise and blame, happiness and misery. The edited Sanskrit text reads *siddha* instead of *middha* (= torpor; Tibetan *gnyid*).

[117] Extracted from the *Prajñopayaviniścarasiddhi* of Anaṅgavajra, ch. 5, vv. 9-26. The corresponding Tibetan version is in T.T. vol. 68, pp. 241-1-7 ff. See B. Bhattacharyya, *Two Vajrayāna Works*, in Bibliography. His edition, useful as it is, would have been greatly improved if he had checked unsatisfactory Sanskrit terms against the Tibetan. Similar teachings are found in the same volume in the *Jñānasiddhi* of Indrabhūti, ch. 1, specifically vv. 13-15.

century may be likely. It is even possible that he was connected with Padmasambhava, who played an important part in the introduction of Buddhism into Tibet in the late eighth century, since both are said to have come from the Swat Valley (Uḍḍiyāna) and Anaṅgavajra's teacher is named as Mahāpadmavajra, conceivably identical with Padmasambhava.[118] However, whatever the date, the description of the religious life given in this extract corresponds with that of a wandering yogin and certainly not that of a monk in an established celibate community. For several centuries these two ways of religious life must have existed side by side, presumably right up to the last days of Buddhism in India, although the literary works in use on both sides would have exerted an increasing mutual influence. With this in mind it may be helpful to resume in a coherent manner those features of the tantras which have already been described more or less adequately. Certain important features, so far dealt with inadequately or in too disparate a manner, such as Buddha-families, maṇḍalas, and rites of consecration, will be described in more detail in separate sections below.

So far we have clarified to some extent the relationship between the Mahāyāna sūtras and certain tantras, while drawing attention to the very different setting in which such a text as the *Hevajra Tantra* must have been composed. We have drawn attention to the importance for the promulgation of tantric teachings of certain master-yogins, conventionally known as the eighty-four Great Adepts (*mahāsiddha*) who flourished in various successions from master to pupil between the eighth and the twelfth centuries. It was surely during this period that Buddhism in its tantric forms became prevalent in northern India, although its uncertain beginnings may be dated as much as three centuries earlier than this, while many of the tantras, later to be accepted as "canonical," were certainly in existence well before the eighth century, as is proved by the known dates of some of the earlier Chinese translations. Some renowned tantras, as different in content as the *Durgatipariśodhana* ("Elimination of Evil Rebirths") and the *Guhyasamāja*, were among the earliest Buddhist Sanskrit works translated into Tibetan in the eighth century, about the same time that the earliest Chinese translations of tantric works began to make their appearance in the early years of the T'ang Dynasty.[119] Important among these is the "Symposium of Truth" from which several quotations have been drawn already. It has been observed above that the relative datings of Tibetan translations of sūtras and tantras have no relevance to the datings of Indian original texts before the eighth century, because this was when the great work of the Tibetan translators, lasting over the next four centuries, began. But since the work of translating Buddhist sūtras into Chinese dates from the second century A.D. and that of translating tantric works dates generally from the eighth century onward, we

118 See my edition of the *Hevajra Tantra*, Introduction, p. 13.

119 Concerning the eighth-century Tibetan translation of the *Guhyasamāja Tantra*, see Kenneth W. Eastman, "The Tun-huang Manuscript of the *Guhyasamāja Tantra*," a paper presented in Japanese to the Twenty-Seventh Convention of the Japanese Association for Tibetan Studies, 17 November, 1979, Kyoto, Japan (*Nihochibettogakkaikaihō*, no. 26, March, 1980).

have a fair indication when such works were sufficiently in vogue in Buddhist centers in India to attract the attention of foreign translators. It is impossible to date with any semblance of precision a particular tantra, just as it is impossible to date any one sūtra. It has already been remarked that many of the beliefs and teachings expressed in later Mahāyāna sūtras can be traced back to a far earlier period, and the same is true of the tantras. In part, e.g., in so far as tantras were used as protective spells, they belong to a very early phase of Buddhism. In certain other respects, e.g., the theory of self-identification with a chosen divinity who has no obvious earlier Buddhist affinities, we may suspect the teachings to be comparatively late as an acceptable form of Buddhist practice, quite as late as the sixth or seventh century, if we are looking for the actual origins of a text in question. Very early dates have been suggested for the *Guhyasamāja Tantra*, but from my knowledge of its contents I find so early a date as the fourth century hard to accept.[120] This is a well-developed tantra, which has absorbed the "objectionable" practices of tantric yogins into a well-defined Buddhist setting, where the fivefold conception of buddhahood is already accepted and a sixth universal buddha-manifestation is added. A comparatively late Mahāyāna sūtra, later categorized by the Tibetans as a tantra, probably because of the four Buddha-manifestations to the four quarters which it takes for granted, is the *Suvarṇaprabhāsa* ("Sūtra of Golden Light"), and this is most likely dated to the fifth century A.D. in its earliest known Sanskrit version.[121] The development of the theory of Buddha-families from three to four and then to five with eventually a sixth Buddha added, will be discussed below, but in its final form it must belong rather to the eighth century than to the fourth. Here again, however, readers must be reminded that the form in which these works are known to us in Sanskrit scarcely ever represent their earliest versions, and the whole question of datings remains open to speculation and consequent disagreement. For the history of Buddhism in India what is important is not so much the dates of the earliest versions of texts which are only known to us in later versions, but the effects that such texts had on Buddhist beliefs and practices once they went into wider circulation, and for this the eighth century onward must be the period under consideration.

The famous Chinese scholar-pilgrim Hsüan-tsang made between the years 629 and 645 the long journey across Central Asia, entering the Indian subcontinent through the far northwest and visiting all Buddhist sites of importance throughout northern India before returning home, traveling back over the same far-flung regions. His travelog contains detailed information of all the places visited, descriptions of places of pilgrimage and shrines, noting the divinities they contained, as well as the numbers and types of monastic communities and the kinds of religious practice of the inmates. He knows only of the four main "schools," which are classed generally as Hīnayāna and Mahāyāna, and there is no indication that he ever encountered any form of ritualized Buddhism that

120 See Alex Wayman, *The Buddhist Tantras*, pp. 15-19.

121 See R. E. Emmerick, *The Sūtra of Golden Light*, Introduction and references.

might be described as tantric or encountered any of the great tantric sets of divinities, even the set of Five Buddhas, who may be defined as entirely Buddhist in inspiration. He moves in a religious world that clearly relates to the kind of Buddhism known to us from the earlier period (see below, section IV.1.a). It is possible that this was a matter of his own spontaneous choice and that he noted little of forms of Buddhism of which he disapproved, or maybe he did not recognize such religious forms as truly Buddhist. Thus, writing of the Swat Valley (Uḍḍiyāna) in the far northwest, he says that the people have great reverence for the Buddhist Dharma and believe in the Mahāyāna, listing the various schools of the Vinaya tradition that were known, but he also makes the general comment that while learning may be appreciated, there is a lack of application, and that in particular the art of spells is practiced. He also notes the existence of ten temples of divinities, in which dwell a mixed number of unbelievers.[122] These scattered references could well indicate a community where tantric Buddhism has taken root, but in this first half of the seventh century we are apparently still far from the later times when tantric studies will become established in the great Buddhist teaching-centers of eastern India.

The reviewing of the history of Buddhism on Indian soil is inevitably a form of academic reconstruction drawing upon a vast quantity of literary materials, few of which survive in India in the original languages, much surviving in Sanskrit in Nepal, and even greater quantities in Tibetan and Chinese translations and in the biographical writings of visiting scholars, mainly Tibetan and Chinese, as well as occasional ordinances promulgated in their homelands. Considering that Buddhism flourished in India for some seventeen centuries, one notes how very little remains of architectural and iconographic significance apart from the vast quantities of ruins and fragmented images unearthed mainly in the northwestern parts of the subcontinent. Visitors may still be impressed by the restored temples and stūpas at Bodhgayā, Sārnāth, Kāsia (Kuśinagara) and Sāñci, but the great monastic center of Nālandā is a vast tragic ruin with little to show in the local museum, while most of the other great monastic centers that were active until the last days of Buddhism in northern India have disappeared altogether, except where a cluster of archaeological discoveries may indicate some such now unidentifiable ancient site. It is perhaps interesting to note how very scanty is any form of tantric imagery amongst the little that does survive here and there *in situ* in sufficient quantity for one to gain at least an impression of the iconographic predilections of the later inmates. The Indian Museum at Calcutta has received Buddhist remains from all over eastern India, but here too there is very little which does not belong to the more conventional Buddhist world of Buddhas and Great Bodhisattvas. Tantric imagery was certainly represented by a well-advanced production of metal work, as is proved by the continuing development of the craft in Nepal, where a whole variety of tantric divinities

[122] See *Si-yu-ki, Buddhist Records of the Western World*, translated by Samuel Beal, Part I, pp. 120-1. One may refer also to René Grousset, *In the Footsteps of the Buddha*, pp. 111-2, for an interpretative account of this part of Hsüan-tsang's travelog.

have continued to be produced right up to the present day. One may note too that tantric imagery is extremely complex, especially where large sets of divinities arranged as maṇḍalas are concerned, and paintings in the form of large murals are clearly the most suitable form of artistic representation. We know how much the murals that survive in early Tibetan temples of the eleventh and twelfth centuries, as well as the murals from several discovered ancient Central Asian Buddhist sites, drew upon Indian models and inspiration. but the Indian originals no longer exist in those many temples that have long since turned to rubble and dust. Some direct links can be established with miniature paintings on palm-leaf manuscripts from eastern India, which have happily survived in Nepal and maybe also in Tibet (*Pls. 30 & 31*). Furthermore, the Buddhist wall paintings that have survived miraculously at Ajantā are no later than the eighth century, and all we have is the negative evidence that tantric imagery had not yet been developed at this one site.

We have suggested above that some tantras were composed within monastic compounds and others amongst the lay followers of tantric yogins. One group may be characterized by a general conformity to Buddhist Mahāyāna teachings, while the other introduces many concepts for which there would appear to be no Buddhist sanction whatsoever. Tantras classed as Yoga tantras might seem to fall into the first group, while Supreme Yoga Tantras fall into the second. But as we have already observed, it is the latecomers who usually order teachings to suit their own latest productions, placing their own teachings in the highest category and claiming that earlier ones are in some way inferior. Thus the claim that the so called Supreme Yoga Tantras are the only ones to teach the set of higher consecrations is manifestly a false one. They offer in effect nothing higher; they merely provide the same teachings in the more outspoken and deliberately scandalous language and in the unorthodox terminology, which one might well expect of wandering tantric yogins, who claim to have no allegiance anywhere except to their own revered teacher. Presumably it is because they taught the same theories and practices as the more orthodox Yoga Tantras, that it was possible for them to be accepted into the main stream of the Indian Buddhist tradition. It was merely necessary to interpret them in accordance with the theory of "enigmatic" meanings, and this is what the commentators set out to do. Moreover, once they were accepted, much of their terminology might be used in tantras composed in a monastic setting. A possible example of this is the *Guhyasamāja Tantra*, which was first received in Tibet as one of a set of so-called Mahāyoga tantras, and one may note that its literal interpretation was still a cause of anxiety some two centuries and more later, as is shown by an ordinance of King Ye-shes-'od of Gu-ge (western Tibet) who ruled in the tenth to eleventh centuries.

You tantric specialists, who live in our villages,
Have no connection with the Three Ways of Buddhism
And yet claim to follow the Mahāyāna.
Without keeping the moral rules of the Mahāyāna

You say "We are Mahāyānists."
This is like a beggar saying he is king
Or like a donkey dressed in the skin of a lion.

And again below:

O village specialists, your tantric kind of practice,
If heard of in other lands would be a cause for shame.
You say you are Buddhists, but your conduct
Shows less compassion than an ogre.
You are more greedy for meat than a hawk or a wolf.
You are more subject to lust than a donkey or an ox on heat.
You are more intent on rotten remains than ants in a tumbledown house.
You have less concept of purity than a dog or a pig.
To pure divinities you offer faeces and urine, semen and blood.
Alas! With worship such as this, you will be reborn in a mire of rotting corpses.
You thus reject the religion of our Threefold Scriptures.
Alas! You will indeed be reborn in the Avīci Hell.
As retribution for killing creatures with your so-called "rite of deliverance,"
Alas! You will surely be born as an ogre.
As retribution for indulging your lust in your so-called "ritual embrace,"
Alas! You will surely be born as a uterine worm.
You worship the Three Jewels with flesh, blood and urine.
In ignorance of "enigmatic" terminology you perform the rite literally.
A Mahāyānist such as this will surely be born as a demon.
It is truly amazing that a Buddhist should act in this way.
If practices like yours result in buddhahood,
Then hunters, fishermen, butchers and prostitutes
Would all surely have gained enlightenment by now.[123]

Such an ordinance castigates much of the "religious practice" that the texts under consideration clearly associate with free-roving tantric yogins who assemble for their rites and feasts at the sacred places known as *pīṭha* etc. However, despite this general condemnation, texts dealing with such matters are regarded as acceptable, once their "enigmatic" terminology is not misunderstood.[124] Moreover, thoroughly reputable Tibetan translators and scholars were directly involved in the transmission of those very tantras that contain such obnoxious references. Thus Rin-chen bzang-po, known as the Great Translator, whose chief supporter was the same King Ye-shes-'od, was responsible for the translation of the "Symposium of Truth," which contains occasional references to the desirability of slaying, robbing, lying and promiscuous sexual intercourse, and also for an amended translation of the *Guhyasamāja Tantra*, already

123 See Samten G. Karmay, "The ordinance of lHa Bla-ma Ye-shes-'od," *Tibetan Studies in Honour of Hugh Richardson*, pp. 150-62. The Tibetan text, retranslated here, is on p. 156, ll. 6-13, and again p. 156, last eight lines to p. 157, l. 17.

124 The word translated here as "enigmatic" is Tibetan *ldem-dgongs*, which might be rendered literally as "intended as a riddle." It represents Sanskrit *sandhābhāṣa*. For other references see "enigmatic language" in the Index.

translated in the eighth century, which contains throughout references not only to such perverse conduct but also to the whole range of foul sacraments in contexts where the original meaning may well have been literal.[125] There is no doubt that patrons of Buddhism as the new religion of Tibet, as well as members of monastic communities, were perturbed by this class of religious literature; but what were their criteria for judging between one text and another? Such was their unbounded respect (which in the circumstances must surely be judged as naïve) for Sanskrit as the sacred language of the Holy Land where the teachings they were now introducing originated, that it was sufficient to prove the existence of a Sanskrit original for any soi-disant Buddhist text to be accepted as "canonical." This led in due course to many tantras of the Old School (*rNying-ma*) being excluded from the Tibetan Buddhist Canon when it assumed a final form in the thirteenth century, although it is likely that Sanskrit originals had once existed, while at the same time the Canon contains the most obnoxious passages simply because a Sanskrit original version was already known. Tibetan translators and scholars who visited India during this formative period (mainly the tenth to twelfth centuries) surely realized that all that was written in Sanskrit was not necessarily Buddhist, but if anything written was traditionally declared to be a Buddhist work, whatever its actual textual origins, they accepted it in good faith. Once confronted "at home" with all these works fast appearing in Tibetan translation of supposedly unchallengeable authority, religious leaders had no other means of explaining them away than by the theory of "enigmatic" meanings, and so it has been to this day, although nowadays amongst Tibetan Buddhist enthusiasts one hears more of "symbolic" interpretations. In general the problem has been solved fairly simply by replacing the foul sacraments by acceptable substitutes and explaining the perverse teachings in the two ways in which they are already explained in canonical texts, namely as directed—legitimately in certain circumstances—against the enemies of Buddhism or as indicating the state of perfection aimed at, where no distinction can be made between good and evil in that the Five Evils are transmuted into the Five Wisdoms of ultimate buddhahood (see p. 280 below).

Sexual yoga is in a case apart, for it should not necessarily be confused with the promiscuous sexual intercourse as recommended in different although sometimes overlapping contexts. As already observed above, sexual yoga is quite as legitimate as the accompanying yoga of breath-control, although judged unsuitable for those who had taken monastic vows. However, even this becomes in Tibet an internal process of yoga in so far as the conditions for its practice no longer existed. Thus it is said:

> Such teachers and pupils together with their Spells (*vidyā*) possessing all the characteristics as described, do not now exist. So the Knowledge-Symbol which one aspires to receive from one's guru and the series of questions and so

[125] For the life of Rin-chen bzang-po see Snellgrove and Skorupski, *Cultural Heritage of Ladakh*, vol. 2, pp. 83 ff. A long list of his translations is given in G. Tucci, *Indo-Tibetica*, vol. II, pp. 40 ff.

> on are explained as a method. Then by reflecting upon the union of oneself with the Spell as the male and female aspects of one's tutelary divinity in the state of complete mental clarity, one of keen faculties does indeed experience bliss.[126]

One may fairly wonder what purpose sexual yoga may then serve, which is not already served by more conventional forms of yoga based upon the theory of the union of two coefficients, often known as Wisdom and Means. Would the yoga of breath-control be equally effective, if instead of being actually practiced, it was used as an imaginative process? One can certainly appreciate that breath-control, certain forms of sexual control, or indeed the use of certain drugs can produce states of consciousness which those who experience them may identify as an elevated religious experience, but when the process consists of instruction in principles and patterns, followed by meditation upon them, we surely have types of religious experience which differ no way in kind from the meditational practices of nontantric Buddhists. One has the clear impression that the vast variety of tantric imagery, when divorced from the actual tantric practices of the kind we have illustrated, becomes in effect nothing more than new styles for old practices, and Buddhism remains after all very much what it had always been, a retreat from the world for the unworldly and a means of religious livelihood for the more worldly members of the community, with the occasional appearance of some truly great men of religion, who while remaining unworldly, continue to work effectively for the benefit of those who are immersed in the world. In short, tantric Buddhism seems to offer little new in results, which earlier forms of Mahāyāna Buddhism do not already supply. Nonetheless, some more detailed account of its complex imagery remains to be given.

11. BUDDHA-FAMILIES

There have been several references throughout the last section to "families" of various kinds. Thus we are informed in the *Guhyasamāja Tantra* (see section III.8) that: "Those belonging to the families of Passion, Wrath and Delusion, being well versed in the meaning of nondiscrimination, achieve the very best success in the supreme and highest way." These three will be recognized as the three fundamental evils which keep the Wheel of Existence, interpreted as the continual round of rebirths, in circulation according to early Buddhist theories (see section I.3.a). Elsewhere the same tantra (III.2 above) relates them directly with various kinds of perverse actions, with the Buddhist trilogy of Body, Speech and Mind, and with the Hindu trilogy of Brahmā, Śiva and Viṣṇu. The fact that

126 Extracted from mKhas-grub-rje's *Fundamentals of the Buddhist Tantras*, p. 323; the passage is retranslated with acknowledgements to the editors of the text and to their earlier translation. One may note that *'dod-lha* is a literal translation of Sanskrit *iṣṭadevatā*, more often translated by Tibetan *yi-dam* (= tutelary divinity).

it is those "well versed in the meaning of nondiscrimination" who achieve the promised success, suggests at once the notion, so often met with in tantric texts, that the perfected yogin transcends in his thought all concepts of good and evil. According to the philosophical concepts of the Mahāyāna one finds this expressed as the essential identity of nirvāṇa and saṃsāra, so clearly and unequivocally stated by Nāgārjuna and his successors. We have already noticed how this cross-identification of good and evil is used to explain the continual beneficent activity of a would-be Buddha (Bodhisattva) in this world of suffering and sin. Such ideas are also expressed in the sūtra entitled "Concentration of Heroic Progress," in the "Teaching of Vimalakīrti," and especially perhaps in the doctrinal verses of Śāntideva:

> The bodhisattvas who understand such connections,
> gladly accept the sufferings of others,
> Plunging into the deepest hell like swans into a lotus-covered lake.
>
> (See II.3.c-d)

But we have also noticed how in the later Mahāyāna a rather different idea is expressed, namely that since we ourselves by our very nature have no choice but to operate through the phenomenal world (saṃsāra), so it is by the transformation, even the manipulation, of the three fundamental evils that we ourselves gain release. In this respect Asaṅga's verses concerning extrication from the emotions (*kleśa*) by means of the emotions were quoted (III.1). This theory that release from passion and the others (primarily wrath and delusion) are achieved by means of passion etc. is indeed fundamental to tantric practice. The theory is rationalized by the further assumption that training should be adapted to suit candidates in whom the evils of passion, wrath and delusion predominate, and these come to be referred to as "families."

The idea of placing potential practitioners of Buddhist doctrine into different categories is a very ancient one. Thus Śākyamuni, surveying the world with his Buddha-vision immediately after his enlightenment saw "beings of little impurity, of much impurity, of keen or dull faculties, of good or bad conditions, easy or hard to teach."[127] Later the followers of the Mahāyāna distinguished the "ways" (*yāna*) of the Early Disciples (*śrāvaka*), of Lone Buddhas (*pratyekabuddha*) and Bodhisattvas, sometimes equated with the possession of dull, medium or keen faculties. We have noticed how the term *gotra*, literally meaning "fold," comes into use, referring to those who belong to the Buddhist fold, and later how five such "folds" are distinguished, including the three accepted "ways," those who have not made up their mind and those who miss final salvation altogether (II.4.d). All such categories are clearly conceived of as Buddhist, even the last mentioned one in certain respects. In tantric literature the term "family" (*kula*) appears frequently, and so gradually the whole structure of Buddhist tantric symbolism, as expressed most clearly in the maṇḍala or mystic circle, becomes directly related to such Buddha-families. One

[127] See E. J. Thomas, *Life of the Buddha*, p. 82.

may note in passing that the term *kula*, while appearing frequently in Mahāyāna works, occurs in such combinations as *rāja-kula* (= of royal family or lineage), *brāhmaṇa-kula* (= of priestly family), *nīca-kula* (= of low lineage), *ucca-kula* (= of high lineage) etc., thus having no specific Buddhist application. In tantric works, however, its use becomes specifically Buddhist, just as the term *gotra* had been adopted to Buddhist usage in Mahāyāna works. Thus both terms come to have the same meaning, as recognized by the Tibetan translators who used a single term for them (viz. *rigs* = lineage or family), and are distinguished only by the contexts, Mahāyāna or Vajrayāna, where they are used.

The tantra entitled "The Fundamental Ordinance of Mañjuśrī," which for reasons that should become ever clearer as we proceed, may be assumed to be—at least in its oldest parts—one of the earliest tantric works, uses the term *kula* to distinguish the already traditionally accepted Buddhist higher beings (viz. those many Buddha- and Bodhisattva-names which we have met in our quotations from Mahāyāna sūtras) from originally non-Buddhist divinities, whether gentle or fierce, who were then in the process of being accepted into the Buddhist fold both as objects of devotion as well as forms of symbolic imagery. Thus three main families are clearly distinguished: the Buddha Family (*Tathāgata-kula*), the Lotus Family (*Padma-* or *abja-kula*) for gentle divinities and the Adamantine or Vajra Family (*Vajra-* or *kuliśa-kula*) for fierce and powerful divinities. The use of the term Buddha Family (for such a term inevitably retains an exclusive sense) acknowledges in effect the earlier non-Buddhist associations of the members of the other two families, although all three come to be treated as adherents of the Buddhist fold. It may be noted, however, that there is a clearly defined gradation of importance, namely Tathāgata, Lotus, Vajra, in the first category of tantras (*kriyā-tantra*) where these three families are generally the only three well-defined ones. Thus one who has received consecration in the Tathāgata Family is authorized to practice the rituals of the other two; one who has received consecration in the Lotus Family may also practice the rituals of the Vajra Family, while consecration in the Vajra Family limits one to rituals of that family only.[128] The formulation of these three families thus represents a conscious effort to incorporate divinities who are originally non-Buddhist, and the benign ones were more readily acceptable than the fierce ones. The main argument justifying their incorporation is the traditionally accepted one of Bodhisattvas appearing in any guise whatsoever, so long as this conduces to the conversion of living beings.

> Other Bodhisattvas, those Great Beings, appear in the form of women, for they do not withdraw from the world, such being their endless activities; for the purpose of establishing all living beings in the irreversible path which is their aspiration, they assume the form of unaccountable spells (*vidyā*), of mantras and mnemonics (*dhāraṇī*) and various kinds of medicinal herbs, or they take the form of different sorts of winged creatures, of *yakṣas* and ogres (*rākṣasa*),

128 See mKhas-grub-rje's *Fundamentals of the Buddhist Tantras*, p. 149.

> of Gem-mantras and Jewel-rājas, thus adapting themselves to the activities of living beings by entering into such categories of living beings and of non-beings, so doing whatever is suitable for converting living beings in accordance with their aspirations, and adapting themselves to all those assumed forms, for they understand the teaching of the "Mighty Ones of Magical Power" (*vidyā-raja*) and are perfected in the Dharma, appearing in the families of the Buddha (*Tathāgata*), the Lotus (*abja*), the Vajra, in worldly and celestial forms, so without transgressing their vows, they establish living beings in the path of instruction, thus acting without parting from the lineage of the Three Jewels.[129]

The *Mañjuśrīmūlakalpa* is a voluminous and composite work; thus one can expect no very clear formulation of the various "families." However, the three that are clearly defined are those of the Buddha, the Lotus and the Vajra, and it is precisely these three that continue to hold their own in Buddhist tantric tradition despite the later formulation of a set of five "families." This particular tantra is interesting in that it reveals the theory of these "families" in a formative process, with three already defined and others still in a state of uncertainty. As many as eight are named rather incoherently, and some of the terms involved reappear integrated into the later fivefold arrangement.[130] For present purposes we need only be concerned with the generally accepted form of the three-family arrangement as preserved in Indo-Tibetan tradition. In what may well be its earliest formulation, it is described thus in the second chapter of this early tantra:

> Then the master of the maṇḍala, evoking the Buddhas and Bodhisattvas, lighting incense accompanied by the incense-mantra as previously taught, making a gesture of homage as he bows before the Buddhas and Bodhisattvas, and a salutation to Mañjuśrī in his princely form, takes the colored powders

[129] *Mañjuśrīmūlakalpa*, p. 9, ll. 9-16. Those who are interested in the disagreements of interpretation which may exist in the elucidation of a difficult passage such as this, should refer to my *Buddhist Himālaya*, p. 63, and Ariane Macdonald's *Maṇḍala du Mañjuśrīmūlakalpa*, pp. 36-7. I have now retranslated the passage in full, rejecting her complaint that I take as subject throughout the "missionary Bodhisattvas." The whole complex sentence is bound together by a series of long compounds all ending with instrumental plural grammatical endings, which must relate to the same subject throughout, namely the Bodhisattvas. I thank Professor J. C. Wright for checking the structure of the phrases and happily confirming my interpretation. Mme Macdonald also argues the existence of four "families," the fourth one being "the worldly and celestial." This is grammatically possible, but quite unnecessary in the whole context of the first three chapters, with which she is mainly concerned. The word for "family" does not occur in the Sanskrit version, but only in the Tibetan, where its position at the end of the list signifies no more than its position at the beginning, as required in the English or French translations. Concerning the "Mighty Ones of Magical Power" (*vidyārāja*) see above p. 135.

[130] For a list of these eight "families" see Ariane Macdonald, *op. cit.*, pp. 42-3. As will be seen later, the Gem Family is retained as one of the eventual five and the Elephant remains as one of the Buddha-vehicles, although their directions are changed. Families of Early Disciples and Pratyeka-buddhas by their very nature are excluded from the later set of Buddha-families, and their appearance here demonstrates a connection, only to be expected in the early tantric period, between "families" (*kula*) and "folds" (*gotra*) as described above. The different contexts are not yet clearly distinguished.

and traces the images which are to be filled in by the painters. In this manner he draws first the Lord Buddha Śākyamuni with all his fine attributes seated on a bejewelled lion-throne in the divine palace of the Pure Abode, as he teaches the Dharma. . . . Then to the right side of the image of the Lord Śākyamuni he should draw two Pratyekabuddhas seated cross-legged in the lotus-posture, and below these he should draw two great disciples listening to the Dharma. Still further to the right there is the Lord Avalokiteśvara adorned with all his finery, white as autumnal reeds, seated in the lotus-posture, holding a lotus-flower in his left hand and making the gesture of giving with his right. On his right is the Lady Pāṇḍaravāsinī holding a lotus in her right hand and making a gesture of salutation toward the Lord Śākyamuni; she is seated in the lotus-posture; her hair is arranged as a headdress; she wears a white garment with a shawl of white muslin around her and she has a triple mark made with ashes (on the forehead). Likewise he should draw Tārā and Bhrukuṭi seated with their appropriate postures and stance. Above these one should draw the Lady Prajnāpāramitā, Tathāgata-Locanā and Uṣṇīṣarājā. One should draw the Sixteen Bodhisattvas, namely Samantabhadra, Kṣitigarbha, Gaganagañja, Sarvanivaraṇaviṣkambhin, Apāyajaha, Maitreya holding a chowrie while looking at the Lord Buddha, Vimalagati, Vimalaketu, Sudhana, Candraprabha, Vimalakīrti, Sarvavyādhicikitsaka, Sarvadharmeśvararāja, Lokagati, Mahāmati, Patidhara. These sixteen Great Bodhisattvas should be drawn in a tranquil aspect and adorned with all their finery. The chief of the Mighty Ones of Magical Power and the Queen of Magical Power should be drawn with their features and symbols as one recalls them for the Lotus Family and the rest in their proper places according to tradition. In the last position one should put a square space adorned with lotus-flowers, and let those Gods of Magical Power who have been forgotten take up their position in this place.

Thus on the right side of the Lord Śākyamuni there should be two Pratyekabuddhas, namely Gandhamādana and Upāriṣṭha. A maṇḍala should always be made with its main entry toward the East. On the other side of the Lord Śākyamuni two other Pratyekabuddhas should be drawn, namely Candana and Siddha. Below them one should draw two great disciples, Mahākāśyapa and Mahākātyāyana.

To their left is the noble Vajrapāṇi, of dark hue like that of a blue lotus-flower, of gracious appearance, adorned with all his finery, waving a chowrie in his right hand, while with his left he makes the wrathful gesture of the Vajra-Fist. He has as entourage Vajrāṅkuśi, Vajraśṛṅkhalā, Subahu, Vajrasenā and all the Mighty Ones of Magical Power, both male and female, all with suitable dress, accouterments, postures and thrones; they should be drawn as one recalls them with their proper features and symbols. To the left of them one should draw a square marked with crossed-vajras, and having drawn it, one says: "Let those Hosts of Magical Power who have been forgotten take up their position in this place."

Above them the Six Perfections and the Lady Māmakī should be drawn adorned with all their finery and in tranquil aspect.

Above them are the Eight Uṣṇīṣa-rājas who should be drawn completely encircled with flames and in the guise of Great Universal Monarchs all with their appropriate symbols. They are golden in color; their sense-faculties are at rest and their gaze is raised slightly toward the Tathāgata (Śākyamuni). Their names are: Cakravarty-uṣṇīṣa, Abhyudgatoṣṇīṣa, Sītātapatra, Jayoṣṇīṣa, Kamaloṣṇīṣa, Tejorāśi and Unnatoṣṇīṣa. Such are the eight Uṣṇīṣa-rājas who are to be to the left of the Pratyekabuddhas.

. . . Below the lion-throne one should draw the Wheel of the Doctrine, entirely encircled with a ring of flames, and then beneath that a palace of gems where reposes the Great Bodhisattva the Lord Mañjuśrī, the Prince in princely form, of yellowish saffron-like hue, tranquil and graceful, with a somewhat smiling expression, holding a blue lotus-flower in his left hand, while his right hand makes the gesture of generosity and holds a myrobalan fruit. He is adorned with all the finery of a youngster and decorated with five crests, while he wears a string of pearls in place of the sacred thread (of a brahman). He wears an upper and a lower garment of fine material, and he is quite splendid, entirely surrounded by a ring of flames, seated in the lotus-posture, as he glances at Yamāntaka, the Lord of Wrath, while facing the main entrance of the maṇḍala with a graceful expression. On his right side below the lotus one should draw Yamāntaka, the Lord of Wrath, terrible in appearance, entirely surrounded by a ring of flames, with his gaze fully directed toward the Great Bodhisattva, on whose command he attends.[131]

I have quoted this passage at some length since it includes important sets of divinities, such as the Eight Uṣṇīṣa (although only seven are listed) and the Sixteen Bodhisattvas, who will appear later on in well-defined maṇḍalas. But its main interest at present is the description, however seemingly disordered, of three predominant groups of divinities under the leadership of Mañjuśrī, associated with the symbol of the Wheel of the Doctrine and placed immediately under the Buddha Śākyamuni; Avalokiteśvara with the symbol of the Lotus-flower to the right; and Vajrapāṇi with the symbol of the Vajra to the left. It is interesting to note that Śākyamuni has in effect an entourage of Pratyekabuddhas and Early Disciples, thus relating him directly with the Buddhist categories of the earliest period, while Mañjuśrī as his primary representative requires no special entourage despite his clearly suggested preeminence. The wrathful divinity Yamāntaka ("Destroyer of Death"), who is explained according to later theories as his own fierce manifestation, alone awaits his commands. The two other leading Bodhisattvas, Avalokiteśvara and Vajrapāṇi, each has an entourage of feminine divinities, tranquil for the one and fierce for the other. The "Mighty Ones of Magical Power" (*vidyārāja*), representing the new divinities now in the process of being introduced into the tantric pantheon, are allocated to one group or the other depending upon whether their nature is tranquil or fierce. This is clearly the formulation intended, although the whole maṇḍala, even envisaged as a painting, might be difficult to execute merely

[131] For the Sanskrit text see *Mañjuśrīmūlakalpa*, p. 39, ll. 10-16; p. 40, l.2-p. 41, l. 13; p. 41, l. 20-p. 42, l. 3. The complete French translation will be found in Ariane Macdonald, *op. cit.*, pp. 105 ff. The only noteworthy divergence is Vajrapāṇi's hand-gesture and the sex of his small entourage.

from the directions which are given here. Certainly there is no very symmetrical arrangement, usually fivefold or eightfold, so typical of the maṇḍalas which will be considered below. The text goes on to describe three presiding Buddhas, named as Saṅkusumitarājendra ("Beflowered Lord of Kings"),[132] who is placed above Śākyamuni, Amitābha ("Boundless Light") placed above Avalokiteśvara, and Ratnaketu ("Gem Banner"), presumably placed above Vajrapāṇi, but even this is not made clear in the text. Of these only Amitābha retains in later tradition his position as presiding Buddha of the Lotus Family, and I mention the others here partly to illustrate the fluctuating efforts at formulation in this presumably early tantra, and partly because we shall meet them again later in a regular fivefold maṇḍala. Although references to Three Families continue to occur, they are effectively eclipsed by the later Five Family arrangement, which has a so much greater symbolic application. We have already drawn attention above to the reference in the *Guhyasamāja Tantra* to the three families of Delusion, Passion and Wrath, although this tantra operates generally within the fivefold system. It will be explained below how the Three Evils, extended to five to fit a fivefold scheme, are identified with a set of Five Buddhas. Probably the most significant survival of the earlier threefold scheme is the cult of the three Great Bodhisattvas, Mañjuśrī, Avalokiteśvara and Vajrapāṇi, referred to as the "Lords of the Three Families" (Tibetan: *rigs-gsum mgon-po*). Shrines to these three will be found throughout the Himalayas, wherever Buddhism prevails, and this popular cult surely derives from Buddhist India, although all trace of it, like so much else, has disappeared there (*Pl. 33b*). They may be represented by painted stone images, or by a simple row of three wayside shrines (chöten) painted usually red, white and black.[133] Far more commonly they are represented by their mantras or "spells" (*vidyā*) inscribed on flat stones, piled up into sacred walls, usually known as maṇi-walls after the first word of this little set of invocations:

OṂ MAṆIPADME HŪṂ	= O thou with the jewelled lotus![134]
OṂ VAGĪŚVARI HŪṂ	= O thou Lord of the Word!
OṂ VAJRAPĀṆI HŪṂ	= O thou with the vajra in hand!

It is a fairly easy matter to set down in tabulated form the names of Five Buddhas as presiding over five families together with all the other fivefold equations; five evils (an extension of the earlier three), five aspects of wisdom, five aggregates of personality (*skandha*), five material elements, etc., thus giving the impression of an overall uniformity throughout Buddhist tantras. Yet not

[132] His name in Tibetan should be corrected to *Me-tog kun-nas rgyas-pa'i rgyal-po*; cf. Ariane Macdonald, *op. cit.*, p. 158, l. 28.

[133] White for Avalokiteśvara, red for Mañjuśrī (according to Tibetan tradition; he is in fact described as "reddish," *dmar-skya*, in the passage just translated, where the Sanskrit states "yellowish"), and dark blue or black for Vajrapāṇi.

[134] These "spells" (*vidyā*) are all feminine in form, which is entirely normal, and the oft seen translation of "Jewel in the Lotus" is a later misunderstanding of someone who is unaware of the nature of such "spells" and the whole feminine context of their application.

only are there several different sets of Five Buddhas, but even their association with families was clearly a gradual process. We have already seen from the excerpts just quoted that the lords of the earlier set of three families are Bodhisattvas, not Buddhas, and that presiding Buddhas are a later addition. In origin the notion of Five Buddhas need have nothing to do with families at all, but signifies as a symbolic pattern the universality of buddhahood in a cosmic sense. We have already observed how the Mahāyāna sūtras tell of innumerable Buddhas presiding over their paradises throughout space and how all these Buddhas are in essence manifestations of a single Buddha, inevitably identified with the Buddha Śākyamuni, around whom all Buddhist doctrine had developed from the earliest recorded period onward. In its simplest form this idea is expressed by a central Buddha with one other in each of the four main directions. Thus in the *Suvarṇaprabhāsa* four such directional Buddhas manifest themselves, declaring the infinite life-span of the glorious Buddha Śākyamuni. They are: Akṣobhya (East), Ratnaketu (South), Amitābha (West), Dundubhisvara (North). With a slight change in the name of the southern Buddha (Ratnasambhava for Ratnaketu) and with the replacement of Dundubhisvara ("Lord of the Drum") by Amoghasiddhi ("Infallible Success"), this is the set which eventually predominates (*Pls. 33a, 62*). Two titles attach themselves specifically to Śākyamuni as central Buddha, namely "Omniscient" (Sarvavit) and "Resplendent" (Vairocana). The second of these becomes the usual name of the central Buddha throughout the whole class of Yoga tantras. As Śākyamuni says in the *Śūraṅgamasamādhi Sūtra*: "That Buddha (namely 'Resplendent One, Adorned with Rays, Transformation-King') is myself with a different name, preaching the Dharma in that universe and saving living beings" (see p. 78). As will be noted below, the gesture of preaching or "turning the Wheel of the Doctrine" becomes the typical iconographic feature of Vairocana when the Five Buddhas come to be differentiated by their hand-gestures. A presumably early tantra of the Yoga Tantra class, where Vairocana or Mahāvairocana (Great Vairocana) as he is also known, presides is precisely the *Mahāvairocana Sūtra*. Here the four other Buddhas are: Ratnaketu (East), Saṃkusitarāja (South), Amitābha (West), Dundubhisvara (North). It may be interesting to note that we have already met three of these Buddhas in our excerpt from the *Mañjuśrīmūlakalpa*, and so Ratnaketu's presumed position over Vajrapāṇi has some semblance of confirmation for whatever this may be worth. However, reasons might be hard to find for Saṃkusitarāja's elevation above Śākyamuni. Some of these rearrangements are seemingly so wayward that Śākyamuni may find himself occupying one of the four directions, while remaining in essence at the center under one of his other titles. Thus in the *Sarvadurgatipariśodhana Tantra* we find the Omniscient One (Sarvavit) at the center with the following arrangement: King-Eliminator of Evil Rebirth (East), Ratnaketu (South), Śākyamuni (West), Saṃkusitarāja[135] (North). This arrange-

135 To avoid confusing a patient reader with too many variations of these names, I use one particular form of any particular name. Thus this Buddha is also known as *Vikasitakusuma* ("Flower in

ment of the Five Buddhas has no explicit association with Buddha-families, which scarcely enter at all into the teachings of this particular tantra. Also it is noteworthy that in the main tantra of this Yoga class, namely the "Symposium of Truth," where the Five Buddhas emerge in their generally accepted dispositions, the rituals are arranged according to a theory of just four families. Vairocana/Sarvavit presides universally, manifesting himself in the four directions as: Akṣobhya (East), Ratnasambhava (South), Amitābha/Amitāyus (West), Amoghasiddhi (North). Their main entourage consists of a set of Sixteen Bodhisattvas, a variation of the set already encountered in the *Mañjuśrīmūlakalpa*, and which is disposed in groups of four around each of the four directional Buddhas. This arrangement then has to be brought into relationship with a set of four families, which is an extension or perhaps further rationalization of the three families met with in the *Mañjuśrīmūlakalpa*, and which clearly does not correspond to the fivefold arrangement of Buddha manifestations. Moreover, the Five Buddhas ultimately preside over all the four families, which are led, as in the earlier tantra, by Bodhisattvas thus:

Tathāgata Family: Samantabhadra *alias* Vajrapāṇi/Vajradhara
Vajra Family: Vajrapāṇi *alias* Vajrasattva
Lotus Family or *Dharma*: Avalokiteśvara *alias* Vajranetra
Gem Family or *Action*: Ākāśagarbha *alias* Vajragarbha

Aware of the later accepted pattern of Five Buddha-families and unaware of the possibility of historical development as an explanation of such anomalies, commentators explain such an arrangement as a deliberate amalgamation of two families, the Gem Family (of Ratnasambhava) and the Action Family (of Amoghasiddhi).[136] The more likely explanation is that the Gem/Action family brings together those divinities and living beings who were not included in the early three-family arrangement, and that such categories are in origin a separate development from the scheme of Five Buddhas. In the last part of the "Symposium of Truth" there is indeed the appearance of a recurring arrangement of five families, as represented by five leaders who speak in turn, but here the five are:

Sarvatathāgata (All Buddhas) represented by the Lord Buddha,
Tathāgata (Buddha Family) represented by Vajrasattva/Vajrapāṇi/Samantabhadra,
Vajra represented by Vajradhara/Vajrapāṇi,
Lotus represented by Avalokiteśvara,
Gem represented by Ākāśagarbha.

There are several variations in the names of the five leaders, and Mañjuśrī who has no substantial aprt to play in this tantra, appears exceptionally as the

Bloom"), while Dundubhisvara ("lord of the Drum") is known as *Divyadundubhimeghanirghoṣa* ("Divine Thunder of Drums").

136 See mKhas-grub-rje's *Fundamentals of the Buddhist Tantras*, p. 217. For the alternative names of the Sixteen Bodhisattvas see section III.12.

spokesman of all Buddhas.[137]

The significant change which has now taken place is that all these families may be regarded as legitimized Buddha-families, although the specific name of Tathāgata (= Buddha Family) continues to adhere to one of them. So far as rites in the maṇḍalas are concerned, there is no separate Sarvatathāgata (All Buddha) Family, and such is the powerful symbolism of the term *vajra* that Bodhisattvas with *vajra*-names predominate, and thus the maṇḍala for the Buddha Family is known as the Maṇḍala of the Vajra-sphere, being all but identical with Vajrapāṇi's Vajra Family maṇḍala, known as the Maṇḍala of Victory over the Threefold World. This represents a totally different situation from the one which we noticed in the "Fundamental Ordinance of Mañjuśrī," where the Vajra Family tends to be regarded as the inferior one of the then accepted three main ones. The divinities of the Lotus/Dharma and Gem/Action families, which make up the four families of the "Symposium of Truth," are simply variations with suitable Lotus (*padma-*) names or Gem (*maṇi-*) names as the case may be of Vajrapāṇi's Vajra Family maṇḍala. At the same time the older tradition of non-Buddhist divinities being converted to the Buddhist fold is preserved and a special Vajra Family maṇḍala is created by Vajrapāṇi for their benefit, as described in translated extracts earlier on (see section III.3). However, all family members may now be accepted on equal terms as aspirants to final enlightenment, and thus family membership comes to be rationalized according to rather different principles, controlled by the cosmic conception of buddhahood as expressed in all maṇḍalas that are arranged according to the symbolism of the Five Buddhas. Thus this further development is best explained within that enlarged context.

12. THE MAṆḌALA

In normal Sanskrit usage *maṇḍala* simply means "circle" or any form of circular array, precisely as we might speak of a circle of attendants. In magical arts, with which the tantras have so many connections at their more popular level, it is used in the sense of "magic circle," while in a more elevated sense it may refer to an enclosure, not necessarily circular, which separates a sacred area from the everyday profane world. Thus it represents the special domain of any particular divinity:

> And all should cry, Beware! Beware!
> His flashing eyes, his floating hair!
> Weave a circle round him thrice,
> And close your eyes with holy dread,
> For he on honey-dew hath fed,
> And drunk the milk of paradise.[138]

137 For some examples see the *STTS, Facsimile Edition*, my introduction, pp. 59-67.

138 The final lines of S. T. Coleridge's poem *Kubla Khan*.

In the modern world we have become generally so divorced from ideas and practices that were all part of common knowledge in earlier centuries, that it may be helpful to recall such associations of similar ideas, which many readers will have simply taken for granted. It is precisely in the sense of sacred enclosure that the term *maṇḍala* is used throughout tantric works, and so it comes about that it is represented often enough as a set of concentric circles, set within a square, and then further enclosed by a circular boundary. The "square," which is regularly described as having a door on each of its four sides, the main one being toward the East, and all adorned with an elaborate portal (tympanum is the more accurate term), represents the normal Indian four-sided temple, many of which survive in Himalayan areas and especially in Nepal, as seen from above. Since a temple is primarily conceived of as the domain of a particular divinity, the significance of the maṇḍala as a stylized two-dimensional pattern with identical intention becomes quite explicit.

The center of the enclosure is its most sacred spot while the outer ring borders on the profane world. Thus a set of concentric circles can represent various stages of accommodation to the not so sacred. There is an exact analogy with the gradations of chief ministers, lesser ministers, serving staff and messengers, with which a great king seated in state might be supposed to be surrounded. However, maṇḍalas can often be very much more simple than this; they may be a simple symbolic pattern with or without a single central divinity, or there may be a central divinity, surrounded by an entourage of four or eight lesser divinities. A more elaborate one consists of the central Buddha, attended by four high-ranking goddesses, with his four emanations in the four directions, each of these surrounded by a group of four Bodhisattvas, while four more goddesses occupy the intermediate points of the compass, and the whole assembly is waited upon by a further set of goddesses with offerings and four fierce guardian divinities, each keeping one of the four portals. Simple or elaborate, the significance of the maṇḍala as enclosing the radiating power of the central divinity remains constant.

However in Buddhist usage the maṇḍala has yet a further significance deriving from the more general Mahāyāna teaching that nirvāṇa (here identifiable as the sacred sphere) and saṃsāra (the profane everyday world) are essentially the same, their identity being recognized in the state of final enlightenment, where all discriminations disappear. Thus one who is properly prepared by being trained to recognize the significance of the symbols of which the maṇḍala is composed, discovers by means of it the whole mystery of existence, as interpreted in the traditional Buddhist terms. Once again this idea should not be unfamiliar to Western readers. In the opening scene of Goethe's greatest poetic drama the learned scholar Faust, oppressed by the seeming vanity of all academic learning, suddenly throws open a volume of a famous sixteenth century astrologer, Nostrodamus, where he sees the symbolic pattern of the macrocosm. At the first glance he exclaims:

What joy arises at this sight,
Flowing suddenly through all my senses!
I feel a sacred youthful vital bliss
Now glowing through my veins and nerves.
Was it a god who drew these signs
Which tranquilize the inner turmoil
And fill the stricken heart with gladness,
And by some quite mysterious impulse
Reveal the powers of nature all around me?
Am I a god? Such light there is!
I see in these pure traits
The natural world unfolded to my inner being.[139]

We find here both the idea of blissful awareness associated with that brilliant light, known to Buddhist tantric adepts as the pure light of the Void, as well as that of self-identification with the surrounding world. Faust may hesitate to believe that he has become one with the god of the maṇḍala, but this is precisely the objective of the Buddhist practitioner. Belief in one's chosen divinity, with whom such self-identification is sought, is the tantric coefficient of the Mahāyāna teaching of the Void. Such knowledge represents divine wisdom, but without the divinity who provides the means toward its realization, belief in the essential emptiness of all concepts would be mere nihilism, from which no salvation is possible. Used in this extraordinary manner, the maṇḍala becomes the most potent expression of pantheistic realization that has ever been devised.

> Whatever things there are, whether moving or motionless, grass and shrubs and creeping plants, they are conceived of as the final quiddity (*tattva*) and having the same nature as oneself. In them there is just one without a second, great bliss which is self-experiencing. Final perfection (*siddhi*) is self-experiencing, and likewise thought-creation (= the imagined world) is self-experiencing. *Karma* consists of this same self-experiencing, for *karma* comes about from opposition (viz., the positing of all such opposites as delusion and knowledge, etc.). One is oneself the Destroyer, the Creator, the King, the Lord. Passion and wrath, envy, delusion and pride, cannot prevail one sixteenth part (viz., even by a single phase of the moon) against this blissful central point. It is Wisdom, where like space, the elements (*dharmas*) have their origin, thus comprising Means. It is there that the threefold world arises, possessing the nature of Wisdom and Means.[140]

Thus the maṇḍala represents the self-identification of the microcosm (the human person) with the macrocosm, which has the nature of saṃsāra for the unenlightened mind; conversely, it reveals itself as the perfect expression of buddhahood when all misleading distinctions disappear in the enlightened state of nonduality. The whole conception develops from a variety of separate

139 I have devised my own translation from the German of Brill's edition, 1936, vol. I, p. 21. For those who do not read German the translation by Bayard Taylor (Chandos Classics, F. Warne & Co., London, no date) may be commended.

140 *Hevajra Tantra*, I.viii, 45-9.

patterns, some already fivefold and thus readily adaptable to the simple cosmic pattern of a center and four directional points, while others need to be extended or truncated, as the case may be, so that they may fit. Readily adaptable are the five great elements, representing the macrocosm, and the five aggregates of personality, representing the microcosm. The three fundamental evils, delusion, wrath and passions, one of the oldest Buddhist triads, are extended to five with the addition of malignity (*paiśunya*) and envy (*īrṣyā*).[141] Likewise the Buddha-families receive a fixed fivefold formulation. Sometimes the six senses (sight, hearing, smell, taste, touch and power of thought) are accommodated to the four quarters, the zenith and the nadir. In a similar manner the Ten Perfections can be included by apportioning them to the directions of the quarters and intermediate points and zenith and nadir. Thus the maṇḍala is the repository of all truth as interpreted in the concepts of Mahāyāna doctrine. It represents both the means of reintegration into the state of buddhahood, and also the outward movement of saving grace of one's chosen divinity, who conjoins the central Buddha with the aspirant through the medium of his guru.

> The maṇḍala is wisdom's noblest form.
> Unlike the moon it does not wax and wane.
> But like the sun that shines alike on all
> The same compassion holds us all in thrall.
>
> Wisdom supreme, Buddha ineffable,
> Thou glorious Buddha-body, now fivefold,
> As human Buddha, whether stern or kind,
> You suit your method to a convert's mind.
>
> Evoked by thought, conceived as having form,
> Intangible, O Lord, you change your norm.
> To offer salutation we make bold
> And worship you with offerings untold.
>
> Yet worshipper and worshipped join as one.
> Who lifts his thoughts to buddhahood is Buddha's son.[142]

A maṇḍala, drawn on consecrated ground, becomes the sacred place where an aspirant is consecrated by his teacher. Painted as a mural or as a temple-banner, it serves both as instruction to a pupil in the intricacies of its parts, and as a means of calling to mind a particular set of divinities in the meditative practice known as the Process of Emanation. Every tantra has its presiding divinity with his or her traditional entourage arranged as a maṇḍala, and some tantras have

[141] An attentive reader may note that in the passage just quoted from the *Hevajra Tantra*, instead of "malignity," "pride" (Sanskrit *māna*) occurs in this extended set of five. This suggests the inevitable uncertainty associated with its eventual formulation.

[142] These jingling verses are my adaptation of a passage translated by me far more literally in my *Buddhist Himālaya*, p. 250, from the rNying-ma ritual known as "Union of the Precious Ones" (*dKon-mchog spyi-'dus*). I have used it together with two other quotations reused here, in an article "Cosmological Patterns in Buddhist Tradition," contributed to *The Origins of the Cosmos and Man*, pp. 87-110.

alternative arrangements of divinities or sets of quite different maṇḍalas. But although the variety is enormous, their function of serving as the means of integration of the religious practitioner with the chosen divinity remains generally the same. It is recounted that when the famous Indian Buddhist teacher Atiśa came to Tibet in 1042 he met the Great Translator Rin-chen bzang-po who had worked on the translations of numerous texts, and he said to him:

> "O Great Translator, do you know this and this and this?" thus questioning about the Buddhist Canon and all the sūtras and tantras.
>
> "These I know," he replied.
>
> "Well then," said Atiśa, "there was no need for me to come here."
>
> When they retired that night, they were in a three-storey temple. On the ground floor there was the circle of divinities of the Guhyasamāja, on the next floor the circle of divinities of Hevajra, and on the top floor the circle of Cakrasaṃvara divinities. At twilight the Translator practised meditation on the ground floor, at midnight on the next floor and at dawn on the top floor. The following morning when they were having a meal, Atiśa asked: "O Great Translator, how was it that you practised meditation yesterday at twilight on the ground floor, at midnight on the next floor and at dawn on the top floor?"
>
> The Translator replied: "In that way I can produce separately and reabsorb the different sets of divinities."
>
> Atiśa's face darkened as he said: "There was indeed need for me to come."
>
> The Translator then asked: "How do you understand it?" and Atiśa replied: "I don't understand it like that. Even if one practises all these religious ways with one's thoughts quite subdued, yet fundamentally they all have the same single flavour. It is quite sufficient to experience in one single spot all production and reabsorption."[143]

This story well illustrates the different attitude of the scholar and the religious teacher. The latter often professes a lack of interest in academic work, forgetting that the religious practices to which he is so devoted would not have reached him in an intelligible form if it had not been for the previous work of scholars and translators. In this case too the disparaging tone used by Atiśa is hardly fair. Rin-chen bzang-po was certainly familiar with a great variety of tantric cycles, and it was doubtless all the same to him whether he meditated upon three of them or only one, for he knew quite as well as Atiśa that the result would be the same. The story is probably apocryphal in any case, but it makes the point very well that any of these maṇḍalas would have served the same purpose. It is also true that the great variety of tantric traditions that were adopted by the Tibetans result in a vast unmanageable quantity of literary and artistic materials, to the embarrassment of anyone who wants to write in a comprehensible way about Buddhist tantras. Tibetan exegetes (and they have been many despite Atiśa's dictum) devote much of their discussions on the subject to explaining disagreements of interpretation between the followers of their own school and those of

[143] From the biography of Rin-chen bzang-po, see our *Cultural Heritage of Ladakh*, vol. 2, p. 96.

others. We for our part might list the many varied sets of divinities, describing their iconographic features and doctrinal interpretation.[144] This is helpful to the keepers of museums of Oriental art and to commercial art collectors, but it would serve no purpose in a book such as this, even if the present writer were to claim the required far-reaching competence. He tends to regard the vast concourse of tantric divinities like a large assembly of guests at some private reception. Many of them one may have met before, some well known, some known but imperfectly. Others one may not know at all; to these one may be introduced, and of this number some will be remembered on a future occasion and some hardly remembered at all. In many cases the ones remembered will be those with whom some common interests were established, and the one or two with whom one becomes really intimate can become friends or partners for life. We are often told that a perfect partner should assist us toward the realization of our whole inner potential, and although this remains perhaps a rather vague concept, it may help to explain the theories of tantric Buddhists concerning the choice of one's religious teachers, one's companions, and one's favorite divinity. The possibility of such a choice is formulated according to the pattern of a maṇḍala conceived as fivefold. Thus the aspirant may throw a flower or a toothpick onto such a maṇḍala drawn on the ground, while led toward it blindfolded by his teacher, and wherever the object falls, this shall be his Buddha-family, indicating in his unregenerate state a preponderance of delusion, wrath, passion, envy or malignance. Such a theory is logically applied in a tantra such as the "Symposium of Truth," where the various maṇḍalas suitable for several different "families" are given; but for many aspirants the choice might seem to be already made once he is accepted by a particular religious teacher or even by his entering a religious order, where certain tantric cycles are in vogue and others not. In practice two families become predominant, those of the Tathāgata, centering on the Buddha Vairocana, and those of the Vajra, centering on the Buddha Akṣobhya. The first group includes generally those tantras that are related rather more closely with traditional Mahāyāna teachings and thus were the more readily approved of in China and Japan, while the second group comprises those that center on the more horrific deities such as Hevajra, Cakrasaṃvara, Guhyasamāja and Kālacakra, who have become especially dear to the Tibetans. To the group centering on Vairocana, often referred to as the "Omniscient," belong mainly the Yoga Tantras of which the "Symposium of Truth" is undoubtedly the most important. Reaching China, mainly by the sea route, already by the eighth century, their popularity is attested by the rapid development of tantric sects both in China and Japan. Under Tibetan influence they also flourished at Tun-huang in far northwestern China (see section IV.2.c) where many painted scrolls and manuscripts were discovered at the beginning of this century. Thus numerous painted maṇḍalas have survived, of which examples can be seen in the National Museum of Delhi or in the British Museum

144 The most notable work of such a kind is that by Marie-Thérèse de Mallmann, *Introduction à l'iconographie du tantrisme bouddhique*.

in London, and it will be noted that wherever the set of Five Buddhas is portrayed, it is Vairocana who is central, in accordance with the general tradition of the Yoga Tantras. Likewise in the ancient temples of the old kingdoms of western Tibet, dating from the tenth to twelfth centuries, we find the same tradition prevailing. Northwestern India and especially Kashmir, which was then still a Hindu-Buddhist kingdom, clearly provided the routes through which the texts and the artistic techniques were transmitted into Central Asia as well as into western Tibet.

The tantras of the Supreme Yoga category were certainly not unknown in Central Asia and China, but there is little artistic representation of their horrific divinities. These prevail in Central Tibet, where they arrived direct from northeastern India and Nepal. These are the tantras that center on Akṣobhya, the Imperturbable Buddha of the eastern quarter, who is typified iconographically by the so-called "earth witness" hand-gesture, deriving from the traditional account of Śākyamuni Buddha's final realization of enlightenment at Bodhgayā (II.2.a). This was by far the most popular image of a Buddha in eastern India, as is shown by the many still to be seen in Indian museums, and his close association with the Buddhist tantras promulgated in that area need cause no surprise. Thus he comes to be accommodated at the center, while Vairocana is relegated to the eastern quarter. It is noteworthy, however, that although such a maṇḍala is often described in exegetical works, it does not seem to be so often depicted, and thus it may be mainly a theoretical structure relating to the maṇḍalas of horrific divinities such as Hevajra, Guhyasamāja and the rest. Such a maṇḍala is described in these tantras, but what we see depicted is not a central Akṣobhya, but Hevajra, Guhyasamāja or whoever else it may be, identified as a manifestation of Akṣobhya. To emphasize the transcendence of buddhahood as a counteraction to the pantheistic involvement of the Five Buddhas in the phenomenal world, a sixth Buddha is sometimes mentioned as though transcending the other five. In the *Guhyasamāja Tantra*, Vairocana is thus duplicated as Great Vairocana (Mahāvairocana) and so returns to his position of preeminence over Akṣobhya, here the central Buddha of the set of five. In the *Hevajra Tantra* there is a passing reference to Vajrasattva as this sixth Buddha. As Hevajra himself explains:

> In full the families are six, but they are also five and three. Just listen, Yoginī: Akṣobhya (wrath), Vairocana (delusion), Ratnasambhava (malignity), Amitābha (passion), Amoghasiddhi (envy), Vajrasattva (bliss). They should be conceived in this order with their spheres of purification. By omitting Vajrasattva we have a fivefold set of families. Then they become three with Wrath, Delusion and Passion. But these six or five families are comprised in one, that one family which has Mind as Lord and consists in the Wrath of Akṣobhya. Such is the adamantine power of Wrath.[145]

Thus for Hevajra the Buddha Akṣobhya, of whom he himself is a horrific mani-

[145] *Hevajra Tantra*, II.iv.100-3.

festation, remains supreme in essence. As we have already observed, Vajrasattva (Adamantine Being) is an epithet of absolute power such as pertains to Vajrapāṇi (Vajra-in-Hand) at the summit of his successful career when he is effectively identified with Vajradhara (Vajra-Holder), a title of the sixth Buddha favored generally in traditions associated with the Eighty-Four Great Adepts. An iconographic distinction comes to be drawn between Vajrapāṇi as Bodhisattva and Vajradhara as Supreme Buddha, but since both names are earlier used of this all-powerful Bodhisattva, it is clearly he and no one else who attains this high rank. Although the *Hevajra Tantra* refers vaguely to the existence of six families, there is no sixth family of bliss existing on the same plane as the families of the five evils, since these are transmuted into bliss in the supreme state of self-experiencing knowledge. In tantras of the Supreme Yoga class all the earlier distinctions that were made between the different families seem to disappear, and they may be referred to as six or five or three as suits the symbolism of the ritual. Thus according to the *Kālacakra Tantra* a preliminary consecration of a pupil is described in this manner:

> Then the teacher makes the pupil enter the maṇḍala (which is marked) on the ground and imprints him with the six families (using the mantras) OṂ ĀḤ HŪṂ HOḤ HAṂ AḤ on the forehead, throat, heart, navel, top of the head (*uṣṇīṣa*) and genitals, then he invokes Vajrasattva with the mantra: OṂ A Ā AṂ AḤ VAJRASATTVA MAHĀSUKHA VAJRA-KĀLACAKRA ŚIṢYASYA-ABHIMUKHO BHAVA SANTUṢṬO BHAVA VARADO BHAVA KĀYAVĀKCITTĀDHIṢṬHĀNAM KURU KURU SVĀHĀ (OṂ A Ā AṂ AḤ Vajrasattva Great Bliss Vajra Wheel of Time be present to this pupil, be pleased with him, be beneficent and empower him in body, speech and mind SVĀHĀ).[146]

Here the reference to six families suits the context of six vital parts of the body, and "family" has come to mean "buddha-sphere." Elsewhere in this tantra the Supreme Buddha is referred to as Ādibuddha (Prime Buddha) defined in this way:

> The word "prime" (*ādi*) means without beginning or end, and "enlightened" (*buddha*) means being enlightened with regard to the elements of existence (*dharmas*), free of all false conceptions. So being primary and being buddha, he is Prime Buddha, with no origin and no decease, omniscient. It is said in the Eulogy of Names (*nāmasaṅgīti*):
>
> Buddha without beginning and end, Prime Buddha with no associates;
> He embodies Compassion (Means) and Void (Wisdom), and he is known
> as Kālacakra (Wheel of Time),
> For Kāla (Time) expresses his relative aspect
> And Cakra (Wheel) expresses the Void,
> But he is beyond duality and he is eternal.[147] (*Pl. 79*)

146 See the *Sekoddeśaṭīka*, ed. M. E. Carelli, p. 10, ll. 17 ff.

147 *Ibid.*, p. 7, ll. 25 ff. Dr. Carelli has translated this same passage on p. 21 of his Introduction, introducing the term *śakti* for which there is no equivalent in the original Sanskrit version of the text.

Another title for this Supreme Buddha, later used by the followers of the Old Order (*rNying-ma*) of Tibetan Buddhism as well as by Bonpos, is Samantabhadra (Universal Goodness), and this is presumably an elevated form of the Bodhisattva Samantabhadra who is the leader of the Tathāgata Family in the "Symposium of Truth" (*Pls. 31c, 78,* and p. 197) where he alternates with Vajrapāṇi/Vajradhara).

The student of tantric Buddhism must accustom himself to a bewildering variety of Buddha-names, many of which relate to distinctive iconographic forms, but which in their true essence know of no diversity. Scarcely any other religion can display so many different divinities, some appearing singly, some appearing in sets, all treated by the simple Tibetan believer as the many gods (*lha*) of his religion, yet recognized by the true adept as mere expressions of absolute buddhahood adapted to his own special circumstances. Thus all these divine forms are dissolved by him into the luminous state of the Void, and it is out of the Void that they are duly summoned by means of his meditative practice. The tantras usually open with just such an emanation of supreme buddhahood, and the aim of the practitioner is to identify himself with the dual process of emanation and reabsorption of the Buddha-forms with whom his teacher has familiarized him by the due processes of initiation. It may be helpful to quote the actual beginning of the *Guhyasamāja Tantra*:

> Thus have I heard: at one time the Lord reposed in the vaginas of the Vajra-maidens—the heart of the Body, Speech and Mind of all Buddhas. He was accompanied by Bodhisattvas, those Great Beings, as innumerable as the atoms of dust of which the sacred mountains of innumerable Buddha-fields are composed. Thus there were the Bodhisattva Vajra-Union (*Samaya*) as well as:

Vajra-Body	Vajra-Earth	Vajra-Form
Vajra-Speech	Vajra-Water	Vajra-Sound
Vajra-Mind	Vajra-Fire	Vajra-Smell
Vajra-Concentration	Vajra-Air	Vajra-Taste
Vajra-Recitation	Vajra-Space	Vajra-Touch
		Vajra-Thought

> and all the others, as many as the atoms of dust of which the sacred mountains of innumerable Buddha-fields are composed. Moreover he was accompanied by the (Five) Buddhas who pervade the realms of Space, namely: Akṣobhya (Central), Vairocana (East), Ratnaketu (South), Amitābha (West) and Amoghavajra (North), all the size as it were of a sesame seed, and the whole of space seemed filled.
>
> Then the Lord the Great Vairocana relapsed into the state of repose known as the "Great Passion-Method of All Buddhas" and thus reabsorbed that whole host of Buddha-forms into his own Vajra-Body, Vajra-Speech and Vajra-Mind. Then all those Buddhas, in order to please the Lord, the Foremost of the Vajra Body, Speech and Mind of All Buddhas, assumed feminine forms as they reemerged from the body of the Lord Great Vairocana. Some took the form of Buddha-Locanā, some of Māmakī, some as Paṇḍaravāsinī

and some as Samaya-Tārā. Some appeared in the nature of Form, some of Sound, or of Smell or Taste or Touch.

Then the Buddha Akṣobhya consecrated the immaculate four-sided maṇḍala in the vagina of the Vajra-Maiden—the heart of the Body, Speech and Mind of All Buddhas.

Translucent and "just so" by nature,
Yet manifest in varied forms,
Pervaded by a host of Buddhas,
Brilliant with its shooting rays,
With translucent circles such as these
The resort of All Buddhas is thus composed.

Then the Lord, the Foremost of the Vajra Body, Speech and Mind of All Buddhas, took his place at the center of the Great Maṇḍala of All Buddhas, and the (Five) Buddhas Akṣobhya, Ratnaketu, Amitāyus, Amoghasiddhi and Vairocana dwelt in the heart of the Buddha Vajra Thought of Enlightenment.

Then the Lord Buddha Vajra Thought of Enlightenment relapsed into the state of composure known as "Vajra Subjugation of All Buddhas," and immediately the whole realm of space was established in the adamantine nature of All Buddhas and all living beings throughout the whole realm of space experienced the bliss and happiness of All Buddhas as a result of their empowerment in Vajra-Being (Vajrasattva).[148]

The Supreme Buddha is here referred to as Great Vairocana, as Vajra Thought of Enlightenment and (at least by implication) as Vajrasattva. He is said to reside at the center of the maṇḍala in the sense that the set of Five Buddhas emanate from him, but in practice it is Akṣobhya who occupies the central place amongst the five in any schematic arrangement of this Supreme Yoga Tantra. We have already noted that Vairocana occupies the central position in the Yoga Tantras with Akṣobhya in the East, and it may be presumed that a certain lingering notion of Vairocana's primacy results in the sixth all-comprehending Buddha having as one of his titles "Great Vairocana" in some Supreme Tantra Tantras. So far as the *Guhyasamāja Tantra* is concerned, the supreme divinity is Guhyasamāja (Secret Union) himself, just as Hevajra is supreme in the *Hevajra Tantra*, Cakrasaṃvara in his tantra, Kālacakra in his etc. All these divinities may be conventionally identified as horrific forms of Akṣobhya as the central one of the Five Buddhas or equally well as manifestations of a sixth supreme Buddha, whether known as Primary Buddha (*Ādibuddha*) or Great Vairocana or Vajra-Being (*Vajrasattva*) or whatever title may be used. These names merely represent different tantric traditions which have originated in the manner suggested above in different monastic communities and different groups of yogins.

148 *Guhyasamāja Tantra*, ed. B. Bhattacharyya, p. 1 (beginning) to p. 3, l. 20. One may refer back to p. 132 for the continuation of this quotation. One may also refer to another quotation from this tantra in section III.8, where the Five Buddhas are identified with the "perverse teachings" of slaying, robbing, promiscuity, falsehood and abusive language, thus "purifying" the Five Evils (delusion, wrath, passion, malignity and envy).

The names of the various Bodhisattvas, as listed in the above passage, also require some elucidation. Body, Speech and Mind are the three main aspects of human personality as well as of supreme buddhahood, representing a form of Buddhist trinity, which is identifiable on different planes. Thus, Body may refer to a manifested particularized Buddha, divine or human, Speech may then refer to his teaching and Mind to his intention of leading all living beings to buddhahood. An interesting analogy might be drawn between this set and the Christian Trinity of God, Word (*Logos*) and Holy Spirit, while noting the differences of interpretation arising from their separate cultural backgrounds. On the plane of the religious cult, Body, Speech and Mind are represented by all Buddhist images, signifying Body; all sacred literature, signifying speech; and all shrines, especially stūpas, signifying Mind. Thus there is frequent mention in religious biographies of the merit acquired by creating "supports (in the sense of instruments) of Body, Speech and Mind," which means that the person concerned paid for images to be made and consecrated, religious books to be copied or printed, and shrines to be built.[149] However, once translated in these realistic terms, the subtlety of the religious intention behind the actions is lost. It must always be understood that Body, Speech and Mind are the main aspects of buddhahood, manifesting themselves in the phenomenal world. However, like other sets of three (e.g., the three evils or the earlier set of three families) they too are extended to five in some contexts in conformity with the cosmic conception of buddhahood as fivefold. Thus it comes about that among the Bodhisattvas listed in the opening passage of the *Guhyasamāja Tantra* we have Vajra-Body, Vajra-Speech, Vajra-Mind, Vajra-Concentration and Vajra-Recitation, followed by another set of five, beginning Vajra-Earth, representing the five elements. These are followed by a set of six, representing the six senses, visual, auditive, olfactory, gustatory, tactile, and the "sphere of the elements," viz. mental (see section II.4.c). The first of all these Bodhisattvas as listed here is Vajra-Samaya, representing here the whole divine manifestation understood as the "sacramental pledge" of the "union," literally "coming together" of the essentially inexpressible transcendent plane and its symbolic expression as a conventionalized maṇḍala.

The Five Buddhas must be thought of here as including all other Buddha- and Bodhisattva-manifestations, who fill space in all directions, and it may be wondered why their feminine manifestations should be limited to replicas of just four goddesses, Locanā, Māmakī, Paṇḍaravāsinī and Tārā. The numbers are dictated by the maṇḍala, for while the Five Buddhas occupy the center and four main points of the compass, the four goddesses occupy the intermediate points, southeast, southwest, northwest and northeast. The four named are perhaps the set most commonly met with and their names have been explained elsewhere (III.6.a). A fifth goddess is sometimes mentioned as partner of the chief Buddha-manifestation at the centre of the maṇḍala. She may be known simply

149 See for example my *Four Lamas of Dolpo*, p. 271, where many items are listed under the three headings of "images" (*sku-rten*), "books" (*gsung-rten*) and "shrines" (*thugs-rtem*).

as the Lady (*Bhagavatī*), as Just So (*Tathatā*), as Voidness (*Śūnyatā*), as Perfection of Wisdom (*Prajñāpāramitā*), as Limit of Reality (*Bhūtakoṭi*), or as Absence of Self (*Nairātmyā*), for she possesses the true nature of Vajrasattva and is Lady of the Vajra-sphere (*Vajradhātvīśvarī*).[150] In the so-called Yoginī Tantras of the Supreme Yoga class, where all the main divinities of the maṇḍala may be feminine, there will be a set of nine goddesses, occupying the center, the four main directions and the four intermediate directions, as in the *Hevajra Tantra*. Here Nairātmyā (Absence of Self) holds the center, surrounded by an entourage of yoginīs named after low-caste women such as Pukkasi, Śavarī, Caṇḍālī and Ḍombinī, and other miscellaneous names such as Gaurī (Blonde or Virgin, one of the titles of the spouse of Śiva), Caurī (Thief), Vetālī (Vampire) and Ghasmarī (Rapacious). These eight also represent the entourage of Hevajra, who usually embraces Nairātmyā as his partner at the center of the maṇḍala. Other names can be added in order to accommodate all the various sets, viz., the aggregates of personality, the five evils, the elements, the six senses etc., all of which are symbolized in the layout of the maṇḍala.[151] If one chooses to follow through the various combinations and permutations given by this tantra and its various commentaries, fairly consistent cross-identifications can be made. Thus for instance the four low-caste yoginīs named above reveal themselves as equivalents of the more regular four, Locanā, Māmakī, Paṇḍaravāsinī and Tārā. Well may one ask, if all maṇḍalas are in essence the same, why should there be such a vast variety of them. The only answer to this is to say that they were thus traditionally received as variously devised in different places and times.

It may be useful to illustrate one or two maṇḍalas according to the traditions of Yoga Tantras, as these are so often represented in the old temples of western Tibet and amongst the paintings discovered at Tun-huang, thus arguing strongly for their prevalence in northwestern India and in Kashmir, if not elsewhere in northern India (*Pl. 34*). These traditions, introduced into Tibet by Rin-chen bzang-po and his colleagues, were maintained at first by the Tibetan religious order of the Ka-dam-pa (*bKa'-gdams-pa*) and subsequently by the Sa-kya-pa (*Sa-skya-pa*). The main groups of divinities of which most of these maṇḍalas are composed are the following:

Five Buddhas with Vairocana (Resplendent) as central one.

Four Buddha-Goddesses: (Buddha-)Locanā (Buddha-Eye), Māmakī (My Very own), Pāṇḍaravāsinī (Lady with White Garment), Tārā (Saviouress).

Sixteen Bodhisattvas, arranged in groups of four and thus associated with the four Buddhas of the main directions.

150 See the short treatise of Advayavajra entitled "Fivefold Manifestation" (*Pañcākāra*) as translated by me in *Buddhist Texts through the Ages*, ed. E. Conze, pp. 249-52.

151 See *Hevajra Tantra* I.ix and the diagrams in my vol. I, pp. 126-7. The equivalents for Locanā etc. may be identified by bringing this chapter into relationship with Kāṇha's commentary on the opening words of the tantra "Thus by me 'twas heard" (*evaṃ mayā śrutaṃ*) of my edition (vol. II, p. 104).

Eight Goddesses of Offerings: Vajralāsyā (Vajra Love-Play), Vajramālā (Garland), Vajragīti (Song), Vajranṛtyā (Dance), Vajradhūpā (Incense), Vajrapuṣpā (Flower), Vajrālokā (Lamp), Vajragandhā (Scent), whose names like
Four Door-Guardians: Vajrāṅkuśa (Vajra Hook), Vajrapāśa (Noose), Vajra sphoṭa (Fetter), Vajraghaṇṭa (Bell) also known as Vajrāveśa (Persuasion).

These are all fairly constant in name except for the Sixteen Bodhisattvas, although many of the variations are simply synonyms thus:[152]

Akṣobhya's group:		
Vajradhara (Vajra-Holder)	=	Vajrasattva (Vajra-Being)
Vajrākarṣa (Vajra-Coercion)		Vajrarāja (Vajra-King)
Vajradhanu (Vajra-Bow)		Vajrarāga (Vajra-Passion)
Vajraharṣa (Vajra-Joy)		Vajrasādhu (Vajra-Good)
Ratnasambhava's group:		
Vajragarbha (Vajra-Embryo)		Vajraratna (Vajra-Gem)
Vajraprabha (Vajra-Light)		Vajratejaḥ (Vajra-Splendor)
Vajrayaṣṭi (Vajra-Standard)		Vajraketu (Vajra-Banner)
Vajraprīti (Vajra-Happiness)		Vajrahāsa (Vajra-Mirth
Amitābha's group:		
Vajranetra (Vajra-Vision)		Vajradharma (Vajra-Religion)
Vajrabuddhi (Vajra-Knowledge)		Vajratīkṣṇa (Vajra-Sharp)
Vajramaṇḍa (Vajra-Essence)		Vajrahetu (Vajra-Cause)
Vajravāca (Vajra-Word)		Vajrabhāṣa (Vajra-Speech)
Amoghasiddhi's group:		
Vajraviśva (Vajra-Universal)		Vajrakarma (Vajra-Action)
Vajramitra (Vajra-Friend)		Vajrarakṣa (Vajra-Protection)
Vajracaṇḍa (Vajra-Wrath)		Vajrayakṣa (Vajra-Yakṣa)
Vajramuṣṭi (Vajra-Gesture)		Vajrasandhi (Vajra-Implicitness)

As may be seen from the accompanying diagrams, these sixteen Bodhisattvas may be arranged in groups of four around their particular Buddhas, or else arranged around the maṇḍala, four to each side nearest to their own Buddhas, or again they may be arranged in a circle, in which the first one (Vajradhara *alias* Vajrasattva) is placed by Akṣobhya and then so on round the circle.

The Tantra entitled "Elimination of Evil Rebirth" has variant names for the Five Buddhas, as already noted above. Otherwise all the other divinities remain the same. This same tantra also uses a maṇḍala consisting of a central Buddha (Śākyamuni) and eight Uṣṇīṣa-Buddhas, known as:

Vajra-uṣṇīṣa	(East)	Tejaḥ-	(Northeast)
Ratna-	(South)	Dhvaja-	(Northwest)
Padma-	(West)	Tīkṣṇa-	(Southwest)
Viśva-	(North)	Chatra-	(Southeast)

The names of those of the main directions are just Buddha-family names, as

[152] Other variations will be found in my introduction to STTS, Facsimile Edition, pp. 26-8.

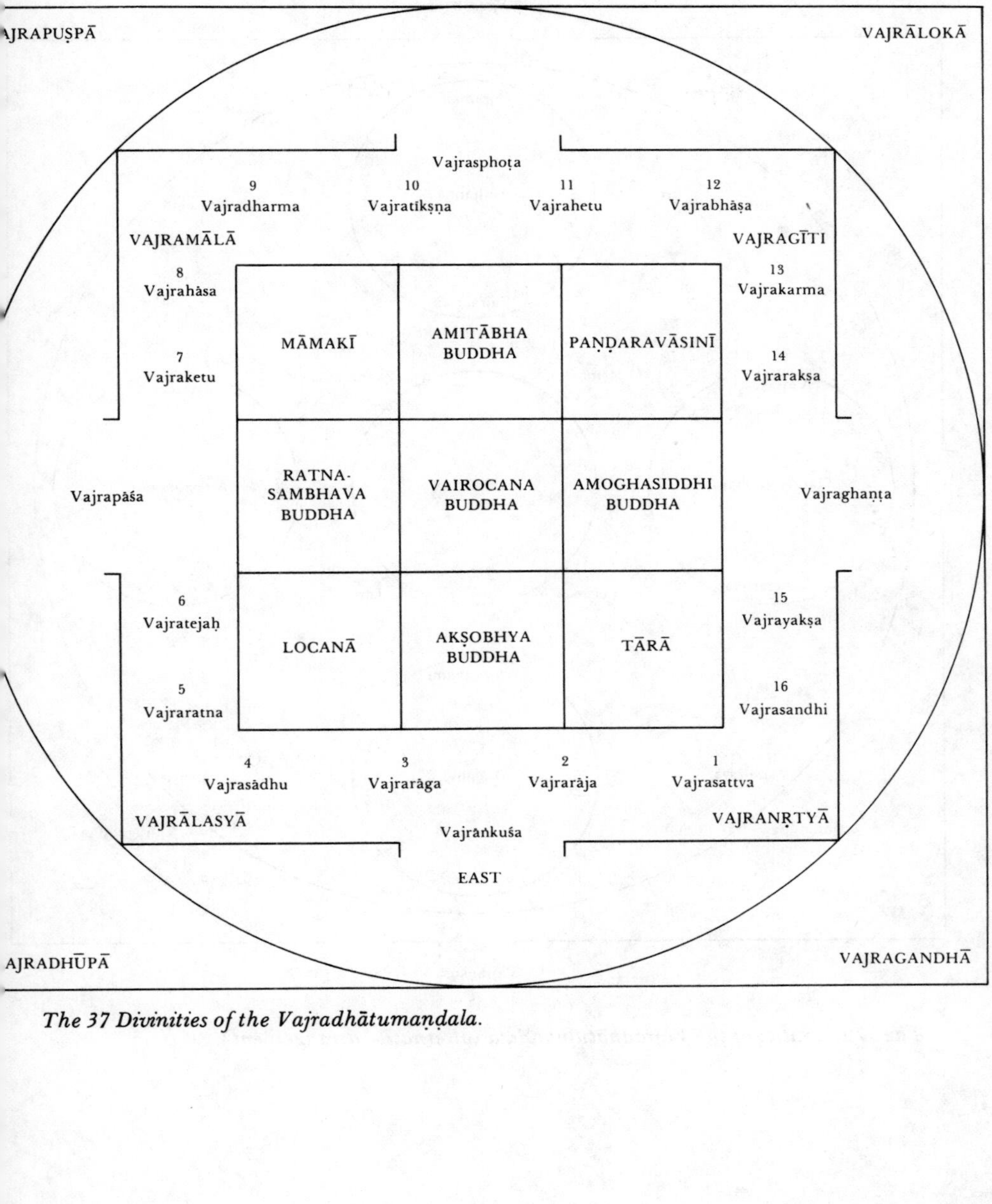

The 37 Divinities of the Vajradhātumaṇḍala.

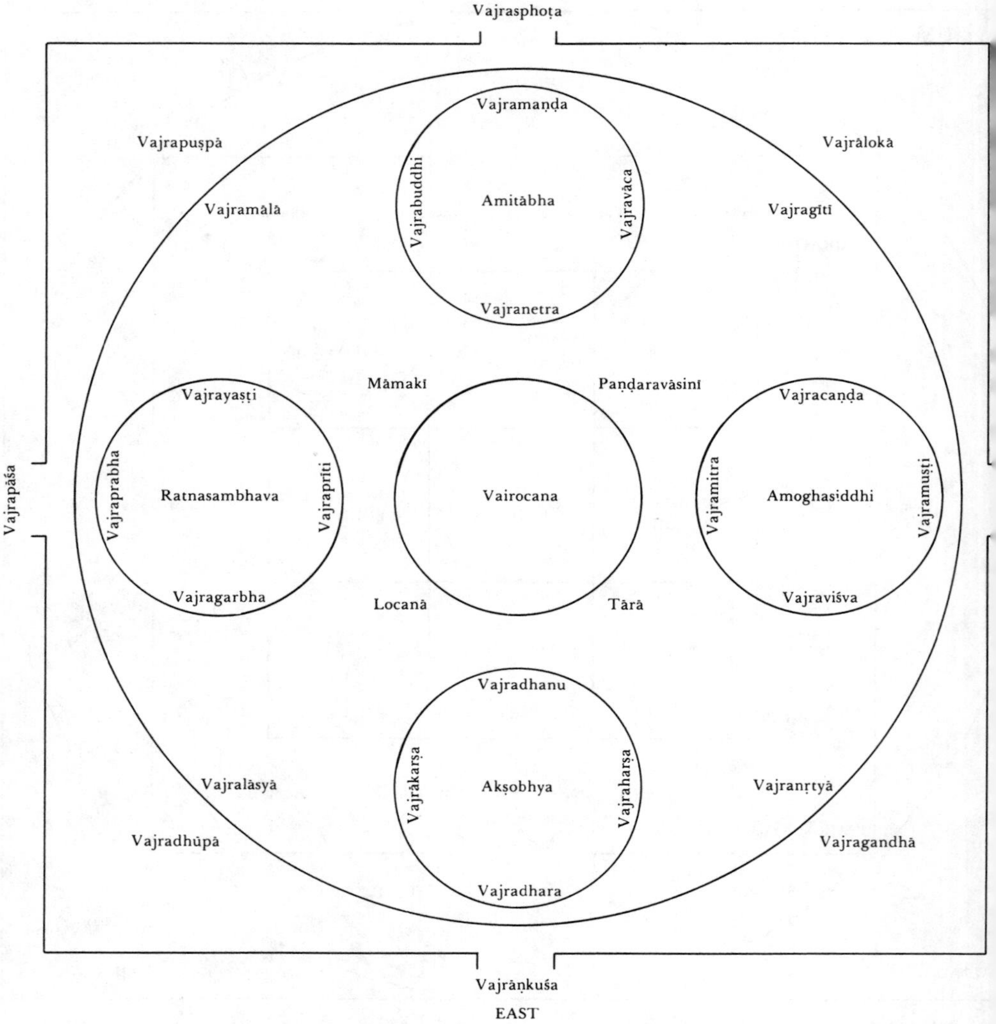

The 37 Divinities of the Vajradhātumaṇḍala (alternative arrangement).

used also for the four main Bodhisattvas (Vajrapāṇi, Ratna-, Padma-, Viśva-). The other four are translated: Splendor-, Banner-, Sharp-, Parasol- (*Pl. 35*). There are no Buddha-Goddesses in this maṇḍala and the set of sixteen Bodhisattvas is an entirely different one, consisting of four sets thus: Maitreya, Amoghadarśin, Apāyajaha, Sarvaśokatamonirghātanamati (East); Gandhahastin, Śūraṃgama, Gaganagañja, Jñānaketu (South); Amṛtaprabha, Candraprabha, Bhadrapāla, Jāliniprabha (West); Vajragarbha, Akṣayamati, Pratibhāṇakūṭa, Samantabhadra (North).[153] Despite variations in names, both the set of eight Buddhas and these Sixteen Bodhisattvas are clearly related to the sets already listed as they occur in the *Mañjuśrīmūlakalpa* (section III.11, pp. 193-4 above).

13. INITIATIONS AND CONSECRATIONS

a. *Initiation as Distinct from "Ordination"*

The word "initiation" suggests the ritualized acceptance of an "outsider" into a community which reserves to itself certain privileges and responsibilities that are often regarded as secret so far as the outside world is concerned. In Buddhist tantric practice this English term may fairly be used to translate Sanksrit *praveśa*, "act of entry," especially when referring to the act of entering a maṇḍala as a privilege bestowed upon a worthy disciple by a suitable teacher, that is to say, one who is already initiated himself and possesses all the necessary attributes. The initiation ceremony (*maṇḍala-praveśa-vidhi*) requires certain rites of "consecration" (Sanskrit *abhiṣeka*) with the result that the two terms are often confused in discussion of the subject, although there is no reason why they should not be kept apart. Used in this tantric context, both terms should be kept distinct from the earlier nontantric rite of the taking of monastic vows, a universal and almost entirely open performance fundamental to Buddhist practice as an organized religion. Thus becoming a monk, for which the Indian term "going forth" (Sanskrit: *pravraj-* "from home to homelessness") was regularly used in the earlier period, was open to any physically and mentally fit person, who was prepared to renounce the ordinary life of the world and agree to keep the rules as a celibate member of a Buddhist monastic community.[154] This involved as in Christian usage a ceremony of the "taking of vows," in which the postulant committed himself as one who "takes refuge in the Buddha, his Religion (*Dharma*) and his Community (*Saṅgha*)," allowed his head to be shaved as a sign of his renouncing the world, assumed the appropriate garments of a monk and formally took the vows that were binding on the community.[155] In

153 See the *SDPS Tantra*, ed. Skorupski, translation on pp. 25-31.

154 On the early use of this term see S. Dutt, *Buddhist Monks and Monasteries*, pp. 43 ff. It is used of the actual rite of "ordination" (Skr: *pravrajyā*, Pāli: *pabbajjā*).

155 For a description of the rite as performed in seventh-century India, see I-Tsing, *A Record of the Buddhist Religion*, pp. 95 ff., noting that the term "priest" instead of "monk" is misleadingly used in his account as translated by J. Takakusu.

the Western terminology of those who write on this subject, this formal act is often referred to as an "ordination," a term that is quite appropriate if one allows for an extension of the usual Christian use of this word, where it applies not to monks, but to priests, whether married or celibate. It is also sometimes referred to as an initiation, and even this term may be appropriate in so far as the would-be monk is being initiated into a new way of life, and especially perhaps in the unusual case of the *banras* of Nepal, who take the vows of monkhood in order to negate them four days later so that they may be initiated as youngsters into the same caste as their parents.[156] There is no evidence of this occurring elsewhere and the Tibetans who followed the accepted Indian practices in all such matters have preserved on a vast scale the tradition of communities of celibate monks and nuns as the main upholders of Buddhist traditions. As already noted above the whole Mahāyāna movement left intact the ideal of monkhood while at the same time recognizing laymen, who lived suitable lives, also as aspirants toward buddhahood. With the further developments of tantric theories the same situation continued to apply, with the result that monks as well as layfolk might choose as teacher a tantric master, receive initiation into the maṇḍala of his chosen divinity, receive the necessary consecrations and perform the appropriate religious practices. The only difference between them was that whereas laymen might practice rites of sexual yoga in accordance with the theories of the tantras of the Supreme Yoga (*anuttarayoga*) class, monks clearly could not do so without breaking their vows. However, in so far as the use of actual feminine partners was considered unsuitable, the tantras even of this so-called highest class came to be practiced through the mental powers of visualization, with the final result that all tantras have become available to all and sundry, if only a tantric master can be found to perform the required initiation.

Because of the terminology of "taking vows" the essential difference between the "vow taking" of a monk and initiation into tantric rites may be obscured to some extent in later Buddhist tradition, since certain vows are judged suitable for a tantric postulant, just as there are vows for a monk and also, let it be recalled, for a Bodhisattva. Thus there are said to be three grades of vows (Tibetan *sdom-pa*; Skr. *saṃvara*), namely for a monk, for a Bodhisattva and for the practitioner of "secret mantras," and these are thought of as corresponding to the three main "ways" (*yāna*), the Hīnayāna, Mahāyāna and Mantrayāna. However, in Mahāyāna Buddhism, wherever it may have been practiced exclusively in India (for it must be remembered that in some communities Hīnayāna and Mahāyāna monks lived together), and certainly as practiced in Tibet, there are in effect only two grades, for no simple monk is likely to admit that he is following an "inferior way" (Hīnayāna) which does not involve at least potentially the career of a Bodhisattva as portrayed so lavishly in the Mahāyāna sūtras. Thus Tibetans commonly refer to the two ways of the sūtras (meaning

[156] See section IV.3.b below, and especially J. K. Locke, "Newar Buddhist Initiation Rites," in *Contributions to Nepalese Studies*, vol. 2, no. 2, pp. 1-2.

Mahāyāna sūtras only) and the tantras, as practicable courses.

Despite this use of a similar terminology of "vow taking," "ordination" as a monk and "initiation" into a maṇḍala or tantric cycle remain very different in kind, as is clear from the life story of any Tibetan monk or man of religion, whether recorded from the past as a form of religious biography, a genre of literature very popular in Tibet, or told today by any contemporary practitioner.[157] The vows of monkhood are taken normally once only in accordance with ancient formulas, while tantric initiations may be performed according to different tantric cycles for as long as the practitioner is interested in "collecting" them and so long as he can find tantric masters qualified to bestow them. In theory only one such initiation with the appropriate consecrations and religious practices is required, if the postulant is seriously concerned to experience the moment of final enlightenment by this very means and no other, but in practice many are often sought and received, each involving visions of different sets of divinities, who in essence are all one and the same. Thus whereas ordination as a monk transforms one's whole way of life at least outwardly, tantric initiations admit one to the possibility of acquiring what are most easily described as psychic powers leading to the realization of enlightenment as a state of spontaneous achievement. This may well have the effect of changing one's way of life, but it is clearly envisaged as operating on an entirely different plane. It corresponds in fact to the various techniques of meditation that are known to have been performed in the earlier periods of Buddhism and for which careful training may have been required but certainly no initiatory rite.[158] In what then does the power of the rite consist if not in its psychological effect? As an example of the whole process we may take the initiation of an acceptable pupil into the maṇḍala of the Vajra-Sphere (*Vajradhātumaṇḍala*), as briefly described in the fundamental tantra of this group. First the maṇḍala itself must be drawn on a specially prepared site, which has been suitably purified and cleared of all adverse influences:

> With a good new thread, well woven and of proper length, the maṇḍala should be measured out by one well skilled who strives his best. It must be four-sided with four entrances adorned with four portals, hung with four cords and bewreathed with garlands and flowers. Then one should draw the outer circle of the maṇḍala, decorating it with vajras and gems, thus filling the spaces between the four corners and the ends of the gates. Then coming inside this outer ring, one should make a circle with a ring of vajras like a wheel. It is equipped with eight pillars and on the inside of these vajra pillars it is fitted with five lunar disks. At the center of the central disk one should

157 One may quote as a few of many examples, *The Life of Bu-ston Rin-po-che*, transl. D. S. Ruegg, pp. 77-8; the lives of *Four Lamas of Dolpo*, my translation, pp. 87, 133, 248; or the life of Atiśa, for which see Helmut Einer, *rNam-thar rgyas-pa*, vol. 1, p. 193. One may note that for such "ordination" the Tibetan expression *bsnyen-par rdzogs-pa*, lit. "perfecting one's approach" (for Skr. *upasampadā*) is often used, as well as *rab-tu 'byung-ba*, lit. "going forth" (= Skr. *pravrajyā*).

158 For references, see L. de la Vallée Poussin, *Bouddhisme, études et matériaux*, pp. 94-7, and for examples Buddhaghoṣa, *The Path of Purification*, translated by Bhikkhu Ñānamoli, pp. 126-84.

place the Buddha-image (viz., Vairocana). Then in the center of the disks of the Buddha-directions one should place the four guarantors (*samaya*, viz., of buddhahood).[159] Thus approaching with a vajra movement this fourfold set of maṇḍalas, one should place there all four Buddhas, Akṣobhya and the others.

Akṣobhya's maṇḍala is rightly made with Vajradhara and the others (Vajrākarṣa, Vajradhanu and Vajraharṣa).
Ratnasambhava's maṇḍala is filled with Vajragarbha and the others (Vajraprabha, Vajrayaṣṭi and Vajraprīti).
Amitāyus's maṇḍala is refined with Vajranetra and the others (Vajrabuddhi, Vajramaṇḍa and Vajravāca).
Amoghasiddhi's maṇḍala is drawn with Vajraviśva and the others (Vajramitra, Vajracaṇḍa and Vajramuṣṭi).
In the intermediate spaces of the circle one should draw the Vajra-Goddesses (Locanā, Māmakī, Pāṇḍaravāsinī and Tārā).
In the corners of the outer maṇḍala one should draw the (eight) goddesses of Buddha-worship (Vajralāsyā, Vajramālā, Vajragīti and Vajranṛtyā; Vajradhūpā, Vajrapuṣpā, Vajrālokā and Vajragandhā).
In the middle of all four gates one should place the four door-guardians Vajrāṅkuśa, Vajrapāśa, Vajrasphoṭa and Vajraghaṇṭa).[160]
One should place the "great beings" as residing in the outer maṇḍala.
Then making correctly the excellent sacramental hand-gesture, the Vajra-Teacher enters and performs the gestures of divulgence.
The spell for effecting the possession (of the maṇḍala by the divinities) is: AḤ!
Being properly authorized and having performed self-consecration and the rest, announcing his own name, he coerces (the divinities) with the vajra.
Making the hand-gesture (known as) Being-Vajra-Hook, the Vajra-Teacher by snapping his fingers a number of times assembles all the Buddhas.
At that moment all the Buddhas together with Vajrasattva and the others join as an assembly in the maṇḍala so that the whole maṇḍala is full.
Then meditating on the Great Symbol of Vajrasattva, he should recite just once the litany of the One Hundred and Eight Names,[161] and pleased with the assembly, the Buddhas stay firm (in position), while Vajrasattva who is self-effective keeps close by as a friend.
Then making the excellent sacramental hand-gestures of Being-Vajra and the rest, he should coerce the Great Beings, reciting JAḤ HŪṂ VAṂ HOḤ!
Thus all the Great Beings, the Buddhas and the others are summoned,

[159] For the range of meaning of the term *samaya*, see references in the Index. It may be noted that the same word occurs below translated as "sacramental" in the phrase "excellent sacramental hand-gesture" (*samayāgrīṃ mudrāṃ*).

[160] Altogether these represent the thirty-seven main divinities of the cycle of the Omniscient One as already listed in *The Cultural Heritage of Ladakh*, vol. 1, pp. 34-5. The variations in the names of the Sixteen Bodhisattvas, headed in the present extract by Vajradhara (= Vajrapāṇi), Vajragarbha, Vajranetra and Vajraviśva is best explained by referring to my translated extracts of the STTS, pp. 26-8. The "great beings" residing in the outer mandala comprise another set of Sixteen Bodhisattvas (of the Good Age), Sixteen Arhats, Twelve Pratyekabuddhas and Sixteen Fierce Divinities.

[161] This refers to the "litany" of one hundred and eight names of Vairocana/Vajradhara as All in All. It is repeated in every part of the STTS and will also be found at the end of the SDPS Tantra, T. Skorupski's edition, pp. 107-8.

drawn in and bound as an assembly, so entering his power.[162]
Then contenting these great ones with forms of secret worship (viz., by envisaging the eight goddesses of the offerings) he requests them, saying: "Act on behalf of all beings for our general success!"

The passage that follows immediately upon this request has already been translated above (section III.5), where it was said that entry into the maṇḍala is for saving the whole sphere of living beings without exception, and having elaborated this statement, the text goes on to describe the way in which a pupil should enter the maṇḍala.

Now first he should make four salutations to all the Buddhas in this manner. Bending the whole body forward with the supplicatory vajra-gesture he should pronounce this mantra:

OṂ SARVA-TATHĀGATAPŪJOPASTHĀNĀYA-ĀTMĀNAṂ NIRYĀTAYĀMI /
SARVA-TATHĀGATA-VAJRASATVA-ADHITIṢṬHASVA MĀṂ //
(I offer myself as the place of worship for all Tathāgatas.
May Vajrasattva of All Tathāgatas empower me!)

Then standing, he makes the supplicatory vajra-gesture level with his heart, and bowing down with his forehead to the ground, he pronounces this mantra:

OṂ SARVA-TATHĀGATA-PŪJĀBHIṢEKĀYA-ĀTMĀNAṆ NIRYĀTAYĀMI /
SARVA-TATHĀGATA-VAJRARATNA-ABHIṢIÑCA MĀṂ //
(I offer myself for consecration in the worship of All Tathāgatas.
May Vajraratna of All Tathāgatas consecrate me!)

Then standing up again, he makes the supplicatory vajra-gesture at the level of his head, and bowing down with his face to the ground, he pronounces this mantra:

OṂ SARVA-TATHĀGATA-PŪJAPRAVARTANĀYA-ĀTMĀNAṂ NIRYĀTAYĀMI /
SARVA-TATHĀGATA-VAJRADHARMA PRAVARTAYA MĀṂ //
(I offer myself for the promoting of worship of All Tathāgatas.
May Vajradharma of All Tathāgatas promote me!)

Then standing up again, he makes the supplicatory vajra-gesture, lowering it from his head to his heart, and bowing down with the top of his head to the ground, he pronounces this mantra:

OṂ SARVA-TATHĀGATA-PŪJA-KARMAṆE ĀTMĀNAṂ NIRYĀTAYĀMI /
SARVA-TATHĀGATA-VAJRAKARMA KURU MĀṂ //
(I offer myself for the act of worship of All Tathāgatas.
May Vajrakarma of All Tathāgatas act upon me!)

He is wearing a red upper garment with a red scarf covering his face and he should make the Being-Vajra hand-gesture, as this mantra is said:

SAMAYAS TVAṂ (You are the sacrament!)

Then as he holds the garland of flowers with his two middle fingers, one leads him to the maṇḍala with this mantra:

SAMAYA HŪṂ (Sacrament indeed!)

162 The four syllables recited here relate to the functions of the four door guardians (see p. 222-3).

Then making him enter, one should say: "Today you enter the family of All Tathāgatas. I shall arouse in you that vajra-wisdom, through which you will gain the success (*siddhi*) of All Tathāgatas, not to mention other successes. When such wisdom has been aroused in you, do not tell those who have not seen the great maṇḍala, or the bond will certainly be broken."

Then the Vajra-Teacher himself makes the Being-Vajra hand-gesture, showing it toward the inside of the pupil's mouth and outside, next placing it on his head, as he says: "This is your bond-vajra; it will split your head apart, if you tell anyone."

Then he blesses water with a sacramental gesture and a single pronouncement of the oath-mantra and makes the pupil drink it. Now this is the mantra of the oath:

VAJRASATVAḤ SVAYAM TE 'DYA HṚDAYE SAMAVASTHITAḤ /
NIRBHIDYA TATKṢAṆAṂ YĀYĀD YADI BRŪYĀD IMAN NAYAṂ //
(Today Vajrasattva has established himself in your heart.
May it disintegrate the moment that you speak of this rite!)
OṂ VAJRODAKA ṬHAḤ (O vajra-water ṭhaḥ)[163]

Then he says to his pupil: "From today I am Vajrapāṇi to you. If I tell you to do anything, it is to be done. You must never contravene me. If you fail to avoid this transgression, you will fall into hell when you die."

Then he commands the pupil to say:

SARVA-TATHĀGATA-ADHITIṢṬHANTU VAJRASATVO ME ĀVIŚATU
(May all Tathāgatas empower me and Vajrasattva pervade me!)

Then the Teacher quickly makes the Being-Vajra gesture and says:

AYAṂ TAT SAMAYO VAJRAṂ VAJRASATVAṂ ITI SMṚTAṂ /
ĀVEŚAYATU TE 'DYAIVA VAJRAJÑĀNAM ANUTTARAṂ //
(This is the sacramental vajra known as Vajrasattva.
May the supreme vajra-wisdom pervade you this very day!)

Then he should make the wrathful hand-gesture and divulge the symbolic gesture of Being-Vajra. He causes (the pupil) to recite a vajra-verse of his choice pertaining to intuitive knowledge of the Mahāyāna.[164] Thus it pervades him, and as soon as it does so, divine wisdom becomes manifest. By means of that wisdom he knows the thoughts of others; he knows all events in past, present and future; his heart is confirmed in the teaching of all Buddhas; all sufferings are ended; all fear is dispersed; he is invulnerable to all beings;[165] all Buddhas empower him; all achievements lie before him; joyful events, happy, pleasurable, delightful, previously unknown and without special cause, will come about, and because of these some will experience states of mental calm, some will bring spells (*dhāraṇi*) to fruition, some all their hopes, while some

[163] If one seeks a dictionary meaning for the syllable *ṭha*, one will find such a variety as: sun-disk or circle, a sacred spot, a divinity, a name of Śiva, and (when used repetitively) the sound of a jar rolling down steps.

[164] I follow the Tibetan version here; the Sanskrit may be translated as "he pronounces his intuitive knowledge of the Mahāyāna with a vajra-verse."

[165] The Tibetan version appears to understand *avadhya* (invulnerable) as though it meant "all" (TT, p. 230-3-4), and one may note also Egerton's *Buddhist Hybrid Sanskrit Dictionary*, p. 72. However, here the Sanskrit as translated is surely correct.

will attain to universal buddhahood.

Then making the hand-gesture, he releases it at his heart, as he pronounces this mantra:

TIṢṬHA VAJRA DṚḌHO ME BHAVA / ŚĀŚVATO ME BHAVA /
HṚDAYAM ME 'DHITIṢṬHA / SARVA-SIDDHIṂ CA ME PRAYACCHA /
(O stay vajra! Be stable, be eternal for me!
Empower my heart and grant me all success!)
HŪṂ HA HA HA HA HOḤ

Then he should throw the garland into the maṇḍala, saying:

PRATĪCCHA VAJRA HOḤ (Receive, O vajra!)

Wherever it falls, that (section of the maṇḍala) is effective for him. Then taking up the garland, the Teacher binds it on the pupil's head, saying:

OṂ PRATIGṚHṆA TVAM IMAṂ SATVAṂ MAHĀBALAḤ
(Receive thou this being, O mighty one)

By the action of tying it on, he is pervaded by that great being, and success is quickly his. One then removes the scarf from his face when he is thus pervaded, saying:

OṂ VAJRASATVAḤ SVAYAṂ TE 'DYA CAKṢŪDGHĀṬANA TATPARAḤ /
UDGHĀṬAYATI SARVĀKṢO VAJRACAKṢUR ANUTTARAṂ // HE VAJRA PAŚYA //
(Vajrasattva himself, concerned to open your eyes this day,
now opens them, the all-eyed, the vajra-eyed, the supreme, see HE-VAJRA!)

Then one shows him the great maṇḍala in the regular manner, and as soon as he sees it, he is empowered by All Tathāgatas and Vajrasattva abides in his heart. Because of this empowerment he sees miraculous forms variously manifest in circles of brilliant light-rays, and the Lord, the Great Vajradhara, will reveal himself or some other Tathāgata. From that time on he will succeed in all things from whatever he may want up to the state of Vajradhara, or (in other words) the state of buddhahood. Then when he has been shown the great maṇḍala, one consecrates him with scented water from the vajra-empowered jar, using this mantra:

VAJRĀBHIṢIÑCA (Vajra consecrate!)

Then binding him with the particular gesture and garland, one should fix his appropriate mark on his hand, saying:

ADYA-ABHIṢIKTAS TVAM ASI BUDDHAIR VAJRĀBHIṢEKATAḤ /
IDAN TE SARVABUDDHATVAṂ GṚHNA VAJRAṂ SUSIDDHAYA //
(Today you are consecrated by the Buddhas with the vajra-consecration.
Take this vajra, (symbol of) universal buddhahood for total success!)
OṂ VAJRĀDHIPATI TVĀM ABHIṢIÑCĀMI TIṢṬHA VAJRA SAMAYAS TVAṂ
(I consecrate you Vajra-Lord. Stay O vajra! You are the sacrament)

Then one consecrates him with the Vajra-Name Consecration with this mantra:

OṂ VAJRASATVA TVĀM ABHIṢIÑCĀMI VAJRANĀMĀBHIṢEKATAḤ HE-VAJRA *N*
(I consecrate you as Vajrasattva with the name of HE-VAJRA *N*!)

Whichever name is applied to him, HE! must be said.
Such is the ritual in detail for the entry into all maṇḍalas.[166]

An account such as this is in fact rather brief. but it contains all the essential elements of the rite. Essential to an understanding of the whole practice is the interıretation of the term *samaya*, which has already been discussed in some detail (section III.7). As observed there, a variety of possible translations offer themselves, such as union, pledge, sacrament, and even guarantor. But it must be emphasized that these are not so much different meanings as illustrations of the fact that we lack in English the one single appropriate term. The Tibetans possess it (*dam-tshig*) only because they coined the term specifically to translate *samaya*. When discussing the term previously, we tended to stress the meaning of "sacrament" in so far as the term is applied to sacrificial offerings. It is possible to retain this meaning in translating the above extract concerning the pupil's consecration, so long as the primary meaning of "coming together" or "union" is kept in mind. A sacrament may be described as a "coming together" of the object offered and the divine element that pervades it. In precisely this sense the pupil becomes the sacrament, when he is pervaded by divine wisdom. Hence we have the exclamation: "You are the sacrament!" In other words this may be expressed as: "You are now the union of your own human body and the supra-mundane element of buddhahood." An understanding of *samaya* may also be assisted by the following section.

b. *The "Descent" of Absolute Wisdom*

Mahāyāna Buddhism in all its forms takes for granted the absolute state of perfection, known as enlightenment, as buddhahood, or as the state of "just so" (*tathatā*), or more precisely as the state of one who has achieved such a state (*tathāgatvaṃ*). In philosophical terms this state is often referred to as "void" (*śūnya*) or as "voidness" (*śūnyatā*) in so far as it is entirely free from all demonstrable characteristics. Eschewing the literal meaning of "void," some Western interpreters have used the term "relative," thus considerably weakening its force. This is really unnecessary if one remembers that this same "voidness" is also the "embryo" or "enclosure" or "essence" of all Tathāgatas or Buddhas (see section III.4.e). Even though this particular terminology may appear comparatively late in Buddhist philosophical developments, it is certainly taken for granted in the earlier Madhyamaka period, in that Buddhas of necessity emerge from thus such a "void" and in due course return to it. Represented as cosmic pattern on a single plane, it corresponds to the maṇḍala of the Five Buddhas, whether conceived of as imminent or transcendent. As already observed above, their transcendence is sometimes represented by a (sixth) Supreme Buddha, known as Vajra-Being (Vajrasattva), Great Vairocana, Vajra-Holder (Vajradhara) etc. (*Pl. 36*). Envisaged and experienced at such a level of attainment, the whole group is

166 Extracted from the STTS, Yamada's edition, pp. 63-72 and the Tibetan version in TT vol. 4, pp. 229-3-2 to 230-4-8. A parallel version, rather longer, will be found in the SDPS Tantra, Skorupski's edition, translation on pp. 100 ff.

referred to as "deities of the final result" (Sanskrit *phala* = fruit, and thus the result of maturation). Here a quotation may be helpful:

> At the outset one should always envisage Vajrasattva, we are told, and this is the reason. In general the chief of all families and all maṇḍalas is the Lord Vairocana, and he has two aspects: Vairocana and Great Vairocana. The difference is this: the true nature of the bodies of the Five Tathāgatas who abide fully enlightened in the Akaniṣṭha Heaven, that is Vairocana. His Mind, where without any duality between thinker and thought Vairocana and Vajrasattva and the rest are produced, is characterized as the Dharma-Sphere, beginningless and endless, and this is Great Vairocana. Thus Vairocana is a Glorious Body (*saṃbhoga-kāya*) and his Mind, namely Great Vairocana, is a Dharma-Body. It is precisely Śrī Vajrasattva who is vested as the bodily form of Great Vairocana. Thus in the "Symposium of Truth" it is said:
>
> Oho! I, Samantabhadra, absolute being, am self-existent.
> Although bodiless because of this absolute nature, yet I assume a body as (Vajra-)sattva.
>
> Although some say that this is the same person as the Vajrasattva who is one of the Sixteen Bodhisattvas, the Precious Lama bSod-nams rTse-mo (1142-82) says that he is Chief on account of his power to cause all the family manifestation or again because of his sovereignty. So it is the Vajrasattva from the context of the One Hundred and Eight names where he is the Lord, the Chief of all Tathāgatas. Also in the (section of the) "Victory over the Threefold World," he is proclaimed as Father of All Tathāgatas, Chief of All Tathāgatas. If one wonders whether he is not the Vajrasattva who appears before Akṣobhya, indeed he is, for there is no difference between them. So in this matter it would be good to follow the Tantra (viz., the "Symposium of Truth") and our above mentioned Lama.[167]

I referred above to the maṇḍala as the most potent expression of pantheistic

[167] As nearly always our quotations serve more than one purpose, it is relevant in the present context to refer to what was written above concerning Vajrapāṇi's gradual rise to preeminence during the Mahāyāna period and the manner in which the names Vajrapāṇi, Vajrasattva and Vajradhara are often used interchangeably during this formative period. While the title Vajrasattva (Adamantine Being) certainly relates to the absolute state of supreme buddhahood (viz., the Dharma-Body), it is frequently used as a synonym for Vajrapāṇi conceived of as a Bodhisattva. In the verse quoted above from the "Symposium of Truth" (STTS, Yamada's Sanskrit ed., p. 12 and my introduction to the facsimile ed., p. 17, where it is translated) it clearly refers to Vajrapāṇi as one of the Sixteen Bodhisattvas. Our author may be quoting the verse from memory or maybe if he is aware of the context then he is clearly at pains to refer it forcibly to Vajrasattva as absolute being. The "litanies" of one hundred and eight names will be found in Yamada's ed., pp. 5-6 and again pp. 154-6 at the start of the tantra Part II dealing with the maṇḍala of Victory over the Threefold World, for which see the STTS facsimile ed., introduction, pp. 39 ff. One may mention that Vajrapāṇi is frequently referred to in this tantra as "Lord of All Tathāgatas." Resuming all this one may note that Vajrapāṇi *alias* Vajrasattva *alias* Vajradhara may be (i) the embodiment of the absolute as envisaged in the present extract, (ii) one of the Sixteen Bodhisattvas, and (iii) one of the set of four Bodhisattvas when he appears before Akṣobhya.

The above quotation is taken from the *Kun-rig cho-ga rnam-bshad*, fo. 64, l. 3-fo. 66, l. 3.

realization that has ever been devised. Here pantheistic is used in the sense that all phenomenal manifestations at all levels of existence are expressions of the supreme being (e.g., Vajrasattva). The implied immanence of such a supreme being does not necessarily contradict his absolute transcendence, and Indian religion generally, whether Hindu or Buddhist, clearly asserts such transcendence.[168] We emphasized the concept of the two planes of existence, nirvāṇa being transcendent and saṃsāra being immanent, according to early Buddhist beliefs. Now while the Mahāyāna asserts the identity or rather the essential non-duality of nirvāṇa and saṃsāra, it continues to distinguish between transcendence as the absolute state of quiescent buddhahood, and immanence as the sphere of Buddha- or Bodhisattva activity. It is from this transcendent sphere that the divine power must be summoned in order to enliven the maṇḍala or indeed any image or symbol of divinity. All these are means toward the final result, which is the aspiration of the practicing yogin. Without means there can be no realization of wisdom; without cause there can be no result. Thus as means toward the result he must first place in position in the maṇḍala the *samaya*-beings, the symbols or guarantors of the divine beings who are identified in their ultimate state as pure wisdom. At a second stage he induces the descent of pure wisdom, which then pervades the *samaya*-beings, transforming them into "wisdom-beings" (*jñāna-sattva*). This process is essentially the same whether applied to *samaya*-beings in front of oneself as a form of external yoga, or to oneself as a *samaya* so that one may then be consubstantiated in buddhahood as a "wisdom-being." It will be now more readily understood how this term *samaya*, which means literally a coming together or conjunction, may in some contexts be suitably translated as sacrament.[169] Thus, addressing his pupil at one point, the teacher says:

> This is the *samaya*-vajra known as Vajra-Being.
> May the supreme vajra-wisdom pervade you this day.

Here the particular hand-gesture referred to as "Being-Vajra" (*sattvavajrī*) combined with the appropriate mantra (OṂ VAJRĀVEŚA AḤ) should produce the desired result if the pupil is properly prepared.

One may note that the four door guardians represent the four stages of introducing the divinities into the maṇḍala, which are effected by the mantra JAḤ HŪṂ VAṂ HOḤ! *Vajrānkuśa* (Vajra-Hook) summons them; *Vajrapāśa* (Vajra-

[168] The term "pantheistic" is sometimes applied to Indian religion by Western writers in a derogatory sense, as though the immanence of divinity conflicts with all possibility of transcendence. Although Christian theology makes a sharp division between uncreated and created being, thus asserting the absolute transcendence of God, mystical religion knows of no such clear distinction, although the two corresponding levels of existence, mundane and supramundane, remain known for what they are, that is to say, the everyday state of existence as contrasted with the state of divine rapture.

[169] There is surely an analogy between such a Buddhist rite as this and the descent of the Holy Spirit, effected by the appropriate words and gestures of the priest, which transform ordinary bread and wine into the "real presence" of Christ. What is a sacrament in Christian terminology but "an outward and visible sign of an inward and invisible grace"?

Noose) draws them in; *Vajrasphoṭa* (Vajra-Fetter) binds them and *Vajrāveśa* (Vajra-Penetration) *alias Vajraghaṇṭa* (Vajra-Bell) completes the pervasion of the maṇḍala by wisdom. This fourfold process is clearly defined in our extract from the "Symposium of Truth" just above, when it is said that "all the Great Beings, the Buddhas and the others, are summoned, drawn in, bound, so entering his power." The teacher follows the same four stages when he introduces his pupil into the maṇḍala according to the *Durgatipariśodhana Tantra*:

> Taking a garland of flowers with his two thumbs, he should be led in with this spell: OṂ I enter upon the vajra-*samaya*! He should be led to the eastern door with Vajra-Hook, made to approach on the southern side by means of the Noose; he should be bound on the western side with the Fetter and made to enter at the north by means of Vajra-Penetration. Leading him in once more by the eastern door, he should say this: "Follow through! Now you have followed through with the Vajra Family of all the Tathāgatas, I will produce for you the Vajra-Wisdom."[170]

This fourfold function of the door guardians fully explains their names, which might otherwise appear quite arbitrary. The names of the eight goddesses of the offerings are self-explanatory. All these divinities, Buddhas, Buddha-Goddesses, Bodhisattvas, Door Guardians and Goddesses of the Offerings, together making up a total of thirty-seven, will be represented in their traditional postures and colors with their specified accouterments on a maṇḍala that is painted as a mural or a temple-banner, but when the maṇḍala is laid out on the ground, mere symbols suffice, such as their written seed-syllables, or again the whole process of their manifestation may be entirely mentally produced. Even so, one must go through the due process of first envisaging the *samaya*-divinities and then empowering them as wisdom-divinities.

c. *The Use of Jars in Consecration Ceremonies*

The consecration of the pupil, with which we are dealing immediately, is composed of a set of subsidiary consecrations, which will be considered in due order. This whole set comes to be known as the Jar Consecration (*kalaśābhiṣeka*) for reasons that will become clear below, but first a description of the way in which the sacred jar is empowered will serve to illustrate very well the whole process of envisaging all these divinities in front of oneself, whether in a maṇḍala or jar.

> As for the sacramental jar, it should be made of gold or silver, copper or even clay. Its capacity should be about two pints (Sanskrit *droṇa*, a rather vague measure); its circumference should be sixteen "inches" (Sanskrit *aṅgula*, a finger-breadth) and its height thirty "inches"; the neck and the spout should each be two "inches"; it must not be black and in any way defective. It may be

170 See SDPS Tantra, Skorupski's edition, p. 103 and the corresponding Sanskrit on p. 290. I have changed the translation slightly in order to bring out the connections with the Door Guardians and what is being done to the pupil. In the last sentence the Tibetan text is preferable, as has been shown by Dr. Skorupski.

filled with pure water possessing the twenty-five "essences," or it may contain the five medicaments, the five types of grain and the five kinds of gems.[171] It should have a mantle made of silk of five colors marked with the signs of the Five Families. Its mouth should be decorated with foliage.

Such a jar symbolizes the Buddha-Wisdom which knows of no duality. It must not be black around its base as this Wisdom is pure by its very nature. Its girth suggests the profundity and vastness of Wisdom. The length of its neck suggests that the depth of such Wisdom is difficult to measure. The five kinds of gems indicate that it fulfills the aspirations of all beings. The five medicaments indicate that it removes all their afflictions. The five kinds of grain indicate that it produces a great harvest of virtues in their life-series. Thus the water (with which it is filled) is sanctified with all the twenty-five "essences." Its mouth is decorated (with foliage) because by practicing virtues in one's life-series, one gains the salvation which is the fruit, etc.

As for the actual empowering of the jar, first one disposes of evil forces by reciting the mantra and making the gesture of Vajrayakṣa. Then one recites the mantra: OṂ pure by nature are all elements; pure by nature am I! From this mantra (which recalls the Void) one envisages the seed-syllable PAṂ, from which a lotus-flower (*padma*) emerges, and then the seed-syllable A, whence arises a lunar disk, on which one envisages the seed-syllable BHRUṂ. One envisages this as transformed into the jar as described above.

In the center of this Victorious Jar one envisages a jewel-throne supported by eight lions; to the east there is one supported by elephants, to the south by horses, to the west by peacocks and to the north by griffons (*garuḍa*). All have lotus-flowers and lunar disks on them. As for the places for the divinities of the entourage, in the case of there being no circle below (the jar) with the resulting absence of center and spokes, one should envisage their various places on an expanse of water just as though it were before one. Then in a single moment one should produce all the thirty-seven divinities from the Omniscient Vairocana on the central throne to Vajraghaṇṭa (the last named of the four Door Guardians). Sending forth rays from one's own heart, one envisages all the Buddhas in the pattern of the thirty-seven-fold basic group of the Omniscient One invited from the self-existent realm, the pure abode, by means of the mantras and gestures for this Vajra assembly. Then reciting three times the verse that begins: "For the benefit of all beings etc." and the mantra JAḤ HŪṂ VAṂ HOḤ! one presents the (prepared) thrones to them as they appear in the sky before one.[172]

Once empowered in this way, such a jar expresses the same totality of Fivefold Wisdom as does a similarly empowered maṇḍala, although in the case of the jar the whole process is one of pure visualization. A maṇḍala is usually produced by

171 The twenty-five "essences" are theoretically combinations of five kinds of metals, gems, medicinal herbs, grains and scents. A complicated dissertation on the subject will be found in M. E. Carelli's edition of the *Sekoddeśaṭīka*, p. 17, l. 22-p. 19, l. 15. Here are listed alternative sets of the five kinds of grain, gems etc., often with a concluding comment that they should be accepted as available. One may note that for most of the items the Tibetan translators (see T.T., vol. 47, pp. 111-4-5 ff.) found no equivalents and so contented themselves with transliterating the Sanskrit terms. An English translation would scarcely be more helpful.

172 Extracted with abbreviations from *Kun-rig cho-ga'i rnam-bshad*, fos. 128, l. 2-132, l. 5.

a combination of visualization and the symbolic representation of the divinities in their proper positions. Again an appropriate number of jars, often five, representing the Five Buddhas, may be themselves arranged as a maṇḍala. The idea of coercing a particular divinity or a whole set of divinities into a jar is an interesting one, but it is likely that two rather different uses have come together to produce this result. Thus in the *Mañjuśrīmūlakalpa Tantra*, from which a long extract describing the relevant maṇḍala has already been translated above, the jars are used both as offerings to the various divinities and as instruments of consecration. Here we have a far less developed form of symbolism.

> As for the above-mentioned ritual of summoning and dismissing (the divinities), he (the teacher) should enter the maṇḍala again. He should definitely offer eight full jars in which are gold, silver, gems, rice and grain; they are draped with clean mantles and decorated with the leaves and fruit of mango. They are offered (one) to Śākyamuni the Lord, the second one to all Buddhas, the third to Lone Buddhas (Pratyekabuddhas) and to the Noble Disciples, the fourth to all great Bodhisattvas, the fifth to the Great Bodhisattva, the Noble Manjuśrī, the sixth to all gods, while the seventh and eighth are to be placed by the doors of the second (viz., outer) circle; of these the first is for all demons (*bhūta*) and the second is to be dedicated to all living beings in general. Then one should summon (them all) in accordance with the aforementioned rite.

The jars are not only offered to these various classes of divinities, but also clearly serve as "supports" for their presence in the maṇḍala, although this is not specifically stated in accordance with the later theory of coercing them into the jars. One may add that the jars are full of pure water, impregnated with precious, medicinal and nutritious substances, conventionally numbered as twenty-five, as we have just noted. There are many different kinds of separate offerings presented to the divinities, lamps and flowers and incense, a whole variety of cakes and sweetmeats and so on, all specified in the text. Thus the account continues:

> The master of the maṇḍala performs, as previously described, the main rite for gratifying them with offerings, whereby he invokes them, praises them, incenses them and so on. Then his assistant who is skillful and quick (takes) a meatless sacrificial cake intended for all the demons, and having circumambulated the outer maṇḍala, which is adorned on all sides and above and below with incense and flowers, lamps and garlands, he should scatter far and wide the cake for the demons, while the joyful sound of the music of drums and conch shells resounds. Then after his ablutions he (presumably the teacher who is master of the maṇḍala) should make a burnt offering (*homa*) of boiled rice mixed with curds, honey and clarified butter, as he recites the basic six-syllable mantra one thousand and eight times.[173] Having made this burnt offering, he performs a rite of protection for the Great Beings who have been brought into the maṇḍala and established there previously. Then he should show the maṇḍala to those whom he has accepted as his pupils, who

[173] Concerning burnt offerings (*homa*) see section III.13.e below.

have produced the thought of enlightenment and made their confession, who have offered their own bodies to the Buddhas and Bodhisattvas and who hold their possessions in common with all living beings with perfection as their object, who are capable of advancing toward the place of enlightenment and are desirous of obtaining the state of omniscient buddhahood; such as these are freed from all sin by the mere sight of the maṇḍala, and even those who have committed the most terrible sins are freed that very moment.

Then the Master of the Maṇḍala should cover the faces of those who will enter the maṇḍala with new cloth, of which the threads have been removed, which are free of fluff, which have been consecrated by a sevenfold recitation of the basic mantra and perfumed with sweet-smelling sandalwood and saffron. First he should cause to enter the maṇḍala children from the age of three years to sixteen, who are adorned with the five crests or the single crest or the topknot, those who are king's sons who have been anointed on their heads, or the sons of noble families or those who are desirous of great sovereignty. Then as they stand in the second maṇḍala with face covered, they form the hand-gesture representing a blue lotus-flower and recite just once the basic mantra of Mañjuśrī the Prince, and he gives them a sweet-smelling flower in both hands, which have been totally purified with a mixture of sandalwood and camphor. They should throw these flowers, and wherever the flower falls, one should give the one concerned the (corresponding) mantra. It is esteemed as his mantra. It is linked to him for a series of eight births. It is his religious friend for it accomplishes his advance to the place of enlightenment resulting in the omniscience of a Great Bodhisattva. It produces great wealth, great kingship, great fame and singleness of purpose.

The consecration itself begins with the pupils paying their master royal honors:

Then having made all preparations as for the consecration of universal sovereignty (*sarvarājyābhiṣeka*), they honor their teacher. They spread the great canopy; they set up flags and banners of victory; they hold a white parasol over his head and wave white fly-whisks. With great ceremony they cause the conch shells and the great drums to make a joyous sound and they praise him with cries of victory, with auspicious verses, with verses of praise and good fortune such as declare a conqueror. Then having bowed before the Buddhas and Bodhisattvas, they should say: "O Master, I wish to enter upon the mantra practice of the Buddhas and Bodhisattvas; I wish to enter the secret circle of salvation that transcends all that pertains to this world; I wish to attain buddhahood involving universal sovereignty in the Dharma. In brief, may I be a Buddha!"

Then the pupil should be seated on a bundle of *kuśa* grass, facing the East and looking toward the maṇḍala.[174] As for the Vidyā Consecration which he is given first, he should be made to make the great hand-gesture of the Five Crests. Then he should write with bezoar on a piece of birchbark whichever

[174] *Kuśa*-grass, botanical name *Poa cynosuroides*, is a type of Indian grass seemingly much in use by Indian ascetics. It is specified here, because in all the accounts of the Buddha Śākyamuni's enlightenment, he is said to have made a seat of this same grass. For a brief mention see E. J. Thomas, *Life of the Buddha*, p. 71, but rather see André Bareau, *Recherches sur la biographie du Buddha*, pp. 57-61.

mantra pleases him; having written it, he should cleanse his hands with sandalwood and saffron and placing the mantra inside a covered dish, he should place it in the maṇḍala at the feet of the Bodhisattva Mañjuśrī. Then seated on the *kuśa* grass he should first of all recite the basic Vidyā mantra one hundred and eight times. Then he should receive the consecration while still seated on the grass. The teacher should take the jar which was for all living beings in general and was placed near the door in the outer circle, and reciting the basic mantra consecrate him on the head. Then the others receive the water (of consecration) just as he wishes. Next he should give the covered dish to him (the pupil) and make him recite the mantra toward a lamp. If it is precisely that one, making effort he will gradually be successful. But if it is another one, he will succeed by the mere recitation of the mantra. But if the syllables are given short or in excess there is no doubt that he will be successful just at this first evocation.[175] Thus there is no doubt of his success with the three evocations which the teacher wrote down before. So in that way the Vidyā Consecration is to be given.

As for the consecration in the second circle, one should give the consecration with the jar that was offered previously to all the gods. By performing the rite just as before on his head, he is freed from the whole morass of evil, he is accepted by the Lord Buddhas, he is empowered by all Buddhas and Bodhisattvas to perform the sacraments (*samaya*), maṇḍalas, mantras and hand-gestures relating to everything mundane and supramundane and he may receive the Master Consecration.

In the third circle he receives consecration on his head with the rite using the jar that was offered to Lone Buddhas and Disciples, and he should be told: "You are authorized by all the Buddhas and Bodhisattvas of great miraculous power to recite the mantras and tantras, to draw and to teach the maṇḍalas, to practice and to teach hand-gestures, thus yourself both performing and teaching." Moreover in this very life or in one of his next eight lives he will attain the state of buddhahood.[176]

Likewise for the aforementioned rite of the Royal and Victorious Consecrations he should be consecrated with the full jars previously offered to the Lord Śākyamuni and the jar offered to the Bodhisattvas. He is told: "You have been accepted by the Lord Buddhas, the Bodhisattvas and the Disciples. Sprites (*bhūta*) cannot prevail over you; no bodily creature can overcome you; may you have power over all spells and achieve whatever you desire."

So the master of the maṇḍala should give to each the five consecrations just as he wishes. Having brought them finally into the maṇḍala, he dismisses them after they have offered themselves to all the Buddhas and Bodhisattvas and then circumambulated the maṇḍala three times.[177]

175 The intention here remains obscure, but Sanskrit and Tibetan versions agree.

176 I follow the Tibetan here. Sanskrit says: "He will always obtain the state of buddhahood in this very life or during successive lives up to (what will be) a last rebirth."

177 For these three closely related texts see MK, p. 47, ll. 20-7 (Ariane Macdonald, p. 130 for French translation and p. 165, ll. 23ff. for edited Tibetan text); then MK, p. 48, l. 24-p. 49, l. 21 (A.M., pp. 132-7 and p. 167, l. 2-p. 168, l. 15); then MK, p. 50, l. 5-p. 51, l. 24 (A.M., pp. 138-42 and pp. 169 top-171 top). I have earlier translated some of these extracts in my article "The Notion of Divine Kingship in Tibetan Buddhism," pp. 206-8 and in *Buddhist Himālaya* (several references).

This extract has been chosen to illustrate the use of such sacramental jars in a context where their symbolism is not yet expressed in so complex a manner as in the description above. The tantra from which the extract is taken, the *Mañjuśrī-mūlakalpa*, being classed as an Action Tantra (*kriyā-tantra*) is one where the whole theory of Buddha-families is in an early formative phase (see section III.6.a, where the relevant maṇḍala is described), and where we find ourselves in an early Mahāyāna environment, occupied by Buddhas, Pratyekabuddhas, Early Disciples (*śrāvaka*), Bodhisattvas, gods and demons. By contrast in the later tantras of the Yoga class the stage is occupied, as we have seen, by the five cosmic Buddhas, their Buddha-Goddesses and sets of Bodhisattvas, attended by the symbolic offerings and door guardians. At this later stage, the Pratyekabuddhas and Disciples have a quite secondary importance, and if represented at all, are placed outside and around the maṇḍala. The jars are then inevitably imbued with all this later symbolism. In our extract just quoted there is reference to five consecrations, and this would simply appear to mean the pouring of water on the head of the pupil from the five jars, which are specified in a rising order of importance, namely the jar offered to all living beings, the one offered to the gods, the one offered to Disciples and Pratyekabuddhas, the one offered to Bodhisattvas and the one offered to the Buddha Śākyamuni, although reference to the last two is rather cursory. They appear to have some kind of progressive effect. The first one concerns the Vidyā (see section III.3 for an earlier interpretation), which I have left untranslated here. It doubtless refers here to the spell of the disciple's chosen divinity, whom he should now be able to invoke. The second consecration enables him to perform the sacraments etc. of this particular cycle; the third one authorizes him to teach so that he becomes a "master" in his own right; the last two would seem to consecrate him as a Bodhisattva and potential Buddha. One must note that the same terms are used with different meanings at the various stages in the history of the development of tantras, and this causes difficulties to the later Indian and Tibetan interpreters, who do not always take historical development into account. Thus although we have five consecrations here, they are all consecrations performed with water and so have to be interpreted all as just the first one of the later formulated set of four (see III.14.c). Also it has to be made clear that the consecration as Master performed here is different from the Master-Consecration bestowed in the higher tantras, for which the name Jar Consecration or Vidyā Consecration is still used (III.14.a). The garland, which is practically indispensable, may be thrown into the maṇḍala to discover the pupil's special association with a particular Buddha-family, or in this usage it may be replaced by a flower or even a toothpick. Also the garland may be used for crowning the pupil as may be the case in our extract above (III.13.a) from the "Symposium of Truth."

d. *The Order of Consecrations in Various Classes of Tantras*

In our example of a consecration (p. 218 f.) the pupil was led to the maṇḍala where his master first administers the oath of secrecy. The oath is confirmed by the appropriate mantra and by the pupil accepting a drop of water from a sacrificial jar consecrated to Vajrasattva. Thus the teacher says: "Today Vajrasattva has entered your heart," and the pupil is theoretically pervaded by the transcendent wisdom of buddhahood. Then the garland, which was previously put into the hands of the pupil as he approached the maṇḍala, is thrown by him into the maṇḍala, where it may be expected to fall into one of the Family segments. The teacher takes it up and binds him round the head with it, thus crowning him in his appropriate Buddha Family. He is then shown the maṇḍala, after which he receives three consecrations, one with a "vajra-empowered" jar, one with an actual vajra, and finally a renaming consecration.

Exegetical works often suggest far more regularity in the ordering of these consecrations than one would expect to find amongst such a vast miscellaneous collection of tantric rites, which were developed by different masters often in quite different religious settings, as we have tried to show above. Bearing this in mind, we may however refer to some of these theoretical schemes, for even if they do not fit in every case and also sometimes impose later interpretations, they certainly assist toward an understanding of these traditions, as subsequently received by Tibetan converts.

A succinct interpretation of the so-called Jar Consecration is given in a short work by Advayavajra, one of the eighty-four Great Adepts, which is entitled "Brief Account of the Process of Consecration," and an extract from this may be helpful:

> Firstly we deal with the Jar Consecration, which is in fact characterized as six jar-consecrations, viz., those of water, crown, vajra, bell, name and master. As one washes away exterior dirt with water, so one sprinkles water for the purification of the impurity of ignorance; for this reason it is called a "sprinkling" (*seka*).[178] As the jar is used in all of them, the name used is "jar-consecration" (*kalaśa-abhiṣeka*). These are consecrations from which there can be no backsliding because they are of the nature of the Six Tathāgatas, thus:
>
> The Water Consecration corresponds to the Mirrorlike wisdom of Akṣobhya,
> The Crown Consecration to the Wisdom of Sameness of Ratnasambhava,
> The Vajra Consecration to the Discriminating Wisdom of Amitābha,
> The Royal Consecration to the Active Wisdom of Amoghasiddhi,
> The Name Consecration to the Wisdom of the Pure Absolute of Vairocana being the wisdom that puts an end to ignorance,
> While the Master Consecration corresponds to Vajrasattva.
>
> Of them (the first) five are (also) known as Vidyā Consecrations because they make use of the Five Vidyās, Buddha-Locanā and the others.[179]

The Water Consecration is bestowed by the Vajra-Master personifying

[178] The noun *seka*, "sprinkling," of which *abhiṣeka* is a derived form, makes this play on words possible in Sanskrit, but not so easily in a Tibetan or an English translation.

[179] These are the four Buddha-Goddesses with Vajradhātvīśvarī (Lady of the Vajra-Sphere) as the fifth. Here Vidyā as female partner represents the later interpretation. Compare Vidyā on p. 228.

Akṣobhya upon the pupil whom he envisages as Vairocana. Such is his total assurance.

The Crown Consecration imparts the seed which develops into the wisdom-bump (*uṣṇīṣa*) of this future Buddha.

As for the Vajra Consecration,[180]

Firm, substantial and solid, of uncuttable, unbreakable character,
Unburnable, indestructible, the Void is said to be Vajra.

In the *Hevajra Tantra* (I.1.4) the vajra is said to be unbreakable. The bestowal of the Vajra Consecration gives, as it were, an infusion of the seed which grows into this unbreakable wisdom.

As for the Bell which resounds in such a way as to make known the whole supreme Dharma, although it thus manifests its superiority and is really the agent productive of causality, nonetheless the Consecration of the Vajra-Bell is preceded by the Vajra Consecration.[181]

The Name Consecration consists in giving up one's own name so that one may understand the namelessness of all *dharmas* while obtaining a name suitable for a Lord Buddha that accords with the lineage of one's own family-divinity.[182]

As for the Master Consecration, it is characterized by the Vajra Sacrament, the Bell Sacrament, the Mudrā Sacrament, Worthiness, Sanction, Vow, Prophesy and Encouragement.

The Vajra Sacrament consists in understanding the words: "You are the Sacrament," so understanding (the change) from a contingent body to the final union which is noncontingent and knows of no distinctions.

The Bell Sacrament consists in the resolution to proclaim the eighty-four thousand teachings of the Dharma.

The Mudrā (Symbol) Sacrament consists in understanding the words: "You are of the self-nature of your chosen divinity."

The Sacrament of Worthiness comprises the quiddity (*tattva*) of the maṇḍala, the particulars of the purification of the maṇḍala, the quiddity of the divinity, the particulars of the purification of the divinity, the action of a teacher, knowing how to produce the maṇḍala mentally, the five lights and eating the (five) ambrosias.[183]

The Sacrament of Sanction is for the purpose of turning the Wheel of the Doctrine, which viewed from the Process of Realization is void of all self-existence.

The making of the Vajra Vow is for the undoing of all heretical vows.

The Prophecy refers to the defining of the nature of the Earth and the rest. Thus the atmosphere contains the earth etc.; the sky is self-existent; the world is in a state of becoming; such is the meaning of earth, atmosphere and

[180] The passage describing the vajra. omitted here, is translated in section III.2, pp. 133-4.

[181] The Bell (*alias* Sovereign) Consecration is preceded by a description of the bell similar to the passage quoted above about the vajra (III.2). Thus it is said: "To show that it is the cause of the knowledge where there is no distinction between Voidness and Compassion, the countenance of the (Goddess) Prajnā is shown above (on the handle)," thus arguing for the superiority of the bell as symbol.

[182] I follow the Tibetan version here, as the Sanskrit is obscurely corrupted.

[183] Concerning the meaning of "purification" in this context, see the Index for references.

heaven.[184]

The Encouragement relates to the understanding of words that begin thus: "You are freed from all impediments and have been accepted by all Buddhas and Bodhisattvas."[185]

It should be observed that such generalizing statements on the correct ordering of the various consecrations are usually made from the viewpoint of one who looks back over the whole range of tantric developments and whose concern is to bring order into the apparent confusion of various traditions. They are also written with all the different classes of tantras in mind, as they were later arranged, with scant regard to historical realities of time and place. Thus it must be kept in mind that the rite of consecration as extracted from the *Manjuśrī-mūlakalpa* or the "Symposium of Truth" is in each case conceived of as self-sufficient within its own particular context of time and place. There is no consciousness on the part of the participants of performing a rite that can be categorized as higher or lower. What is true of the standpoint of the later Indian interpreters is even more true of Tibetan interpreters, who, having received the whole tantric tradition when it was more or less complete, were understandably at pains to discover why it should exist in so many variant forms. Thus those who promoted Supreme Yoga tantras, which have had such a vogue in Tibet, have reinterpreted the whole concept of consecration in accordance with their theories of sexual yoga, and they teach a set of four such consecrations, which will be described below in the next section. At the same time they demonstrate an apparent superiority to all other classes of tantras by accepting as their first consecration the whole set of consecrations which were already all in all for the practitioners of the earlier tantras, referring to this set, as we see from the above quotation as the Jar or the Vidyā Consecration. It is also referred to as the Master Consecration (*ācārya-abhiṣeka*) because when a pupil had received the whole set, he could become "master of the maṇḍala" in his own right. It was precisely in this way that the particular tradition was carried forward from master to pupil, who once trained and consecrated becomes a master in turn. It must be clear that the idea of mastership can only relate to the particular sphere in which one becomes a master, and thus sanction (*anujñā*) to teach according to an Action Tantra is different from the sanction to teach a Yoga Tantra. However, for these as well as for Performance Tantras, viz., all the first three categories, such mastership represents a kind of finality, while for the tantras of the Supreme Yoga class it is the lowest of four consecrations and thus cannot bestow mastership in the normal sense of this term, so in this case it becomes a mere name for which some suitable interpretation needs to be found. A commentary on the term occurring as the first of the set of four in the *Hevajra Tantra* may be

184 Here we have another play on like-sounding words which is lost in translation.

185 The Sanskrit text would mean: "You are the sacrament (*samaya*) of all Buddhas and Bodhisattvas." For this whole extract see the *Advayavajrasaṃgraha*, p. 36, l. 7-p. 38, l. 23. The correct Sanskrit title of this short work is *Sekatākāryasaṃgraha* according to the Tibetan. My translation continues on pp. 243-4 below.

quoted in illustration of this:

> The first is called the Jar Consecration or the Master Consecration. It is called a "sprinkling" because impurity is washed away. It is called the Jar Consceration because it is characterized by a jar, and the Master Consecration because it proceeds far from evil and wickedness. It is also called the Vidyā Consecration, because it overthrows ignorance and arouses an awareness of the five spheres of knowledge.[186]

With such a shift in meaning one understands how misapprehensions can arise when all the various consecrations are listed for all classes of tantras as though they were to be treated as a progressively higher series of related items. Such a classification of higher and lower can also be misleading when applied to the tantras generally, as separated into the four grades of Action, Performance, Yoga and Supreme Yoga. Thus one often finds it asserted that these four grades have been taught to suit the capabilities of various beings, whose faculties may be categorized as inferior, mediocre, superior or truly excellent, as though all four grades were available at all times rather like our present-day grades of university degrees. Even this comparison, however, is misleading, for it is clearly and quite rightly taught that all grades of tantras have the same goal, namely the winning of buddhahood, so that as a final result there can be no difference between them. We have already noted above how those who come latest onto the historical scene tend to grade the various phases that preceded them as descending stages of inferiority, and it is precisely this that occurs with the later categorizing of all the accumulated masses of tantras and the various consecrations that they bestow. Thus in order to make some sense of the various explanations offered by traditional scholars for the existence of such a variety, one needs to keep in mind the all-important factor of historical development. The consecration ceremony extracted from the tantra *Mañjuśrīmūlakalpa*, subsequently classed as an Action Tantra, would have to be classified according to some later theories as primarily suitable for those of "inferior faculties." The nonsensity of this is surely self-evident, unless one takes one's stand resolutely on the side of class distinctions, the essential artificiality of which is adequately argued in Buddhist philosophical treatises without our need to turn to modern Western reformers. In terms of historical considerations, as already treated in some detail in this present work, the question of why there should be different kinds of tantras is more easily answered, namely that they were part of a quite natural religious development that affected Buddhist beliefs and practices in the course of its long history on Indian soil. Thus it is not without significance that the so-called Action Tantras describe maṇḍalas and rites relating to those divinities and higher beings who were part of the early Mahāyāna scene, namely

186 See H.T., vol. 1, p. 95 n. The verbal connection between "master" (*ācārya*) and "proceeds far" (*āráddūryaṃ carati*) on which this otherwise apparently strange interpretation is based, cannot be reproduced either in the Tibetan text, which I am here translating, or in the English. The same play on words is found in Kāṇha's commentary, translated on p. 132 (top lines), where the Sanskrit is available.

Buddhas with names already familiar to us from early Mahāyāna sūtras and related Bodhisattvas, Pratyekebuddhas and Early Disciples, as well as some feminine divinities whose cult already forms part of Buddhist practice, as well as some fierce protecting divinities. We have already noticed the tendency to arrange these into the three main families of the Tathāgata, the Lotus and the Vajra in this clearly specified order of importance. In short we find ourselves in a normal Mahāyāna world and the ritual works that were later categorized as Action Tantras were not then even thought of as being part of the different sphere of tantras as opposed to sūtras. Indeed at this earlier stage they were usually referred to generally as sūtras and not as tantras at all. Much the same situation would seem to apply to the rather smaller group of so-called Performance Tantras, which continue to belong to the same kind of Mahāyāna setting, although in so far as Vairocana comes now clearly to the fore as the primary Buddha, still presiding, be it noted, over three Buddha-families, and Vajrapāṇi's importance is clearly recognized, we may observe a kind of intermediate development between the Action Tantras, so called, and the later Yoga Tantras with their well-formulated set of five cosmic Buddhas and their well-patterned maṇḍalas. However, we are still in a normal Mahāyāna Buddhist world, even though one might refer to it now as late Mahāyāna, and the fundamental tantra of this class, namely the "Symposium of Truth," was still traditionally referred to as a sūtra. Once buddhahood came to be envisaged as fivefold with the added theory of five Buddha-families, the earlier three-family arrangement might easily be regarded as a less developed theory and certainly less manageable when it came to the drawing of maṇḍalas, where the fivefold arrangement fits perfectly. We have noted above how difficult it is to envisage as a maṇḍala the groups of divinities who go to make up the maṇḍala of the *Mañjuśrīmūlakalpa*, simply because we too have come to conceive of maṇḍalas as symmetrical arrangements of symbols or divinities arranged according to the general pattern of a center and the four main directions.

Thus the point may safely be made that those ritual works known later as Action and Performance Tantras were originally the main ritual texts which formed part of Mahāyāna religious practice at a time when later tantras were unknown. The term *kriyā*, for which I have adopted the conventional translation of Action, simply means a rite of any kind. *Caryā*, translated conventionally as Performance simply in order to suggest some kind of difference between these two groups in accordance with later theories, also means a rite of any kind.[187] In short, there is essentially no difference in meaning at all, and these two groups of works, later differentiated according to the terminology which happened to be in use, viz., *kriyā* or *caryā*, can best be understood if they are accepted as part of the normal Mahāyāna scene. They provided the directions

[187] I have chosen the terms Action and Performance in this book out of deference to Jeffrey Hopkins, whose two books on the *Yoga of Tibet* contain much interesting discussion of the differences between the various classes of tantras as seen from a very much later Tibetan standpoint, where time sequence and historical development are scarcely taken into account.

and the liturgies for the worship of the regular Mahāyāna divinities and they introduced the kind of consecration ceremony for a would-be Bodhisattva of the kind we have already illustrated. Both involve the practice of yoga. No tantric vow of any kind was involved for the straightforward reason that tantric practice, as later conceived, was still unknown in these conventional Mahāyāna circles. Thus the path toward perfection remained that of the Bodhisattva, that self-sacrificing being, who undertook to run his course through aeons of existence. At the same time the appropriate consecration performed by one's teacher in the presence of the Buddha-symbols could have a powerful psychological effect, increasing one's faith in the goal, one's zeal, one's comprehension and so on, thus shortening the time needed to run the course and win one's crown. There appears to be a close relationship between these Buddhist consecrations and those of consecration to kingship, and the connection is easily found in the early Buddhist conception of Śākyamuni Buddha as "universal monarch" (*cakravartin*) and a "great man" (*mahāpuruṣa*) possessed of the thirty-two major marks and eighty minor marks of perfection. One need but quote from a passage already translated above, where it is said that the teacher introduces into the maṇḍala for consecration "children from the age of three years to sixteen" who are "sons of noble families or desirous of great sovereignty." While any young aspirant toward enlightenment might be admitted, the idea of royalty would seem to exercise a special appeal (p. 226).

The later exegetes, who explain for us the nature and limitations of these earlier kinds of consecration within the much later context of fully developed tantric theories and practices, are certainly aware of the differences between what they now regard as lower and higher tantras, but the real reason, namely that the supposedly lower tantras belong to an earlier phase of the Mahāyāna, is obscured for them, because they themselves are already operating within the later phase, and so they interpret according to the later theories. Thus mKhas-grub-rje argues quite rightly that it is wrong to introduce a vow of the Five Families in Action and Performance tantras, quoting cases where this has occurred.[188] He knows that it is wrong for traditional reasons, but as we have noted, the fundamental reason is the historical one that the theory of five families had not yet been formulated in the circles where these works first circulated. He is also aware that the only vows necessary for taking part in the consecrations of the so-called "lower tantras" are those of becoming a monk and of aspiring as a Bodhisattva to buddhahood, no tantric vow being necessary. From the viewpoint of later theories this was a matter which required elucidation, for these rituals had now been clearly classed as tantras.[189] Once again from a historical point of view, the answer is far easier: when these rites were first performed within the traditional Mahāyāna setting, no such thing as a tantric vow had yet been heard of in those circles. Thus it comes about that a great deal of complex argument that one reads in later exegetical works corresponds to the

188 See mKhas-grub-rje's *Fundamentals of the Buddhist Tantras*, Lessing & Wayman, pp. 146-7.
189 *Ibid.*, pp. 154-5.

rather arid and outmoded scholasticism for which earlier Christian scholars are often taken to task. Much of it may be ingenious but hardly enlightening.[190]

In so far as Yoga Tantras represent an advance in symbolic representation and religious practice upon Action and Performance Tantras, so they tended to replace them, and thus we note that precisely the Yoga Tantras provide for the transmission of Tantric Buddhism to China and Tibet in the eighth and ninth centuries. Also it would seem to have been inevitable that the earlier tantric traditions, in so far as they continued to be used, should be interpreted in accordance with later theory. Thus we may note an interesting controversy concerning an essential attribute of the Yoga Tantras, namely their power to enable one to achieve a state of self-identification with a supremely divine form representing the goal of buddhahood, and the extent to which Action and Performance Tantras might achieve a similar effect.[191]

e. *The Power of Coercion*

All tantras claim the power to coerce divinities, for it is by coercing them into an image or symbol that one is enabled to worship them and make them suitable offerings, and it is by coercing them into oneself that one is enabled to act with their assumed assurance (or literally "pride," Sanskrit *māna* or *ahaṃkara*, Tibetan *nga-rgyal*) and thus achieve the objective in view. All tantras of all classes promise both supramundane success (the gaining of buddhahood sooner or later) and mundane successes, such as gaining prosperity, offspring, a particular woman, good harvests or rainfall, overcoming adverse influences such as various kinds of disease-causing evil spirits, curing the effects of poison etc. It is sometimes suggested that while the tantras, later classified as inferior, cater for the more mundane requirements, the superior ones are concerned with more

[190] See e.g., Jeffrey Hopkins, *Tantra in Tibet*, pp. 151 ff., where we have his admirable translation of Tsong-kha-pa's theories on "Identifying the Four Tantras." Here of course the four classes of tantras are intended; I have referred above to the modern rather confusing habit of referring to the Mantrayāna/Vajrayāna generally as "the Tantra." Having disposed of several quite absurd theories, notably that they were promulgated to suit the four Indian castes of Brahmans, Kṣatriyas, Vaiśyas and Sudras, Tsong-kha-pa opts for the strange theory that they are thus subdivided into four groups depending upon whether the divinities with which they deal are (i) smiling at one another, (ii) looking at one another, (iii) embracing and (iv) united. This theory is based upon some Indian commentaries on a verse in the *Hevajra Tantra*. But one should note that the *Hevajra Tantra* itself does not relate smiling, gazing, embracing and uniting with the four classes of tantras at all, but much more appositely with the Four Joys and the Four Consecrations. See the *Hevajra Tantra*, II.iii.10-12. It is true that the commentaries do make this artificial equation, since as we are informed elsewhere in the *Hevajra Tantra* "everything goes in fours" (I.i.30). The supposed quotation from the *Hevajra Tantra* (Hopkins, *op.cit.*, foot of p. 158) is misleading. As a theory for the reason of there being four classes of tantras, this may be ingenious, but historically the whole discussion is irrelevant. My translation of the relevant passage will be found below toward the end of section III.14.b, pp. 252-3.

[191] See e.g., Jeffrey Hopkins, *The Yoga of Tibet*, pp. 47-62: "Controversy about Deity Yoga in Action and Performance," or mKhas-grub-rje's *Fundamentals of the Buddhist Tantras*, ed. Lessing and Wayman, pp. 163 ff.

truly religious objectives. In fact all tantras are interested in precisely the same objectives, whether supramundane or mundane. It must be remembered that from the earliest times the acquisition of miraculous powers (Sanskrit *ṛddhi*, Tibetan *rdzu-'phrul*) was closely associated with the realization of enlightenment. Śākyamuni's own enlightenment was in fact defined in terms of the miraculous kinds of knowledge (*vidyā*) that he achieves, namely the "divine eye" (*divya-cakṣur*) enabling him to see all beings being reborn with their various characteristics in all states of existence, as well as the special knowledge of all his own previous rebirths (see section I.3.a). There are other powers, such as the "divine ear," which hears all sounds everywhere, from the preaching of other Buddhas to the conversations of others however distant, the knowledge of the thoughts of others, together with a whole variety of magical powers, which came to be grouped together as a scholastic set of five (or six) "further knowing" (Sanskrit *abhijñā*, Tibetan *mngon-par shes-pa*) of which the miraculous powers form one quite large group. This includes already many of the so-called mundane powers claimed on behalf of tantric yogins, e.g., the power to become invisible, to pass through solid objects, to fly in a crosslegged position, to assume different appearances, sending forth other emanations of oneself, to coerce others into doing one's will, to bestow material benefits on others etc.[192] Thus neither in the supramundane nor in the mundane sphere do tantric masters offer much else that was not also believed to be within the reach of a successful Bodhisattva who continued to operate within conventional Mahāyāna limitations. The main difference was the time factor, for what took a Bodhisattva aeons of time to acquire might be won by a tantric yogin within the course of a single birth. The small additions to such mundane achievements introduced in the tantras relate to increased scope for coercion and the practice of avowedly harmful rites, such as the destruction of property and the slaying of enemies. In Action and Performance Tantras the three main types of mundane actions, namely those of a pacific kind, those aiming at worldly benefits, and those of a fierce destructive kind, are allocated quite logically to the three primary families of the Tathāgata, the Lotus and the Vajra.[193] Thus the Buddhas preside over such rites as "pacifying" illness and disease or the causes of untimely death; the gods such as preeminently Avalokiteśvara control rites to increase prosperity in various ways, while powerful fierce divinities such as preeminently Vajrapāṇi preside over the rites of coercing, destroying and slaying. This helps to explain the ordering of these three families in the earlier tantras, to which reference was made above. In theory one who has received a consecration in the Vajra Family, thereby becoming skilled in fierce activities, is not fit to perform beneficent ones, whereas one who is proficient in beneficent ones could, if he would, perform fierce ones in case of special need. At the highest level one who has received consecration in the Tathāgata Family should be able to operate effectively on the two lower spheres of activity. Such a view corresponds with conventional

192 See Har Dayal, *The Bodhisattva Doctrine*, pp. 112-6.

193 See above p. 191; also Jeffrey Hopkins, *op. cit.*, p. 174 and mKhas-grub-rje, *op. cit.*, pp. 200-1.

Mahāyāna theories where the Buddhas remain superior to all other beings.

By contrast in Yoga and Supreme Yoga Tantras the Vajra Family comes to the fore as represented in the Yoga Tantras by Vajrapāṇi/Vajradhara/Vajrasattva (see III.2) and in the Supreme Yoga Tantras by the great horrific divinities such as Heruka, Hevajra, Śambara and the rest (III.6.b). Through self-identification with these divinities all achievements of a supramundane and mundane kind are attainable and in this respect all gradation of family allegiance disappears. The Yoga Tantras continue to operate in terms of families and the consecration one receives should fit one's personality, depending upon its inherent tendency to Wrath, Delusion, Passion, Malignity or Envy. However, in whichever family one receives consecration, the same achievements become theoretically possible. although certain family specialities may be noticed. The Vajra Family specializes in slaying and destroying, but it gives also the powers of restoration; the Lotus Family specializes in subduing beings to one's will, as well as in becoming invisible, assuming various bodily forms and flying in the sky; the Gem Family specializes in the gaining of wealth with special facilities for discovering hidden treasure.[194] All such powers are gained through the bestowing of the relevant consecrations. One example from the Vajra Family may suffice:

> Then Vajrapāṇi explained the pledge-maṇḍala of subtle knowledge according to the Vajra Family. "Now I shall explain," he said, "the supreme Dharma-maṇḍala, which resembles the Vajra Sphere and is known as Wrathful Knowledge. One should design the whole maṇḍala in the manner of the great (*Vajradhātu*) maṇḍala, and in the center one should indicate the Buddha centered on the Knowledge-Vajra. To the (four) sides of this Buddha one should indicate all the (other four) Buddhas. Then approaching with a vajra-step one should place within the set of four circles the Victor of the Threefold World (*Trilokavijaya*) and the other divinities, and by their sides the gods of Vajra-Wrath all as prescribed."
>
> Now as for the rite in this maṇḍala of subtle knowledge of the Vajra Family, one should bring in (the neophyte) and say to him: "Today you are consecrated by the Lord Vajrapāṇi in the Vajra-Wrath of All Tathāgatas. Be fully attentive. Until all realms of existence without exception have been saved, it is for the sake of winning that fruit which is the supreme achievement in joyful bliss of All Tathāgatas, that one slays all beings with Vajra-Wrath as a sign of their purification, and how much the more all evil beings." Then one should remove his face-scarf and showing him the whole maṇḍala, place a vajra in his hand and teach him the subtle knowledge of Vajra-Wrath:
>
> Stabilizing the subtle vajra as one stays united with Vajra-Hūṃkāra
> (= Vajrapāṇi), toward whomsoever one directs the syllable HŪṂ, the
> life of that one is destroyed.
> Stabilizing the subtle vajra, one sends it forth in the way prescribed,
> and wherever it is thus sent forth, that enemy is destroyed.
> Stabilizing the subtle vajra as one stays, united with Vajra-Hūṃkāra,

[194] For some examples one may refer to my introduction to the STTS, pp. 45, 52, 55. See also section III.14.c below.

wherever one sends it forth in wrath, one destroys those living beings.
Likewise he can withdraw it and insofar as the yogin wishes,
he can restore all life without exception.[195]

In Supreme Yoga Tantras all family distinctions are in effect transcended, and the successful yogin should be able to practice any rite he pleases. The second chapter of the *Hevajra Tantra* is devoted entirely to such rites, and since this is available in English translation, further examples are scarcely necessary.[196] Other references from the *Guhyasamāja Tantra* have also been given in a previous section of the present work. A major interest of all tantras is the gaining of powers of such a kind and for most practicing Buddhists, whether Tibetans nowadays or the Indian Buddhists of the past, mundane achievements evoke greater interest than those supramundane ones which seem to have little relevance to their everyday lives. Religious experts, whether monks or non-celibate yogins, are expected to be proficient in what are generally referred to as the "Four Rites" (Sanskrit *catuḥ karmāṇi*, Tibetan *las bzhi*), namely tranquilizing, prospering, subduing and destroying. Grouped under such headings, the appropriate ceremonies are described in the Yoga Tantra *Durgatipariśodhana*, and although in other tantras this fourfold arrangement does not emerge so clearly, many commentaries seem to take it for granted, and it is in this form that they were accepted in Tibetan Buddhist tradition.[197] They were presumably arranged as a set of four, because as the *Hevajra Tantra* informs us, "everything goes in fours."[198] While they may be performed by means of mental concentration (such is the implication of the term "subtle vajra" as used just above), they are more usually accompanied by the performance of an appropriate *homa* ceremony, as described in more or less detail in most tantras. In Sanskrit *homa* (connected with the verbal root *hu-* meaning "to offer") means simply an oblation made from Vedic times onward, usually as a burnt offering. The practice of making such an offering to the gods was taken up by Buddhists during the Mahāyāna period, and it was mentioned as we saw above in connection with the consecration ceremony as performed according to the *Mañjuśrīmūlakalpa*. It comes to be closely associated with rites involving "mundane" aspirations, the size and shape of the sacrificial hearth and the items which are consumed in the fire depending upon the kind of rite, tranquil or prospering, subduing or destroying, which is to be performed. While exegetical works go into great detail on the subject of the correct performance of an appropriate *homa* ceremony, the many variant references to be found in the tantras themselves suggest the exercise of much individual discretion in accordance with certain basic rules, such as sweet-smelling wood and useful products of a pleasant kind for beneficent rites and acrid wood and unpleasant items for harmful rites.

195 From the STTS, ch. 8, Yamada's Sanskrit ed., pp. 228-9, TT, vol. 4., pp. 247-4-4 ff.
196 See my edition, vol. I, pp. 50-5.
197 See SDPS Tantra, ed. T. Skorupski, pp. 68 ff.
198 See H.T., I.1.30 and the quotation from Vajragarbha's commentary in my vol. I, p. 88 n.

Concentrated in thought he ignites the fire with sweet-smelling wood
and self-composed in Vajra-Wrath he burns up evils by offering sesame oil.
With the very same wood he ignites the one who consumes the oblation
(= the fire-god) and by offering grain, prosperity for the house is assured.
The sage ignites the fire with mellifluous wood and offering there the young
shoots of millet with clarified butter, he causes an extension of life.
With the very same wood he ignites the one who consumes the oblation
and by offering there the young shoots of *kuśa* grass together with oil,
protection is always assured.

Or again:

First lighting the fire with bitter wood and self-composed in Vajra-Wrath,
by offering thorny branches (the victim is) truly coerced.
Lighting the fire with the very same wood the wrathful one can petrify a
moving man when he offers red flowers and fruits.
Lighting the fire with the very same wood the angry yogin can bind with
vajra-bonds when he offers metal filings.
Lighting the fire with the self-same wood as he concentrates his thought,
with wrath he causes death that moment as he offers peppercorns.

Or again:

Lighting the fire with acrid wood, the sage of wrathful mien offers the fruit
and flowers of the tamarind tree for such is the best way of subduing.
Well composed he lights the fire with the very same wood and with wrathful
mien he offers the "fruit of desire" (a kind of mango) and so gains any
form he pleases.
Lighting the fire with the very same wood, he offers clusters of flowers of the
"invisible plant" and becomes invisible at will.
With thought well composed he lights the fire with the self-same wood,
and offering there flowers of the "sky-creeper" plant, he is able to fly
in the sky.[199]

Generally it may be said that *homa* rites represent an important "additional practice" in all dealings with higher and lower divinities. There is frequent reference to them in the tantras because they serve as a support for the gaining of those powers, whether mundane or supramundane, which the consecration ceremony bestows, as it were, in anticipation. Thus they may be performed by the side of a maṇḍala, in fact the eastern side, as an extra special offering to the divinities of the maṇḍala, who have first been "coerced" into it in the manner described above. They may be offered to other divinities for special purposes who have likewise been brought first into the presence of the practitioner by the same powers of coercion. Some of the items mentioned in the above quotation suggests an element of sympathetic magic in that briars are offered for coercing, metal filings for binding foes, a fruit known as *kāma* (also meaning "desire" in Sanskrit) for gaining the power to assume various forms according to one's

199 From the STTS, ch. 9, Yamada's ed., pp. 240-2, omitting the spells, TT vol. 4, pp. 248-5-2 ff.

desire, and a plant named *adṛśya* (unidentified, but with a name which also means "invisible" in Sanskrit) for gaining the power to become invisible. In this respect, as throughout tantric teachings, we have the strange mixture of popular superstition and higher religious striving. In any case their effectiveness does not depend on the rite itself, and thus any apparent element of sympathetic magic is altogether transcended in Buddhist usage. They are only effective in so far as the one who performs this rite has first achieved a state of self-identification with the higher divinity whose consecration he has received. As a neophyte he will have received the appropriate consecration through the administrations of his religious teacher. As a confirmed practitioner himself, and better still one who cannot go into retrogression (*avaivartika*), having received the Master Consecration (*ācārya-abhiṣeka*) in the maṇḍala of the Vajra Sphere in accordance with Yoga Tantra theory, he can, as it were, summon his chosen divinity into himself any time by a process of self-consecration.

f. *The Process of Self-Consecration*

It is precisely this unshakable or adamantine (*vajra*) element present in the Yoga Tantras which separate their consecrations from those performed in accordance with otherwise similar rituals described in Action and Performance Tantras. Thus only with the Yoga Tantras and consequently with the Supreme Yoga Tantras do we reach a form of Buddhist practice that may be called Vajrayāna as distinct in some way from Mahāyāna. This distinction is clearly shown by the need to reinterpret the enlightenment of Śākyamuni Buddha as realized under the sacred pipul tree at Bodhgayā (see section III.1), thus subtly altering an account which had proved totally adequate for the followers of the early schools, referred to generally now as Hīnayāna, and of the Mahāyāna. This includes the practitioners of the so-called Action and Performance Tantras, which, as has been shown above, are best understood as part of conventional Mahāyāna practice.

The fundamental tantra of the Yoga Tantra class, namely the "Symposium of Truth," after the opening praises proceeds to describe the process of self-consecration into the newly conceived adamantine state which the Bodhisattva Siddhārtha (the future Śākyamuni Buddha), who is here referred to with the variant name of Sarvārthasiddhi, needs to receive in order to attain this further state of enlightenment (*abhisambodhi*).

> The Lord the Great Thought of Enlightenment known as the Great Bodhisattva Samantabhadra (All Good) resides in the hearts of All Tathāgatas. Then this Buddha-Field (viz., our world) became filled with all the Tathāgatas the size of sesame seeds. They all came together as an assembly and approached that great being, the Bodhisattva Sarvārthasiddhi, as he sat on the seat of enlightenment. Going up to him, they displayed their glorious forms (*sambhogakāya*) and said: "O son of good family, how will you realize the highest enlightenment, you who undergo such privations in your ignorance of the Truth of All Tathāgatas?"

Then the great being, the Bodhisattva Sarvārthasiddhi, thus urged by all the Tathāgatas, arose from his state of immobile[200] concentration and making a salutation to all the Tathāgatas, spoke thus: "O Lord Tathāgatas, teach me how I should gain access to such truth." Then all the Tathāgatas said with one voice to the Bodhisattva: "Proceed with this mantra, reciting it as much as you please, which clarifies and composes one's thought and which is spontaneously effective: OṂ CITTAṂ PRATIVEDHAṂ KAROMI (OṂ I penetrate thought)!"

Then the Bodhisattva said to all the Tathāgatas: "I see, as it were, a lunar disk revealed in my own heart." All the Tathāgatas replied: "That, O son of good family, is Thought which is naturally radiant (*prabhāsvara*).[201] As one works upon it, thus it becomes, just like stains (disappearing) on a white garment." Then in order to develop his knowledge of Thought which is naturally radiant, they got him to raise the Thought of Enlightenment with this mantra which is spontaneously effective: OṂ BODHICITTAM UTPĀDAYĀMI (OṂ I raise the Thought of Enlightenment)!

Then the Bodhisattva, having raised the Thought of Enlightenment with the sanction of All Tathāgatas, said: "That appearance of a lunar disk, I see it really as a lunar disk." All the Tathāgatas said: "The heart of All Tathāgatas, that Rising of Thought known as Samantabhadra has become manifest. Proceed with it well! Now in order to stabilize that Rising of Thought known as Samantabhadra of All Tathāgatas, concentrate on the form of a vajra on the lunar disk in your heart, as you recite this mantra: OṂ TIṢṬHA VAJRA (OṂ Vajra stay)!"

The Bodhisattva said: "Lord Tathāgatas, I see a vajra on the lunar disk." All the Tathāgatas said: "Stabilize this Thought-Vajra of All Tathāgatas, known as Samantabhadra, with this mantra: OṂ VAJRĀTMAKO 'HAṂ (OṂ I am Vajra itself)!"

Then the Vajra-elements of the Body, Speech and Mind of All Tathāgatas, as many as there are throughout the whole of space, entered that Being-Vajra with the consecration of All Tathāgatas, and that Lord Sarvārthasiddhi, the great Bodhisattva, was consecrated by All Tathāgatas with the vajra-name consecration, naming him Vajradhātu (Vajra-Sphere).

Then Vajradhātu, the great Bodhisattva, said to all the Tathāgatas: "I see myself, O Lord Tathāgatas, as the Body of All Tathāgatas." All the Tathāgatas said: "O Great Being, envisage yourself as the Vajra of Being, that Buddha-Form that comprises all excellent manifestations, reciting this mantra which is naturally successful: OṂ YATHĀ SARVATATHĀGATĀS TATHĀHAṂ (OṂ I am as All Tathāgatas are)!"

As he said this, the great Bodhisattva Vajradhātu, knowing himself to be a Tathāgata, made salutation to all the Tathāgatas and said: "Empower me, Lord Tathāgatas, and stabilize this state of enlightenment." When he said

200 "Immobile" translates Tibetan *mi-g-yo-ba*; the Sanskrit has *āspharaṇa*, normally translated by the Tibetans as "space-prevading" (*mkha'-khyab-pa*). See also p. 303 below.

201 Up to this point the present passage is also quoted by Indrabhūti in his *Jñānasiddhi* (B. Bhattacharyya, *Two Vajrayāna Works*, p. 81, ll. 18ff. However there he dilates a little on the term *prabhāsvara*, meaning radiant or luminous, which comes much into favor in tantric Buddhism. The Tibetans render it by *'od-gsal*, literally translated as "clear light" but here, as was often the case, they were coining a new word for a Sanskrit Buddhist term for which they possessed no equivalent.

that, All Tathāgatas entered the Being-Vajra of the Tathāgata Vajradhātu, and at that very moment the Lord Vajradhātu became fully enlightened in the wisdom of the sameness of All Tathāgatas; he entered upon the secret pledge of the symbol of the wisdom of sameness of All Tathāgatas; he entered upon the secret pledge of the symbol of the wisdom of sameness of the vajra-gem consecration of All Tathāgatas; his self-nature was purified in his understanding of the wisdom of the sameness of the Dharma of All Tathāgatas; he became the source of the wisdom of that spontaneous brilliance which is the sameness of All Tathāgatas; so he was transformed into a Tathāgata, an Arhat, a perfectly enlightened Buddha.

Then all the Tathāgatas emerged once more from that Being-Vajra, and having been consecrated with the great gem-consecration of Ākāśagarbha, and having manifested the Dharma-wisdom of Avalokiteśvara, and having been established in the Universal Activity of All Tathāgatas, they went to the summit of Mount Meru where there is a palace of gems with tiered roof, and having reached there they empowered the Tathāgata Vajradhātu as the totality of All Tathāgatas and they placed him on the lion-throne of All Tathāgatas and he faced in every direction.

Then the Tathāgata Akṣobhya, the Tathāgata Ratnasambhava, the Tathāgata Lokeśvararāja and the Tathāgata Amoghasiddhi, having received themselves empowerment in the totality of All Tathāgatas, in order to express the universal sameness of the Lord the Tathāgata Śākyamuni with regard to the sameness of all directions, took their places in the four quarters.[202]

As has been shown above, this set of Five Buddhas is fundamental to the maṇḍala of the Vajra-sphere (*vajradhātumaṇḍala*), and now the above quotation makes clear that the whole manifestation is comprised by Śākyamuni Buddha, who has been consecrated as Vajradhātu. While he is of the essence of All Tathāgatas, he is also essentially Vajra-Being (*Vajrasattva*), and thus Vajrapāṇi's Vajra Family, relegated as the lowest of three in Action and Performance tantras, has come to pervade all others as the one essential "family." Reading on in this particular tantra, one notes that Vajrapāṇi himself emerges as an expression of Samantabhadra, named above as the Lord Bodhisattva of the Thought of Enlightenment. It may be worth noting in this respect that when all the Tathāgatas emerge once more from the Vajra of Being (Vajradhātu *alias* Śākyamuni), they receive the gem-consecration of Ākāśagarbha (the presiding Bodhisattva of the Gem Family), they are proficient in the Dharma-wisdom of Avalokiteśvara (the presiding Bodhisattva of the Dharma/Lotus Family) and they are intent on the universal activity of Viśvakarma ("Universal Action," the presiding Bodhisattva of the Karma or Action Family). Logically no mention is made in this context of the Vajra Family, because all these emerging Tathāgatas are already vajra-beings.[203] Thus it may be fairly stated that with the appearance

[202] STTS, Yamada's Sanskrit ed., pp. 7-10; TT vol. 4, pp. 219-4-2ff.

[203] The presiding Bodhisattva of the Vajra Family is in fact Samantabhadra, whence emerges Vajrapāṇi. From Ākāśagarbha emerges Vajragarbha/*alias* Vajraratna (Gem Family); from Avalokiteśvara emerges Vajranetra/Vajradharma (Lotus Family); from Viśvakarma energes Vajrakarma/Vajraviśva (Karma Family). For these various equations see my introduction to the STTS, pp. 26-8.

of the Yoga Tantras we have an effective Vajrayāna. Because of the presence of this "adamantine element" the consecrations received in the Vajradhātu and related maṇḍalas have a different character (whether real or supposed it is not for an outsider to assert) from the very similar consecrations bestowed in the maṇḍalas of Action and Performance Tantras. In these a pupil progresses to mastership in due course, receiving a "master's consecration," but this remains within the conventional Mahāyāna context, and thus is to be distinguished from the *(vajra-)ācārya-abhiṣeka* (Master Consecration) of the Yoga Tantras.

14. FURTHER CONSECRATIONS

a. *Interpretations of the Higher Consecrations, Scholastic, Lyrical and Ritual*

We have already observed that the whole series of consecrations as given in the first three classes of tantras (Action, Performance and Yoga) and there regarded as complete, come to be regarded in tantras of the Supreme Yoga class as representing in combination merely the first of a higher set of further consecrations, and to this primary set a further three are added, thus making a separate set of four. There are variations of a comparatively minor kind in the primary set as formulated by followers of Supreme Yoga tantras, the number of items usually amounting to six or seven. The short work by Advayavajra on the subject, which was quoted above, lists six such primary consecrations, namely: water, crown, vajra, bell (also referred to there as "royal"), name and master.[204] Regarding them all as essentially one consecration, whether known as that of the jar, or the master or the *vidyā*, he goes on to define the three higher consecrations, known as the Secret, the Knowledge of Wisdom and finally the Fourth. His description of these three further consecrations is certainly recondite, and for this very reason it may serve as a suitable introduction to this particular section. The whole matter should become clearer as we proceed:

> The Secret Consecration is the bestowal of the Thought of Enlightenment, which is produced simultaneously on both sides and it is for the purpose of making Wisdom (*prajña*) a ground for faith (*śraddhā*) and for protecting the pledge (*samaya*). One bestows it from the secret places of Wisdom and Means (*upāya*) and so it is defined as secret.[205]
>
> There are two definitions for Knowledge of Wisdom. Knowledge (arises) by Wisdom, and Wisdom is the external knowledge. The intellect (*buddhi*) contains (within itself) the (various) aspects of subject and object; (and at the same time) Wisdom is identifed as woman with the nature of the four elements (earth, water, fire and air), the five aggregates of personality, form etc. and

[204] An admirable article by Per Kværne, "On the Concept of Sahaja in Indian Buddhist Tantric Literature," deals with most of the topics covered in this particular section, with which it may be helpfully read in conjunction. Thus on his p. 93 there is a diagram showing the realationship between the six or seven consecrations of the primary set.

[205] "One bestows" following the Tibetan version, which represents Sanskrit *dāpayate*; Bhattacharyya's edition reads *dīpayate*, "one causes it to shine forth." Either is possible.

the six spheres of sense. It is the knowledge of her (Wisdom's) Thought of Enlightenment, and it is in her that these characteristics have arisen. Such is the first definition. She too is that state of consciousness which is void of the dual aspects of subject and object. This is the other definition.

According to some the meaning of the Fourth (Consecration) is the final objective (*sādhyaṃ*) involving the seven constituents of enlightenment as characterized by the Knowledge of Wisdom. Others say that the Fourth resembles the clear sky of autumn (as deriving from) the Knowledge of Wisdom. Yet others explain the Fourth as the pure state of self-existence (*svabhāva*) conveying that absence of duality where the Knowledge of Wisdom in its natural state is united with its evolved state as produced from the natural state. Other views are not stated through anxiety of writing too much.[206]

We have already met Wisdom (*prajñā*) with the two applications to which Advayavajra here refers. As the Perfection of Wisdom, it (or she) is the absolute, whether defined as the Void (*śūnyatā*) according to Madhyamaka teachings, or as Pure Consciousness, where there is no duality of subject and object, as taught by the Mind Only school. At the same time in accordance with this later tantric terminology she is the feminine counterpart of Means (*upāya*), for without the Means, Wisdom remains unattainable. The Means as we have seen is the form of the practitioner's chosen divinity with whom he must identify himself in the embrace of Wisdom. Depending upon the context, the absolute, neither male nor female, may be referred to as though it were one or another, e.g., as the Perfection of Wisdom, who is certainly feminine, or as one of the several male titles for the absolute such as Vajrasattva, Great Vairocana etc. Envisaged from the male side, Wisdom can be seen as representing the evolving universe, and thus she is described above as having the nature of the four elements, of the aggregates of personality and of the spheres of sense. One may observe in passing that this interpretation of her corresponds with that of the *śakti* in Hindu tantric terminology, for in these Supreme Yoga tantras, as we have already seen, Hindu and Buddhist notions are often intermingled.

Through the union of Wisdom and Means there comes the Thought of Enlightenment (*bodhicitta*), "produced simultaneously on both sides," as defined above, and this is identified ritually with the drop of semen (*bindu*) at the tip of the vajra (the male organ) as it rests in the lotus (the female organ). It is with this "drop" taken "from the secret places of Wisdom and Means" that the master consecrates his pupil in the Secret Consecration by placing it on the tip of his tongue. Thus consecrated, the pupil may proceed to the next consecration, the Knowledge of Wisdom,[207] when he knows Wisdom herself by being united with her. He experiences in her embrace external experience (the external world as defined by the four elements etc. above), which through the ecstatic union

206 Translated from *Advayavajrasaṃgraha*, p. 38, ll. 24ff. The present extract is the direct continuation of the earlier passage translated in III.13.d.

207 While keeping to this translation for *prajñā-jñāna* because it seems to be the most suitable in the context of these consecrations, I remain aware of other translations sometimes employed for these elusive terms.

becomes reabsorbed into the natural nondual state of absolute nonduality, as defined in Mahāyāna philosophical concepts. In our above quotation the term used for "natural state" is *prakṛti-rūpa* as distinct from the evolved state (*vikāra-rūpa*) of absolute being, and this particular terminology belongs rather to non-Buddhist, viz., Sānkhya philosophical theory, but it may fairly be regarded as now belonging to a common Indian cultural heritage. Perhaps one may point out at this stage that the same term in Sanskrit, just as in English, may carry interpretations that appear to be opposites, depending upon the viewpoint of the user. Thus what is defined as "real" in everyday terms may at the same time be described as "unreal" in absolute terms when its transient and contingent nature is taken into account. Likewise the term *prakṛti* may refer to the absolute in its natural quiescent state or it may refer to the natural condition of things in the everyday world.

The Fourth Consecration, a consecration in the sense that it is induced by one's master, is precisely this transcendent state, which resembles the clear sky of the Indian autumn in its utter vacuity after the last of the monsoon rainclouds have finally passed. The relationship between the Third and Fourth Consecrations is expressed in terms of grades of joy, known as Joy, Perfect Joy, the Joy of Cessation and the Natural or Innate Joy. This fourth joy comes about in the Fourth Consecration with which it is effectively identical, and the term used for it—yet one more term for this nonconceptual absolute state— is *sahaja*, meaning inborn, natural, innate.[208]

> The first joy is of this world; the second is of this world; the third joy is of this world, but the Innate exists not in these three.
>
> Neither passion nor absence of passion is found there, nor yet a middle

[208] The meaning of this word in the present context has been well defined by S. B. Dasgupta in *Obscure Religious Cults*, pp. 77ff. He translates it regularly as "Innate," as do M. Shahidullah, G. Tucci and others including myself. More recently Herbert Guenther with his well known zeal for coining new terms has argued for a translation as "co-emergence," followed by Per Kværne (*op. cit.*, pp. 88-9), who prefers "simultaneously-arisen." Both these rather cumbersome circumlocutions are based upon the Tibetan term (*lhan-cig skyes-pa*) which is a literal translation of the Sanskrit *saha-ja*; when broken into its two parts thus, it means "born together with," hence the accepted meaning of inborn, natural, innate etc. It can be a fallacy to base translations of Buddhist Sanskrit terms on the Tibetan equivalents, which often had to be invented with great ingenuity, simply because suitable terms did not already exist in their language. Should we abandon the term "absolute" in translations of Buddhist works because the Tibetans rendered Sanskrit *paramārtha* (supreme reality) as *don-dam-pa* and invent a more literal rendering? Should we renounce the use of the term "relative truth" because the Tibetans devised the term *kun-rdzob* (literally: altogether false) for the Sanskrit *saṃvṛti* (literally: concealment)? Such a proceeding leads to absurdity when the Indian term *Arhat* (literally: worthy) as used of a perfected Buddhist saint of the older schools, appears in English translation as "foe-destroyer" (*taceat*, my friend Jeffrey Hopkins), because the Tibetans chanced to interpret it incorrectly by breaking the Sanskrit into two parts as supposedly derived from *ari-hat* (striker of foes), when they were devising a suitable technical translation. The Tibetan achievement in building up an entirely new vocabulary for their translations from the Buddhist Sanskrit is altogether remarkable, but we seldom find suitable English terms for those same Sanskrit ones by retranslating their skillful inventions. In the present case to translate *sahaja* as coemergence or simultaneously-arisen is rather like taking the English word "inborn" and insisting on interpreting it as in-born and then using such a circumlocution as "born interiorly." It is made quite clear in our texts that the "Innate" is not "born together with" anything; it is totally free in its realization.

state. Because of its freedom from all three the Innate is called perfect enlightenment. The essence of all things and yet free of all things, one may mark it at the beginning of (the Joy of) Cessation, but from those other three joys it is free.[209]

And again:

From Joy there is some bliss, from Perfect Joy yet more; from the Joy of Cessation comes a passionless state, and finally the Joy Innate!

The first comes by desire for contact, the second by desire for bliss, the third from the passing of passion, and by that the Fourth is realized. Perfect Joy may be called saṃsāra, and nirvāṇa the Joy of Cessation, with plain Joy as a middle state. But the Innate is free of all three, for there is found neither passion nor absence of passion, nor yet a middle state.

In the realization of the perfect truth there is no Wisdom and no Means. By no other is the Innate told and from no one may it be received. It is born of its own accord by merit and by due attendance on one's guru.[210]

If exegetical works tend to be reticent on the subject of the Fourth Consecration, this is understandably so when treating of a mystical state that transcends all rationalizing philosophical concepts. Its praises can only be sung by those yogins who have experienced it using the allusive language of which the tantras are so full.[211] If one holds to the view that this ultimate state, whether achieved by tantric means or by the Bodhisattva's practice of the great perfections, remains one and the same, then all the categories of the latter must apply to the realization of the Fourth Consecration. Thus Advayavajra says that it involves the seven constituents of enlightenment, namely mindfulness, discernment with regard to Buddhist teachings, heroism, contentment, serenity, mental concentration and equanimity.[212]

The *Hevajra Tantra* is largely concerned with these four consecrations and their interior realization, which we shall consider below, but the references tend to be scattered through various chapters, thus obscuring much of the procedure. However, in the very last chapter they are listed in the highly abbreviated form of the words of authorization pronounced by the teacher on each of the four occasions:

Then the Adamantine One spoke regarding the four consecrations:

(1) "O you who are already consubstantiated with the Vajra, take up the mighty vajra and the mighty bell and perform today for your pupil the beneficent act of a Vajra-Master."

(2) "Just as Bodhisattvas are consecrated by Buddhas, so in this Secret Consecration you are consecrated by me with the flow of 'Thought' (viz., the

209 H.T., I.x.15, 17-18.

210 *Ibid.*, I.viii.32-6.

211 See also Per Kværne, *An Anthology of Buddhist Tantric Songs*, e.g., nos. 3, 4, 13, 27, 29, 30. For a helpful discussion of the nature of this supreme state, see his article, n. 204 above, pp. 124ff.

212 Concerning these seven constituents of enlightenment (*bodhyaṅga*), see Har Dayal, *The Bodhisattva Doctrine*, pp. 149-55.

Thought of Enlightenment, *bodhicitta*, in its actual and ritualized sense)."

(3) "O thou great being, take, take to yourself this beautiful and delightful goddess, who bestows bliss, who bestows achievement (*siddhi*), and having taken her, pay her full honor."

(4) "Such knowledge is Great Bliss, the Vajra Sphere, immaculate like space, tranquil and salvation-giving. You are your own progenitor."[213]

Such in brief are the four consecrations. When one embarks upon a more detailed description, one becomes immediately aware of what may be regarded as conflicting interpretations in the canonical sources, but what must fairly be regarded of differing traditions as followed by different masters. Buddhists were never disposed to accept a central regulating authority for their beliefs and practices. For this very reason the teachings of Śākyamuni were from the start represented by so many different schools of thought, developing gradually into the rich variety of doctrine as described in previous chapters. Even greater freedom in interpretation of received teachings and in experimenting with techniques of yoga was taken for granted by the followers of the tantras, and one should thus be surprised at the amount of uniformity that was achieved rather than perturbed by conflicting interpretations.

b. *Scholastic Equations in Sets of Four*

At the same time some apparent problems may be caused to us modern interpreters by the interest taken by Indian exegetes in set patterns and lists, so that they bring sets of terms into parallel relationships, especially their favorite sets of four. Thus we are dealing with not only four consecrations and four grades of joy, but four moments, corresponding with the experiencing of the four grades of joy, and four *mudrā* (symbols), all of which have to be brought into some satisfactory mutual relationship. Such equations, which are partly forced in order to produce the desired patterns, are often made without reference to what seems to occur in the actual consecrations as described elsewhere.[214] Thus many of the interpretations are symbolic of the overall unity that is the final objective and so may not be of great assistance as an explanation of a particular passage. This overall preoccupation with sets of four is freely stated in the very first chapter of the *Hevajra Tantra* and it needs to be taken into account whenever these terms occur arranged in similar patterns in the commentaries. The object of all tantric practice, one may well add of all Buddhist practice, is the total reintegration of scattered personality in the pristine state of self-realizing wisdom. Thus the whole process, whatever appears to occur outwardly, takes

213 H.T., II.xii.1-4. See below III.14.c for the full context of these verses.

214 An example of this is provided by Kāṇha's commentary on the four consecrations as translated by me in H.T., vol. I, pp. 131-3 and again by Per Kværne, *art. cit.* n. 204, pp. 122-3. As he observes, "beyond doubt this passage raises as many questions as it answers." These questions relate to the manner in which the various sets of items are correlated, and this particular explanation is further complicated by relating the three higher consecrations with pupils whose faculties are weak, medium or strong, so that they might appear as alternatives. This is scarcely intended, and one may assume that the same pupil's faculties are strengthened as he proceeds. Concerning the correlations of the *mudrā* in this passage, see immediately below.

place within the practitioner's personality as expressed by his actual human body. While the body may be no more real than any other external phenomena, it provides the yogin with the only available means in order to attain his goal. All other means, mantras, maṇḍalas, "symbols" (*mudrā*) of various kinds, as well as philosophical teachings as propounded by different schools, the various kinds of tantric texts etc., all are subservient to the practice of yoga as performed with one's own body as the final means. Thus as we are told, "everything goes in fours," and all these sets of four are arranged symbolically within the yogin's body, corresponding with the four vital nerve-centers (known as *cakra* or "wheels" in Sanskrit), between navel and genitals, at the heart, the throat and the head. The symbolic nature of the whole arrangement is well illustrated by the use made of the Sanskrit words *evaṃ mayā*, which in this particular context are left untranslated by Tibetan translators for reasons which will be apparent. These are the opening words of all sūtras and tantras, followed by the third word *śrutaṃ*, and together the three mean "thus by me ('twas) heard," indicating originally that the canonical work about to be recited was indeed heard from the mouth of the Buddha. However, *śrutaṃ* means not only heard, but also learned and understood. Hence the four syllables E-VAṂ MA-YĀ symbolize the whole truth of that tantra and by implication of all tantras and the whole Buddhist doctrine. Thus they too may be incorporated within the yogin's body. In a different context where the polarity of Wisdom and Means, of female aspect and male aspect, of the lower part of the body and the head, are under consideration, then EVAM alone can express the final truth of unity and so the three words *evaṃ mayā śrutaṃ* are interpreted as "I have understood E (Wisdom) and VAṂ (Means) as a unity." Thus, speaking of himself, Hevajra can say: "I dwell in that Paradise of Bliss in the *bhaga* of the Vajra-Maiden in the casket of Buddha-gems with the form of the letter E" (see below III.15.c). This comparatively simple example illustrates the deliberately affected nature of such equations and the way in which they can be differently applied depending upon the context. Since we are now dealing with fourfold sets, it may be useful to reproduce the various sets listed in the *Hevajra Tantra* (I.i.22-30), adding the other sets which are given later in the same work and a few from elsewhere.

Navel	*Heart*	*Throat*	*Head*	
E	VAṂ	MA	YĀ	
Locanā	Māmakī	Pāṇḍaravāsinī	Tārā	4 goddesses
nirmāṇa	dharma	saṃbhoga	great bliss	4 nerve centers
64-petalled	8-petalled	16-petalled	32-petalled	4 lotus flowers
variety	development	consummation	blank	4 moments
worship	adoration	coercion	achievement	4 requisites
sorrow	its origin	and cessation	the way	4 truths
self	mantra	divinity	knowledge	4 realities (*tattva*)
joy	perfect joy	joy of cessation	joy innate	4 joys
Sthavira	Sarvāstivāda	Sammitīya	Mahāsaṅghika	4 schools

To these we may add:

master	secret	knowledge of wisdom	fourth	4 consecrations
smile	gaze	embrace	union	4 attitudes
Action	Performance	Yoga	Supreme Yoga	4 tantra classes
karma-mudrā	(samaya-mudrā)	(dharma-mudrā)	mahāmudrā	4 symbols

Later we shall meet with:

void	extreme void	great void	universal void	4 voids
light	manifestation of light	perception of light	radiance	
relative thought (*paratantra*)	imagined thought (*parikalpita*)	perfected thought (*parinișpanna*)	omniscience	
mind	mental states	nescience		
awake	dreaming	deep sleep	fourth (*turiya*)	

Before treating the set of four consecrations in detail we should give rather more general considerations to the various sets of four as here listed, distinguishing those which clearly have a prior claim to be considered as fourfold from those that have been reshaped to fit the overall fourfold scheme. We may also note that while some sets consist of graded items with the fourth item usually the supreme one, other sets are composed of four items of equal standing. One may well ask if there can be any logical relationship with sets of such different kind. Perhaps the first question concerns the reasons for this preoccupation with arranging so many items in these fourfold sets. We may note that many already existing patterns cannot be pressed into a fourfold scheme, such as Buddha-families, already recognized as either three, five and possibly six in number, or the five components of personality, or again the six senses and their corresponding spheres of sense, or the six or ten perfections of a Bodhisattva, and many other items. The basic Buddhist set of four items is clearly the set of Four Truths as attributed traditionally to Śākyamuni's early preaching:

> O monks, what are the four noble truths? They are sorrow, the origin of sorrow, the cessation of sorrow and the way leading to the cessation of sorrow.

In this set it is the third item that corresponds with nirvāṇa and thus we might have expected an appropriate rearrangement to have been made. In any case we note that sets of four are quite common in early Buddhism. For there are four recognized magical powers, four stations of mindfulness, four "pure abodes" (*vihāra*) and four kinds of right effort. More significant for present consideration are perhaps the four stages toward perfection:

entering the stream	a once-returner	a non-returner	an arhat
srota-āpanna	*sakṛdāgamin*	*anāgamin*	*arhat*

It is also interesting to note that the four "schools" or religious orders named are those under which all Buddhist monks were traditionally grouped,[215] and not the

215 Concerning these four main groups, Sthavira, Sarvāstivāda, Sammitīya and Mahāsaṅghika, one may refer to I-tsing, *A Record of the Buddhist Religion*, pp. xxiii-v and pp. 1-20. The *Hevajra*

four philosophical schools as later formulated, namely, Vaibhāṣika, Sautrāntika, Cittamātra and Madhyamaka.[216]

Another well-established fourfold set is the one based on the waking state, the dream state, deep sleep and an unnamed fourth, which is described as "incognizant internally, incognizant externally, incognizant both ways, not even cognition itself, not cognitive, not noncognitive, unseen, inexpressible, ungraspable, uncharacterized, inconceivable, unnamable, the single essence of self-realization where all diffuseness is resolved, tranquil, peaceful, free of duality, thus they consider the Fourth to be. It is the Self which should be recognized." In so far as Buddhist tantras display no inhibitions in even using the term Self (*ātman*) for the absolute, this passage might well come from them. Apart from the word Self it describes quite adequately the goal of final enlightenment as conceived by more traditionally minded Buddhists. It comes in fact from the *Māṇḍūkya Upaniṣad*, and apart from the appositeness of the actual wording, the use of the term Fourth for the otherwise unnamable final state is significant.[217] The tantric yogins have transferred the symbolism from the act of falling asleep to the sexual act.

All these sets of four so far considered belong to pre-Mahāyāna conceptions and in Mahāyāna doctrinal formulations no special interest seems to be given to fourfold patterns. Indeed all the other sets of four listed appear to be deliberate tantric Buddhist creations, developed either from Mahāyāna groupings that were not previously fourfold or from parallel Hindu tantric conceptions. Thus if one asks why Buddhist tantras have a predilection for fourfold arrangements, one might answer that they have been based either consciously or unconsciously on the earlier Buddhist fourfold schemes when the number was still felt to be especially significant. Alternatively they might have developed from the wish or the need to assert an even higher state of perfection than the one already formulated in traditional Mahāyāna teachings. This could well be so in the case of the Bodies of Buddhahood. I have already referred in section II.4.f to the way in which the earlier concept of two Buddha-bodies, in effect the human form in which he appears on earth (*nirmāṇakāya* = "transformation body") and the form in which he exists absolutely (*dharmakāya*), was extended to three or even occasionally four Buddha-bodies. However, when four are mentioned, two of them are different kinds of Glorious Body (*saṃbhogakāya* = "enjoyment body") and the Dharma-body, also referred to as the Self-Existent Body, remains supreme. In general it is clear that the generally accepted Mahāyāna conception

Tantra records *Saṃvidi*, but the Tibetan version confirms that Sammitīya (*kun-gyis bkur-ba*) is intended.

216 For a description of these one may refer to Geshe Lhundrup Sopa and Jeffrey Hopkins, *Practice and Theory of Tibetan Buddhism*, pp. 65ff.

217 One may refer to Radhakrishnan, *The Principal Upaniṣads*, pp. 695-705. These four stages, waking, dreaming, etc. are not listed in H.T., but see I.ix.19. Nāropa uses them in his commentary on the Kālacakra Tantra (*Sekoddeśaṭīka*, p. 27 top) in order to theorize on a set of sixteen Joys, produced by combining these four stages with Body, Speech, Mind and Wisdom (*jnāna*). Such are the invented complexities with which one meets in this exegetical literature.

remains a threefold one. In the tantras this is consciously increased to four with the so-called Self-Existent Body placed above the *dharmakāya*. It is also referred to as the Innate Body (*sahaja-kāya*) or as the Body of Great Bliss (*mahāsukha-kāya*) with reference to the experience of the Four Joys as realized through the fourfold consecration. The conception of this tantric fourth Body seems to be the special preserve of Supreme Yoga Tantras, although the way is prepared for it in Yoga Tantras, which often refer to the gaining of a Vajra-Body without however disrupting the accepted Mahāyāna theory of three Buddha-bodies.

As we see from the above table (p. 248) it is as Buddha-bodies that the four main nerve centers within the yogin's body are named, but they are not arranged in the normally ascending order in that the Dharma-Body is placed below the Glorious Body. Some reason for this, of doubtful value it seems, is given in the *Hevajra Tantra*, where the set of Buddha-bodies is significantly still referred to as three, although four are in fact named:

> The Three Bodies are said to be inside the body in the form of "wheels," and the perfect knowledge of them is called the "wheel" of Great Bliss.
> The Three Bodies, transformation, glorious and *dharma*, and the Body of Great Bliss too are situated at the perineum, the heart, the throat, the head.
> The Transformation Body (*nirmāṇa-kāya*) is at the place where the birth of all beings comes about; one is formed (*nirmīyate*) there, and so it is called *nirmāṇa-kāya*.
> *Dharma* is expressed as thought, so the Dharma-Body is at the heart.
> *Saṃbhoga* is said to be the enjoyment of the six kinds of flavor, and so the Enjoyment-Body is in the throat, while Great Bliss resides in the head.[218]

The presence of these four wheels or nerve-centers within the body, identified experimentally, could be another reason for the invention of so many other fourfold patterns to fit this fundamental one. However, the allocation is so arbitrary and displays so many variations that this can scarcely be the case. Firstly the lowest center is sometimes placed at the genitals and sometimes at the navel. According to Hindu tantric theory they are found at both places and the total number may be as many as seven: the top of the head, between the eye-brows, at the throat, the heart, the navel, the root of the penis and the peri-neum. When it suits a particular argument, locating the Five Buddhas within the body, or even all six, five or six wheels are specified.[219]

However, despite such variations, four nerve-centers may be regarded as normal in Buddhist tantras of the Supreme Yoga class. They are described as lotus flowers with differing numbers of petals and a Buddha-Goddess is allocated to each center. One may note that Hindu goddesses are likewise allocated to the seven nerve-centers of Hindu tradition together with the differentiated lotus flowers.[220] The controlling element in this Buddhist tantric arrangement would

218 H.T., II.iv.51-5. We may note at once a certain vagueness concerning the position of the lowest nerve-center: the navel, the genitals and here the perineum.

219 For examples see H.T. vol I, Introduction, p. 38.

220 See further on this S. B. Dasgupta, *An Introduction to Tantric Buddhism*, pp. 161ff.

seem to be the Four Buddha-bodies, fixed at four for the reasons suggested earlier, namely the prevalence of fourfold sets in earlier Buddhism and the impled claim to a higher state of achievement than could be gained by the more conventional Mahāyāna practice. A similar suggestion is implied by the placing of a final (fourth) grade above the three modes of existence postulated by the followers of the Mind Only school, namely the imagined one (*parikalpita*), the relative or conditioned one (*paratantra*) and the perfected one (*parinispanna*), where this third item is the equivalent of buddhahood (see II.4.c). As we shall see below (III.15.d) even the "perfected one" has to be transcended in omniscience.

The above discussion may explain why there are four consecrations, and since there are these four, why there should also be four joys and four moments, although as we shall see, these do not in practice correspond with the four consecrations. It is felt that there should also be four grades of *mudrā*, but when the *Hevajra Tantra* was compiled the only terms of this kind employed are *mudrā* and *mahāmudrā*. Later commentators introduce a *dharma-mudrā* and a *samaya-mudrā*, but there is so much disagreement on how this particular set of four should be arranged that its arbitrary nature is clearly revealed.[221] The "four requisites" and the "four realities" are consistent sets arranged to fit the fourfold scheme and require no special comment. The "four attitudes" go together with the Four Joys, as experienced in the course of the fourfold consecration. To this we may now return.

First a short passage on the general theory may be quoted:

The union of all Buddhas consists in the sound EVAṂ and by consecration the Great Bliss, the sound EVAṂ is known.
That beautifully shaped E adorned at its center with VAṂ is the abode of all delights, the casket of Buddha-gems.
It is there that the Four Joys arise distinguished by the Moments and from knowledge of the Moments there is blissful knowledge in EVAṂ.
So yogins know that this EVAṂ is attainable through Four Moments, Variety, Development, Consummation (known as "rubbing") and Blank (for it lacks all characteristics).
It is called Variety, because it involves different things, the embrace, the kiss and so forth.
Development is different from this for it is the experiencing of blissful knowledge.
Consummation is the reflection: "I have enjoyed this bliss."
Blank is quite other than these three, knowing neither passion nor absence of passion.
The first Joy is in Variety, Perfect Joy in Development, Joy of Cessation in Consummation and Innate Joy in Blank.
These four Joys should be experienced in due order in accordance with the fourfold consecration, Master, Secret, Wisdom, Fourth.

[221] A set of four *mudrā* is already referred to in the STTS; see below pp. 265-9.

The first is clarified by a smile, the Secret by a gaze, the Wisdom Consecration by an embrace, and the fourth by union.
This fourfold set of consecrations is for the purpose of perfecting living beings. The word consecration or sprinkling is used because one is sprinkled and cleansed.[222]

This short passage contains all the essential elements of the main rite, and we shall deal with it in more detail below, separating the fourfold series of consecrations. Commenting on the experiencing of the Four Joys in accordance with the fourfold consecration, Kāṇha relates them in pairs as they appear on the above table, simply because the main text is interpretable in this manner. In fact, as he makes quite clear in his following description of the consecrations, the master (*guru*) experiences the Four Joys in accordance with the Four Moments in the Secret Consecration, and after he has initiated his pupil, the pupil in turn experiences them in the Knowledge of Wisdom Consecration.[223] Thus the arrangement on the table is an artificial one. As for "clarification" by a smile, a gaze etc., the Sanskrit term means literally "purification" (*viśuddhi*), but in Buddhist tantric usage it comes to mean "to represent" or "symbolize." The meanings come together when it is said for instance that the Five Buddhas "purify" the Five Evils, but it can equally well be said that they "purify" the Five Wisdoms, which they effectively symbolize. Once again we note that this set of four, which relates closely to the Four Joys, is artificially arranged to correspond with the set of four consecrations, which is scarcely possible in practice. Even more artificially, it is paired by commentators with the four groupings of tantras (see p. 235, n. 190).

Taking the series of consecrations in due order, we deal first with the Master Consecration, otherwise called the Jar or the Vidyā (Knowledge) Consecration. As was noted above this corresponds in its general form to the whole series of consecrations, which makes up the main consecration ceremony in Action, Performance and Yoga Tantras, where the aim is the consubstantiation of the one consecrated with the chosen divinity. By this means he can not only be empowered as a powerful divinity, but even as we have seen as Vajrasattva himself (in Yoga Tantras), so that he is thereby preordained for buddhahood. Thus the full rite in the maṇḍala completes the intended process. In tantras of the Supreme Yoga class all this is but the first consecration, preparing the neophyte for the two further ones, the Secret and the Knowledge of Wisdom, the last resulting in the spontaneous realization of the Fourth Consecration, which like the final Buddhist goal according to the whole Mahāyāna tradition, is altogether beyond the descriptive power of words. In descriptions of the set of four consecrations, commentators usually deal with the first one in great detail, as can be seen from the short work of Advayavajra quoted above. Its form clearly varied in accordance with the tradition into which the neophyte was to be

222 H.T. II.iii.2, 4-12.

223 The relevant extract of Kānha's commentary has been translated by both Per Kværne and myself, see references in n. 204 above.

received. Thus in the case of the Hevajra tradition he would be initiated into the maṇḍala of Hevajra and the attendant goddesses, whose meaning would be explained to him by his teacher, acting the part of Hevajra, effected by means of self-consecration. Our tantra contains a short chapter on thus consubstantiating oneself with one's chosen divinity and this general process as described by some notable Tibetan scholars is already available in English translation.[224]

c. *The Higher Consecrations According to the Tradition of Hevajra*

As for a description of the whole consecration ceremony we can do no better than follow that given in a short work entitled "The Rite of Consecration" (*Abhiṣekavidhi*) written by one of the scholarly tantric yogins, named as Prajñāśrī.[225] Having no knowledge concerning any possible surviving Sanskrit version, I am translating it from the Tibetan version as available in the Tibetan Canon.[226] In its elaboration of the set of consecrations leading to the Master Consecration it helps to clarify the short work by Advayavajra already quoted above. It serves too as a useful commentary on the *Hevajra Tantra* II.xii likewise quoted above.

> The means of consecration are twofold, external and internal; externally there are eleven and they will be listed. The pupil should ask like this:
>
> Just as Vajrasattva has consecrated former conquerors,
> Do thou, well qualified, feel love for me and bestow the Vidyā consecrations!
>
> Then the master collects water from the Jar of Victory and the other jars, pouring it into a scoop made of shell. He directs his thought toward Akṣobhya, worships and praises him and then envisages him dissolved in light. Then from the three places (forehead, throat and heart) of Hevajra he envisages manifestations coming from lightrays and filling the sky, and the (eight) goddesses thus manifest hold a jewelled jar and they consecrate the pupil on the top of the head with a stream of *bodhicitta*. Thus he envisages it, as he takes the water in the scoop and bestows the Water Consecration, reciting the mantra: OṂ Vajra-Jar consecrate HUṂ! He envisages Akṣobhya on the pupil's head.
>
> Then with water from the general-purpose jar he sprinkles the crown made of gold or other material, and he meditates upon it as void. This void becomes the seed-syllable TRAṂ, yellow in color, and this turns into Ratnasambhava with three faces and six arms, and from him the crown reemerges. So he

224 See mKhas-grub-rje's *Fundamentals of the Buddhist Tantras*, ed. Lessing and Wayman, pp. 159ff., and Tsong-kha-pa as interpreted by Jeffrey Hopkins, *Yoga of Tibet*, pp. 103ff.

225 It is difficult to suggest a plausible personal indentification for a religious name quite as stereotyped as this.

226 T.T., vol. 57, pp. 19-2-3 to 26-2-2, the passage translated being from p. 24-3-7 onward. Unsatisfactory and illegible words have been checked against the Narthang version, Tenjur, *rGyud*, vol. 22 (*za*), fo. 49a, ll. 6ff. A similar work entitled *Hevajrasekaprakriyā* ("Procedure of Consecration in Hevajra") has been edited in the Sanskrit original with a French translation by Louis Finot in "Manuscrits sanskrits de *sādhana* retrouvés en Chine," *Journal Asiatique* (1934), pp. 1-85. This text has many omissions and in the absence of a Tibetan translation its usefulness is limited to the comparisons that it affords with the one here selected.

bestows the Crown Consecration reciting the mantra: OṂ I bestow the Crown Consecration! He envisages Ratnasambhava emerging from behind the right ear of the pupil.

Then he sprinkles the vajra with water of general purpose and meditates upon it as void. From this there emerges the seed-syllable JRIṂ, red in color, and this turns into Amitābha with three faces and six arms, and from him the vajra reemerges. Thus envisaging it, he says this verse:

Consecration with the vajra, the Vajra Consecration of all Buddhas,
Today you receive this consecration, so take this vajra for the purpose of the achievements of all Buddhas!

So saying he touches the pupil with it three times at the heart and then gives it into his right hand, thus consecrating him as he pronounces this mantra: OṂ I bestow the Vajra Consecration! He envisages Amitābha emerging from the back of the pupil's neck.

Then he sprinkles the bell with water of general purpose and meditates upon it as void. From this there emerges the seed-syllable KHAṂ, green in color, and this turns into Amoghasiddhi with three faces and six arms. Thus envisaging things, he recites this verse:

The nondual reality of Wisdom and Means possessing the nature of the Dharma-Sphere,
Take it with your left hand, embracing it, uniting with it,
Such is the reality of the Vajra-Holder!

So saying, he gives the bell into the pupil's left hand, thus consecrating him as he pronounces this mantra: OṂ I consecrate you with Vajra Sovereignty, thou foremost one! He envisages Amoghasiddhi emerging from behind the pupil's left ear.[227]

Then he sprinkles both the vajra and the bell with water of general purpose and meditates upon them as void. There emerges then the seed-syllable HŪṂ, white in color, and this turns into Vairocana with three faces and six arms. He envisages the vajra and bell as emerging from Vairocana and he holds them on the pupil's head as he intones this mantra: OṂ I consecrate you with this glorious name! So saying, he gives him the name of the family-divinity where the flower had fallen.[228] He envisages Vairocana emerging from the top of the pupil's head.

Then he sprinkles the vajra with water of general purpose and meditates upon it as void. Thence there emerges the seed-syllable HŪṂ, dark blue in color. He envisages this as transformed into a blazing vajra. Taking the vajra in his hand, the master recites this verse:

This (vajra) pertains to all Buddhas and it reposes in the hand of Vajrasattva.
You must always remain firmly holding to the vow of Vajrapāṇi!

227 The Tibetan text specifies the right ear, perhaps a copyist's error.

228 The flower has already been thrown as part of the previous rite of the maṇḍala: "Then from the wreath around the scarf which covers the pupil's eyes, he takes a flower and places it in the pupil's hand. Saying 'Receive, O Vajra, ho!' he throws it into the maṇḍala. Then the master takes it up and fixing it on the pupil's head, saying 'Take it, O mighty one!' etc. (pp. 24-2-7ff.).

Then the pupil should hold the vajra at its tip as the master intones this mantra: OṂ Abide in the vajra-pledge (*samaya*), which is the success of All Tathāgatas. It is I who hold you to it. SVĀHĀ HI HI HI HI HŪṂ! Then giving the vajra into his hand, he says: "That Being without beginning or end, Vajrasattva, great rejoicer, Samantabhadra (All Good), Universal Self, Vajragarbha (Vajra-Embryo),[229] Lord of lords!"

Then he sprinkles the bell with water of general purpose and meditates upon it as void. Thence there emerges the seed-syllable ĀḤ, which turns again into the bell. Giving it into the pupil's left hand, he recites this verse:

> This is the supreme reality, wisdom in the form of illusion,
> You should always cleave to it, this primeval enlightenment cleaved to by conquerors.
> It is the knowledge of the supreme vajra, indivisible in form like space.[230]

So saying, he gives it into the pupil's left hand.

Then holding the vajra at his heart and resting the bell against his side, he should meditate in all clarity on Vajrasattva (*Pl. 36*). Then he makes this request: "Granting me the consecration of the irreversible wheel, grant me the substance of the gods of the maṇḍala and the action of a guru, that I may always operate as a guru!" Then the master explains to him the substance of the maṇḍala, the substance of its divinities and the action of a master (guru). Having understood all this, the pupil envisages himself as not passing beyond the phenomenal world (saṃsāra). So this is the irreversible consecration.[231] Then placing the wheel in the pupil's hand, the master recites this verse:

> Turn the Wheel of the Doctrine in whichever way suits your converts,
> Thus benefiting living-beings throughout all the threefold world!

Thus giving into the pupil's hands a vajra, a gem, a lotus flower and a crossed vajra, he recites the above verse. Such is the Consecration of Authorization.

Then with his pupil placed before him, he should envisage a glistening drop, cleansed of impurity by the movement of breath, entering the pupil's right nostril and emerging again by the left one. Envisaging it before him, he makes the prophetic pronouncement. He conceives of himself as Śākyamuni, holding the edge of his religious garb with his left hand at the level of the heart and with his right hand making the all-sacrificing gesture,[232] as he pronounces these verses:

> I prophesy concerning you as the Tathāgata Vajrasattva.[233]

229 In his ed. of the *Hevajrasekaprakriyā*, L. Finot read *vajra*[*ṃ*] *Gavāṃpatoḥ patiḥ* for what must be *Vajragarbhaḥ patipatiḥ* (*op. cit.*, pp. 26 and 41). One may note that in his text this whole verse is wrongly applied to the bell instead of to the vajra. For the close relationship between Vajrasattva *alias* Vajrapāṇi, Samantabhadra and Vajragarbha, see STTS, *Facsimile Ed.*, p. 27.

230 This verse is a variant of the one in L. Finot's text, *op. cit.*, p. 26, where instead of "in the form of illusion" there is a phrase meaning "said to proceed from sound," thus clarifying the relationship between wisdom and the symbol of the bell.

231 With this account of the "irreversible consecration" one may contrast L. Finot's rather different version, *op. cit.*, pp. 43ff., noting that he has misread *avaivartika* (irreversible) for *avaivarṇika* (homogeneous). However this does not affect his translation of the following passage.

232 "All-sacrificing gesture" = Tib. *mchod-sbyin* (skr. *yāyajūka*; see *Mahāvyutpatti* 2847).

233 The opening line of the prophesy occurs in L. Finot's text, *op. cit.*, p. 27, l. 1 and p. 41

Draw forth those who have fallen into unhappy rebirths
thus effecting the salvation of living beings.
You shall be a perfect Tathāgata; you shall be the Sage of the threefold world.
With one voice the Buddhas, Bodhisattvas, the noble ones, prophesy
perfect enlightenment for you, O worthy one.
The fruit of the Great Symbol you shall attain.
Receive this spoken word!

Such is the Consecration of the Prophetic Announcement.

Next one gives the Consecration of Encouragement:

As disciples who enter the maṇḍala are cleansed of defilements at the sight of it,
So today there is no doubt that you are reborn in the family of the Buddhas.
By entering this secret maṇḍala where all defilement is gone,
Hereafter there is no death and rebirth in this Way (*yāna*) of Great Bliss.
Existence is the Perfect Achievement, where both existence and nirvāṇa
are rejected, for you have attained that nirvāṇa of no basis at all.

Such is the Consecration of Encouragement. "O thou who art already consubstantiated with the Vajra, take up the great vajra and the great bell, and perform today for your pupil the beneficent act of a Vajra-Master," so it is said in the *Hevajra Tantra* (see above pp. 246-7).

Afterwards he endows him with the pledge (*samaya*):

This vow of the achievement-pledge (*siddhi-samaya*) must always be observed by you.
You must never let go the Vajra, the Bell, the Symbol, the Thought of Enlightenment.
Have feelings of love toward those who would harm you and treat with respect your Vajra-brethren.
Do not despise simple believers and do not speak ill of your teacher.
Do not practice austerities and (self-inflicted) suffering, rejecting your own body.
Take happiness as happiness comes, for here is a future Buddha.[234]

Thus is he proclaimed and this is the pledge of the external consecrations.

Then clothes and food and drink of different kinds should be placed before the pupil. The clothes should be blessed to represent divine garments,[235] and the food and drink blessed as ambrosia. Desiring good fortune for his pupil, the guru should intone a hymn of blessing. Such are the external consecrations.

As for the internal consecrations, there are three of them, Secret, Knowledge

(translation) followed by the words *bhūr bhuvah svar* (= earth, mid-atmosphere and heaven) but the text is broken at this very point. However, their presence here confirms that they relate to the prophetic statement of the Bodhisattva's activity. See above, pp. 230-1 where Advayavajra includes them in his brief account.

234 For this verse see L. Finot, *op. cit.*, p. 27, ll. 3-4.

235 The divine garments are specified as *pañcālika* etc., the Sanskrit term being transliterated and not translated in Tibetan.

of Wisdom and the Fourth.

On the northern side of the main maṇḍala one prepares a maṇḍala, four-cornered and one fathom across, sprinkling it and dotting it with blood. In each of the four corners one sets an arrow covering it with cloth. On it one spreads a white blanket or a white cotton sheet, scattering flowers inside and outside (the circle). Then the pupil makes his request:

As great honor is bestowed upon Buddhas by the Vajra of Enlightenment,
O You, Celestial Vajra, bestow it today on me for the sake of Salvation.[236]
Great Hero, Vajra of Enlightenment, grant me the Secret Consecration.
Grant me the elixir of wisdom, grant me the emission of the vajra!

Then one places in the center of the maṇḍala the Wisdom-maiden, sixteen years old, who has all the marks of perfection, who has been bathed with water containing sandalwood extract, saffron and camphor, in immaculate garments and adorned with all kinds of jewelry. She is consecrated as Nairātmyā (the feminine partner of Hevajra). Her eyes and other organs of sense are consecrated as Īrṣyavajrā and the others,[237] her body, speech and mind are consecrated as Khecarī and the others,[238] her five limbs are consecrated to the Five Families, the Secret of Space is consecrated. Then envisaging the Family-Head (= Akṣobhya) as resting on his crown, the master honors her with worship, external, internal and secret, praising her with acclamations, and thus he should unite in her embrace. Then he should recite the *anurāga* (enamoring) mantra, and as soon as there is excitation he intones the refrain of HŪṂ; as bliss descends, he recites *pūja* (worship) mantra. Then with an elephant tusk he collects the *bodhicitta* from her pudenda and pouring it into a shell-receptacle, with a gesture of the ring-finger and the thumb, he drops it into the pupil's mouth. The pupil says: "O Bliss!" and drinks it without hesitation.

Just as Bodhisattvas are consecrated by Buddhas, so in this Secret
Consecration you are consecrated by me with the flow of "Thought,"

as is taught in the *Hevajra Tantra* (see above, pp. 246-7). Such is the Secret Consecration.

Then on the southern side of the main maṇḍala one prepares a maṇḍala for the Consecration of the Knowledge of Wisdom, four-cornered and one fathom across, anointing it with sandalwood and other perfumes. On it one places a white blanket or a white sheet, scattering flowers inside and outside. Consecrating the Wisdom-maiden, the worship and so on are as before. The pupil makes his request in this way:

You who abide in blissful wisdom, all hail to you O lord,
Possessing the nature of *āli* and *kāli*, rejoicing ocean of bliss, all hail![239]

236 For this verse see L. Finot, *op. cit.*, p. 30, ll. 7-8, and the *Guhyasamāja Tantra* in the extract quoted below (III.14.f).

237 These are the goddesses symbolizing the Five Evils, *īrṣyā* being "envy." See the *Hevajra Tantra*, vol. I, p. 129 for diagram, and the text, II.iv.16-19 of my edition.

238 These three are Khecarī (speech), Nairātmyā (mind) and Bhūcari (body). See the *Hevajra Tantra*, vol. I, pp. 128-9. "Secret of Space" (*mkha'-gsang*) = pudenda.

239 *Āli* (= *a* etc., viz., the vowels of the Sanskrit alphabet); *kāli* (= *ka* etc., viz., the consonants), reprsenting Wisdom and Means; see H.T. I.i.21.

All hail to you who disport yourself between Perfection and Cessation![240]
Grant me, O excellent lord, the Wisdom-Knowledge Consecration.

Then the master gives the right hand of the Wisdom-maiden into the left hand of his pupil, addressing him thus:

You must take her; the Buddhas declare her suitable in excellence.[241]
Experience the holy bliss by the stages of the three knowledges,[242]
For this is the place of the psychic nerve on the left-hand side of the
precious vessel of buddhahood.
This is the Sky-goers' Mouth (*kha-ga-mu-kha*).
This is the Queen of the Vajra-Sphere.
By no other means but this is enlightenment ever obtained.
Do not fail in cohabitation now and at all times.

Then the Wisdom-maiden speaks:

Boy! Can you eat my faeces and urine, blood and semen and human flesh?
Such is the vow with women. Can you suck the lotus of my pudenda?
Speak, boy, how is it?

He replies:

O goddess! How should I not? I can eat blood and semen and all.
I will always perform this vow with women, and your pudenda too I
shall suck.

Then she says:

My open lotus is the resort of all bliss, hurrah!
You who take possession of here, use the lotus as should be!

Then he kisses the lotus and unites in her embrace. As the *bodhicitta* descends, he should hold it as instructed, and the knowledge that he experiences is the Consecration of the Knowledge of Wisdom. Also quoting from the *Hevajra Tantra*: "O thou great being, take, take to yourself this beautiful and delightful goddess, who bestows bliss, who gives the resort, and having taken her, pay her full honor."[243]

Then on the western side of the main maṇḍala one should prepare the maṇḍala for the Fourth Consecration one fathom across, sprinkling it with sandalwood scent and so on and with *bodhicitta*. On it one places a white blanket and so on and then the Wisdom-maiden, who is consecrated, adorned and honored just as before. Then the pupil makes his request in this manner:

240 Viz., in the Joy Innate between Perfect Joy and the Joy of Cessation; how this comes about is explained in section III.14.d.

241 I have translated this line as it occurs in the Tibetan version, but we probably have here a variant, seemingly inferior, of the text as it occurs in the CMT, C. S. George's edition, p. 22, l. 28, translaton on p. 56, ll. 6-8. Other similarities with our present text may be noted on this page.

242 Concerning the three knowledges, see the extract from the *Pañcakrama* translated in section III.15.d. They correspond to the three modes of "thought" according to the Mind Only school, capped by "omniscience" as the fourth and last stage.

243 For this verse see above, p. 247. One may note that the word for "achievement" (*siddhi*) is replaced by "resort" (*sthāna*). This certainly goes back to some Sanskrit original, precisely the one used by the Tibetan translators. See the H.T. vol. II, p. 100 and Kāṇha's commentary on p. 159, where he explains the "resort" as the resort of *bodhicitta*.

Salutation to you, the inward self of the sensible world,
Salutation to you, inwardly gentle to sensible things
and inwardly released from the sensible world,
inward bestower of sensible things, salutation to you!
O excellent lord, grant to me, the excellent Fourth Consecration.

Then the master speaks thus:

You must slay living beings. You must speak lying words.
You must take what is not given. You must frequent others' wives.
If you do these things, no evil is done; great merit is yours.
If these things you can do, I will give the Fourth Consecration.

The pupil replies:

Great protector, by your gracious favor, I can.

Then he unites in the embrace, performs coition, and as the great bliss descends to the palace of knowledge, he reverses it upward to the level of noncognition, holding it there. This experiencing of noncognitive knowledge is the Fourth in terms of its (psychophysical) support. The Fourth in terms of no support is to be known from one's master's mouth.

Such knowledge is very subtle; it is the Vajra-sphere immaculate
like space, tranquil and salvation-giving. You are your own progenitor.

So it is said in the *Hevajra Tantra*. Such are the means of consecration.

A distinctive feature of this account is the deliberate separation of the Fourth Consecration from the preceding one, each taking place at one of the four sides of the main maṇḍala, the Master Consecration to the East, the Secret to the North, the Knowledge of Wisdom to the South and the Fourth to the West. There may be something artificial in this arrangement in accordance with the above discussed preoccupation with sets of four. Elsewhere it is clearly stated that the Fourth state arises spontaneously from the Third Consecration and thus as a consecration rite they are inseparable. It may be noted that the above description of the Fourth, despite a slightly changed terminology, adds nothing to what was said of the Knowledge of Wisdom.

As seems to be usual in such exegetical works the three final consecrations are treated in a rather less explicit manner than the whole set that makes up the first one. However, they are easily supplemented by extracts from the *Hevajra Tantra* itself, and here it is noteworthy that the whole performance is not described in a coherently consecutive manner. For these three the feminine partner, known as the *mudrā* (symbol) is required, assuming as we are for the present that the rite is actually performed. The yogin will already have received initiation into Hevajra's maṇḍala and so will be empowered to meditate upon Hevajra, absorbing him as it were into himself by the process of "self-consecration." Thus prepared he looks for a suitable girl between the age of twelve and twenty, who may be a relative or not or a girl of any class.

Keeping continually to his meditative practice, having achieved the power of
concentration and altogether self-collected, he should practice for

one month in secret while he still lacks a *mudrā*.
This reciter of mantras receives an order; he is ordered by yoginīs:
"Taking such and such a *mudrā*, O Vajra-Holder, serve the cause of beings!"
Taking this girl with her wide-open arms, endowed with youth and beauty, and who has come of age, he should prepare her with the Thought of Enlightenment (= according to Kāṇha, taking the threefold Buddhist "refuge" etc.).
Beginning with the ten rules of virtuous conduct, he should expound to her the Dharma, how the mind is fixed on the divine form, concerning the pledges (*samaya*, namely those of the maṇḍala) and in one-pointedness of mind.
Within one month she will be fit, of that there is no doubt.
So there is the girl freed of all false ideas and received as though she were a boon.
Else he may produce a *mudrā* by conjuring her forth by his own power from among the gods, the titans or men, or from local divinities (*yakṣa*) or celestial attendants (*kinnara*).
Then taking her one should perform the practice for the realization of one's own composure, for this practice which is alarming in appearance is not taught for the sake of enjoyment, but with intentness on one's own thought, whether the mind is steady or waving. (H.T. II.ii.16-22)

In the following chapter the actual consecrations are described in some brevity:

The sixteen year-old Wisdom (*prajñā*) he clasps within his arms and from the union of vajra and bell we understand the Master Consecration.
She is fair-featured and wide-eyed and endowed with youth and beauty.
With thumbs and fourth finger he lets (the drop) fall into the pupil's mouth.
The taste of universal sameness is thereby brought within the pupil's range.
(This is the Secret Consecration.)

Then having honored and worshipped the Wisdom, the master should consign her to the pupil saying: "O great one, take thou this *mudrā* who will bring you bliss," and knowing his pupil to be fully worthy and free of envy and anger, he further commands him: "Unite, O Vajra-Holder!"
(This is the Consecration of the Knowledge of Wisdom.)

When the pupil has achieved the state of Perfect Joy, that moment which is free from all notions of diversity, the master should say:
"O great one, this great bliss must be held to until enlightenment is won.
O Vajra-Holder, serve the cause of living-beings!"
So speaks the vajra-master as he sees his pupil overwhelmed in compassion.
"This is the great knowledge subsisting in all bodily form, dual in appearance and yet free of duality, the Lord whose nature is both being and non-being.
He abides pervading all things, moving and motionless, and he appears in illusive forms."
(This is the Fourth Consecration.)

(H.T. II.iii.13-17, 22-5)

The intervening verses (18-21) describe the pupil's part and how he begs for consecration:

> . . . how he pronounces words of praise and worship, when he beholds his master with the *mudrā*:
>
> O Lord of great tranquility, singly intent on this vajra-yoga,
> Thou perfector of the *mudrā*, now manifest in the indivisible vajra-yoga,
> As you now do for yourself, may you also do for me.
> Sunk as I am in the thick mud of saṃsāra, save me who am helpless."
>
> Then with pleasing food and drink, with liquor and meat of good quality, with incense, oblations and garlands, with bells and banners and lotions, with all these he should honor his lord.

d. *Consecration as a Psychophysical process*

These later consecrations involving the union of the teacher with the female partner, his consecrating of his pupil with the drop of semen that he exudes in this union, and then presiding over his pupil's union with the same partner, are manifestly of an entirely different kind from the earlier set of consecrations as described in section 13 above. Since they are now referred to as a set of four, there seems to have developed a separate tradition according to which the term Master Consecration, which should include all six or seven earlier consecrations, comes to be applied to the entirely separate acts of the teacher's union with the *mudrā* and the formal introduction of her, which he makes to the pupil by allowing him to touch her breast, referred to in this particular context as the "jar," thus justifying the alternative name of this first consecration as the Jar Consecration. Such at least is the tradition reported by Nāropa in his commentary on the *Kālacakra Tantra*.[244] Despite other complications of interpretation which it will inevitably involve, I quote from a passage in his work that lists all the consecrations and clearly distinguishes the overall set of eleven (according to his tradition) from the special set of four. It will be noticed that the Four Joys are here brought into parallel relationship with the four consecrations, although during the actual rite, both master and pupil must experience them in turn. The extract may also be of interest in that an attempt is made to relate the four consecrations with the gradual movement of the Thought of Enlightenment (*bodhicitta*, whether conceived in its absolute or relative form[245]) from the top of the head to the orifice of the penis, where it must remain stationary at the final moment of the Innate Joy. The description is all the more curious in that more nerve-centers, consisting of variously petalled lotuses, are introduced than might seem to be strictly logical, namely the basic four which as noted above are typical of most Buddhist tantras, but not of the *Kālacakra*.

[244] See M. E. Carelli's ed. of *Sekoddeśaṭīka*, p. 22, ll. 22ff. and Per Kværne, "The Concept of Sahaja," p. 96.

[245] See H.T. II.vi.30: "as relative, white as white jasmine, as absolute essentially blissful, it arises in the lotus-paradise, which is symbolized by the word EVAṂ."

Also in the Tantra known as Vajra-Cage of Ḍākinīs (*Ḍākinīvajrapañjara*)
the eleven consecrations are listed thus:
First the consecration with water, secondly with the crown,
thirdly with the stole, fourthly with the vajra and bell,
fifthly with self-lordship and sixthly with the name,
seventhly with sanction and eighthly with the jar,
ninthly with the secret consecration and tenthly with wisdom.
By applying the vajra of reality he should give all vajra-vows.
The teacher himself should proclaim this as the actual consecration-rite.
One's teacher must not be maligned and the word of the Blessed Ones never
transgressed.

These are the eleven consecrations, which are primary. As for the words "by applying the vajra of reality," meaning by the clear teaching of the Lord, the set of four consecrations and the set of eleven consecrations should be recognized as quite separate by those who are wise. So it is said. Here is the nomenclature in order for these four, (the consecration of) the Jar and the others, together with their associations, changing, unchanging, moving and motionless. Body etc. (viz., Speech, Mind, Wisdom) are easily understood. Then there are also the appellations, childlike, fully grown, mature and lord of creation (*prajāpati*).

As for the Wisdom-maiden (*prajñā*), she is from sixteen to twenty years old. By touching the breast of such a one who is worthy for this consecration and who delights one's mind there is said to be a flow of *bodhicitta*. The bliss that is experienced by this flow of shining nectar (*śukra-amṛta*) from the four-petalled lotus at the top of the head to the sixteen-petalled lotus in the forehead has the nature of Joy of Body, Joy of Speech, Joy of Mind, Joy of Wisdom (*jñāna*), and this is childlike. Since it is obtained in the First Consecration the yogin is consecrated (as it were) with a receptacle of milk, and thus it is called childlike.

Again by a slight up and down motion of the vajra in her pudenda there is said to be a flow of *bodhicitta*, namely from the thirty-two-petalled lotus in the throat to the eight-petalled lotus at the heart. The bliss that is experienced has the nature of the Perfect Joy of Body, Perfect Joy of Speech, Perfect Joy of Mind and Perfect Joy of Wisdom. Since it excels that which preceded it, it is known as fully grown. Such is the Secret Consecration.

Then by a strong up and down motion there is said to be palpitation (*spanda*), and this refers to the drop of shining fluid (*śukra*) as it advances from the sixty-four-petalled lotus at the navel to the thirty-two-petalled lotus in the secret parts. The exceedingly blissful state (produced) by the advance to the orifice of the vajra-gem of that pure flow of the moon-fluid (Literally: the foremost one of the fifteen parts),[246] referred to as "palpitation" (*spanda*), has the nature of the Joy of Cessation of Body, Speech, Mind and Wisdom. This is mature and such is the Consecration of the Knowledge of Wisdom.

As for the meaning of the Great Symbol (*mahāmudrā*), it is the non-

246 A frequent epithet of the moon, which from early times in India is identified with the male element. The edited Sanskrit text requires amendment from *pañcadaśa-kamala* to *-kalā*, viz., from "fifteen lotuses" to "fifteen parts."

> palpitation (*niḥspanda*) that is born of enamorment (*anurāga*) characterized as the external experiencing of the savors of the one who is celestial. Non-palpitation refers to the checking of the outward flow from the vajra-gem, and the bliss that results from the nonemission of the moon-fluid has the nature of the Innate Joy of Body, of Speech, of Mind, of Wisdom. So it is known as Great Wisdom and such is the Fourth Consecration. Then further it is to be explained. He who has attained to this supramundane wisdom that is free of all obscurations (*āvaraṇa*) is lord of creation, and that is because of the perfection achieved by his having the created nature (*prajābhāva*) of the Five Tathāgatas, the Five Buddha-Goddesses etc. as a transformation of the (five) aggregates of personality, the spheres of sense etc.[247]

To translate a passage such as this is very much a *tour de force*, but it serves to illustrate how the Four Joys, paralleled by four consecrations, may be interpreted as an internal psychophysical process. Externally the pattern of events is thus rather different, when a master in the art is actually initiating his pupil by means of the requisite consecrations. But can the internal process of the descent of the *bodhicitta* really be intended as an actual one? This question may well be asked doubtingly, when one notes that its descent from the forehead to the throat and again from the heart to the navel remains unaccounted for. The Tibetan version seems to be partly aware of this discrepancy, for in the case of the second consecration it refers incongruously to "the eight-petalled heart-lotus at the navel," thus covering both nerve-centers in one. The more normal set of four nerve-centers would solve the problem, but the *Kālacakra Tantra* appears to remain more closely attached to recognizable Hindu terminology than other tantras. One may note that the use of the term "lord of creation" (*prajāpati*) and the related term "created nature" (*prajābhāva*) might appear slightly awkward in a Buddhist context where all notion of a creating divinity and created beings is anathema, but such is inevitably the connotation of such terms from Vedic times onward, and only deliberate reinterpretation can make them suitable for Buddhist ways of thought. But we have already noted above that Supreme Yoga Tantras are not overconcerned with this problem.

The *Hevajra Tantra* is reasonably consistent in its application of fourfold patterns. The most noteworthy discrepancy concerns the ordering of the Four Joys, for in certain contexts (II.ii.40 and II.v.66, 70) the Innate Joy is said to come between Perfect Joy and the Joy of Cessation. I suggested long ago that this reordering conforms with the ritualistic embrace and a return to normal experience. Thus this arrangement could apply to their actual experience as distinct from their rather more artificial order in parallel with the four consecrations, where the Joy Innate is inevitably linked with the Fourth Consecration. We cannot expect complete consistency in matters of this kind, and dogmatic

[247] For the Sanskrit text, see M. E. Carelli, *Sekoddeśaṭīka*, p. 27, ll. 20ff.; for the Tibetan text see TT vol. 47, pp. 115-5-3ff. Compare a similar passage from the same work translated by Per Kværne, *op. cit.*, pp. 112-13.

assertions on such subjects are quite out of place.[248] Even greater hesitation affects the ordering of the set of four *mudrā*, once these were introduced. In this context the *Hevajra Tantra* uses only the terms *mudrā* in the sense of feminine partner and *mahāmudrā* (Great Symbol) as an expression for the absolute truth as realized through her. However, she is also referred to as *Mahāmudrā*, presumably with the result in mind, and she is also the *Avadhūti*, the central artery, of which we shall say more below. The two other *mudrā* which are introduced to make up an evolved set of four are the *samaya-mudrā* and the *jñāna-* or *dharma-mudrā*. We have already met these terms in discussing the manner in which the divinity is absorbed into oneself or into its right position in a maṇḍala, where *samaya* (pledge) refers to the external expression or "guarantee" of the divine presence, and this has to be fulfilled by the descent of "wisdom" (*jñāna*) from above. When brought into parallel relationship with the four consecrations and joys, the artificiality of any suggested arrangement would seem to be apparent. *Jñāna-* or *dharma-mudrā* can only refer to the same ultimate reality as does the term *mahāmudrā* already in use, but they are placed below it much as the *dharma-kāya* comes to be placed below the "Self-Existent" or the Innate Body in another set of four. They are thus explained as the truth that is realized as a result of the union with the *mudrā* (now referred to as *karma-mudrā*, "Action-Mudrā") either at the second or the third stage. The *samaya-mudrā* can logically only come last and then only in relationship with the "Joy of Cessation" when that too is placed last. It can then be explained as the expression of supreme wisdom, which emerging from the absolute state (= *mahāmudrā* here as third stage) becomes manifest in the maṇḍala in the form of the Five Buddhas, as Vairocana or one's chosen divinity.[249] Efforts to place it third or fourth do not seem to be very satisfactory.

As already stated, these disagreements and apparent contradictions in the ordering of the Four Joys, Moments and Four Symbols arise from their artificial arrangement in parallel with the four consecrations as shown above. In fact they apply to the rite of sexual union, whether practiced by the master in the second consecration or by the pupil in the third one. It must be assumed that if the master is proficient, as is clearly intended, he is capable of realizing the whole series of Joys etc. in the course of the second consecration, which is performed on behalf of his pupil. Properly prepared, the pupil in turn should experience the whole series of Joys in the third consecration, resulting in his realization of the fourth state of Great Bliss. But even if this final state is achieved as "fourth," there has to be a return to the world of everyday experience, including the realization that "he has enjoyed such bliss," and his continuing activity, or

248 I have in mind the assertions of tantric exegetes to be found in the *Advayavajrasaṃgraha*, pp. 28 and 32. For more recent discussion see my Introduction to the *Hevajra Tantra*, pp. 34-5, and especially Per Kværne, *op. cit.*, pp. 109ff., where the whole matter is argued in great detail.

249 This is how the tantric exegete Nāgārjuna explains it in a short work *Caturmudrāniścaya* (in the *Advayavajrasaṃgraha*, p. 34 for this particular passage). For further discussion see the *Hevajra Tantra*, vol. I, pp. 136-7 and Per Kværne, *op. cit.*, pp. 115ff.

supposed activity, on behalf of other living beings.[250] He then lives ideally in the state of the free-roving yogin who is freed of all worldly conventions, as so often described in our texts and celebrated in tantric songs. Seen from this point of view the Four Joys, Moments and Symbols might logically be arranged thus:

joy	perfect joy	joy innate	joy of cessation	4 joys
variety	development	blank	consummation	4 moments
mudrā	*dharma-mudrā*	*mahā-mudrā*	*samaya-mudrā*	4 symbols

With this order established as valid in a psychophysical sense we may refer back to the verses concerning "reversals" as quoted from an important work of the great Asaṅga (see p. 128):

> Supreme self-control is obtained in the reversal of sexual intercourse
> in the blissful Buddha-poise and the untrammelled vision of one's spouse.
> Supreme self-control is obtained in the reversal of spacial perceptions
> resulting in the supernatural production of thought-forms and in material manifestation in phenomenal spheres.

The realization of this process where "material manifestation" (*vibhāvana*) in the various spheres of existence follows upon the attaining of blissful knowledge, seems to correspond with the later arguments of these tantric exegetes who place the Joy Innate, *alias* the Great Symbol (*mahā-mudrā*), third and the manifestation in divine form (*samaya-mudrā*) last. Sexual yoga appears to be more firmly established in Indian Buddhist practice than has been generally conceded.[251]

e. *References to Higher Consecrations in Yoga Tantras*

While it appears to be only in the tantras of the Supreme Yoga class that the theories and symbolism associated with sexual yoga are elaborately developed, it is wrong to assume, as done by most later Tibetan interpreters, that sexual yoga was unknown in other tantras, precisely in those that can be related with orthodox Mahāyāna sūtras. Thus in the *Durgatipariśodhana Tantra* all eleven consecrations are specifically listed, including the Secret Consecration and what is here known as the Consecration of the Union of Wisdom and Means. Vajravarman's commentary explains these in terms which accord completely with the interpretations of Supreme Yoga Tantras.[252] The only noticeable difference in emphasis in this tantra, normally classed as a Yoga Tantra although some would assign it to the Performance class, is the overriding concern for achieving "long life" and the state of a "universal monarch" (*cakravartin*). The main Yoga

250 See H.T. vol. I, Introduction, p. 35 and Per Kværne, *op. cit.*, p. 114; see above near end of section III.14.b for the phrase "Consummation is the reflection: 'I have enjoyed this bliss.' " Thus the yogin scholar Maitṛpa argues: "How can it then be third?" (*Advayavajrasaṃgraha*, p. 28, l. 5).

251 For references to the Four Symbols (*mudrā*) in the Yoga Tantra, "Symposium of Truth," see immediately below.

252 See SDPS, Skorupski's ed., pp. 46-8, 78-80. It is interesting to note that the great Tsong-kha-pa who wrote a commentary on this tantra (see Skorupski's reference) explains this as the Master Consecration and no more. So easily is clear evidence ignored, if it does not fit other preconceived theories.

Tantra, "Symposium of Truth," contains references throughout the several parts into which it is arranged to "secret yoga," although there appears to be no specific reference to the so-called "higher consecrations" and the achievements gained tend to be listed according to the groupings of the four (or five) Buddha-Families, which underlie the whole arrangement of this voluminous tantra. Thus in the fourth chapter, which lists the achievements gained according to the different kinds of worshipful offerings made, the benefits of "secret worship" find their place:

> The self-producing blissful worship where the whole body is embraced,
> offering this, he should quickly become the equal of Vajrasattva.
> The bliss of holding her hair in the state of fervent enamorment,
> offering up this to the Buddhas, one should be the equal of Vajra-Gem.
> The greater bliss of kissing clung to in fervent joy and bliss,
> offering up this to the Buddhas, one should be the equal of Vajra-Dharma.
> The blissful joys of the yoga of the union of the two organs, always
> offering up this as one worships, one should be the equal of Vajra-Action.

One need not therefore be surprised to read a few folios later:

> There is no sin in the threefold world such as absence of passion,
> so you should never practice the nonimpassioning of desire.[253]

Or again from the twentieth chapter, which belongs to the Part IV dealing with the maṇḍalas of the combined Gem-Action Family (see section III.11 last paragraph), one may quote the "secret knowledge of the Pledge-Symbol of the Gem Family":

> Positioning the great vajra-gem, one places the gem in the woman's pudenda
> and meditating upon the Great Symbol one achieves success (*siddhi*).
> Positioning the gem of the foremost Pledge in the woman's pudenda,
> by the positioning of this foremost Pledge there is always success in the consecrations.
> Positioning the great vajra-gem and meditating on the Dharma-Symbol,
> inserting the gem in the woman's pudenda, the highest success is achieved.
> Inserting the Action-Symbol gem in the woman's pudenda, by the positioning
> of the Action-Symbol there is supreme success in all one's action.
>
> For these the mantras are: OṂ Great Success! OṂ Pledge Consecration Success! OṂ Dharma Success! OṂ Action Success![254]

I observed in section III.8 that the tantras of the Supreme Yoga class are not the

253 See STTS, Yamada's ed., pp. 139 and 150 for the Sanskrit; Tibetan, TT vol. 4, pp. 237-5-8ff. and p. 239-1-7. The leading Bodhisattvas of the Four Families, as named here, are on p. 210.

254 STTS, Yamada's ed., p. 412, TT vol. 4, p. 264-2-4. It may be noted that these verses are arranged to correspond with the four symbols (*mudrā*), which were discussed above. Here we appear to have *Mahā-mudrā*, *Samaya(-mudrā)*, *Dharma-mudrā* and *Karma-mudrā* all specifically mentioned and ordered in accordance with the four families of Tathāgata/Vajra, Gem, Dharma and Action, which are all subservient in this part of the STTS to the Gem Family. These rather complex arrangements are explained by my Introduction to the STTS, *Facsimile Edition*.

only ones which preach perverse teachings as suitable for those who have achieved the highest spiritual attainments as understood by tantric yogins. The example given there from the "Symposium of Truth" (pp. 175-6) is typical of many more and it is within this context that so many references to sexual gratification as a means toward enlightenment occur. One more should suffice.

> Then Vajrapāṇi the Great Bodhisattva recited the Secret Tantra of the Pledge-Perfection of All the Tathāgatas:
> "Now this is the Secret Tantra of the Pledge-Perfection of All Tathāgatas: Saying you are the Pledge, you should gratify all women. Do not turn away from the affairs of living beings. Thus one soon gratifies the Buddhas." So says the Lord, the Great Vairocana.
> "This is the Secret Tantra of the Pledge-Perfection of the Tathāgata Family: Gratification should not be despised; one should gratify all women. Holding to the Secret Pledge of the Adamantine One (*vajrin*), one succeeds." So says the Lord Vairocana.
> "This is the Secret Tantra of the Pledge-Perfection of the Vajra Family: Slaying, one slays the world for the purpose of purifying it. With beneficent actions of body and speech and with the sounds of HŪṂ the Pledge achieves its objective." So says the Lord "Victor over the Threefold World" (viz., Vajrapāṇi).
> "This is the Secret Tantra of the Pledge-Perfection of the Lotus Family: Gratification is pure for those of a pure disposition, but is impure in the case of heretic yogins. Holding to the Pledge of the pure-minded, one obtains perfection." So says the Lord Avalokiteśvara.
> "This is the Secret Tantra of the Pledge-Perfection of the Gem Family: Positioning the Vajra-Gem in concentration (*samādhi*) on Vajragarbha (Vajra-Embryo) and seizing the possessions of evil folk, this Pledge bestows perfection." So says the Lord Vajra-Gem.[255]

The arrangement of the teachings in this last part of the "Symposium of Truth" according to five families of All Tathāgatas, Tathāgata, Vajra, Lotus and Gem (this one including Action) has been mentioned above, but the actual teachings may not always appear to be so logically arranged, unless one bears continually in mind a variety of associated ideas. Clearly the whole present set of verses is concerned either with sexual yoga or the innocence of sexual bliss for the right-minded. Thus the reference to slaying in the third verse and to seizing others' property in the last one might seem irrelevant unless one remembers that converting by terrible means is an attribute of the Vajra Family and acquiring wealth is one of the main successes promised to members of the Gem Family. The wealth acquired, however, may be the treasure of enlightenment:

> With the two organs joined together one should seek for treasure, for meditating upon the Great Symbol one obtains the treasure by interpenetration.
> Positioning the foremost Pledge, causing delight to woman, there where

255 For this excerpt see STTS, *Facsimile Edition*, p. 63; similar examples on pp. 37, 46, 51, 59 etc.

the symbol is firm, one obtains the treasure.
With the two organs joined together one should seek for treasure, for
meditating on the Knowledge-Symbol, one gets the treasure-knowledge.
Positioning the Action-Symbol with concentration on the two organs,
there where the Symbol is manifest, one should find the treasure.[256]

Coming upon such passages as these, which occur throughout this foremost of Yoga Tantras, one may well wonder to what extent one may be justified in distinguishing between this class of tantras and those of the Supreme Yoga class, and even how far Tibetan exegetes are right in insisting that the three higher (or internal) consecrations are taught only in tantras of the Supreme Yoga class. It may be truer to say that while they are taught explicitly (albeit with implicit meanings according to some interpreters) in tantras of the Supreme Yoga class, there is an implicit understanding of them according to a Yoga Tantra tradition, related to the very practices mentioned in Asaṅga's treatise. There is nothing particularly secret about sexual yoga in Supreme Yoga Tantras; one merely has to read the texts. It is possible that they continue to refer to it as though it were secret, simply because it was really so in more orthodox Buddhist circles, while the tantric yogins have brought censure upon themselves by the flamboyant manner in which they parade their teachings. Their "enigmatic language" (*sandhābhāṣa*) to which we have referred above conceals nothing from intelligent outsiders and it was probably never intended that it should, while at the same time their carefree way of life was plain for all to see.

At the same time all the distinctions that I have made between some tantras of the Supreme Yoga class and the many other tantras that are relatable to Mahāyāna sūtras seem to remain valid. The former group had their origin amongst groups of tantric yogins possessing limited Buddhist associations, while the others form an entirely acceptable part of Mahāyāna Buddhist practice and were composed in well-established Buddhist centers. But it is not an interest in sexual yoga that distinguishes them, and the so-called "higher consecrations" need not be regarded as a speciality of followers of Supreme Yoga Tantras. The ease with which these tantras, which seem to have shocked many non-Indian Buddhists, Chinese, Japanese and even the Tibetans, became accepted as a valid part of Indian Buddhism, suggests that their teachings brought nothing essentially new, but simply improved methods and a wealth of symbolic expression aiming at the same kind of goal. One notes that whereas the tantras, grouped as Action, Performance and Yoga Tantras, consist largely of instructions for the per-

256 See STTS, Yamada's ed., p. 398; Tibetan, TT vol. 4, p. 262-4-7. The Sanskrit word translated as "is manifest" in the last line is *sphuṭet*, which means "it bursts open, comes into view," or "it separates." The Tibetan translation has: "Where the Symbol becomes two (*gnyis gyur pa de na*) there the treasure is found." The word translated as the verb "to position" throughout all these recent quotations is Sanskrit *bandh* meaning "to bind, fix," etc. It is used of "fixing" (viz., "making") a hand-gesture (*mudrā*). Hence there may be ambiguities of meaning that cannot be expressed in translation, whether Tibetan or English. Tibetan translates the term rigidly with a word meaning "to bind" while I have sought deliberately an ambiguous interpretation. Here we have yet one more good example of the problems these texts present to any translator.

formance of rituals with little or no philosophical and speculative intrusions, tantras of the Supreme Yoga class are filled with speculations of all kinds, philosophical, mythological, cosmological, psychophysical—an interesting subject in itself, which must be treated separately in the next section. The reason for this difference between them can only be that those other tantras were the ritual counterparts of the Mahāyāna sūtras; there is no need for them to deal with Buddhist philosophical teachings, fully taken for granted and easily available to them. But these Supreme Yoga Tantras introduce certain basic theories and patterns of thought that are clearly extraneous to traditional Mahāyāna teachings and these require explanation and justification, if the identity of the one goal is to be maintained.

f. *The Problem of Textual Obscurity*

It thus comes about that commentaries and exegetical works of all kinds play an essential part in any study of tantras of the Supreme Yoga class. By contrast, Mahāyāna sūtras and all the other tantras (Action, Performance, Yoga), which as we have attempted to show are related to them, are for the most part clear enough in meaning without the aid of commentaries. With Yoga Tantras problems of interpretation begin to arise and with Supreme Yoga Tantras the use of commentaries becomes essential, not only to establish meanings but also to obtain preferable versions of an otherwise corrupt text.[257] As distinct from the tantras themselves, the commentaries and exegetical words are usually clear in meaning and coherently written. They are normally attributed, at least in their Tibetan translations (for the Tibetans were careful to check on such matters with the help of their Indian masters), to a named author. But the tantras, being supposedly "Buddha-Word," are altogether anonymous; one may surmise that their contents comprise the direct teachings of tantric masters, either as learned by heart or maybe recorded immediately in writing, and also what pupils recall of their master's teaching, as they have learned it, well or perhaps not so well, at their master's feet. To end this section on consecrations I translate a short section from an exegetical work entitled *Prajñopāyaviniścayasiddhi* ("The Attainment of the Realization of Wisdom and Means") by Anangavajra, well written and lucid, followed by a contrasting passage concerning consecration extracted from the *Guhyasamāja Tantra* as an example of the problems that confront any would-be interpreter of such a work. Tibetans have always insisted that one

[257] In the introduction of his admirably produced work to which I have already referred (*The Saṃvarodaya-Tantra*) Shinichi Tsuda appears to quibble about the virtues of establishing a text by making primary use of what the Tibetan translators have preserved for us. Perhaps I should take this opportunity of stating more clearly the points made in my "Note on the texts" at the beginning of my edition of the *Hevajra Tantra*, part II. Most Buddhist tantras have several commentaries by Indian interpreters, often lost in their Sanskrit originals, but happily preserved in Tibetan translations. These commentaries often quote the text word for word, thus providing us with valuable parallel versions of the actual tantra as they had it before them when writing any time between the eighth and the twelfth centuries A.D. Such versions, albeit in Tibetan translation, thus have greater authority than a corrupt nineteenth century MS, copied and copied again in Nepal. In some cases (e.g., the STTS) we do have an early Indian MS available, and that fact one takes fully into account.

cannot hope to understand these texts except under the direction of a qualified lama, and indeed that it is sacrilegious and a sure way to hell even to attempt to do so. However, solving textual problems and experiencing the Great Bliss are not quite the same things, although it might be foolish to deny all connection between the two. The Great Translator Rin-chen bzang-po had to wrestle with the former, and although Atiśa may have taken him to task for dealing with tantras as if they were separate works (see. p. 202), one has no choice in a work such as this but to follow rather feebly in his footsteps. So here follows the first of the two above-mentioned extracts.

For the benefit of aspirants (*sādhaka*) whose objective is the rank of Vajrasattva, the rite of consecration will be explained, firm-set (Tibetan: preeminent) in the threefold world. When an intelligent man is consecrated according to the Mantra Path in the maṇḍala which is the resort of the Blessed Ones and in the presence of all the Buddhas, then the Lord of the sphere of limitless worlds is comprehended by him, as he reaches the grade of self-consecration, thoughtful and anxious that he should not violate the pledge. In all truth it has been said by those who are fully enlightened in the Mantra Path, that the pledge of Vajrasattva and like divinities is hardly transgressible. So the offspring of the Buddhas (viz., the student) for the sake of this consecration serves his Vajra Teacher, that ocean of good qualities, both in the correct manner and with all his effort. Having obtained a fair-eyed Symbol (*mudrā*), possessed of youth and beauty, he adorns her with fine clothes, with garlands and sandalwood scent, and makes a presentation of her. Then zealously he adores and worships his Teacher together with the Symbol, honoring them with perfumes and garlands and so on, and making offerings of milk (Tibetan: liquor) and other things. Placing one knee on the ground and making a beseeching gesture, he makes his request of his Teacher with these words of praise:

Salutation to you, who free of all false imaginings encompass the Void!
Salutation to you the omniscient, the totality of wisdom, the very form of wisdom!
Eliminator of the folly of the world, revealer of the pure truth,
Salutation to you, Vajra-Being, born of the nonselfhood of *dharmas*!
From you there arise Buddhas and Bodhisattvas, possessed of perfections and virtues, salutation to you, O Thought of Enlightenment!
From you are the Three Jewels, the Mahāyāna and this whole threefold world, all that is stable and all that moves, salutation to you, the seed of the world![258]
As wonderful as a wish-granting gem for achieving what is desired by the world, glorious performer of the ordinances of the Blessed Ones, Son of the Buddhas, salutation to you!
It is by your favor that I may know the supreme reality, O Ocean of good qualities; do me the favor now, O Omniscient One, of the Vajra-Consecration.

258 The edited Sanskrit text reads "hero" (*vīra*) of the world. The Tibetan version representing Sanskrit *bīja* is probably correct for this context.

Favor me, O Lord, with the secret of all Buddhas, even as it was revealed by the Glorious Thought-Vajra to the Dharma-Vajra.
If I leave your lotus-feet there is no other course for me, so have compassion on me, O Lord, you who have vanquished hostile saṃsāra.[259]

Then the glorious Vajra Teacher, sympathetic and intent on good,
Feels compassion for the pupil and summons him to the circle of offerings.
It is filled with the five kinds of desirable things, resplendent with the canopy spread above, the place for union with the yoginī, resounding with bells and tinkling chimes.
It is a delightful place filled with flowers and incense, blissful with garlands and divine perfumes, the resort of Vajrasattva and other divinities, wonderful indeed.
Then the blissful Teacher, having united with the Symbol, lets fall into the lotus-vessel, the resort of the Buddhas, his Thought of Enlightenment.
Then as lord of the world he should consecrate his pupil who (in turn) is united with the Symbol, while chowries are waved, parasols held high and auspicious hymns are sung.
Having bestowed the excellent gem of consecration, the Teacher as supreme lord should give him the sacrament, delightful, divine and pure by nature, the great gem consisting of "camphor" joined with "red sandal," prepared of vajra-water, having its origin in the fifth prescription.[260] "This is your sacrament, dear one, as taught by all Buddhas; hold to it always, my friend, and attend now to the vow. Do not harm living beings. Do not abandon the Three Jewels. Never forsake your Teacher. Such a vow is hardly transgressible."
Then he should give this admonition to his pupil, who having received the consecration of the Thought of Enlightenment, is freed of sin and is become a foremost son of the Buddhas:
"Until you finally reach the Place of Enlightenment, turn the supreme Wheel of the Doctrine everywhere throughout the whole world. Personally formed of Wisdom and Means, magnificent like a wish-granting gem,[261] unwearying and free from all attachments, work now for the good of living beings."
Having received the consecration and the admonitions, joyful in that he has completed all that had to be done, he (the pupil) pronounces these pleasing words which cause everyone to rejoice:
"Today my birth has become fruitful. Today my life is fruitful. Today I have been born into the Buddha-Family. Now I am a son of the Buddhas. I have been rescued by you, O Lord, from the terrible ocean of the aeons, so hard to cross because of the mud of the emotions and where one is overwhelmed with continual rebirths. I know myself to be as perfect thanks to your gracious favor, and I am free from all latent tendencies, since my heart is set on enlightenment."[262]

259 Sanskrit reads not the *saṃsāra-enemy*, as does Tibetan, but destinies of rebirth (*gati*) of samsāra, which does not fit so well with "vanquishing."

260 The fifth tantric prescription is *maithuna* (copulation).

261 This follows the Tibetan version with *rgya-che* (= *udāra*) instead of *ucyate*.

262 Following the Tibetan, thus correcting the Sanskrit to *bodher yena ca me kāskā*. For the

In contrast to the above and as an example of how very allusive the description of consecrations may be, I now quote from the sixteenth chapter of the *Guhyasamāja Tantra* ("Secret Union"). A choice of interpretations is available, whether relating to an actual performance or a meditational exercise, where the whole process is envisaged, or again as a combination of both.

Then the Lord Tathāgata Vajrapāṇi relapsing into the state of concentration known as Origin of All Maṇḍala-Circles, announced the Sacred Vajra of the Body, Speech and Mind of all maṇḍalas from his own adamantine Body, Speech and Mind:

"These are the fundamental syllables for laying down the threads, the essential mantras for a vajra maṇḍala: OṂ ĀḤ HŪṂ.

The laying of the vajra-threads and the application of the colors should not be done by the mantra-being.[263] If he does this, enlightenment is hard to obtain.

So one who understands the system of pledges (*samaya*) should introduce the mantra-divinities, and concentrating upon this place of empowerment, he envisages the mystic circles (for the various divinities).

He should introduce the Great King Vairocana and the (Buddha-Goddess) Locanā. Their delightful resort is the maṇḍala of Body and it bestows the qualities of the Vajra of Body.

He should introduce the Great King Vajradharma (= Amitābha) together with his Dharma-consort (= Pāṇḍaravāsinī). This is the secret place of all mantras in all eternity.

He should introduce the Great King Vajrasattva (= Akṣobhya) together with (the Buddha-Goddess) Māmakī. This is the secret place of all mantras, altogether amazing.

By acting thus one secures their presence, and being themselves possessors of the gem (of consecration), they approach joyfully and reveal the supreme secret."

He said too:

"The wonderful vajra-secret (= the maṇḍala ritual) should be performed by one who is accomplished in mantras. As King of Wrath he coerces all the Buddhas and worships them.

These pure adamantine beings of the Threefold Vajra require sacramental worship during the three time-periods and by the union of the Threefold Vajra success in mantras is achieved."

He said too:

"One should make a wondrous offering to all these mantra(-divinitie)s, thought-produced urine and faeces, flesh and oil and the fifth item, for with semen all mantras are delighted, they say. This is the very best sacrament,

Sanskrit version of the whole excerpt see B. Bhattacharyya, *Two Vajrayā Works*, pp. 11ff; for the Tibetan, TT, vol. 68, pp. 239-5-3ff.

263 The term "mantra-being" might have several interpretations, but here it seems to refer to the pupil. Candrakīrti's commentary interprets as "one who is intent on mantra and attached to dualistic knowledge," perhaps a rather belabored interpretation.

perfecting a Buddha's enlightenment.

One should proceed to the laying down of the threads, envisaging oneself as Vairocana and the neophyte as Vajrasattva or he is known as Amṛtavajra (Elixir-Vajra) of adamantine brilliance. One should lay the adamantine thread of the Great Kings, the Five Buddhas. This is the supreme secret of all Buddhas. As for the application of the color with its twenty-five distinctions, this is the secret of all adamantine ones, the highest enlightenment.[264] In the case of all these mantra(-divinitie)s one evokes Vajra-HŪṂ-kāra (a fierce form of Vajrapāṇi), evoking this divine sacrament, bodily and vocally, in the five sections (of the maṇḍala).

By effecting their presence in this way, the Vajra-Born of the unbreakable vajra (viz., the main divinities of the maṇḍala) act with fear toward the attentive Vajrasattva (viz., the pupil).

The placing of the vajra-jars is done as recorded by the masters of mantras and tantras, and so he should envisage things, firm in mind, as he abides in the concentration of Vajrasattva.

The knower of mantras, desiring the fruits of all achievement (*siddhi*) should make the sacrificial offering (*homa*); he should present the sacrificial offering of urine and faeces, flesh and oil and the rest.

He should give the full vajra-offering to the kings (*cakrin*) of the unbreakable threefold Vajra, and concentrating upon his own chosen divinity in the centre he should put it into the mouth (of the pupil).[265]

These are the vajra-syllables for entering the great maṇḍala: ĀḤ KHAṂ VĪRA HŪṂ! This is the Mantra-Vajra which is the essence of the Body, Speech and Mind of all sacraments (*samaya*).

Now this is the secret of the hidden knowledge of the Great Vajra Consecration. One who belongs to the Vajra lineage (*gotra*) should envisage the celestial sphere filled with all the Buddhas, worshipping them with music and clouds of perfume."

He said too:

"The one firm in his vow (= the teacher) should inflict them (the Buddhas) with mustard-seeds, which have been infused with the mantras of the threefold vajra body; then they will bestow of their own accord the consecration upon him (the pupil).

Or with the concentration of Vajrasattva he should envisage the Buddhas; the wise one should envisage the jars borne by the foremost of pledges (again the Buddhas or their consorts).

264 The number twenty-five presumably refers to five divinities in each of the five circles of the maṇḍala.

265 I follow Francesca Fremantle (*A Critical Study of the Guhyasamāja Tantra*, p. 356) in attaching this half verse of the Sanskrit (in English: "and concentrating etc.") at this juncture, although any such rearrangement of the text must be regarded as tentative. This means that using B. Bhattacharyya's edition from p. 115, ll. 3ff., one jumps from p. 117, l. 5 (correcting the last part of this line to *trivajrābhedyacakriṇām*) to p. 119, l. 2. One continues from here to the foot of p. 120 and then returns to p. 117, ll. 6ff. I take this opportunity of acknowledging the great help received from Francesca Fremantle's work in dealing with this intractable text. Her thesis contains a greatly improved edition of the Sanskrit presented side by side with the Tibetan translation.

Conceiving of his disciple, who is always firm-minded, the knower of mantras should consecrate him with them, the one who is adamantine in Body, Speech and Mind.[266]

Now this is the secret of all consecrations, the Speech-Vajra pronouncement of all teachers:

'I bestow (upon you) the Consecration of the Great Vajra, born of the threefold secret Vajra, honored throughout the threefold world.'

Now this is the secret rite for all disciples requesting the Great Vajra: 'As great honor is bestowed upon Buddhas by the Vajra of Enlightenment, O You, Celestial Vajra, bestow it today on me for the sake of salvation.'

Then he should joyfully give him the consecration and in union with his chosen divinity, he should deposit the Lord (*adhipati*) in his heart. Revealing the maṇḍala to his attentive disciple, he should recite to him the secret pledge announced by all Buddhas:

'You must slay living beings; you must speak lying words; take what is not given; be available to women.'

He should incite all beings with this Vajra Way, for this is the supreme eternal pledge of all Buddhas.

With words which urge the use of mantras, he should then give him the mantra, and having bestowed upon him the mental composure of that king of mantras, he should proceed with the Secret (Consecration).

Having consecrated in accordance with the rite semen or faeces, the vajra-teacher should make him eat it, and so success is without difficulty attained."[267]

I have already referred above to the disjointed nature of much of the material of which some tantras of the Supreme Yoga class are composed. This may be unintentional, simply as a result of the rather haphazard manner in which these teachings were put together from earlier oral transmissions, and I suspect this is the case. It could conceivably be intentional, if the object was to conceal the sequence of events from noninitiates. One may note that the intruding words "he said too" may change the context in many cases, thus suggesting that what we now have is the later written record made by a disciple or group of disciples of their master's words. This could easily have resulted in certain verses being omitted because they were forgotten, or wording changed because the original wording became confused in transmission. It may be of interest to analyze such possibilities in regard to the extract just quoted, as an example of the vast amount of critical work of a literary nature still required before such works can be adequately translated. As is well known, traditional religious scholarship

266 The phrase "adamantine in Body, Speech and Mind" is best referred to the pupil if one follows the rather doubtful Sanskrit grammatical construction, but the Tibetan translation, I suspect rightly, refers it to the teacher.

267 Here we have a clear example of the choices open to a translator or interpreter of this text. We can choose "vajra-teacher" (*vajrâcârya*), "vajra-yoga" or "vajra-mind," all of which are supported textually in one way or another. From this point on, we are informed of the rites in which the pupil should now be skilled; they are of the kind already described in extracts quoted above in section III.8.

tends to be uncritical in a modern literary sense, because the main interest centers upon the religious content of a text that is already regarded as sacred and so inviolate. Thus the Indian commentators and their Tibetan successors were at pains to interpret the text as they had received it, and although they were sometimes aware of alternative readings and made choices between them, and although they could be critical of one another's interpretations, one can hardly expect them to declare a canonical text actually defective. A meaning must be found for it somehow, and in texts such as these, where interpretations are so fluid, there is little difficulty in finding a suitable one.

At the start of the above quotation Vajrapāṇi announces the "Sacred Vajra of the Body, Speech and Mind of all maṇḍalas." But before announcing them, the text refers to the laying out of the maṇḍala with threads, and it must be remembered that the maṇḍala is fivefold (see above) and not threefold as is the "Sacred Vajra of Body, Speech and Mind," which is about to be announced. This Threefold Vajra as now announced corresponds as we have already seen above with the three Buddha-Families of the Tathāgata, the Dharma or Lotus, and the Vajra. The first bestows the qualities of the Vajra of Body, the second of Speech (thus it is called the secret place of all mantras) and the third surely of Mind, but here we have the almost identical repetition of the verse just above. Was this the original wording, one may well wonder. Difficulty is also caused to the uninitiated reader by substitute names, e.g., Vajradharma for the Buddha presiding over the Dharma-family, so that the more regular pattern of names is slightly disrupted. It is well established that the teacher must first be self-constituted as a Vajra-Being (*Vajrasattva*), and for coercing the divinities he should display a fierce aspect; thus he is referred to as King of Wrath, or again as Vajra-HŪṂ-kāra, both of which are titles of Vajrapāṇi in wrathful form. The *Guhyasamāja Tantra* refers frequently to the coercing of Buddhas and forcing them to do one's will as though in a state of subjection, so one should not be surprised at the act of hurling mustard-seeds at them, a rite that is more frequently performed to reduce evil spirits to subjection. One may note in passing that in Candrakīrti's commentary mustard-seed is interpreted as the sacrificial semen, the Thought of Enlightenment in its relative/absolute form which is in a sense superior to all Buddhas, for it is their essence.[268]

The list of five items of which the offering is said to consist may appear doubtful. Oil occurs where blood would be expected and the fifth item is surely semen. Yet the Tibetan translation, which must have been based upon an early Sanskrit text, has: "faeces and urine, flesh and oil and self-produced sandalwood.[269] Such variations need cause no problem to the traditional scholar, Indian or Tibetan, for whatever the items, they can be interpreted as "enigmatic language," actually meaning symbolically offerings representing the five sense-spheres.

268 For the references to Candrakīrti's commentary, the *Pradīpodyotana-nāma-tīka*, I am indebted to Francesca Fremantle.

269 Here "oil" would refer to semen and "self-produced sandalwood" to blood. One may compare the parallel use of "camphor" and "red sandalwood" with those meanings in the previous extract.

As for the general relationship of the extracts translated, the second clearly overlaps with the first. They appear to be separate accounts of the same event, which have been simply placed more or less together. What is being described is the Secret Consecration, as well known from other Supreme Yoga Tantras, but here the account is arranged as a kind of meditational exercise, and little or no account is taken of a precise order of events. My two extracts are in fact separated or linked, depending upon one's overall interpretation, by three verses, which contain a general comment on the whole proceeding:

> And he said: With the two organs united the wise one should make offerings one hundred and eight times. This indeed is the pledge of all Buddhas, which is hard to transgress. In union with Vairocana and meditating upon one's disciple, who is born of the Threefold Vajra, with the seed-syllable ĀḤ in Body, Speech and Mind, he is grasped by the vajra.[270] The Great King Vajrasattva and the illustrious Vairocana grant the empowerment which is the pledge of (their) Body, Speech and Mind.

I have dealt in some detail with this passage as an example of the difficulties confronting anyone who writes about the tantras, making use of original sources. Apart from irregularities in the texts which often allow variant interpretations, one has the problem of keeping in mind a wide range of overall interpretations and conventionalized sets, whether of Buddha-families, of Buddhas, of their related Bodhisattvas and female partners if any, of sacrificial items, of philosophical conceptions, etc., so that one can identify a whole context before beginning to interpret a particular passage. It is for this reason that so few tantric texts have been translated into any European language and that the slightly more Sanskrit editions of such texts that are available find so few readers amongst those scholars, worldwide, who are proficient in Sanskrit. Brahmanical literature and the more regular Mahāyāna sūtras and their commentaries, despite their particular difficulties, present nothing like the same problems. Combined with this there is an understandable distaste for much of the subject-matter. It is thus likely that for a long time to come the tantras will remain chiefly the preserve of traditional Tibetan interpreters, and since they claim to be the only true interpreters, we may perhaps rest content with this situation. At the same time we probably have a sufficiently clear idea of what was involved in these "higher" tantric consecrations and what kind of achievements were claimed by their adepts. What the Tibetans have made of them since may in some respects be something different, and their claims can be tested by anyone who is seriously interested in joining their following, wherever obliging lamas may be found in these unhappy days of their exile.

270 I am aware that this sentence is ungrammatical in English, but such is the Sanskrit structure, and if one changes it, one enforces a particular meaning. The Tibetan translation, as recorded in the Derge Canon as opposed to the Narthang, translates as "he grasps with the vajra," which would at least give a grammatical English construction. For the Sanskrit, see Bhattacharyya's edition, p. 119, ll. 3-9.

15. SPECIAL CONCEPTS OF TANTRIC YOGINS

a. *Buddhahood as Twofold Rather than Fivefold*

I observed above that tantras of the Supreme Yoga class are filled with speculations of all kinds, philosophical, psychophysical, cosmological and mythological, while by contrast other tantras that are more easily relatable to Mahāyāna sūtras are concerned almost exclusively with prescriptions for rites, usually in the appropriate maṇḍalas, details of the requisite mantras and the various pronouncements to be made by the master and his pupils, descriptions and hymns of praise of the special divinities, etc. Much of this material might be described as mythological, especially the fivefold set of Buddhas, the attendant Buddha-Goddesses, carefully specified sets of Bodhisattvas, and the miscellaneous groups of minor divinities who are pressed into service. I have also referred to the set of Five Buddhas as a cosmological one, relating it to the more general Mahāyāna conception of innumerable Buddhas presiding over Buddha-fields in all the directions of space. However, all these mythological and cosmological ideas are to be found already in Mahāyāna sūtras, and the tantras that are classed as Action, Performance and Yoga merely take them for granted as the basis for their ritual provisions.

In dealing with tantras of the Supreme Yoga class, one has the impression that all this more general mythological and cosmological material is relegated to the background of their interests, except where it can be reinterpreted in accordance with their own special theories of existence, and at the same time other concepts are freely introduced, which are in direct conflict with traditional Buddhist teachings. Attention has already been drawn to several of these, and certainly the most notable is the blatant manner in which the existence of a Self is proclaimed with names that are as much Hindu as Buddhist (see, e.g., section III.6.b). At the same time Madhyamaka teachings concerning truth of the Void are upheld, and the special theories of the Mind Only school are used and developed. This will be illustrated below, but first one needs to clarify those patterns of thought that are special to tantric yogins, thus distinguishing their form of Buddhism from all that had gone before and which continued to go on around them so long as Buddhism survived in India. A form of amalgamation was subsequently achieved in Tibet with the result that it is very difficult for a present-day Tibetan religious teacher, who lives fully within the Tibetan Buddhist tradition that he has received, to distinguish between tantric and non-tantric Buddhism in the way in which an attempt will be made in this present section.

Having named these general categories of Buddhism as tantric and non-tantric out of deference to a terminology well established in use, I have to qualify these terms almost to the extent of rejecting them altogether. In a literal sense *tantra* means more or less the same as *sūtra*, namely a "thread" of discourse, and it is thus the special application of the word and not its literal meaning that matters. Distinguished in the most general terms, one may say that *sūtras* are concerned with doctrine and *tantras* with rituals, and thus one might freely interpret "tantric" (the adjectival form of the word seems to be a Western creation in any case) as "ritualistic." It is certainly not intended to attempt to distinguish in this section between ritualistic and nonritualistic Buddhism, especially as it may fairly be claimed that there has scarcely ever been any form of Buddhism that has not involved rituals of some kind, even if one thinks only of the cult that surrounded the early stūpas. Certainly no one would dispute the great increase in ritual which took place in Mahāyāna Buddhism with its cult of the Buddhas and Bodhisattvas and other great beings, not to mention the attention that was still paid by faithful Buddhists to local essentially non-Buddhist divinities. All this the Mahāyāna sūtras take for granted, and the tantras classed as Action, Performance and (to some extent) those known as Yoga Tantras fit quite easily into general Mahāyāna philosophical theory and religious practice. Thus it comes about that we are really trying to distinguish between Mahāyāna Buddhism including those tantras that are closely relatable on the one hand and the form of tantric Buddhism, which may accurately be described as Vajrayāna, on the other. Such a distinction has not previously been made to my knowledge in scholarly works on the subject, and the distinction, real as it may be, is obscured in traditional works by the use of the term Mantrayāna, which covers all tantras, as distinct from *Pāramitānaya* (System of the Perfections), which covers the sūtras with their philosophical teachings and their preaching of the Bodhisattva ideal (see section III.1). These traditional distinctions, regarded as the two wings as it were of the Mahāyāna, remain perfectly valid, but they obscure certain other distinction that can be drawn between Mantrayāna and the other term Vajrayāna. "The Vajra Way" has its origins in Yoga Tantras and becomes fully developed in tantras of the Supreme Yoga class. It is thus a special form of Mantrayāna, and it can be misleading when the two terms are used as synonyms,as is often the case. I would scout altogether the entirely untraditional use of the term "The Tantra" as used by several modern writers to cover vaguely what is included under the traditional term Mantrayāna, usually presented with special reference to sexual implications.

If one is to be as precise as possible, one may claim to be attempting to distinguish between the form of Buddhism represented by tantric yogins, as typified by the Eighty-Four Great Adepts (*mahāsiddha*) on the one hand and the Mahāyāna and related Mantrayāna on the other. At the same time we note that the latter already introduce certain novel ideas that are developed still further in Supreme Yoga Tantras. The primary idea that is novel so far as the rest of Mahāyāna Buddhism is concerned is the primacy given to the Vajra as symbol and the resulting preeminence of the Vajra Family of divinities. As we have also noted, secret consecrations involving sexual yoga are referred to, although often only implicitly, in Yoga tantras, and these become one of the main subjects of tantras of the Supreme Yoga class. Tantras of this class provide a speculative basis of a quasiphilosophical kind for their sexual yoga, whether practiced as an actual ritual or as a form of solitary internal yoga. This introduces us at once to the most important of their special patterns of thought.

Yoga Tantras are based upon a theory of buddhahood as fivefold in the manner already described in some detail. The maṇḍala is primarily the expression of the essential identity of saṃsāra and nirvāṇa, where the one is interpreted as the cosmos (composed of five main elements, space, air, fire, water, earth) and the microcosmos as represented by the human person (composed again of five aggregates as defined in section I.3.b), and the other is expressed as the Five Buddhas and the five aspects of wisdom. Now the tantras of the Supreme Yoga class accept this fivefold arrangement in a general way, but it has ceased to be particularly relevant to their changed patterns of thought. As Hevajra says (p. 204), the families can be three or five or six, and so far as he is concerned there is really only one, and that is Aksobhya's Family of Wrath, which is the family of all the great tantric divinities. The final truth may be expressed symbolically by any of these numbers, but the favored expression now is twofold, for the absolute is the union of two. These are normally known as Wisdom and Means, terms often used in our discussion above but without any careful examination of their significance and origin. In that they may be identified with the old terms nirvāṇa and saṃsāra, their need be nothing new except perhaps the strangeness of their use. Hevajra assures us that the "identity of Wisdom and Means remains unharmed by the twofold process of origination and dissolution, for Means is the origination and Wisdom the dissolution and end of existence" (H.T., II.ii.27). Defining the final essence or quiddity (*tattva*) of existence, he says that "passion and wrath, envy, delusion and pride (viz., the Five Evils) cannot prevail one sixteenth part against this blissful central point. It is Wisdom, where spacelike, the elements have their origin, thus comprising Means. It is there that the threefold world arises possessing the nature of Wisdom and Means." Thus his own maṇḍala, which is his own means of self-expression, arises from this same basic duality, whether expressed as Wisdom and Means, Sun and Moon, *āli* (vowels) and *kāli* (consonants).

> The conjunction of these two, Moon and Sun, is the Great Bliss;
> *Āli* has become the Moon while the Sun assumes the form of *kāli*.
> From this mingling of Moon and Sun, Gaurī and her companions (who form Hevajra's circle) are proclaimed to be.
> The Moon is Mirrorlike Wisdom;
> The Sun is the Wisdom of Sameness;
> Seed-syllables and symbols of the chosen divinity are Discriminating Wisdom;
> The merging of all into one is Active Wisdom;
> The manifestation is the Wisdom of the Pure Absolute.
> The wise man should conceive of phenomenal forms in terms of these five modes here listed.
> With features and symbolic implements as before, and brilliant as the magic moon-stone, they all become manifest with the nature of Wisdom and Means.[271]

[271] H.T., I.viii.5-8, 10.

This description of the origin of Hevajra's maṇḍala is significant in that not only is the origin twofold, but also the more conventional fivefold pattern is reinterpreted to represent the process of the original unity of two becoming manifold, instead of being itself the primary expression of a fundamental nonduality.

With reference to the Four Joys as experienced through the set of four consecrations, this fundamental duality is expressed as male and female:

> Therefore twofold is the Innate, for Wisdom is the woman and Means is the Man. Thereafter these both become twofold, distinguished as absolute (*vivṛti*) and relative (*saṃvṛti*). In man there is this twofold nature, the life-force (*śukra*) and the bliss arising from it; in woman too it is the same, the life-force and the bliss arising from it.[272]

Before treating this important aspect of the Wisdom-Means combination, we should perhaps investigate its antecedents in early Mahāyāna teachings.

b. *Wisdom and Means*

The term wisdom (*prajñā*) is so old in Buddhism and so much has already been written about the Perfection of Wisdom (Prajn̄āpāramitā) that nothing more needs to be said about this in the present context. The other term "skilfulness in means" (*upāya-kauśalya*) occurs several times in the "Perfection of Wisdom in Eight Thousand Verses," which is one of the earliest of Mahāyāna philosophical works, datable as was noted above to perhaps the first century B.C. It occurs thus in combination with the Perfection of Wisdom, already forming in effect a pair of necessary qualities for a Bodhisattva, in that they should qualify all the other great perfections, which at this stage of the doctrine are six, namely generosity, morality, patience, heroism, meditation and wisdom. When the list is later extended to ten, "skill in means" becomes the seventh, but it continues to hold a special place, pervading all the others, as does its companion, wisdom. Some earlier quotations are already available (especially in section II.3.c), and so here one or two other short examples should suffice. Thus, the Lord Buddha explains to the chief of the gods, whom he addresses with the brahmanical name of Kauśika:

> When there are no Worthy Tathāgatas, Perfectly Enlightened Buddhas in the world, then Kauśika those Great Beings, the Bodhisattvas who are possessed of skill in means from the flow of the perfection of wisdom previously heard, feel compassion for living beings, and arousing this compassion, they come to this world and foster the ten virtuous ways of behavior, the four states of meditation but without the factors of enlightenment, the four "pure abodes" (*brahmavihāra*), again without the factors of enlightenment, the four formless attainments and the five magical accomplishments, all without the factors of enlightenment. So Kauśika, just as plants and bright stones reflect the light of the moon and the lunar mansions reflect its light, so in the absence of Worthy Tathāgatas, Perfectly Enlightened Buddhas, when there is no holy religion of a Worthy Tathāgata, a Perfectly Enlightened Buddha, whatever holy conduct, good conduct, virtuous conduct is manifested and recognized

272 H.T., I.viii.27-9.

in this world, all that comes about through the Bodhisattvas, is produced by the Bodhisattvas and becomes manifest by their skill in means.[273]

In the above passage skill in means is effectively identified with compassion (*karuṇā*), with the result that the pair Wisdom and Means become synonymous in Mahāyāna usage with Wisdom and Compassion.

Another short extract asserts the equal and primary importance of Wisdom and Means:

> Even if a Bodhisattva, a Great Being, having raised his thoughts to perfect enlightenment, should practice generosity for world-ages as many as are the sands of the River Ganges, should practice morality, operate with patience, display heroism and practice meditation—however great may be his resolve and however great may be the uplifting of his thought for the realization of perfect enlightenment—if he is not encompassed by the Perfection of Wisdom and if he is deprived of skill in means, he will fall to the state of an Early Disciple or a Lone Buddha.[274]

The importance of Wisdom and Means is increasingly urged throughout the Mahāyāna period and quotations might be culled from very many sūtras on the subject. For our immediate purposes it is enough to refer to one of the writings attributed to the Indian monk Kamalaśīla, who represented the case for Indian Buddhism and specifically the teachings concerning the conventional career of a Bodhisattva against the case for a kind of Chinese Buddhism, involving a quietist approach to buddhahood, at a general council that may have been held in Lhasa or bSam-yas Monastery toward the end of the eighth century (see section V.2.a). In order to argue his case Kamalaśīla quoted from a large number of Mahāyāna sūtras in which the importance of Wisdom and Means is mentioned several times:

> In short the practice of a Bodhisattva consists of Wisdom and Means, not Wisdom alone and not Means alone. As it is said in the *Vimalakīrtinirdeśa Sūtra*: "Wisdom without Means or Means without Wisdom is the thwarting of Bodhisattvas; Wisdom combined with Means, Meaṇs combined with Wisdom, this is the prescription for salvation." Again it is said in the *Gayāśīrṣa Sūtra*: "Expressed in concise terms, the way of a Bodhisattva is twofold. Bodhisattvas who follow this twofold way, quickly achieve the supreme and highest enlightenment. What are these two? Means and Wisdom!"

Or again:

> Even so is achieved the nirvāṇa of the Buddhas, where there is no reliance on anything. By the means of their generosity and the other perfections they do

[273] For the Sanskrit see ASP, Vaidya's ed., p. 37, ll. 21ff. Compare E. Conze, ASP (translation), p. 28. The corresponding passage in his *The Large Sūtra of Perfect Wisdom* will be found on pp. 237-8. I may be wrong in translating *tārā* as "bright stones," as "stars" would be a more obvious translation, were not the term linked here with "plants" (*auṣadhi*) which were supposed to flourish under the light of the moon. See S. B. Dasgupta, *Obscure Religious Cults*, pp. 250-1.

[274] See ASP, ed. Vaidya, p. 155, l. 26; E. Conze, p. 116, and also his *Large Sūtra*, p. 380.

not repose in nirvāṇa, for they accept the magnificent results (of their efforts) in the enjoyment of their manifestation-body (*rūpa-kāya*), their Buddha-field, their entourage etc. But because of their wisdom they do not repose in saṃsāra, for they have renounced all false notions, and false notions are the basis of saṃsāra. According to a process that consists of Wisdom and Means, they eschew over emphasis and undervaluation, thus evincing a medial process, and so avoiding overemphasis on Wisdom and undervaluation of Means. So it is said in the *Dharmasaṅgīti*: "He delights in the perfection of a manifestation-body with the thirty-two major and eighty minor marks of perfection, and he does not delight only in the realization of his Absolute Body (*Dharma-kāya*)." Furthermore it is said: "The arising of Buddhas occurs when Wisdom and Means are produced in mutual dependence."[275]

These last few extracts illustrate the special significance of Wisdom and Means in traditional Mahāyāna doctrine, although the mere making of such a selection may suggest that as a pair they are more prominent in such teaching than may be the case.[276] At all events it must be emphasized that here Means remain a doctrinal concept, serving as means to an end, and in no sense can this concept be construed as an end in itself, as is certainly the case with the Perfection of Wisdom, which is identified with the Void (*śūnyatā*) as a metaphysical absolute. However, in terms of the evolving thought patterns of Buddhist tantric yogins, Means as a concept is elevated to this high position, thus providing them with the dual form of metaphysical absolute which is required if their whole theory of existence as the state of "two-in-one" is to be philosophically justified. The previous extracts from the *Hevajra Tantra* have already illustrated how this "two-in-one" concept is taken for granted. As in the case of other developments of theory and practice that have been described as taking place within the general context of Indian Buddhism, this latest one might claim to be a restatement of what was already asserted in Madhyamaka teaching, namely the essential identity of nirvāṇa and saṃsāra as equally void (*śūnya*). Indeed, the extract from Kamalaśīla quoted just above suggests a parallel between nirvāṇa/saṃsāra and Wisdom/Means, but this certainly does not raise the latter pair to the state of metaphysical absolute. For this we must turn to another Buddhist scholar, who is also a renowned tantric yogin, namely Anaṅgavajra, from whose work "The Attainment of the Realization of Wisdom and Means" I have already quoted (III.10 & 14.f). He and Kamalaśīla may well have been contemporaries, and one may take this occasion to observe that the older and the newer interpretations of Buddhist doctrine continued to exist side by side throughout the history of Indian Buddhism, and thus references to tantric Buddhism as the last phase of Buddhism in India should not suggest that this phase eclipsed all that

275 See G. Tucci, *Minor Buddhist Texts*, II, for the *Bhāvanākrama* of Kamalaśīla, pp. 155ff. The Sanskrit version of the above extracts occurs on p. 194, ll. 6ff. and p. 197, ll. 1ff. (Tibetan: p. 238, ll. 26ff. and p. 243, ll. 12ff.). There is no English translation but only a résumé.

276 See e.g., Har Dayal, *The Bodhisattva Doctrine*, pp. 248-79, where he discusses skill in means as the seventh of the set of ten Perfections, but without any reference to its special relationship with Wisdom.

had gone before.[277] Anaṅgavajra's interpretation of Wisdom/Means is interesting in that it deliberately links the more traditional version with the enhanced tantric one:

> The nonsubstantiality of things which is realized by reflection and by discriminating between the act of knowing and what is known, is called the essence of Wisdom.
>
> Because one is passionately devoted to all beings who have failed to extricate themselves from a whole flood of suffering, this passionate devotion of which their suffering is the cause is known as Compassion. In that one thereby brings a man to the desired end by a combination of appropriate measures; it is also called the Means.
>
> The mingling of both, which is like that of water and milk, is known as Wisdom-Means in a union free of duality. It is the essence of Dharma, to which nothing may be added and from which nothing may be withdrawn. It is free from the two notions of subject and object, free from being and nonbeing, from characterizing and characteristics; it is pure and immaculate in its own nature. Neither duality nor nonduality, calm and tranquil it consists in all things, motionless and unflurried; such is Wisdom-Means, which may be known intuitively. It is this that is called the supreme and wondrous abode of all Buddhas, the Dharma-sphere, the divine cause of the perfection of bliss. It is Nirvāṇa Indeterminate (*apratiṣṭhitanirvāṇa*) and is frequented by the Buddhas of the Past, Present and Future; it is the blissful stage of self-empowerment (*svādhiṣṭhāna*), the beatitude of the Perfection of Wisdom. The three Buddha-bodies, the three Buddhist vehicles, mantras in their innumerable thousands, *mudrās* and maṇḍala-circles, phenomenal existence and that which transcends it, all arise from the same source; gods and titans and men, disembodied spirits and whatever else exists, all spring from here and return here to their cessation. It abides always in all things like a wish-granting gem; it is the final stage of Enjoyment and Release. It is here that the Blessed Ones met in times past and so became Buddhas, and it is here that those intent on the good of the world become Buddhas now and will always do so in future. It is called the Great Bliss, for it consists of bliss unending; it is the Supreme One, the Universal Good, the producer of Perfect Enlightenment. The great sages define this truth, which is the supreme bliss of self and others, as the union of limitless Compassion, which is intent alone on the destruction of all the world's suffering, and of perfect Wisdom, which is free from all attachment and is an accumulation of knowledge that may not be reckoned, so great is its diversity.[278]

The *Hevajra Tantra* might be regarded as the *locus classicus* for references to Wisdom and Means as the fundamental pair of coefficients, whose union

277 B. Bhattacharyya and I seem to agree in placing Anaṅgavajra round about the eighth century; see the introduction to his *Two Vajrayāna Works*, pp. xi-xii and my introduction to the *Hevajra Tantra*, vol. I, p. 13.

278 For the Sanskrit see B. Bhattacharyya, *Two Vajrayāna Works*, p. 4, verse 14 to the end of this first chapter. For the Tibetan, see TT, vol. 68, pp. 239-1-1ff. I translated the whole chapter many years ago in *Buddhist Texts through the Ages*, pp. 240-2.

produce the state of Great Bliss which is essentially innate to the whole of existence. With these terms the tantric yogins are able to link their theories and practices directly with the more conventional Mahāyāna teachings while endowing them with interpretations of a rather different kind. Furthermore, by identifying their union with the Void of the Perfection of Wisdom teachings they achieve an appearance of orthodoxy which has been readily accepted by their Tibetan successors, whatever names with more positive or even theistic implication they may use whenever it suits them.

> Then the quiddity (*tattva*) is declared as a form of knowledge purified,
> where there is no separation between saṃsāra and nirvāṇa.
> Nothing is mentally produced in the highest bliss and no one produces it.
> There is no bodily form, neither object nor subject,
> Neither flesh nor blood, neither dung nor urine,
> No sickness, no delusion, no purification,
> No passion, no wrath, no delusion, no envy,
> No malignity, no conceit of self, no visible object,
> Nothing mentally produced and no producer,
> No friend is there, no enemy,
> Calm is the Innate and undifferentiated.[279]

This central truth of the Mahāyāna is expressed in more scholastic terms in Nāropa's commentary on the *Kālacakra Tantra*:

> From the absence of self-nature a thing is void and the state of something thus void is voidness (*śūnyatā*). Knowledge of past and future is void. The vision of this is a state which is voidness profound and vast. In that past and future are void, it is profound. In that there is this vision of past and future, it is vast. The purification resulting from it is the Great Bliss which is changeless because of the inviolate Fourth State. Of this bliss it is said "it arrests," its mark being compassion, while it is the adamantine state of knowledge. It is truly the Body of the Innate personified as Wisdom and Means and it is described as Yoga Purified.[280]

The technical term used to express this notion which I have translated as "two-in-one" is Sanskrit *yuganaddha*, meaning literally "bound to a yoke," and the usage by tantric yogins doubtless derives from the sight of two oxen bound to a yoke. The Tibetan translators devised the term *zung-'jug* meaning "combine as a pair," and "two-in-one" seems an acceptable English translation. The last chapter of a short work entitled *Pañcakrama* (Fivefold Series) written by a certain Nāgārjuna, whom Tibetan tradition identifies with the renowned Madhyamaka teacher, is devoted entirely to definitions of the "two-in-one", and the opening verse may be quoted:

> Bowing before the Lord who personifies both cause and effect
> and is yet free of all duality, I write this final section on "two-in-one."

279 H.T., I.x.32-4.

280 M. E. Carelli, *Sekoddeśaṭīka*, p. 5, ll. 19ff.; TT, vol. 47, pp. 107-2-5ff.

Where there is freedom from the dual conception of saṃsāra and nirvāṇa,
in the state where they are one, this then is called the "two-in-one,"
Knowing emotional disturbance (*saṃkleśa*) and its assuaging in terms of
absolute truth, whoever thus recognizes their unified state, he knows
the "two-in-one."
The yogin who goes his way unifying the concepts of things with form
and yet as formless, he knows the "two-in-one,"
The wise man does not think of subject and object as distinct,
and where there is no such distinction, this is the "two-in-one," I say.
The one who has cast aside thoughts of eternity and noneternity,
who knows this truth we call as "series two-in-one," he is a *paṇḍita* indeed.
Where there is the knowledge of the unity of Wisdom and Compassion,
that is proclaimed as "two-in-one" and this series is the Buddha-sphere.
Knowing Wisdom and Means as altogether joined in union, there where
a great yogin takes his place, that is the "two-in-one."[281]

This dual concept of "two-in-one" expressed as Wisdom/Means, Voidness/ Compassion, Female/Male, Lotus/Vajra, is fundamental to the thought patterns of tantric yogins. In their songs of the kind quoted above (see *Songs* in the Index) other pairs, such as Sun and Moon, the Rivers Ganges and Jumna, are frequent, and we have also encountered the pair *āli* (vowels)/*kāli* (consonants) used with the same general meaning, but with particular reference to the series of letters envisaged as moving with the control of breath to the two sides of the practicing yogin's body.[282] The use of the names of the two rivers, Ganges and Jumna, may be regarded as confirming the general area, namely the central and lower Ganges Valley, where many tantras of the Supreme Yoga class were probably compiled. We may note in passing that at least one famous tantra, the *Guhyasamāja*, does not make use of this fundamental dual concept, but continues to use the threefold concept of Body, Speech and Mind or of the Three Buddha-families, and the fivefold one of the Five Buddha-families, as already illustrated by several quotations already available. The basic maṇḍala of this tantra is also the regular Five-Buddha maṇḍala with Akṣobhya to the center and all subsumed by the supreme (sixth) Buddha, the Great Vairocana. In this too it differs subtly from the tantras which center on Heruka in one of his horrific forms, Hevajra, Cakrasaṃvara, Caṇḍamahāroṣaṇa etc. These divinities have their more personal circle of attendant divinities and are themselves

[281] See L. de la Vallée Poussin's ed. of the *Pañcakrama*, p. 46, vv. 1-8. This is in fact the fifth chapter although he lists it as sixth, having published a short separate work of the same Nāgārjuna as a supposed first chapter. See also S. B. Dasgupta, *Obscure Religious Cults*, pp. 29-30 for a loose translation of the same verses and some more general useful observations. See also Per Kværne, *op. cit.*, pp. 132-3 where many more of the verses are translated. The Tibetan translation of the work (TT, vol. 61, pp. 288-3-7ff.) was done by the great Rin-chen bzang-po and his Kashmiri teacher Ratnākaraśānti around A.D. 1000. It is generally agreed by non-Tibetan scholars that the two Nāgārjunas, Madhyamaka (?first century A.D.) and tantric yogin (?ninth-tenth century), cannot be confused.

[282] For an example of this see Kazi Dawa Samdup's translation of the relevant passge in W. Y. Evans-Wentz, *Tibetan Yoga and Secret Doctrines*, pp. 180-1.

represented as embraced at the center of their maṇḍala by their particularized feminine partner, thus symbolizing the Wisdom/Means concept as the essence of existence. As is well known, this concept is carried over in Buddhist iconography in the form of a pair of such divinities, usually horrific in appearance, shown in close embrace. Few such images have survived in India, but they are well represented in Nepal and Tibet. Their maṇḍala continues to be identified with the more regular Five-Buddha maṇḍala, but may claim to transcend it in that all the earlier family distinctions are united in the one Vajra family. Thus at the beginning of the *Caṇḍamahāroṣaṇa Tantra* the "Fierce and Wrathful One" and his spouse "Queen of the Vajra-Sphere" announce themselves thus:

> Then the Lord Vajra-Being, entering the state of composure of the Black Imperturbable One (Acala = Akṣobhya) proclaimed this:
>
> Intent only on the Four Joys I am freed from existence and nonexistence.
> My true form is nondiversified (*niḥprapañca*) avoiding all conceptualizations.
> Deluded men do not recognize me as present in all males
> and it is for their benefit that I appear in fivefold form.
>
> Then the Lady Queen of the Vajra-sphere, entering the state of composure known as Black Adamantine, proclaimed this:
>
> I am undifferentiated Void and Compassion, manifest as the bliss of divine desire.
> I am free of all concepts, nonevolving and unencumbered.
> Foolish men do not recognize me as present in all females
> and it is for their benefit that I appear in fivefold form.[283]

As may have been noted from the quotation from the *Hevajra Tantra* just above, not only does this pair represent a unity, but each one of the pair comprises the fundamental duality within itself. Since all these tantric texts now under consideration have clearly been produced primarily for the benefit of male practitioners, the transference of the whole sexual symbolism to the human body is regularly described in terms of the male, although in theory at least it should also be applicable to the female. In the descriptions of the "Further Consecrations" given above, the feminine partner known as the Wisdom-Maiden (*prajñā*) and supposedly embodying this great perfection of wisdom, is in effect used as a means to an end, which is experienced by the yogin himself. Moreover, once he has mastered the requisite yoga techniques he has no need of a feminine partner, for the whole process is reenacted within his own body. The reverse situation is scarcely suggested, namely that a woman requires a male partner in order to experience the Four Joys and that having mastered the technique, she can do it alone. Thus despite the eulogies of woman in these tantras and her high symbolic status, the whole theory and practice is given for the benefit of males.

283 See C. S. George, *The Caṇḍamahāroṣaṇa Tantra*, p. 18, ll. 10ff. for the Sanskrit text. For his translation see p. 45. I have retranslated the passage in order to keep as close as possible to the terminology in use throughout the present book; e.g., he refers to "four blisses," in itself an acceptable translation, whereas I and others refer to "four joys," retaining "bliss" for *sukha*, which he translates perhaps too feebly as "happiness."

While the relative neglect of woman's interests in pursuing a higher religious life is typical of Buddhism of all periods, simply because her ability to do so is doubted so long as she is encumbered with a female body, this form of tantric Buddhism appears to offer her hope at last, but in the actual event seems to fail to do so.[284] As should already be clear from the above quotations, her body comprises Wisdom and Means as well as the expression of their unity known as *bodhicitta* ("thought of enlightenment") just as much as does the male, but as might well be expected, when one takes account of the time and place of their origin, the practical descriptions normally assume that the actual practitioner is male. This must already be clear from all the quotations throughout this long chapter on the tantras. However, it is sufficiently clearly stated that the human body, whether male or female, comprises the essential elements for the realization of enlightenment, as understood by these tantric yogins.

c. *The Cult of the Human Body*

Care of the human body as the means for the practice of meditation need not be anything new in Buddhism, but the overt cult of the body that now finds expression during the later tantric period is certainly soemthing new. Early Buddhist teachings insist upon the need for carefully controlled use of the body, but these are accompanied by vivid descriptions of the foul aspects of the living organism in order to inculcate a sense of detachment from one's self and aversion to contact with others, especially with women. This tradition continues right through the Mahāyāna period, and for the later examples one need only turn to the eighth chapter of Śāntideva's famous work "Entering upon the Career toward Enlightenment" (*Bodhicaryāvatāra*) or the thirteenth chapter of his "Compendium of Instruction" (*Śikṣāsamuccaya*). For easier reference one may turn to a short work attributed to the great Nāgārjuna entitled "The Precious Garland of Advice for the King," as recently translated by Jeffrey Hopkins:[285]

> Lust for a woman mostly comes
> From thinking that her body is clean,
> But there is nothing clean in a woman's body.
> The mouth is a vessel filled with foul saliva and filth between the teeth,
> The nose with fluids, snot and mucus,
> The eyes with their own filth and tears. . . .

A favorite theme is to compare live bodies with dead ones, especially those rotting in cemeteries:

> If you still harbor doubts about the nature of such filth
> even when before your own eyes,
> Then go and look at the bodies of others

[284] A rare case of special provision for female disciples being cited occurs in C. S. George, *op. cit.*, pp. 54-5 (Sanskrit p. 21, ll. 41ff.), but this is only for the first consecration, as already catered for in the MK; see pp. 225-6 above.

[285] See his *The Precious Garland and the Song of the Four Mindfulnesses*, p. 39.

so dreadful to see when thrown into the cemetery.
When the skin is torn apart, one has a feeling of great horror.
Once you know that, how can you thereafter take delight in that object?[286]

All such morbid thoughts are totally strange to tantric yogins, since for them the human body is a means of delight and the source of all bliss. Thus Saraha can sing:

Don't concentrate on yourself, restricting your breath.
Fie, yogin, don't squint at the end of your nose.
O fool, hold fast to the Innate,
And abandon the clinging bonds of existence.
Bring together in thought the restless waves of breath.
Then know the true nature of the Innate,
And this becomes still of itself.
When the mind goes to rest
And the bonds of the body are destroyed,
Then the one flavor of the Innate pours forth
And there is neither outcaste nor brahmin.
Here is the sacred Jumna and here the River Ganges,
Here are Prayaga and Benares, here are Sun and Moon.
I have visited in my wanderings shrines and other places of pilgrimage
But I have not seen another shrine blissful like my own body.[287]

Hevajra proclaims even more clearly:

In the absence of the body how could there be bliss?
Of bliss one could not speak. The world is pervaded by bliss,
which is itself both the pervader and the pervaded.
Just as the perfume of a flower depends upon the flower
and without the flower becomes impossible,
Likewise without form and so on bliss could not be perceived.
I am what exists, yet I am not what exists; I am the Enlightened One
because I know things for what they are.
But those fools who are afflicted with indolence do not know me.
I dwell in that Paradise of Bliss (*sukhāvatī*) in the *bhaga*
of the Vajra-Maiden, in the casket of Buddha-gems
with the form of the letter E.[288]

The identity of the world of phenomenal forms (saṃsāra) with the absolute truth which transcends them and yet is involved in them is an essential part of Mahā-yāna teaching. What is new therefore is the explicit identifying of this duality within the human body, whether of the male and female in union as practiced in the "higher" consecrations, or within the single human body, envisaged as com-

286 *Bodhicaryāvatāra*, VIII, vv. 63-4.

287 See *Buddhist Texts through the Ages*, ed. E. Conze, p. 230.

288 H.T., II.ii.35-8. The term *bhaga*, which I leave untranslated in accordance with the tradition of the early Tibetan translators, means not only vagina, but also blessednesss or good fortune (usually spelt as *bhāga* in this sense with a long *ā* sound) and it is often interpreted as this by commentators when explaining it in the present context. See also p. 248.

prising within itself the two vital coefficients, Wisdom/Means and female/male, expressed most succinctly in the term EVAṂ (thus). As we have seen, E (the Sanskrit letter is shaped as a narrow triangle ▽) indicates the female organ (lotus) and VAṂ the male (vajra). Within the single body of a practicing yogin E represents the general area of the genitals up to the navel and VAṂ is the head. The same thought-pattern is also represented by the word AHAṂ, meaning I myself, where A is below the navel and HAṂ is in the head. Their reunion may be represented in Jungian terms perhaps as the reintegration of the self, but in Buddhist terms it is final truth, devoid of self, referred to technically as the "Process of Realization" (*sampannakrama*).

The expression of their union is the *bodhicitta* ("thought of enlightenment"), which in the more conventional Mahāyāna setting depends upon the Wisdom and Means of a Bodhisattva for its effective existence. In such a context it means literally the aspiration toward enlightenment, which is the driving force for his heroic activities throughout so many rebirths in all spheres of saṃsāra. While continuing to retain this meaning throughout the remaining period left to Buddhism in India, it was used by tantric yogins to refer to that vital force resulting from the union of Wisdom and Means, understood as the perfect union of the male and the female elements. Thus in terms of consecration rites described in the last section it refers to *semen virile* and especially the drop retaken from the vagina of the feminine partner, with which the pupil receives the Secret Consecration. It is likewise the drop that reaches the "vajra-gem" in the Consecration of the Knowledge of Wisdom, and of which there must then be no emission. Vajragarbha, who is Hevajra's main interlocutor in the *Hevajra Tantra*, says:

> So one must not eject this "camphor," which arises from all the yoginīs.
> Its nature is the Joy Innate, indestructible and luscious, pervasive as the sky.
>
> The Lord replies: "It is even as you say."
>
> Vajragarbha asks: "By what means should one arouse this 'thought of enlightenment?"
>
> The Lord replies: "One should arouse the 'thought of enlightenment' in its relative and absolute aspects by means of the maṇḍala-circle and so on and by means of the process of self-empowerment. As relative white as white jasmine, as absolute essentially blissful, it arises in the Paradise of Bliss (*sukhāvatī*) in woman's *kakkola* as symbolized by the word EVAṂ. We call it Paradise of Bliss, because of bliss it is the keeper, being the resort of all Buddhas, Bodhisattvas and Vajra-holders."[289]

Regarded under these relative and absolute aspects, this "thought of enlighten-

[289] H.T., II.iv.23-31. "Camphor" is enigmatic language (*sandhābhasa*) for *śukra* (semen); *kakkola* means the female organ, pairing with *bola*, the male one. The *yoginīs*, whence the "camphor" arises, mean here the "nerves" or psychic channels (*nāḍi*), which will be discussed immediately. As further explained by Kāṇha (H.V., vol. II, p. 147), the *bodhicitta* is aroused in its relative form by the maṇḍala and so on (viz., the Process of Emanation) and in its absolute form by the process of self-empowerment (viz., the Process of Realization). Thus despite the sexual symbolism there is no actual sexual involvement.

ment" becomes yet one more name for the "two-in-one," and so regarded, it exists as much in woman as in man (H.T., I.viii.27-9). Thus the pair Wisdom/Means is also comprised within the human body with the result that we have a doubling of the imagery, and one may well ask what may be the sense of "thought of enlightenment" when envisaged as the union of Wisdom/Means within a female body. It can no longer be *semen virile* it its relative form. Once the imagery is transferred within the body, we are clearly concerned with the control of breath regarded as the carrier of fragmented thought. When the breath, passing as envisaged up and down the two sides of the body, is brought under control, then discursive thoughts are stilled, thus entering the state referred to as "thought of enlightenment," which still retains however its sexual association. The breath as gradually controlled is envisaged as traversing two psychic channels situated to the sides of the body, which come together near the sexual organ where the "thought of enlightenment" in its relative sense is produced. From here there rises the central channel, which connects the four "nerve-centers" (*cakra*, i.e., wheels represented by lotus flowers, see above pp. 251-2) at the navel, heart, throat and head, named, as we have seen, after the four Buddha-bodies. The "thought of enlightenment" ascends this channel, thus assuming its absolute aspect and so pervading the whole body with bliss. The thought pattern of Wisdom/Means and all the equivalent pairs are transferred into the body by identifying the channel on the left side as Wisdom and so as feminine, and the one on the right side as male and so as Means. They are known by the strange names of Lalanā and Rasanā, of which the literal meanings are perhaps "wanton woman" and "organ of taste," specifically the tongue. The central channel, which unites the other two, is known as Avadhūtī, meaning literally "anchoress." However, all these terms may be accepted as enigmatic language (*sandhābhāṣa*) whatever their literal meanings. Continuing the sexual symbolism, the two other channels are said to carry the uterine blood and semen, which unifies as the thought of enlightenment, which in this context becomes a mingling of the two. One may note that likewise *vajra* may refer to the absolute itself, thus being identical with the two-in-one, or paired with "lotus," it may refer to the male coefficient alone. One must be prepared for a certain capriciousness in all these identifications and cross-identifications. The central channel is also identified with the Wisdom-Maiden. Thus it is known on the one hand as the Great Symbol (*mahāmudrā*) and on the other nicknamed as Ḍombī. Again she is known as Caṇḍālī (Outcaste), which the Tibetans have translated as *gTum-mo*, meaning "raging" with the notion of raging heat. She is so named in the concluding verse of the first chapter of the *Hevajra Tantra* with direct reference to the other identifications within the body that we are now considering:

> Caṇḍālī blazes at the navel.
> She burns the Five Tathāgatas.
> She burns Locanā and the others.
> HAṂ is burnt and the Moon dissolves.

Various interpretations may be given, but the most direct identifies the Five Tathāgatas with the five aggregates (*skandha*) of personality, viz., the human being as microcosm, while Locanā and the other three goddesses stand for the elements of earth, water, fire and air, namely the macrocosm. Caṇḍālī blazing at the navel corresponds to the Sun as distinguished from the Moon in the head, the fusion of the two resulting in the bliss of the two-in-one. The same polarity identifies her with the syllable A corresponding with HAṂ in the head, thus producing together AHAṂ (I myself) as yet another term for the two-in-one. It may be noted that the commentaries often interpret *Caṇḍālī* as a composition of *caṇḍa* meaning "fierce" and identified with Wisdom in that it cuts away all emotional disturbances, and *ālī* corresponding with Means. Thus Caṇḍālī corresponds with the thought of enlightenment produced by the union of Wisdom in the left channel and Means in the right. Here one may note a further example of innocent capriciousness, for when the two-in-one is expressed as a union of *āli* (vowels) and *kāli* (consonants), *āli* corresponds with Wisdom and *kāli* with Means. It may also be noted that the term Mystic Heat has come into vogue in some English versions of Tibetan works, where *gTum-mo* (= *Caṇḍālī*) is under discussion, and this form of yoga has been described as though its main purpose were to produce actual physical warmth. It is described quite explicitly in these terms by Alexandra David-Neil, probably representing popular Tibetan ideas on the subject.[290] W. Y. Evans-Wentz describes *gTum-mo* as "meaning Psychic (or Vital or Secret) Heat (or Warmth), which is the necessary driving force for the devotees seeking spiritual development, and the means for the solitary hermit, in the very severe cold of the snowy ranges of Tibet, to be comfortable without fire." The following treatise on the subject makes it quite clear that the sensation of heat is only one of the many factors involved, and that this is not primarily a warmth-producing exercise.[291]

290 Her book *With Mystics and Magicians in Tibet* contains a chapter on "Yogic Sports," where competitions in keeping the body warm by tantric methods are described. While I remain rather skeptical of some of her stories, there is no doubt that Tibetans generally believe that the body can be kept warm by such methods.

291 See W. Y. Evans-Wentz, *Tibetan Yoga and Secret Doctrines*, pp. 172ff. See also H. V. Guenther, *The Life and Teaching of Nāropa*, pp. 53ff. where there is a detailed description of symbols and signs involved in this Caṇḍālī yoga, which he follows the others in referring to as the "mystic heat," thus overemphasizing again the significance of heat in accordance with later Tibetan tradition. In this respect one might refer to a short article in the *Times of India*, 8 Feb. 1982, p. 5, entitled "Monks Can Raise Body Temperature" and where we are informed that "A team of scientists who recently witnessed for the first time Tibetan 'heat meditation' rituals, have reported that the claims are true—the monks can will their bodies to heat up by as much as 8.5 degrees C in less than an hour. . . . The team monitored vital signs and temperature of three lamas as they practiced yoga meditation known as 'tum-mo' or 'heat meditation'. Small temperature-sensing wires were taped to the skin of the monks in a number of locations—the spine, calf, navel, palm, toe and finger. Measurement monitored throughout the one hour of meditation revealed that the temperature deep in the body remained normal while skin temperature of the lamas rose all over by 1 to 1.5 degrees C. Said Dr. Benson, leader of the group and also a researcher at the Harvard Medical School in the U.S.: 'The meditation is part of a ritual in which the lamas produce heat in the body to burn away the emotional defilements that interfere with a proper outlook on life.' " One may comment that at least the concluding words place the matter in a proper context and that the suggested heat increase

The whole concept of heat and fire, suggested by the name Caṇḍālī, is surely just figurative, for Caṇḍālī, like Ḍombī, is one of Hevajra's circle of eight goddesses. This is clear from several references all couched in poetic style. Thus when Hevajra remains entranced in the embrace of his leading lady Nairātmyā ("Selfless"), four of his entourage arouse him with these verses:

> Arise, O Lord, whose mind is compassion, and save me Pukkasi.
> Embrace me in the union of Great Bliss and leave this state of voidness.
>
> Without you I die. Arise O Hevajra! Leave this state of voidness
> and bring me Śavari to fruition.
>
> O Lord of Bliss who are at the service of the world, why remain in the void?
> I Caṇḍālī entreat you, for without you I cannot burn the (four) quarters.
>
> O Wonder-worker arise, for I know your thought.
> I Ḍombī am quick-witted. Do not interrupt your compassion.[292]

She appears with the same attribute in one of the songs of the tantric yogins:

> She arises between the Lotus and the Vajra.
> Caṇḍālī blazes through the union of sameness.
> Ḍombī puts fire to the house and burns it.
> Taking moon-water I sprinkle it.
> No flaring thatch or smoke is seen.
> Reaching the top of Mount Meru, it goes into space.
> The Lords Viṣṇu, Śiva and Brahmā are all burned.
> The nine qualities and the dominion (of the senses) are consumed.
> I Dhāma say, receive this and understand clearly.
> Through the five channels water has risen.[293]

Despite detailed problems of interpretation, the general meaning is clear. The fire of passion resulting from the union of Lotus and Vajra (Wisdom and Means) produces the thought of enlightenment (in its relative aspect) referred to here as "moon" or "water." This is conceived of as ascending the central channel through the various nerve-centers (referred to here seemingly as *nāḍi*, which we translate normally as "channel") and becoming transmuted into the absolute thought of enlightenment at the top of the head (Mount Meru) producing the transcendent state of Great Bliss. Thus the fire is extinguished in so far as it ever really exists. It should be noted that Caṇḍālī and the figurative suggestion of her consuming fire is the tantric Buddhist equivalent of Kuṇḍalinī, the coiled serpent-goddess, who lies dormant in the lowest nerve-center (*cakra*) of the human body, waiting to be raised into activity by the vital breaths passing along

of 8.5 degrees C, seemingly purely speculative, is far in excess of that recorded in this extraordinary experiment.

292 See H.T., II.v.20-3. These verses are in the same Middle Indian dialect of eastern India as the songs quoted above and the one that now follows.

293 As before, my translation is based upon Per Kværne's edition of *An Anthology of Buddhist Tantric Songs*, no. 47 (pp. 255ff.). One may note that here as in no. 18, Caṇḍālī and Ḍombī are one and the same.

the two channels, Piṅgalā (corresponding to Rasanā) and Iḍā (corresponding to Lalanā of the Buddhists) and meeting in the central channel, known as Suṣumnā (corresponding to Avadhūtī).[294] The "serpent-power" of the goddess that ascends the central channel to unite finally with Śiva in the head, corresponds to the consuming power of Caṇḍālī which dissolves the "moon-fluid" in the head, pervading the whole body with bliss. Although Buddhists may urge the superiority of their theories and practices, no detached observer can detect any essential difference between the Buddhist techniques of "supreme yoga" and the exactly corresponding practices of avowedly non-Buddhist tantric yogins.[295] An artificial difference is achieved simply by the use of different terminologies, but as has already been noted, a basic terminology common to all tantric yogins still remains.

d. *The Coalescence of All Concepts through the Practice of Tantric Yoga*

In the exegetical works of Buddhist scholars we expect to find a predominantly Buddhist terminology, and as an example of this we may quote the second chapter of the short work known as the "Fivefold Series" (*Pañcakrama*). Here the two coefficients of enlightenment, Wisdom and Means, together with their union (*bodhicitta*) taken as the third item, are brought together in the fourfold scheme outlined in detail above (III.14.b), thus emphasizing the absolute transcendent state of the fourth stage. This is not a matter of ascending stages, but rather the union of three resulting in the final fourth. This may be clarified by extracting one verse (no. 5) and commenting upon it in advance:

> From the union of Wisdom and Means perfection is accomplished
> and from this accomplished perfection comes the radiance of the Universal Void.

Here three parallel sets of four are brought into play, introducing an item from each set, thus making it essential that the reader should be acquainted with the parallelism of all the items that make up the sets. One notes too how easily the necessary clues may be further concealed in translation. Thus the word translated as "perfection" above represents Sanskrit *niṣpanna* (for the fuller form *pariniṣpanna*), which is the third item in the fourfold set: relative thought, imagined thought, perfected thought and omniscience, as listed above. Radiance (*prabhāsvara*) belongs to another set of four, expressed as light, its manifestation, its perception and fourthly its overwhelming radiance. The concept of enlightenment as thought purified of all its accidental defilements

[294] Like the terms Lalanā and Rasanā, Iḍā and Piṅgalā must be treated as mere names. The first is an ancient Vedic term referring to a kind of libation; the second means reddish-brown or tawny with a host of derived meanings to be found easily in Monier-Williams, *Sanskrit Dictionary*, p. 624. Suṣumnā is a feminine form (as are the other two) of a name for a sun-ray. For the whole theory of these psychic channels see S. B. Dasgupta, *An Introduction to Tantric Buddhism*, pp. 169ff. and also his *Obscure Religious Cults*, pp. 88ff.

[295] For the same subject-matter in a Hindu context one may refer to G. W. Briggs, *Gorakhnath and the Kanphata Yogis*, chapter 14, pp. 284-304, consisting of the text and translation of "The Hundred Verses of Gorakṣa," who like his teacher Mīnanāth or Matsyendranāth was numbered among the Eighty-Four Great Adepts.

and manifest as pure radiance can be traced back to the earliest Buddhist period, and it became a favorite theme of the Mind Only school, since their whole theory of existence was based upon thought interpreted at graded levels of experience (see section II.4.c). Many quotations could be given, but one will suffice:

> Being free of all defilement and all conceptualization,
> It is pure radiance of the self-nature of the Dharma-sphere
> and so within the reach of yogins.[296]

We may recall too that in the "Symposium of Truth" the Bodhisattva Sarvārthasiddhi, who is going through the process of self-consecration, envisages a lunar disk in his heart. All the Tathāgatas say to him: "That, O son of good family, is Thought which is naturally radiant. As one works upon it, thus it becomes, like stains (disappearing) on a white garment" (see section III.13.f). Using this fourfold terminology of light, verse 5, as quoted above, could be restated thus:

> From the union of Light and its manifestation, the perception of
> Light is accomplished, and from this accomplished perception
> comes the radiance of the Universal Void.

Parallel with the other fourfold sets, we are given a rather arbitrarily named set of four voids, namely void (*śūnya*), extreme void (*atiśūnya*), great void (*mahāśūnya*) and universal void (*sarvaśūnya*), which provide the framework for the structure of this rather complicated chapter.[297] Verses 7-14 describe the Void, identified with relative thought, with Wisdom and all its associations. Verses 15-22 describe the Extreme Void, identified with imagined thought, with Means and all its associations. Verses 23-35 describe the Great Void, identified implicitly with the union of Wisdom and Means, and with perfected thought. Verses 36-43 identify this third state explicitly as the union of lotus and vajra (i.e., Wisdom and Means) interpreted within the context of sexual yoga, where the third state passes directly into the fourth (compare section III.14.c). Verses 44-52 continue with an analysis of the first three, regarded as meditational yoga aiming at producing the form of one's chosen divinity, i.e., as a Process of Emanation (*utpattikrama*). Verses 53-68 describe the fourth state, as the radiance that purifies the other three in a state of "perfected yoga," taking Śākyamuni as the prime example. Contrasted with the other three, the fourth state may be identified as the Process of Realization (*sampannakrama*). It is said in the *Hevajra Tantra* (II.ii.29-31):

[296] From the *Ratnagotravibhāga*, Sanskrit text, ed. E. H. Johnston, p. 87, ll. 1-2. See also Takasaki's translation, p. 327, and note a similar extract from the same work on p. 144 above. For the whole subject of this "radiance" or luminosity, see D. S. Ruegg, *La théorie du Tathāgatagarbha et du Gotra*, part 4, pp. 409ff. entitled "La luminosité naturelle de la pensée."

[297] The concept of a plurality of aspects of the Void (*śūnyatā*) is also found in more conventional Mahāyāna works, attributed to the great Asaṅga. See e.g., Stcherbatsky, *Discourse on Discrimination*, pp. 186ff. or D. L. Friedmann, *Analysis of the Middle Path and the Extremes*, pp. 72ff., where sixteen "voids" are listed. One should note that Stcherbatsky translates as "modes of relativity" and Friedmann as "nonsubstantialities."

> The yogin conceives of the diversity of existence as the Process of Emanation, and realizing the dreamlike nature of this diversity, he renders it undiversified by means of its diversity. Like a dream, like a mirage, like the "intermediate state," so the maṇḍala appears from continuous application to the practice. The Great Bliss is known in the consecrations of the Great Symbol (*mahāmudrā*); of that the maṇḍala is the true expression and nowhere else does it have its origin.

As Kāṇha explains elsewhere in his commentary: "The process is one of meditation. Emanation refers to the manifestation of the forms of the divinities. The meditation in which this consists is the Process of Emanation. Realization means being substantiated in the very essence itself, and the practice by which the yogin meditates, who is intent only on this, is called the Process of Realization."[298]

It should be observed that the same terminology is applied, whether these processes are achieved by means of sexual yoga as practiced in accordance with the four higher consecrations, or by means of self-consecration as practiced in accordance with the visualization of the maṇḍala of one's chosen divinity and the consequent self-identification with him, or by means of the yoga of breath-control where the sexual symbolism is transferred within the yogin's body. As we have seen, the body is then envisaged as a structure maintained by psychic channels. These are said to be as many as seventy-two thousand, of which thirty-two are specially named in the *Hevajra Tantra*. In order to emphasize the essential identity of the outer world (the macrocosm) and the inner world of the yogin's body (the microcosm) these veins are equated with the twenty-four or thirty-two meeting-places scattered over the Indian subcontinent, where yogins and yoginīs came together (see section III.7). By the very nature of the case the cross-identifications are arbitrary, for it is the overall identification that matters and not the details.[299] For practical purposes only three seem to come into play, Lalanā to the left, Rasanā to the right and Avadhūtī in the middle, with which we have already dealt in some detail. For the purpose of the yoga of breath-control now under consideration these channels are treated as the transmitters of thought-bearing breath. Breath carries with it discursive thought, and as the breath is stilled so thought becomes tranquilized, assuming its pure pristine state.

Thought is here expressed in terms of eighty "natural states" (*prakṛti*), thirty-three of which are associated with Void and its various equivalents, forty with Extreme Void etc., and seven "moments of nonknowledge," associated with Great Void, adding up to a total of eighty, a figure that is arbitrarily doubled to one hundred and sixty since these natural states are said to be operative both day and night. While referring back to the sets of four, we should attempt to clarify

298 See H.T., vol. I, p. 75, n.4 for the reference.

299 See H.T., vol. I, pp. 69-70 for a discussion on the problems involved in making these cross-identifications. See also S. Tsuda, *The Saṃvarodaya Tantra*, ch. 7. Here seventy-two thousand veins are mentioned, of which one hundred and twenty are said to be main ones. "The Hundred Verses of Gorakṣa" (see Briggs in Bibliography) refer to three hundred thousand veins of which seventy-two are main ones. The H.T. is content with thirty-two (I.i.13ff.); but all agree that three are essential.

by means of a new list various other items which now are named:

void (*śūnya*)	extreme void (*atiśūnya*)	great void (*mahāśūnya*)	universal void (*sarvaśūnya*)
light (*āloka*)	manifestation of light (*ālokābhāsa*)	perception of light (*ālokopalabdhi*)	radiance (*prabhāsvara*)
relative thought (*paratantra*)	imagined thought (*parikalpita*)	perfected thought (*parinispanna*)	omniscience (*sarvajñatvaṃ*)
Wisdom (*prajñā*)	Means (*upāya*)	Wisdom/Means	
night	day	night/day	
woman	man	woman/man union	
left side	right side	center	
moon	sun		
lotus flower	vajra		
gentleness & other states	fierceness & other states	impassivity & other "moments of nonknowledge"	

For some of these sets no fourth state need be named simply because it is the essentially nameless "fourth." Where no third state is named one might insert the union of the two already named. If the absence of a fourth state as well as a third appears at all anomalous, one must bear in mind that several concepts that are fundamentally threefold (e.g., Wisdom, Means and their union, which is the thought of enlightenment) are here brought into relationship with a transcendent unnamed fourth as in the set of the four higher consecrations. Thus the union of sun and moon or the union of lotus and vajra already express the finality of enlightenment.[300]

The so-called "natural states" (*prakṛti*) and "moments of nonknowledge" (*avidyākṣaṇa*), which it would be superfluous to list, correspond in many respects to the traditional Buddhist conception of *dharmas* as "elements" of existence or perhaps more specifically to the *saṃskāras* ("impulses"), which represent one of the main aggregates of personality (I.3.b), but a non-Buddhist conception is also involved and this accounts for other apparent anomalies. *Prakṛti*, which I have translated here as "natural state," is used in the Sānkya school of Indian philosophy to refer to the universal cosmic substance, thus effectively corresponding to the totality of "elements of existence" (*dharmas*) of the early Buddhist schools.[301] But whereas the Buddhists envisaged existence as an ever-fluctuated plurality, the Sānkhya school conceives it as a unity under the

[300] See e.g., H.T., I.iii.11: "There is Moon and Sun and between them the Seed; this is the True Being, they say, whose nature is Joy Supreme." Or again see the references to Sun and Moon, left and right, in the song quoted above on p. 159. At the same time the "fourth state" may be suggested by the absence of sun and moon, or where there is no right, no left, no center, thus emphasizing its total transcendence. In passing one may note that Sun and Moon are reversed in the chapter of the *Pañcakrama* that is now being analyzed, since usually Moon corresponds with the right and the male side, and Sun with the left and the female side.

[301] S. Dasgupta discusses this same chapter from the *Pañcakrama* that we are now considering in his *Obscure Religious Cults*, pp. 45ff. Rather oddly he translates *prakṛti* as "impure function,"

three modalities of *sattva* (goodness), *rajas* (activity) and *tamas* (inertia). These three modalities correspond in a general way to the "natural states" as allocated to the Void (equated with woman), Extreme Void (equated with man) and Great Void (equated with their union). In the first category gentleness predominates and other supposedly feminine characteristics; in the second manly virtues and vices are listed, while in the third category all seven items are clearly relatable to the general concept of inertia. We thus have an application of these three non-Buddhist concepts to the tantric Buddhist conception of the absolute as the union of Wisdom and Means, of female and male and all the other pairs, of which the union results in the state of two-in-one. Thus it comes about that the third state is already the absolute with the result that the "moments of non-knowledge," forgetfulness, vagary etc. are also "the moment between passion and nonpassion." "There is no seed-syllable with its dot; no air issues from the exits. Such perception of the Light is the mark of perfected (thought)" (verse 26 below). Such ambivalence between the third and the fourth stages is inevitable when the terminology used can suggest nothing else but the absolute state for followers of the Mind Only school. Thought once perfected (*pariniṣpanna*) is already for them the supreme goal. As has already been noted, the distinction between the third and fourth stages in many of these sets of four is very difficult to draw, whether it is between the "self-existent" (*svabhāvika*) Buddha-Body and the Dharma-Body of a Buddha, or the third consecration, known as "Knowledge of Wisdom," and the fourth consecration, which is all part of the same process. Here the third stage, named Great Void, is described as comprehending all the "natural states" of the previous two stages, while it has no actual "natural states" of its own, but rather the seven "moments of non-knowledge." However since these seven are mental states they are added to the "natural states" to give a total of eighty and then doubled for day and night presumably to emphasize the third stage as the union of the other two. This may not seem very logical, but we have already met with so many anomalies in the thought patterns of these tantric yogins, that there need be no cause for surprise.

As well as helping to clarify so much complex terminology, this one chapter illustrates two other aspects of the essential tantric conception of the final goal as two-in-one. These are the relationship between sexual yoga and the yoga of breath-control and once again the close relationship that exists between Buddhist and more general Hindu concepts in theories and practices as expounded in tantras of the Supreme Yoga class. Thus the text passes at verse 36 direct from the subject of breath-control, where the control of breath coincides

adding the Sanskrit term *doṣa* (= defect) in brackets as though this were the term used and not *prakṛti*, and nowhere throughout his discussion is *prakṛti* mentioned. Elsewhere (especially in chapter XIV) the most helpful references to *prakṛti* in its more generally accepted sense will be found. Per Kværne also discusses the same chapter in *An Anthology of Buddhist Tantric Songs*, pp. 32ff., translating *prakṛti* as "opacity" while recognizing its Sāṅkhya associations. By using the term in the plural the author of the *Pañcakrama* deliberately detaches it from the normal Sāṅkhya usage, yet retains, as we shall note, something of the three modalities, associated with the Sāṅkhya concept of *prakṛti* as the "stuff of the universe." For a brief account of the system, see M. Hiriyanna, *The Essentials of Indian Philosophy*, pp. 106-128.

with the control of thought, to that of sexual yoga. Thought, consciousness, knowledge—all these are said to be threefold, corresponding to the categories of the Mind Only school as relative, imagined and perfected, or again as subject and object and the realization that there is neither subject nor object. These are now expressed as the male (vajra) and the female (lotus flower) and their union, and it is said that this need not be experienced in a relative (meaning here physical) sense, since the desired objective can be obtained by skill in yoga, if only one has experienced the physical union just once. This surely implies that when a pupil has been fully consecrated by his teacher by means of the fourfold consecration, as described in the last section, he may continue to practice as a solitary yogin, of which there are so many examples in later Indian and Tibetan Buddhism. That is one aspect of the matter.

The other revealing statement occurs in verse 41, where it is said that "the yogin should always identify her as pertaining to nature." Literally translated the text says "identify her as *prakṛti*," where this term is clearly used in its more regular Sāṅkhya sense of the fundamental "stuff of the universe," which exists in close relationship with "universal spirit" (*puruṣa*). Previously it was used in this chapter in the plural as "natural states" corresponding to some extent to the Buddhist concept of *dharmas* in the sense of "elements of existence." Once the full Sāṅkhya sense is restored to the term and it is identifed with the feminine partner in her relationship with the yogin, then we have an interpretation of the two-in-one exactly equivalent to the thought patterns of the Hindu tantras where the pair of Śiva and Śakti are identified with *puruṣa* and *prakṛti*.[302] In short, the tantric Buddhist concept of Wisdom (feminine) and Means (male) is deliberately reversed, thus effectively separating this fundamental thought pattern of some Buddhist yogins from the philosophical concepts of generally accepted Mahāyāna teachings. If the feminine aspect of the two-in-one is no longer *prajñā* (wisdom), but *śakti* (power), one is no longer operating with Buddhist thought patterns but with Hindu ones, and it must be quite clear from which side the borrowing has taken place. There can be no doubt of the considerable extent to which Buddhist tantras of the Supreme Yoga class are imbued not only with Hindu terminology but also with the corresponding non-Buddhist ways of thought. There have already been so many examples of this, but one more from the *Hevajra Tantra* on the theme immediately under discussion will not be amiss:

> From self-experiencing comes this knowledge, which is free from ideas of self and other.
> Like the sky it is pure and void, the supreme state of being and nonbeing.
> It is a mingling of Wisdom and Means, a mingling of passion and the absence of passion.
> It is the breath of living beings, the Supreme Unchanging One.
> It pervades all things, abiding in all bodily forms.

302 This has already been clearly shown by Shashibhusan Dasgupta in the chapter referred to in n. 301, especially pp. 337-342.

It is the Great Spirit (*mahāprāṇa*); it is what the world is made of.
Being and nonbeing have their origin there and whatever else may be.
It is the All. It has the form of consciousness. It is primeval *puruṣa*.
It is the Lord (*īśvara* = Śiva). It is the Self (*ātman*), the life-force (*jīva*),
The true being (*sattva*), time (*kāla*) and the Person (*pudgala*).
It is the self-nature of all being and illusory in its forms.[303]

After this introduction to the verses that are now about to be quoted, an introduction that has become rather longer than originally conceived, ending with a quotation of a rather non-Buddhist flavor, readers may be surprised to find that the whole process of yoga at present under discussion is foisted upon the Buddha Śākyamuni by means of a supposed quotation from one of his earliest "biographies," the Mahāyāna sūtra entitled *Lalitavistara* (meaning literally "Extended Version of his Display").[304]

1. Praise be to you! Praise be to you! Praise, praise to you!
   Thus praising: praise to you, who is the praiser and what the praised?
2. As water merges into water and melted butter into butter,
   where knowledge sees the self as self, that indeed is worship.
3. But without recourse to omniscience this is not to be realized,
   for it is covered with a veil of darkness and it is through grace that one obtains the light.
4. Void and Extreme Void (*atiśūnya*) and Great Void (*mahāśūnya*), these three, as well as Universal Void (*sarvaśūnya*) as fourth, are distinguishable by effect and by cause.
5. From the union of Wisdom and Means realization is accomplished and from such accomplished realization comes the radiance of the Universal Void.
6. Purified of causal process the highest stage is gained by application of the three states of consciousness and from the union of the three (other) Voids.
7. The Void is Light, Wisdom, Thought in its relative aspect (*paratantra*), and I shall now explain clearly the manifestations of its natural state.
8. It is free from passion, whether light, medium or advanced, and likewise free of regrets of the same three gradations, both with regard to the past and the future.
9. It is gentle, hesitating, timorous, whether slightly, moderately or extremely. It is desirous, whether slightly, moderately or extremely, and thus grasping.
10. It is nonvirtue, hunger, thirst, slight feeling, moderate feeling, extreme feeling, knowing in a moment the basis of a topic.
11. It is attentiveness, bashfulness, compassion and three grades of affection, and it is known too as fear, doubt and envy.
12. Such are the thirty-three natural states recognizable in human beings,

[303] H.T., I.x.8-12. Primeval (*purāṇa*) *Puruṣa* is also a title of Visnu and so could refer to him.

[304] Reference to the *Lalitavistara* has been made already in section I.2. There is a French translation by Foucaux (see Bibliography) but no English one to date. The account of Śākyamuni's enlightenment, which has been deliberately reworded in the *Pañcakrama* quotation, will be found in Foucaux's translation, pp. 224 and 287-8. The passages have been quoted falsely in the *Pañcakrama* so that the unwary reader may be misled into believing that Śākyamuni was accomplished in tantric practice as indicated by such comparatively early biographical material.

and because of their manifest form as relative truth, they are explained as a concept of night,

13. or again as the concept of woman, or again as gentle in form, or again as the concept of the left or as the lotus flower on a lunar disk.
14. Because it is the cause of stabilization it is the first letter (of the Sanskrit alphabet) with a dot on it (= the syllable AṂ), and it is the source of the knowledge of Light like the (cool) rays of the moon.
15. The Extreme Void is explained as the Manifestation of Light, as the Means, as what is imagined (*parikalpita*), as mental activity.
16. It is passion, attachment, the three grades of pleasure, mild, moderate and extreme. It is happiness and joy, wonderment and laughter.
17. It is the satisfying embrace and kissing and sucking. It is valor and strength and pride and the power of the doer and taker.
18. It is energy and force, whether slight, extreme or moderate.[305] It is fierceness, sportiveness and antagonism.
19. It is acquisition, clear speech, truth, untruth, and also conviction, It is the urge to give where there is no receiving, so it is heroism too.
20. It knows no shame, for it is crafty, violent and cunning. Such are the forty natural states, which arise in a moment from the Extreme Void.
21. It is represented by the concepts of day and of male, of severity and of the right, and again those of the solar disk and of the vajra.
22. It is to be known as the digit with the two dots (= A:)[306] and being born of the Manifestation of Light it resembles the rays of the sun.
23. Being both the perception of Light as well as what is perceived, it is perfected (*parinispanna*) and so is known as nonknowledge.
24. Such are the categories of the Great Void as explained by the Buddhas. It is the moment between passion and nonpassion, thus forgetfulness and vagary.
25. It is the state where silence falls; it is exhaustion, sloth and idleness. It is known by the practitioners of subtle yoga as the seven moments of nonknowledge.
26. There is no seed-syllable with its dot; no air issues from the exits. Such perception of the Light is the mark of perfected (thought).
27. One hundred and sixty natural states are in motion day and night with air (= breath) as their vehicle.
28. In a moment, a trice, a second, an eye-twinkle, or an instant— where a moment equals a snap of the fingers, a trice the turning of
29. a mustard seed, a second the intake of breath, an eye-twinkle the moment of the eye, and an instant the clapping of the hands—
30. Such knowledge is mere consciousness, uncharacterized like space, but its division is like the twilight separating day and night.
31. Thought is said to be threefold as Light, the manifestation of Light and as its perception, and so its basis is explained.

305 For "force" (*sāhasa*) the Tibetan version has "innate" (*sahaja*) which is nonsense.

306 The "two dots" shown here as a colon refer to the Sanskrit *visarga*, a light aspiration added to vowels. In transliteration we usually show it as *-ḥ*, but shown thus here, the reference to two dots becomes unintelligible.

32. By means of breath in its subtle form knowledge becomes commingled;
issuing from the paths of the sense-organs it relates with the spheres of sense.
33. When it is linked with Light, breath becomes the vehicle,
carrying all those natural states here and there.
34. Wherever the breath happens to stay, it carries that kind of natural state.
In so far as breath does not arise, the Light is motionless.
35. The imaginary idea of a self has as its cause the two aspects of Light
(viz., Light itself and its manifestation) and the perception of the
Light is part of both of them.
36. Of all illusions the illusion of woman is a special case,
for the distinction between the three kinds of knowledge is here most
clearly marked.
37. Passion and the absence of passion and the state between them
make a set of three. By the coming together of the two organs
38. and from this union of vajra and lotus the resulting encounter is
known as the union of the two kinds of knowledge. By this union of the
two kinds of knowledge, for the reason as explained, that
39. knowledge which is carefully acquired is the perception of Light (viz.,
the third kind of knowledge). The one for whom the union of vajra
and lotus is not available in the relative (= physical) sense, can
40. succeed by his skill in yoga, having experienced it (physically) just once.
Understanding the operation of (the three kinds of) knowledge
41. according to their differences, the yogin should always identify her (the
female partner) as pertaining to nature. Just as clouds with their different
42. hues and shapes arise in the expanse of the sky and relapse there
again, so all these qualities which have as their cause the three
43. aspects of Light, disappear into the spheres of sense and are
resolved in the radiance (of the Universal Void).
44. Not recongizing their true nature and so immersed in the mire of ignorance
people do good and evil deeds, transmigrating through the five realms
45. of rebirth. Having done virtuous deeds such as gift-giving and so on, a man
rejoices in heaven, and then having committed one of the heinous sins,
46. he burns in hell. So he obtains endless thousands of rebirths, and in
his folly laments his fate saying: "This is the ripening of former karma."
47. Living beings suffer because of their attachment to the manifestations
of natural states and it is precisely by knowing these that wise men
become freed from the cage of existence.
48. The lunar disk that one imagines has the self-nature of wisdom,
and one should envisage thought itself as having the form of the moon.
49. Then concentrating on the moon one should produce the sign of the vajra.
This is identified as means for yogins who practice this production of
the vajra etc.
50. From the union of lunar vajra etc. and the amalgamating of thinker and
thought and the union of Wisdom and Means the divine form is born.
51. Signed with the four symbols (*mudrā*) and adopting the confidence of his
(chosen) divinity, so the yogin who is intent on the process of emanation
(*utpattikrama*) proceeds.
52. As it is often stated in the *Śrī Samāja* and elsewhere, so long as

there is still meditational yoga, one is still a beginner.
53. Now I shall describe perfected yoga,
which is here defined as the radiance that purifies the (other)
three Voids. By purifying the three aspects of knowledge there
54. comes this stage of the Universal Void, which is supreme omniscience,
the quiddity which is the state of knowledge purified. It is the perfect
state of tranquility, free of all duality, changeless, nonmanifest.
55. It neither is nor is not, for words cannot apply to it.
But it is from this pure radiance (*prabhāsvara*) that the three
56. aspects of knowledge arise in the form of one who possesses the
thirty-two major marks and the eighty minor marks (of buddhahood) and
thus is born the Omniscient One in all his perfect manifestations.
57. So it is said in the Mahāyāna sūtra *Lalitavistara*:
The Tathāgata Śākyamuni desirous of supreme enlightenment and
58. in the conceit that he would obtain buddhahood by means of the Great
Void, went to the bank of the Nairañjana River and relapsed into
immobile concentration.[307]
59. Then the middle atmosphere was filled with Buddhas the size of
sesame-seeds, and snapping their fingers they addressed with one
voice that best of conquerors.
60. "Impure is such meditation; it will not bring what you desire.
One must be in touch with the supreme radiance which is like the
61. celestial expanse, and having gained that stage you may prevail in any
form you will. Thus obtaining universal lordship, you will rejoice in
a Vajra-body."
62. Hearing this, the best of conquerors abandoned his immobile
concentration, and at the hour of midnight touched the truth (quiddity)
63. with his body being neither rigid nor slack, neither breathing
64. nor breathless, neither mute nor vocal, with eyes neither closed
65. nor open, and so by the grace of a teacher he saw clearly the
wonderful Universal Void, the Great Knowledge.
66. As a purified comprehender of radiance he beheld in that moment the
whole of existence in the threefold form of past, present and future,
and he was graced with those illusive visions of the moon in water and
sparks and so on.
67. Then at dawn he took his seat at the place of enlightenment in a
state of adamantine repose and so destroyed the Evil One (*Māra*).
68. Having obtained this supreme knowledge of the truth, the Śākya Lord
has taught it here for the good of the threefold world.[308]

[307] Tibetan: *mi-g·yo-ba'i ting-nge-'dzin*; Sanskrit: *āsphānakaṃ* = *āspharaṇa* (Edgerton's *Buddhist Hybrid Sanskrit Dictionary*, p. 111). The same term will be found in the passage quoted in III.13.f. See above p. 241, n. 200.

[308] For the Sanskrit text, see L. de la Vallée Poussin's ed. of the *Pañcakrama*, pp. 27-31. This is in fact chapter II, although marked as III. The corresponding Tibetan version will be found on TT 61, pp. 289-5-2ff.

Padmasambhava
(drawn by Robert Beer)